TIME FOR KIDS®

ALMANAC 2005

with
Fact Monster™

Beth Rowen
Editor

Curtis Slepian
Managing Editor

FACT MONSTER™
from Information Please®
a Pearson Education Company
http://www.factmonster.com

Unless otherwise noted, all information in
this book comes from FactMonster.com

W9-AWC-616

with
Fact Monster™

FACT MONSTER/INFORMATION PLEASE

EDITOR: Beth Rowen
CONTRIBUTORS: Borgna Brunner, Christine Frantz
FACT-CHECKING AND PROOFREADING:
Christine Frantz
DESIGNER: Sean Dessureau
INDEXING: Marilyn Rowland
EDITORIAL DIRECTOR: Borgna Brunner
VICE PRESIDENT AND GENERAL MANAGER: George Kane

TIME FOR KIDS ALMANAC

MANAGING EDITOR: Curtis Slepian
COPY EDITOR: Peter McGullam
PHOTOGRAPHY EDITOR: Sandy Perez
MAPS: Joe Lertola
ART DIRECTION AND DESIGN: R studio T, NYC:
Raul Rodriguez and Rebecca Tachna
COVER DESIGN: Elliot Kreloff
EDITORIAL DIRECTOR: Keith Garton

TIME INC. HOME ENTERTAINMENT

PRESIDENT: Rob Gursha
VICE PRESIDENT, BRANDED BUSINESSES: David Arfine
VICE PRESIDENT, NEW PRODUCT DEVELOPMENT:
Richard Fraiman
EXECUTIVE DIRECTOR, MARKETING SERVICES:
Carol Pittard
DIRECTOR, RETAIL & SPECIAL SALES: Tom Mifsud
DIRECTOR OF FINANCE: Tricia Griffin
ASSISTANT MARKETING DIRECTOR: Ann Marie Doherty
PRE-PRESS MANAGER: Emily Rabin
RETAIL MANAGER: Bozena Bannett
BOOK PRODUCTION MANAGER: Jonathan Polsky
ASSOCIATE PRODUCT MANAGER: Kristin Walker

SPECIAL THANKS: Alexandra Bliss, Bernadette Corbie, Robert Dente, Gina Di Meglio, Anne-Michelle Gallero, Peter Harper, Suzanne Janso, Robert Marasco, Natalie McCrea, Mary Jane Rigoroso, Chris Rowen, Steven Sandonato, Grace Sullivan

SPECIAL THANKS TO IMAGING: Patrick Dugan, Eddie Matros

Published by TIME For Kids Books
Time Inc.
1271 Avenue of the Americas
New York, New York 10020

ISSN: 1534-5718
ISBN: 1-931933-67-7

We welcome your comments and suggestions about TIME For Kids Books. Please write to us at:
TIME For Kids Books
Attention: Book Editors
PO Box 11016
Des Moines, IA 50336-1016

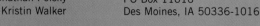

CONTENTS

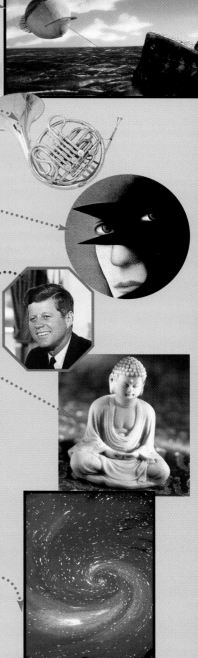

Homework
TIP

• Find information for school assignments in your *TFK 2005 Almanac*

WHO'S NEWS

The U.S. Armed Forces

More than 110,000 men and women in the U.S. Armed Forces are on duty in Iraq. That's the largest number of U.S. troops stationed overseas in American history. With help from other nations, they successfully removed Saddam Hussein from power and captured the former Iraqi leader. After months of searching, American soldiers found Hussein in December 2003, hiding in a hole near his Iraqi hometown.

Soldiers continue to fight for freedom for the people of Iraq. As they work to bring security to Iraq, the troops face struggles and resistance from some Iraqis and outside terrorists. Many soldiers have lost their lives trying to help the cause.

In Afghanistan, U.S. troops are working to bring stability to the war-torn nation. An American-dominated military force of about 12,000 is helping to rebuild Afghanistan and fight what is left of the Taliban.

About 165,000 National Guard and Reserve troops are on active duty all over the world to help fight the war on terrorism. That number is expected to increase. For their courage and commitment to defending freedom in the U.S. and around the world, the U.S. Armed Forces were chosen the TFK People of the Year in 2003.

Robot Explorers Land on Mars

NASA scored a touchdown when its exploring robotic rover, *Spirit*, landed on Mars in January 2004, six months after its takeoff from Cape Canaveral, Florida.

Spirit landed in the giant Gusev Crater, which is about the size of Connecticut.

A second rover, called *Opportunity*, landed on the opposite side of Mars a few weeks later. Soon after they landed, the rovers began sending images of Mars's landscape to scientists 106 million miles away on Earth. "It was so gorgeous to see the horizon in the pictures," said Julie Townsend, a researcher on the project.

In March, scientists working with the rovers reported some big news: The cold and dry red planet once had enough water to support life. But Steve Squyres, a scientist working on the *Opportunity* mission, cautioned, "That doesn't mean life was there. We don't know that." At least not yet!

A SCARE FOR BEEF EATERS

In the winter of 2003, the U.S. Department of Agriculture (USDA) reported the first case of mad-cow disease in the country. The sick cow was brought to Washington State from Canada. Officials took steps to protect the nation's beef supply. The USDA banned the use of sick animals in food.

Mad-cow disease, or bovine spongiform enceph-alopathy, is carried in a cow's brain and spinal cord. The USDA says the risk to humans is very low. Still, more than 30 nations banned the sale of U.S. beef. And the U.S. continued its ban on beef and live cattle from Canada.

Major Earthquake Rocks Iran

Rescue teams from all over the world pored through piles of rubble that covered the city of Bam in southeastern Iran. They searched for signs of life in the ancient city. In the winter of 2003, a major earthquake had struck, destroying much of the city and killing more than 25,000 people.

In addition to the deaths, at least 10,000 people were hurt and tens of thousands left homeless and hungry.

U.S. military planes delivered blankets, medical supplies and water. The U.S. also sent medical teams and a search-and-rescue crew. International relief workers from 26 countries helped the people of Bam.

Terror Strikes Spain

In March 2004, a series of bombs exploded on commuter trains and at stations while people were on their way to work in Madrid, Spain. More than 200 people were killed and at least 1,400 were wounded. It was the worst terrorist attack in Spain's history.

Leaders from nations worldwide expressed their outrage at the terrorist attacks. President George W. Bush called Spain's then Prime Minister José María Aznar to express sympathy and said the U.S. would support "the people of Spain at this difficult moment." Secretary of State Colin Powell said the U.S. stands "with Spain in the fight against terrorism in all its forms."

An Icy World

NASA scientists reported in March 2004 that they had discovered a distant object in our solar system. They named the "planetoid" Sedna, after an Inuit goddess who created sea creatures of the Arctic.

Made out of ice and rock, Sedna is the largest object found in the solar system since Pluto was discovered in 1930. It's also the coldest, with its highest temperature -400°F. Eight billion miles from the Sun, Sedna is the most distant object in the solar system.

Scientists term Sedna an "object" because they are not sure what to call it. Some think that Sedna may be large enough to be called the 10th planet. Others think it is just one of many objects in the outer reaches of the solar system.

POLE POSITION

In winter 2004, after 58 days in the snow and ice, English adventurers Pen Hadow and Simon Murray reached the South Pole. Murray, 63, became the oldest person to walk to the pole. Hadow, 41, also set a record. He is the first person to walk unassisted to both the North and South Poles. He reached both ends of the Earth in less than a year. "I'm always interested in doing things that haven't been done before," Hadow told TFK.

The pair walked 680 miles, most of it uphill. Each man set out pulling a 400-pound sledge full of gear and food. Their favorite daily event: dinner! Hadow says that his son, Wilf, 5, "is very pleased" that his dad is back. Now, Hadow is planning his next big adventure.

13

KING OF THE COURT

Minutes after stepping onto the basketball court at the start of the 2003–2004 NBA season, 18-year-old LeBron James slam-dunked any doubts about his abilities. The guard for the Cleveland Cavaliers scored 12 points during the first 12 minutes of his professional career. By the end of the game, James had earned 13 more points—and had managed to live up to the hype surrounding his debut.

Many critics argue that few teenage athletes are mature enough to deal with the mental and physical pressure of the pros. That's one reason the NBA says it would prefer a minimum age requirement of 20. But now that King James is ruling the court in Cleveland, no one is jumping to change the rules.

Top Dogs

The kings and queens of college hoops hold court at the University of Connecticut. In 2004, UConn became the first school to capture the Division 1 men's and women's basketball titles in the same year. In San Antonio, the men, led by super center Emeka Okafor, beat Georgia Tech University 82–73. The next day, in New Orleans, the dynamic play of Diana Taurasi helped UConn defeat the University of Tennessee 70–61. The UConn Huskies are dog-gone amazing!

A Big Talent!

Hilary Duff, look out! Lindsay Lohan may be gaining on you. Alr__
a TV and movie star, Lindsay is aiming to become a singing
sensation. She played a pair of crafty twins in the 1998 movie __
Parent Trap and starred in the Disney TV movies *Life-Size* and __
Clue. The Hollywood hitmaker appeared in the flicks *Freaky Fri__*
and *Confessions of a Teenage Drama Queen.* Her impressive sin__
debut with "Ultimate," the feature song from *Freaky Friday*, led __
a record deal with a major label. What's in this teen megastar's __
future? Check her out in the film *Mean Girls.*

HOORAY for HOLLYWOOD

Among the movie highlights of the year was the return of Shrek. Shrek 2 adds the comic voice of John Cleese to those of Mike Meyers and Eddie Murphy.

The wizards of Pixar brought their magic to The Incredibles. In this animated extrava-ganza, over-the-hill superheroes come out of retirement to fight the bad guys.

You can find "real" wizards in Harry Potter and the Prisoner of Azkaban. This installment brings back Harry for his third year at Hogwarts.

Another popular book series is being turned into a movie. In Lemony Snicket's Series of Unfortunate Events, Jim Carrey plays Count Olaf, who is trying to steal the inheritance of the three Beaudelaire orphans.

Star on the Rise

What a whale of a tale! Keisha Castle-Hughes became, at 13, the youngest person ever nominated for a best-actress Academy Award. Castle-Hughes was honored for her role in the film *Whale Rider*. She says the nomination was "something a Kiwi [New Zealand] girl would never dare dream about." Castle-Hughes didn't win the Oscar (it went to Charlize Theron), but her nomination did make Academy history.

Oh! Oh! It's Yu-Gi-Oh!

Yu-Gi-Oh is still on the go! The popular animated TV show revolves around Yugi, a high schooler who morphs into an evil-fighting warrior. Yu-Gi-Oh has morphed itself from a comic book in Japan to a Saturday-morning 'toon to video games to sets of trading cards. And now there's *Yu-Gi-Oh!: The Movie*. It's about an ancient, evil being that threatens to destroy Yugi and take over the world. What's next—*Yu-Gi-Oh: the Broadway Musical*?

ANIMALS

DADDY DAY CARE

Dad to the rescue! A father shields his baby from a baboon bully.

At the foot of Mount Kilimanjaro, in Kenya, wild savanna baboons spend their days lounging next to elephants, antelopes and buffalos. Mother baboons groom their babies and protect them.

But baboon moms aren't on the job alone. Scientists recently made the surprising announcement that many baboon dads also recognize and care for their young. Researchers had assumed that male baboons didn't know which babies were theirs, because the males live in groups and have several partners. A three-year study shows that baboon dads recognize, and often protect, their offspring.

By using samples of DNA, the chemical that genes are made of, scientists matched 75 baboon babies with their fathers. Half the dads that were observed stuck around and played Mr. Mom until their babies reached age 3.

With their sharp teeth, male baboons are "designed to be dangerous," says Joan Silk, a professor who worked on the study. "But they can be sweet with infants." What's more, the researchers found that dads don't monkey around about defending their own. They rush to protect their offspring in fights more often than they help other baboon babies.

"Life is pretty tough for young baboons," says Jason Buchan, who was also involved in the study. When the fathers are on the scene, it decreases the babies' chances of getting hurt. The scientists believe some of the ways the male baboons identify their young are by appearance and smell. Silk is thrilled that animal dads show similarities to human dads. Says Silk: "It's always fun to find out that animals are smarter than you thought!"

By Elizabeth Winchester

DEDICATED DADS

Baboon males aren't the only proud papas in the animal kingdom. Some other animal dads are good parents, too. Here's a look at some of the critters that take part in parenting in extraordinary ways.

CATFISH A father sea catfish keeps the eggs of his young in his mouth until they are ready to hatch. He will not eat until his young are born, which may take several weeks.

COCKROACH A father cockroach eats bird droppings to obtain precious nitrogen, which he carries back to feed to his young.

MARMOSET Marmosets are tiny South American monkeys. The fathers take care of their babies from birth. When the marmoset is born, the father cleans it, then carries it to the mother only when it needs to be nursed. When the baby can eat solid food, the father will feed it.

RHEA Rheas are large South American birds similar to ostriches. Father rhea takes sole care of his young. From eggs to chicks, he feeds, defends and protects them until they are old enough to survive on their own.

SANDGROUSE A father Namaqua sandgrouse of Africa's Kalahari Desert flies as far as 50 miles a day in order to soak himself in water and return to his nest, where his chicks can drink from his feathers!

WOLF When the mother wolf gives birth to pups, the father stands guard outside their den and brings food to the mother and pups. As they grow, he not only plays with them but also teaches them how to survive. Wolves continue to live together much as human families do.

FROG The male Darwin frog hatches his eggs in a pouch in his mouth. He can eat and continue about his business until his tadpoles lose their tails, become tiny frogs and jump out of his mouth!

ANIMALS

EMPEROR PENGUIN

A penguin pop balances the mother's egg on his feet. He uses his skin and feathers to protect the egg from the bitter Antarctic cold. Dad does this for nine weeks—without eating—until the egg is ready to hatch.

SEA HORSE

A female sea horse lays her eggs in a pouch located in the front of the male's stomach. The daddy sea horse carries the eggs until they hatch. When the babies are big enough, they swim free.

Top 5 Insect Groups

Three out of every four creatures on the planet are insects.

1. Beetles 400,000 known species
2. Butterflies and moths 165,000
3. Ants, bees and wasps 140,000
4. True flies 120,000
5. Cicadas, leafhoppers and related bugs 90,000

Source: *Top 10 of Everything*, DK

19

Animal Groups

Almost all animals belong to one of two groups, **VERTEBRATES** or **INVERTEBRATES**. Adult vertebrates have a spinal column, or backbone, running the length of their bodies; invertebrates do not. Vertebrates are often larger and have more complex bodies than invertebrates. However, there are many more invertebrates than vertebrates.

Vertebrates

REPTILES are cold-blooded and breathe with lungs. They have scales, and most lay eggs. Reptiles include turtles and tortoises, crocodiles and alligators, snakes and lizards.

FISH breathe through gills and live in water; most are cold-blooded and lay eggs (although sharks give birth to live young).

AMPHIBIANS are cold-blooded and live both on land (breathing with lungs) and in water (breathing through gills) at different times. Three types of amphibians are caecilians, salamanders and frogs and toads. Caecilians are primitive amphibians that resemble earthworms. They are found in the tropics.

Crocodiles are reptiles, and frogs are amphibians.

DINOSAURS were reptiles, although some scientists believe that some dinosaurs were warm-blooded.

BIRDS are warm-blooded animals with feathers and wings. They lay eggs, and most birds can fly. Some, including penguins and ostriches, cannot fly.

MAMMALS are warm-blooded and are nourished by their mothers' milk. Most are born live, but the platypus and echidna are hatched from eggs. Most mammals also have body hair.

Platypuses are mammals.

Sponges are invertebrates.

Invertebrates

SPONGES are the most primitive of animal groups. They live in water, are sessile (do not move from place to place) and filter tiny organisms out of the water for food.

ECHINODERMS, including starfish, sea urchins and sea cucumbers, live in seawater and have external skeletons.

WORMS come in many varieties and live in all sorts of habitats—from the bottom of the ocean to the inside of other animals. They include flatworms (flukes), roundworms (hookworms), segmented worms (earthworms) and rotifers (philodina).

MOLLUSKS are soft-bodied animals, some of which live in hard shells. They include snails, slugs, octopuses, squid, mussels, oysters, clams, scallops and cuttlefish.

ARTHROPODS are the largest and most diverse of all animal groups. They have segmented bodies supported by a hard external skeleton (or exoskeleton). Arthropods include insects, arachnids (spiders and their relatives) and crustaceans (such as shrimp and lobster).

Lobsters are arthropods.

Sea anemones do not have backbones.

COELENTERATES are also very primitive. Their mouths, which take in food and get rid of waste, are surrounded by stinging tentacles. Some coelenterates are jellyfish, corals and sea anemones.

Warm-Blooded and Cold-Blooded Animals

Snakes are cold-blooded.

Warm-blooded animals regulate their own body temperatures; their bodies use energy to maintain a constant temperature. Cold-blooded animals depend on their surroundings to establish their body temperatures.

Fascinating ANIMAL Facts

☆ While humans get by with **FIVE SENSES**—touch, taste, sight, smell and hearing—animals have developed additional ways to navigate and survive the world:

• Some **DOLPHINS, WHALES** and **BATS** navigate and track prey using **ECHO-LOCATION.** This is a very advanced form of hearing that allows them to "see" their surroundings by listening to and analyzing the way sound reflects off objects in their environment.

• Many fish sense their surroundings with a **LATERAL-LINE SYSTEM,** which detects changes in water pressure. This allows them to feel the movement of other animals in the water nearby.

☆ Animals' lives are not peaceful! They must be able to find food for themselves and their young and avoid becoming food themselves:

• Self-sacrificing **ANTS** explode in the face of the enemy to save their colonies.

• A **SOUTH AMERICAN LIZARD** squirts blood from its eyes to repel enemies.

• Both **CUTTLEFISH** and **SQUID** eject black inky fluid that helps them hide from predators.

• The **SEA CUCUMBER** squirts its insides out to defend itself! (It then grows a new stomach.)

☆ Check out these impressive numbers:
• There are 200 million **INSECTS** for each person on Earth.

• An **ELEPHANT** eats 250 pounds of plants and drinks 50 gallons of water a day.

• The **MIDGE,** a tiny insect, beats its wings 62,000 times a minute.

• Most starfish have five arms, but the **BASKET STARFISH** may have 50 or more arms!

• One **BEEHIVE** can hold up to 80,000 bees.

☆ Talk about an identity crisis! These animals didn't get the names they deserve:
• The **AMERICAN BUFFALO** is not a buffalo; it is a bison.
• The **BALD EAGLE** is not bald; it has a cap of white feathers on top of its head.
• The **KOALA** is not a bear; it is a marsupial, which is a mammal with a pouch.
• The **PRAIRIE DOG** is not a dog; it is a rodent similar to a squirrel.

bat

koala

go For the answers to fascinating animal FAQs, www.FACTMONSTER.COM

Classifying Animals

There are billions of different kinds of living things (organisms) on Earth. To help study them, biologists have created ways of naming and classifying them according to their similarities and differences. The system most scientists use puts each living thing into seven groups, organized from most general to most specific. Therefore, each kingdom is composed of phylums, each phylum is composed of classes, each class is composed of orders, and so on.

From largest to smallest, the groups are

Kingdoms are huge groups, with millions of kinds of organisms in each. All animals are in one kingdom (called Kingdom Animalia); all plants are in another (Kingdom Plantae). It is generally agreed that there are five kingdoms: Animalia, Plantae, Fungi, Prokarya (bacteria) and Protoctista (organisms that don't fit into the four other kingdoms, including many microscopic creatures).

Species are the smallest groups. In the animal kingdom, a species consists of all the animals of a type who are able to breed and produce young of the same kind.

Kingdom
Phylum
Class
Order
Family
Genus
Species

ANIMALS

TIP

● **To remember the order for classification, keep this silly sentence in mind:**

King Philip
came over
for good soup.

A Sample Classification:

The Gray Wolf

Kingdom: Animalia includes all animals

Phylum: Chordata includes all vertebrate, or backboned, animals

Class: Mammalia includes all mammals

Order: Carnivora includes all carnivorous, or meat-eating, mammals

Family: Canidae includes all dogs

Genus: Canis includes dogs, foxes and jackals

Species: lupus the gray wolf

Fast Tracks

Forget about challenging a cheetah to a race. The fastest human sprinter only reaches a speed of about 18 m.p.h.

Animal	Speed (m.p.h.)
PEREGRINE FALCON	200+
CHEETAH	70
LION	50
ZEBRA	40
GREYHOUND	39
DRAGONFLY	36
RABBIT	35
GIRAFFE	32
GRIZZLY BEAR	30
CAT	30
ELEPHANT	25
SQUIRREL	12
MOUSE	8
SPIDER	1
GARDEN SNAIL	0.03

Source: James G. Doherty, general curator, Wildlife Conservation Society

Animal Gestation & Longevity

Here's a look at the average gestation (the time an animal spends inside its mother) and longevity (life span) of certain animals.

Animal	Gestation (days)	Longevity (Years)
CAT	52-69	10-12
COW	280	9-12
DOG	53-71	10-12
HAMSTER	15-17	2
HORSE	329-345	20-25
KANGAROO	32-39	4-6
LION	105-113	10
PIG	101-130	10
PIGEON	11-19	10-12
RABBIT	30-35	6-8
WOLF	60-63	10-12

TFK Puzzles & Games

A Long Trip

Each year, millions of monarch butterflies fly south for the winter. Help these monarchs on their trip. Starting from Canada, find an unblocked path along the borders of the states that leads to the Finish in Mexico.

CANADA

FINISH

MEXICO

(See Answer Key that begins on page 340)

Extinct, Endangered and Threatened Species

Many species of animals are disappearing from our planet. **EXTINCT** means that the entire species has died out and can never return. **ENDANGERED** animals are those in immediate danger of becoming extinct. **THREATENED** species are likely to become endangered in the future.

Humans are largely responsible when animals become extinct, endangered or threatened. Here are some of the things that can lead animals to become endangered.

DESTRUCTION OF HABITAT

Humans destroy precious habitat—the natural environment of a living thing—when they fill swamps and marshes, dam rivers and cut down trees to build homes, roads and other structures or developments.

POLLUTION

Oil spills, acid rain and water pollution have been devastating for many species of fish and birds.

HUNTING AND FISHING

Many animals are over-hunted because their meat, fur and other parts are very valuable.

INTRODUCTION OF EXOTIC SPECIES

When animals or plants arrive into a new habitat from a foreign place, they sometimes introduce diseases that the native species can't fight. "Exotic" species can prey on the native species, and they often have no natural enemies.

There are 1,072 endangered and threatened species of animals in the world. The list includes:

- 342 species of mammals, such as the red wolf, the right whale and the mountain gorilla

- 273 species of birds, such as the California condor, the whooping crane and the northern spotted owl

- 126 species of fish, such as coho salmon

- 115 species of reptiles, such as the green sea turtle

- 48 species of insects, including the mission blue butterfly

- 30 species of amphibians, including the Houston toad

whooping crane

northern spotted owl

mountain gorilla

coho salmon

mission blue butterfly

California condor

Did You Know?

No one knows for sure how many species of animals there are on Earth. In fact, scientists identify new species every day. But most scientists agree that the total number of animal species is about 1.5 million.

Where in the World
Do Animals Live?

Animals live only where they can survive. Koalas, for example, eat only the leaves of certain eucalyptus trees, so they must live in Australia, where these trees grow. All of the animals listed below can survive in only one place on Earth—and many of these animals are endangered.

NORTH AMERICA
alligator, Arctic fox, Arctic tern, bald eagle, bison, California condor, California sea tern, Dall sheep, musk ox, North American gray squirrel, raven, snapping turtle, wild turkey

SOUTH AMERICA
alpaca, Darwin's finch, flightless cormorant, giant tortoise, llama, marine iguana, sloth, torrent duck, toucan, vicuña

EUROPE reindeer, Scottish wildcat, wild goat

AFRICA aardvark, aardwolf, aye-aye, camel, chimpanzee, giraffe, green gecko, hippopotamus, hyena, indri, lion, ruffed lemur, spitting cobra, tsetse fly

ASIA Asiatic lion, giant panda, Komodo dragon, Przewalski's horse, snow leopard, Mongolian gazelle

AUSTRALIA and NEW ZEALAND dingo, duck-billed platypus, echidna, emu, kakapo, kiwi, koala, quokka, short-nosed rat kangaroo, short-tailed wallaby, Tasmanian devil

ANTARCTICA Adélie penguin, penguin, Ross seal, Weddell seal

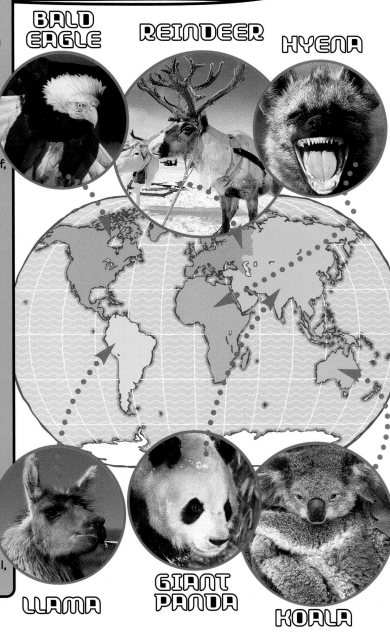

BALD EAGLE

REINDEER

HYENA

LLAMA

GIANT PANDA

KOALA

TFK NEWS

One Big Guinea Pig

Imagine a 9-foot-long, 4.2-foot-tall, 1,500-pound guinea pig. It may sound like something out of a bad horror movie, but paleontologists have proof such a creature actually existed. They recently uncovered the fossil of an extinct rodent that was as big as a buffalo!

The discovery was made in a dry region of Venezuela, about 250 miles west of Caracas, the country's capital. It is believed that Goya, as scientists are calling the rodent, lived about 6 million to 8 million years ago in a South American swamp. This is the largest rodent ever discovered!

Goya lived alongside giant turtles and catfish, chewing on grass with its long teeth. The furry creature had small ears and eyes and a long tail that helped balance its weight as it moved and hunted for predators.

The scientific name of the rodent is *Phoberomys pattersoni*. The term pattersoni was given to the animal in honor of Brian Patterson, a professor who led a fossil-collecting expedition to Venezuela in the 1970s.

Homework TIP

Don't be impatient if you are having trouble with your work. Mistakes are normal. Take a short break, and then begin again. Ask for help if you get stuck.

Animal Names

ANIMAL	MALE	FEMALE	YOUNG
bear	boar	sow	cub
cat	tom	queen	kitten
cattle	bull	cow	calf
chicken	rooster	hen	chick
deer	buck	doe	fawn
dog	dog	bitch	pup
duck	drake	duck	duckling
elephant	bull	cow	calf
fox	dog	vixen	cub
goose	gander	goose	gosling
horse	stallion	mare	foal
lion	lion	lioness	cub
pig	boar	sow	piglet
sheep	ram	ewe	lamb
swan	cob	pen	cygnet

Hello! My name is MOLLY!

Top 10 DOG Breeds

1.	LABRADOR RETRIEVER
2.	GOLDEN RETRIEVER
3.	GERMAN SHEPHERD
4.	BEAGLE
5.	DACHSHUND
6.	YORKSHIRE TERRIER
7.	BOXER
8.	POODLE
9.	CHIHUAHUA
10.	SHIH TZU

Source: The American Kennel Club

Top 10 Cat Breeds

1.	PERSIAN
2.	MAINE COON
3.	EXOTIC
4.	SIAMESE
5.	ABYSSINIAN
6.	ORIENTAL
7.	BIRMAN
8.	AMERICAN SHORTHAIR
9.	TONKINESE
10.	BURMESE

Source: Cat Fancier's Association

TOP PET NAMES

Did you know your furry friend was destined to be a "Smokey" the moment you looked into its soulful eyes? You're not alone.

The American Society for the Prevention of Cruelty to Animals (ASPCA) conducted a veterinarian survey to find out which pet names are most popular in the United States.

HERE ARE THE TOP 20:

1. Max	11. Ginger
2. Sam	12. Baby
3. Lady	13. Misty
4. Bear	14. Missy
5. Smokey	15. Pepper
6. Shadow	16. Jake
7. Kitty	17. Bandit
8. Molly	18. Tiger
9. Buddy	19. Samantha
10. Brandy	20. Lucky

Hello! My name is GINGER!

Fish FAQs

How many species of fish are there?

An estimated 20,000 species exist. But there may be as many as 20,000 more.

What is the smallest fish?

The smallest fish is the tiny **goby,** an inhabitant of fresh-to-brackish waters in Luzon, Philippines. It grows to a mere half inch at adulthood.

How long do fish live?

Some fish (small reef fishes) live just a few weeks or months; others (sturgeons) live up to 100 years. In temperate (moderately warm) waters, there are many species that live 10 to 20 years.

Do fish breathe air?

Yes, but not using lungs as mammals do. Actually, fish breathe oxygen, not air. As water passes over a system of very fine gill membranes, the fish's blood absorbs the water's oxygen content.

Do sharks prey on people?

Sharks rarely pose a danger to humans. But humans are a risk to sharks! Fishers kill millions of sharks every year. About 75 shark species are in danger of becoming extinct. Often, when an attack on a human occurs, the shark has mistaken the human for a fish or a seal. A human is too bony to be a good meal for a shark.

How fast do fish swim?

Tunas, billfishes and certain sharks are the speed champions, reaching 50 miles per hour in short bursts. When these strong swimmers swim long distances, their speeds generally range from about 5 to 10 miles per hour.

What is an exotic fish?

One not native to an area, but one introduced either by accident or on purpose is called an exotic. Some such species can cause problems. Many foreign species have no natural enemies in the new environment. This allows them to spread rapidly and threaten the survival of native species.

What's the biggest shark?

The whale shark is the biggest fish of any type. It earned its name not just for its size—it can grow 50 feet long—but also because its dark body, like that of some whales, is sprinkled with white spots. This gentle giant has teeth no bigger than a human baby's and eats only small fish and plankton.

ANIMALS

TFK Mystery Person

CLUE 1: Ever since I was a 10-year-old girl living in England, I dreamed of living with animals in Africa.
CLUE 2: I grew up to become one of the world's most respected researchers on animal behavior.
CLUE 3: I have lived among chimpanzees in Africa for more than 40 years and have gained insights into the similarities between humans and chimps. I have campaigned around the world to save these wonderful animals.

WHO AM I?

(See Answer Key that begins on page 340.)

David Turns 500

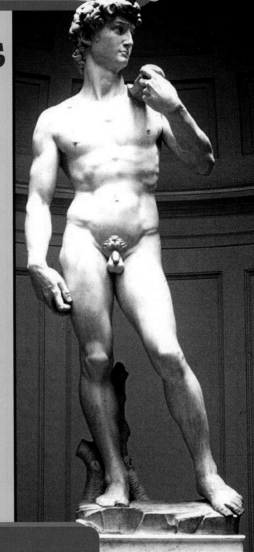

Michelangelo Buonarroti, known simply as Michelangelo, remains one of the most important artists of all time. Born in Tuscany, Italy, in 1475, the Renaissance sculptor, painter, architect and poet created some of the world's most famous works of art.

Dozens of celebrations are planned throughout 2004 to commemorate the 500th anniversary of Michelangelo's most famous sculpture, **David.** In the Bible, David fearlessly conquered the giant Goliath using only a slingshot and a rock. Michelangelo's *David* is regarded as a masterpiece because the marble statue is an ideal representation of the male figure. *David*, which measures nearly 14 feet tall, is on display in Florence, Italy.

Art conservationists caused a controversy in 2003, when they decided to clean up *David* for his 500th birthday. Art restorers used distilled water and a mud pack to lift the dust that had built up on *David*'s body. Opponents of the method said it could destroy some of the details of the statue. It took months to complete *David*'s bath.

TFK Top 5 Most Expensive Paintings

PAINTING	ARTIST	SALE PRICE
1. *Portrait of Dr. Gachet*	Vincent Van Gogh	$82,500,000
2. *Au Moulin de la Galette*	Pierre Auguste Renoir	$78,100,000
3. *Portrait de l'Artiste Sans Barbe*	Vincent Van Gogh	$70,500,000
4. *Massacre of the Innocents*	Peter Paul Rubens	$68,400,000
5. *Still Life with Curtain, Pitcher and Bowl of Fruit*	Paul Cezanne	$60,500,000

Source: Soyouwanna.com

Major Types of PAINTING

Have you ever painted a portrait or a still life? Some paintings combine types.

A **PORTRAIT** is an image of a person or an animal. Besides showing what someone looks like, a portrait often captures a mood or personality. This portrait, the *Mona Lisa*, is one of the most recognizable paintings. Leonardo da Vinci completed it in 1506. ● ● ● ● ● ● ● ►

A **STILL LIFE** shows objects. It reveals an artist's skills in painting shapes, light and shadow. Vincent van Gogh painted many still-lifes of sunflowers. He painted this one in 1889. ● ● ● ● ● ● ● ● ● ►

A **LANDSCAPE** is an outdoor scene. An artist can paint land, water, clouds, air and sunlight, as Claude Monet did in *The Beach at Sainte-Adresse*. ● ● ● ● ● ● ● ● ● ● ● ● ►

A **REAL-LIFE** scene captures life in action. It could show any place where living occurs.

A **RELIGIOUS WORK OF ART** shares a religious message.

The World of Art

A **MOSAIC** is a picture or design made by gluing together small stones, pieces of glass or other hard materials. In ancient times, grand homes sometimes had mosaic floors. ● ● ● ● ● ● ● ● ● ● ● ►

PHOTOGRAPHY was invented almost 200 years ago. We see photographs every day in newspapers and magazines, on billboards and buses and in museums and galleries. Ansel Adams and Mathew Brady were famous photographers.

For thousands of years, people all over the world have made **MASKS** to use in rituals, in their work, the theater and just for fun. Have you ever made a mask from a paper bag? ● ● ● ● ● ● ● ►

In prehistoric times, people wore **JEWELRY** even before they wore clothing. Jewelry has been created using everything from berries to gold.

People have made **SCULPTURE** from materials such as clay, marble, ice, wood and bronze. Some artists today create sculptures that move with the wind. Alberto Giacometti and Louise Nevelson were important sculptors.

As technology changes, the tools artists use change too. **NEW MEDIA** include video, performance, computer-generated imagery and installation (where an entire room may be made into a work of art).

Warm and Cool Colors

Artists use color to create a mood for their works. **WARM COLORS** are made with red, orange, yellow or some combination of these. They tend to make you think of sunlight and warmth.

In *The Fighting Temeraire* by William Turner, the warm colors of the sunset give a feeling of brightness and heat. • • • • • • •

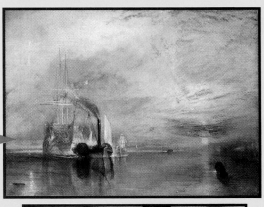

COOL COLORS are made with blue, green, purple or some combination of these. These colors might make you think of cool and peaceful things, like winter skies and still ponds.

In Georgia O'Keeffe's *Red Barn,* the cool • • • blue background contributes to the quiet feeling.

Perspective and Focal Point

PERSPECTIVE is a way of showing space in three dimensions. By using perspective, a flat picture can seem to show depth and distance. Look at the painting *Cape Cod Evening* by Edward Hopper. Notice how the straight lines on the house seem to move on a diagonal away from you, toward a • • • • background point? This is called **LINEAR PERSPECTIVE.**

Another way of showing perspective is **ATMOSPHERIC PERSPECTIVE.** The dark green area on the left seems farther away than the lighter green trees because light colors "jump out" while darker colors seem to fade away.

The **FOCAL POINT** is the part of the painting that catches your eye first. In the painting *The Wedding Feast* by Pieter Brueghel, your eye probably goes to the right, to the person in the blue shirt carrying the tray of pies. The bright blue shirt and white apron (and the two white pies) stand out against the dark colors of the rest of the painting. • • • • • •

Art movements

ABSTRACT EXPRESSIONISM

A style developed in the mid-20th century, Abstract Expressionism emphasizes form and color rather than an actual subject. Jackson Pollock and **WILLEM DE KOONING** were Abstract Expressionists.

BAROQUE

A form of art and architecture that was popular in Europe in the 17th and early 18th centuries, baroque art was very ornate, dramatic and realistic. Peter Paul Rubens and **REMBRANDT** were Baroque painters.

CUBISM

Cubism is a style of art that stresses basic abstract geometric forms and often presents the subject from many angles at the same time. **PABLO PICASSO** was a Cubist painter.

IMPRESSIONISM

Impressionism developed in France during the late 19th century. The Impressionists tried to capture an immediate visual interpretation of their subjects by using color rather than lines. Claude Monet and Edgar Degas were Impressionist painters.

POP ART

Pop art emerged in England and the U.S. after 1950. Pop artists use materials from the everyday world, such as comic strips and canned goods. **ANDY WARHOL** and Roy Lichtenstein were Pop artists.

ROMANTICISM

Romanticism was popular in the early 19th century. Romantic artists produced exotic, emotional works that portrayed an idealized world and nostalgia for the past. **WILLIAM BLAKE** was a member of the romantic school of painters.

TFK Mystery Person

Clue 1: I was an American photo-journalist born in Hoboken, New Jersey, in 1895.
Clue 2: I became famous for my photographs of the Great Depression of the 1930s.
Clue 3: My photos of people created a social record of those difficult times. Photojournalists around the world have followed my example.

WHO AM I?

(See Answer Key that begins on page 340.)

33

BOOKS

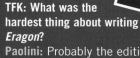

ERAGON
Christopher Paolini

Christopher Paolini, author

By Elizabeth Winchester

Twenty-year-old Christopher Paolini has always loved adventure books. In fact, he plotted out his first book, *Eragon*, when he was just 15! TFK talked to this storytelling teen about his books and how he ended up being one of the best-selling authors of all time!

TFK: What inspired you to write *Eragon*?
Paolini: I love fantasy. I love the sense of awe and wonder that you always get at the end of a great book or movie. *Eragon* was an attempt to capture that.

TFK: Where do you get your ideas?
Paolini: I'm definitely influenced by authors who have a fairly inventive use of language, imaginative worlds and a sense of wonder — authors who write about things that other people don't.

TFK: What was the hardest thing about writing *Eragon*?
Paolini: Probably the editing because I wasn't used to it. I had to learn a huge amount about grammar and commas and other things I had never paid much attention to before.

TFK: What kinds of books did you like to read when you were a kid?
Paolini: The Redwall books, all the Nancy Drew books, the Tom Swift books and the Ramona books (when I was much younger). The local library says I've checked out 3,000 or 4,000 books and my sister has checked out just as many. We read each other's books, so I definitely read a lot!

TFK: Do you have to be a good reader to be a good writer?
Paolini: If you are going to be creating art, you need to be familiar with different forms of that art. I like to know what other people are doing. I'm creating books because I love books. I hope that the more I know about them, the better writer I'll be.

TFK: What advice would you give to aspiring young writers?
Paolini: Write about what you enjoy the most or what touches you the most, otherwise you'll never be able to endure a book-length project. It's hard enough as it is writing about something you truly care about.

TFK: What kind of readers do you think will love *Eragon*?
Paolini: Anyone who is looking for a bit of magic in the world.

BOOK AWARDS

The Caldecott Medal honors an outstanding American picture book.

2004 Winner:

The Man Who Walked Between the Towers, Mordicai Gerstein, writer and illustrator

The Newbery Medal honors an outstanding example of children's literature. The Newbery winner is not a picture book.

2004 Winner:

The Tale of Despereaux: Being the Story of a Mouse, a Princess, Some Soup and a Spool of Thread, Kate DiCamillo

2003 National Book Award for Young People's Literature

The Canning Season, Polly Horvath

The Coretta Scott King Awards recognize black authors and illustrators whose works have promoted an understanding and appreciation of all cultures.

2004 Winners:

Writer: Angela Johnson, *The First Part Last*

Illustrator and Writer: Ashley Bryan, *Beautiful Blackbird*

2003 Boston Globe Horn Book Award

Nonfiction: *Fireboat: The Heroic Adventures of the John J. Harvey,* Maira Kalman

Picture Book: *Big Momma Makes the World,* Phyllis Root, writer; Helen Oxenbury, illustrator

Fiction and Poetry: *The Jamie and Angus Stories,* Anne Fine, writer; Penny Dale, illustrator

The Dewey Decimal System

Imagine walking into a house where room after room is filled with shelves, all packed with books in no specific order. Imagine trying to find the one book you want! That's what happened every day to Melvil Dewey, an American librarian who lived from 1851 to 1931. He became so unhappy trying to help people find books that he invented the Dewey Decimal System of Classification, which is still used in libraries today. The system numbers books by their subject matter in the following way.

000-099	General Works (encyclopedias, magazines, almanacs)
100-199	Philosophy and Psychology
200-299	Religion and Mythology
300-399	Social Science
400-499	Language
500-599	Math and Science
600-699	Medicine and Technology
700-799	Arts and Entertainment
800-899	Literature
900-999	History and Geography

The Big Read

The **British Broadcasting Corporation (BBC)** compiled a list of the most popular novels in England. The kids' titles ranged from classics to the Harry Potter books, from Dickens to Dahl. Check out what your peers across the Atlantic recommend.

Alice's Adventures in Wonderland
by Lewis Carroll

Alice falls down a rabbit hole and finds herself in Wonderland. Her odd encounters with such characters as the White Rabbit and the Queen of Hearts have enchanted readers since 1865.

Anne of Green Gables
by Lucy Maud Montgomery

The Cuthberts of Prince Edward Island planned to adopt a boy orphan, but Anne Shirley arrived instead. Redheaded, imaginative and mischievous, Anne provides the family with a daily dose of adventure. This is the first installment in a series of eight books.

The BFG by Roald Dahl

Although most children are terrified of giants and their wicked ways, Sophie has nothing to worry about when she's abducted by the BFG. The Big Friendly Giant blows happy dreams through children's windows.

Black Beauty by Anna Sewell

This classic follows Black Beauty as it matures from a young colt into an overworked cab horse. The story, told from the viewpoint of the horse, also teaches lessons about humane animal treatment.

Charlie and the Chocolate Factory
by Roald Dahl

After five children find a golden ticket in their chocolate bars, they're treated to a private tour of Willy Wonka's famous candy factory. Charlie Bucket, the most decent of the lot, will never be the same after the adventure.

Double Act by Jacqueline Wilson

Identical twins cope with the death of their mother, a new town, a new school and their father's new girlfriend.

Goodnight Mister Tom
by Michelle Magorian

With World War II looming, Willie Beech, an abused child from London, is sent to the countryside, where he experiences a very different life with "Mr. Tom."

The Hobbit
by J.R.R. Tolkien

Hobbit Bilbo Baggins dislikes adventure. But when Gandalf the Grey Wizard arrives at his door, he finds himself one of 13 dwarves who seek to reclaim a lost treasure from a dragon. *The Hobbit* is considered the prequel to Tolkien's *Lord of the Rings* trilogy.

Holes by Louis Sachar

Stanley Yelnats, accused of a crime he didn't commit, is sentenced to Camp Green Lake, a detention center where boys dig holes to build character. Stanley soon realizes that they are digging for more than just character.

The Lion, the Witch and the Wardrobe
by C.S. Lewis

Peter, Susan, Edmund and Lucy discover a magical land, called Narnia, through the back of a wardrobe. In Narnia, the siblings help the golden lion Aslan fight against the evil White Witch.

go Read an interview with Holes author Sachar at *www.timeforkids.com/holes*

Little Women
by Louisa May Alcott

The March sisters come of age while their father is away during the Civil War. Told in two parts, the book describes how beautiful Meg, adventurous Jo, sensitive Beth and romantic Amy bond as young sisters and then pursue their individual dreams as they mature into adults.

Lord of the Flies
by William Golding

A group of English schoolboys stranded on a deserted island must fend for themselves. At first the boys work together to make shelters, light fires and hunt for food. The cooperative environment is shattered when resentment and cliques give rise to violence.

 Peek at some Potter magic at www.timeforkids.com/potter

The Princess Diaries
by Meg Cabot

Mia Thermopolis is like any normal ninth grader in New York until her father tells her that he's the Prince of Genovia and she's the crown princess. (Other books in the series include *Princess in the Spotlight*, *Princess in Love* and *Princess in Waiting*.)

The Secret Garden
by Frances Hodgson Burnett

Orphaned Mary Lennox arrives at her uncle's Misselthwaite Manor convinced that she'll hate living there. But she's pleasantly surprised when she and her cousin discover a magical garden.

Treasure Island
by Robert Louis Stevenson

After a pirate shows up at his mother's inn, young Jim finds a treasure map and sets out in search of buried treasure on a faraway island.

Reference Books: You Could Look It Up

Atlas
A book of maps with or without text
Example: *Time For Kids World Atlas*

Biographical Index
A book of information about people who are well known in a particular field
Example: *Who's Who in America*

Dictionary
Definitions, spellings and pronunciations of words, arranged in alphabetical order
Example: *The Merriam-Webster Collegiate Dictionary*

Encyclopedia
Information on just about every subject, arranged in alphabetical order
Example: *Encyclopædia Britannica*

Guidebook
Information and directions, often for travelers
Example: *Let's Go Europe*

Thesaurus
Synonyms, or near synonyms, for words as well as related terms
Example: *Roget's Thesaurus*

Yearbook/Almanac
Current information on a wide range of topics. You're reading one now!

Types of Literature

Here are some examples of kinds of fiction (made-up stories) and nonfiction (books about real-life events and people).

An **autobiography** is the story of a person's life written or told by that person.
Example: *A Girl From Yamhill: A Memoir* by Beverly Cleary

A **biography** is the story of a person's life written or told by another person.
Example: *Langston Hughes: American Poet* by Alice Walker

A **fable** is a story that teaches a moral or a lesson. It often has animal characters.
Example: "The Tortoise and the Hare"

A **folktale** is a story that has been passed down, usually orally, within a culture. It may be based on superstition and may feature supernatural characters. Folktales include fairy tales, tall tales, trickster tales and other stories passed down over generations.
Example: "Hansel and Gretel"

A **legend** is a story that has been handed down over generations and is believed to be based on history, though it typically mixes fact and fiction. The hero of a legend is usually a human.
Example: Robin Hood

A **myth** is a traditional story that a particular culture or group once accepted as sacred and true. It may center on a god or supernatural being and explain how something came to be, such as lightning or music or the world itself.
Example: The Greek story of the Titan Prometheus bringing fire to humans

TFK Top 5 Books Kids Like to Read

What's the best book you have ever read? That's the question the National Education Association asked in a recent survey of 1,800 students ages 7 to 15. Here are their top picks.

1. Harry Potter (series)
   J.K. Rowling

2. Goosebumps (series)
   R.L. Stine

3. Green Eggs and Ham
   Dr. Seuss

4. The Cat in the Hat
   Dr. Seuss

5. Arthur (series)
   Marc Brown

SOURCE: NATIONAL EDUCATION ASSOCIATION

Puzzling Potter

Test your knowledge of the latest installment in the Harry Potter series, *Harry Potter and the Order of the Phoenix.*

1. What career does Harry tell Professor McGonagall he is interested in pursuing?
   a. Training to become an Auror
   b. Teaching at Hogwarts School of Witchcraft and Wizardry
   c. Playing professional Quidditch

2. Who lives at 12 Grimmauld Place?
   a. The Weasleys rent it as a summer home
   b. Albus Dumbledore
   c. Sirius Black—it is his family's estate

3. Who sent the Dementors to attack Harry on Privet Drive?
   a. Voldemort
   b. Dolores Umbridge
   c. Wormtail and the Death Eaters

4. Who is the Secret-Keeper for the Order of the Phoenix?
   a. Severus Snape
   b. Cornelius Fudge
   c. Albus Dumbledore

5. What reward does Ron choose for being named a Prefect?
   a. A new owl
   b. A new broom
   c. A new set of dress robes

(See Answer Key that begins on page 340.)

A Series of Series

Harry Potter isn't the only young hero to star in a series of books. In fact, there are dozens of other series that are equally adventurous. Check these out while you wait for book No. 7.

Artemis Fowl **by Eoin Colfer**
Boy genius Artemis Fowl has crime in his blood, but you can't help but cheer for him as he takes on modern fairies.

Little House on the Prairie **by Laura Ingalls Wilder**
The author vividly chronicles the triumphs and tragedies she experienced as a pioneer in the Midwest during the 19th century.

Magic Treehouse **by Mary Pope Osborne**
A magic treehouse transports Jack and Annie to another time and place, where they must carry out a daring mission.

Ramona **by Beverly Cleary**
Ramona Quimby has a knack for finding trouble and annoying her older sister, Beezus.

A Series of Unfortunate Events **by Lemony Snicket**
The three orphaned Baudelaire children put their intelligence and resourcefulness to work as they encounter ghastly misadventures.

TFK Mystery Person

CLUE 1: I was born in Joplin, Missouri, in 1902.
CLUE 2: During the 1920s, I became part of a group of talented African American artists and writers who lived in Harlem, part of New York City.
CLUE 3: I wrote more than 50 books, and also worked as a journalist and playwright. One theme ran through all my books: America is a nation built by many races.

WHO AM I?

(See Answer Key that begins on page 340.)

BUILDINGS
& LANDMARKS

A Sky-High Plan for New York

A glass tower planned for the site of the World Trade Center will be the world's tallest building.

The world's tallest building will stand proudly in New York City by the year 2009. Plans for a 1,776-foot glass "Freedom Tower" will be built on land where the Twin Towers once stood, New York Mayor Michael Bloomberg announced.

What Will the Tower Look Like?
The twisty-shaped tower will have 70 floors of office space, a public observation deck, rooftop restaurants and an open area at the top of the building. Its 1,776-foot height represents the year America signed the Declaration of Independence. The tower will be supported by crisscrossing cables meant to look just like the nearby Brooklyn Bridge.

A 276-foot spire on top of the tower will represent the Statue of Liberty's arm holding the torch of freedom. A 200-foot broadcasting antenna will sit atop the spire. Energy-generating windmills will also be housed above the building. Using wind to make electricity, they will provide 20% to 40% of the building's energy. The tower is expected to cost about $1.5 billion to build.

Safety First
Architects David Child and Daniel Libeskind designed the tower. Childs said the tower will be "the safest building in the world." He said it will include wider staircases, a separate stairway and elevator for firefighters, "blast-resistant glass" and more public stairways with direct access to the street.

At the unveiling of the new design, Libeskind called the building a "beacon of light and hope in a world that is often dark."

New York Governor George E. Pataki said the building "will show the world that freedom will always triumph over terror." Larry Silverstein, the developer of the new World Trade Center site, said the entire five-building complex will be complete by 2013.

By Laura Girardi

Counting its antenna, the Freedom Tower will rise more than 2,000 feet.

Tall Tale

In October 2003, a new office building in Taipei, Taiwan, officially became the tallest building in the world. Called Taipei 101, the skyscraper measures an impressive 1,667 feet. Made of steel, concrete and glass, the skyscraper will house offices for 12,000 occupants, a shopping mall and the Taipei stock exchange. It will also feature the world's fastest elevators.

Until now, the tallest buildings in the world were Petronas Tower 1 and Petronas Tower 2 in Kuala Lumpur, Malaysia. Both buildings are 1,483 feet tall. But Taipei 101's reign as the world's tallest building will be brief. In 2007, China is expected to complete an even taller building, to be called the Shanghai World Financial Center. New York City's Freedom Tower will surpass that in 2009.

Taipei 101 can withstand earthquakes. Its elevators travel at 37 miles per hour.

Impressive Lengths and HEIGHTS

Tallest Buildings in the U.S.

	BUILDING	LOCATION	STORIES	HEIGHT (FEET)
1.	SEARS TOWER	CHICAGO	110	1,450
2.	EMPIRE STATE BLDG.	NEW YORK	102	1,250
3.	AON CENTRE	CHICAGO	80	1,136

Tallest Towers	World:	Canadian National Tower (CN Tower); Toronto, Canada		1,815 feet
	U.S.:	LORAN-C Tower; Port Clarence, Alaska		1,350 feet
Longest Vehicle Tunnel		Laerdal; Laerdal-Aurland, Norway		15.2 miles
Longest Bridges	World:	Akashi Kaikyo; Hyogo, Japan		main span* of 6,529 feet
	U.S.:	Verrazano-Narrows; Lower New York Bay		main span* of 4,260 feet

*The main span of a bridge is the distance between two supports.

TFK Top 5 Longest Rail Tunnels

NAME	COUNTRY	LENGTH (MILES)
1. Seikan	Japan	33.46
2. Channel Tunnel	France/England	31.35
3. Moscow Metro	Russia	19.07
4. London Underground	United Kingdom	17.30
5. Hakkoda	Japan	16.44

Source: *The Top 10 of Everything 2004* (DK)

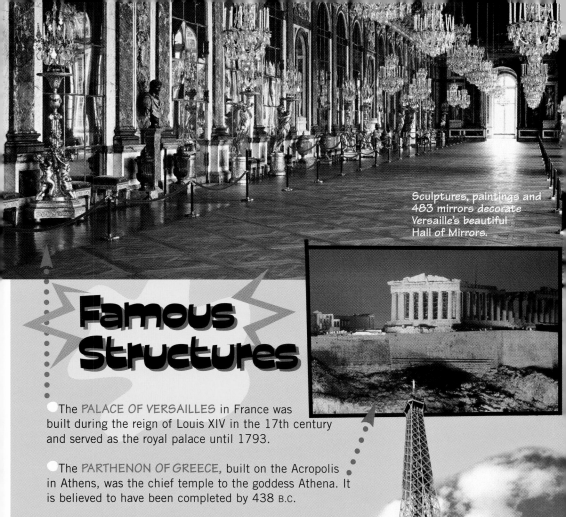

Sculptures, paintings and 483 mirrors decorate Versaille's beautiful Hall of Mirrors.

Famous Structures

● The PALACE OF VERSAILLES in France was built during the reign of Louis XIV in the 17th century and served as the royal palace until 1793.

● The PARTHENON OF GREECE, built on the Acropolis in Athens, was the chief temple to the goddess Athena. It is believed to have been completed by 438 B.C.

● The COLOSSEUM OF ROME, the largest and most famous of the Roman amphitheaters, was opened for use in A.D. 80.

● The PANTHEON at Rome was begun in 27 B.C. It has served for 20 centuries as a place of worship.

● The TOWER OF LONDON is a group of buildings covering 13 acres. The central White Tower was begun in 1078. It was once a royal residence.

● The VATICAN is a group of buildings in Rome that includes the residence of the Pope. The Basilica of St. Peter, the largest church in the Christian world, was begun in 1450.

● The EIFFEL TOWER in Paris was built in 1889. It is 984 feet high (1,056 feet including the television tower).

The Eiffel Tower was built by Alexandre Gustave Eiffel.

The white marble TAJ MAHAL (built 1632–1650) at Agra, India, was built by Shah Jahan as a tomb for his wife.

The 12th-century temples at ANGKOR WAT in Cambodia are surrounded by a moat and have walls decorated with sculpture.

The GREAT WALL OF CHINA (begun 228 B.C.), designed as a defense against nomadic tribes, is so big and long that it can be seen from space!

The ALHAMBRA in Granada, Spain, is a masterpiece of Muslim architecture. Construction of the palace and fortress began in 1248. It was finished in 1354.

The BROOKLYN BRIDGE, built between 1869 and 1883, was the achievement of engineer John Roebling. It was the first steel-wire suspension bridge in the world.

The massive standing stones of STONEHENGE are located in the south of England. Begun some 5,000 years ago, their purpose remains a mystery.

MACHU PICCHU is an Inca fortress in the Andes Mountains of Peru. It is believed to have been built in the mid-15th century.

The DUOMO, with its pink, white and green marble façade, is a symbol of the Renaissance. Construction on the cathedral in Florence, Italy, began in 1296, and it was completed 200 years later.

go> For more about famous structures around the world, www.FacTMoNSTeR.CoM

The words of Martin Luther King Jr. are etched on the Civil Rights Memorial.

Architects and Their Masterpieces

An architect designs homes, libraries, office buildings, museums and other structures and environments. Here are some famous modern architects and their signature creations.

*R. Buckminster Fuller (1895–1983) An engineer and a poet, Fuller was known for his revolutionary designs that were both innovative and efficient. He developed the Dymaxion principle, which called for using the least possible amount of material and energy in construction and manufacturing. His most famous creation was the geodesic dome.

*Antonio Gaudí (1852-1926) Gaudí, a leader of Spain's Art Nouveau movement, was known for his fluid and flamboyant style and his use of color and textures. His surreal designs, often based on Gothic architecture, included countless curves, angles and towers. He spent much of his career designing Barcelona's Temple de la Sagrada Familia (Church of the Holy Family), which resembles a giant sand castle. He started work on the church in 1882, and was still at it in when he died in 1926. In fact, the building still has not been completed.

*Frank Gehry (b. 1929) Many of Gehry's designs are oddly shaped and made from a variety of materials, such as corrugated metal and chain-link fencing. His best-known project is the **Guggenheim Museum** in Bilbao, Spain.

*Maya Lin (b. 1959) Lin earned fame when, as a student at Yale, she won a contest to design the Vietnam Veterans Memorial in Washington, D.C. She also designed the **Civil Rights Memorial** in Montgomery, Alabama.

*Julia Morgan (1872-1957) Morgan was the first woman accepted into the architecture department of Paris's prestigious Ecole des Beaux-Arts. Many of her designs, which include dozens of homes and San Simeon, William Randolph Hearst's palace-like California estate, reflect her interest in Beaux Arts. This style of architecture features well-proportioned buildings covered with intricate ornaments. Her creations are known for their careful detail and craftsmanship.

Frank Gehry's use of curved metal makes his Guggenheim Museum a special building.

The Seven Wonders OF THE ANCIENT WORLD

Since ancient times, people have put together many **"SEVEN WONDERS"** lists. Below are the seven wonders that are most widely agreed upon as being in the original list.

1. Pyramids of Egypt
A group of three pyramids located at Giza, Egypt, were built around 2680 B.C. Of all the Ancient Wonders, only the pyramids still stand.

2. Hanging Gardens of Babylon
These terraced gardens, located in what is now Iraq, were supposedly built by Nebuchadnezzar II around 600 B.C. to please his queen.

3. Statue of Zeus (Jupiter) at Olympia
The sculptor Phidias (fifth century B.C.) built this 40-foot-high statue in gold and ivory. It was located in Olympia, Greece.

4. Temple of Artemis (Diana) at Ephesus
This beautiful marble structure was begun about 350 B.C. in honor of the goddess Artemis. It was located in Ephesus, Turkey.

5. Mausoleum at Halicarnassus
This huge above-ground tomb was erected in Bodrum, Turkey, by Queen Artemisia in memory of her husband, who died in 353 B.C.

6. Colossus at Rhodes
This bronze statue of Helios (Apollo), about 105 feet high, was the work of the sculptor Chares. Rhodes is a Greek island in the Aegean Sea.

7. Pharos of Alexandria
The Pharos (lighthouse) of Alexandria was built during the third century B.C. off the coast of Egypt. It stood about 450 feet high.

 **TFK Mystery Person**

CLUE 1: I am one of America's greatest architects.
CLUE 2: Working in Chicago in the late 19th century, I helped design the world's first skyscrapers. I believed that the form of a building should be based on its function.
CLUE 3: Some of my buildings still stand, including the Auditorium Building and the Krause Music Store in Chicago.

WHO AM I?
(See Answer Key that begins on page 340.)

CALENDARS

& HOLIDAYS

2005

January
S	M	T	W	T	F	S
						1
2	3	4	5	6	7	8
9	10	11	12	13	14	15
16	17	18	19	20	21	22
23	24	25	26	27	28	29
30	31					

1 New Year's Day
17 Martin Luther King Jr.'s birthday observed
21 Eid al-Adha*

February
S	M	T	W	T	F	S
		1	2	3	4	5
6	7	8	9	10	11	12
13	14	15	16	17	18	19
20	21	22	23	24	25	26
27	28					

2 Groundhog Day
2 Ash Wednesday
9 Chinese New Year
10 First day of Muharram*
14 Valentine's Day
21 Washington's Birthday

March
S	M	T	W	T	F	S
		1	2	3	4	5
6	7	8	9	10	11	12
13	14	15	16	17	18	19
20	21	22	23	24	25	26
27	28	29	30	31		

17 St. Patrick's Day
20 Spring begins
25 Purim*
27 Easter Sunday

April
S	M	T	W	T	F	S
					1	2
3	4	5	6	7	8	9
10	11	12	13	14	15	16
17	18	19	20	21	22	23
24	25	26	27	28	29	30

3 Daylight Saving Time begins
24 First day of Passover*

May
S	M	T	W	T	F	S
1	2	3	4	5	6	7
8	9	10	11	12	13	14
15	16	17	18	19	20	21
22	23	24	25	26	27	28
29	30	31				

8 Mother's Day
30 Memorial Day observed

June
S	M	T	W	T	F	S
			1	2	3	4
5	6	7	8	9	10	11
12	13	14	15	16	17	18
19	20	21	22	23	24	25
26	27	28	29	30		

13 Shavuot*
19 Father's Day
21 Summer begins

July
S	M	T	W	T	F	S
					1	2
3	4	5	6	7	8	9
10	11	12	13	14	15	16
17	18	19	20	21	22	23
24	25	26	27	28	29	30
31						

4 Independence Day

August
S	M	T	W	T	F	S
	1	2	3	4	5	6
7	8	9	10	11	12	13
14	15	16	17	18	19	20
21	22	23	24	25	26	27
28	29	30	31			

September
S	M	T	W	T	F	S
				1	2	3
4	5	6	7	8	9	10
11	12	13	14	15	16	17
18	19	20	21	22	23	24
25	26	27	28	29	30	

5 Labor Day
22 Autumn begins

October
S	M	T	W	T	F	S
						1
2	3	4	5	6	7	8
9	10	11	12	13	14	15
16	17	18	19	20	21	22
23	24	25	26	27	28	29
30	31					

4 Ramadan begins*
4 Rosh Hashanah*
10 Columbus Day observed
13 Yom Kippur*
18 Sukkot*
26 Simchat Torah*
30 Daylight Saving Time ends
31 Halloween

November
S	M	T	W	T	F	S
		1	2	3	4	5
6	7	8	9	10	11	12
13	14	15	16	17	18	19
20	21	22	23	24	25	26
27	28	29	30			

3 Ramadan ends (Eid al-Fitr)*
11 Veterans Day
24 Thanksgiving

December
S	M	T	W	T	F	S
				1	2	3
4	5	6	7	8	9	10
11	12	13	14	15	16	17
18	19	20	21	22	23	24
25	26	27	28	29	30	31

21 Winter begins
25 First Day of Hanukkah*
25 Christmas
26 Kwanzaa begins

* All Jewish and Islamic holidays begin at sundown the day before they are listed here.

Federal Holidays

New Year's Day
January 1
New Year's Day has its origin in ancient Roman times, when sacrifices were offered to Janus, the two-faced Roman god who looked back on the past and forward to the future.

Martin Luther King Jr. Day
Third Monday in January
This holiday honors the civil rights leader. It has been a federal holiday since 1986.

Washington's Birthday
Third Monday in February
Although this holiday is sometimes called Presidents Day to honor both George Washington and Abraham Lincoln, the federal holiday is officially Washington's Birthday.

Memorial Day
Last Monday in May
Memorial Day originated in 1868 as a day when the graves of Civil War soldiers would be decorated. Later, it became a holiday dedicated to the memory of all war dead.

Independence Day
July 4
The Declaration of Independence was adopted on July 4, 1776. It declared that the 13 colonies were independent of Britain.

Labor Day
First Monday in September
Labor Day, a day set aside in honor of workers, was first celebrated in New York in 1882 under the sponsorship of the Central Labor Union.

Big balloons are part of the fun at the Macy's Thanksgiving Day parade.

Columbus Day
Second Monday in October
Columbus Day honors Christopher Columbus's landing in the New World in 1492.

Veterans Day
November 11
Veterans Day honors all men and women who have served America in its armed forces.

Thanksgiving
Fourth Thursday in November
The first American Thanksgiving took place in 1621 to celebrate the harvest reaped by the Plymouth Colony after it survived a harsh winter.

Christmas Day
December 25
The most popular holiday of the Christian year, Christmas is celebrated as the anniversary of the birth of Jesus.

47

Other FUN Holidays

Groundhog Day
February 2
Legend has it that on this morning if a groundhog can see its shadow, there will be six more weeks of winter.

Mardi Gras
Last day before Lent
Mardi Gras, or "Fat Tuesday," is a time of carnivals and parades before Ash Wednesday starts the penitent Christian season of Lent.

Valentine's Day
February 14
Named for the third-century martyr St. Valentine, this day is celebrated with candy, cards and other tokens of love.

Mother's Day
Second Sunday in May
Having a day to honor mothers goes back at least as far as 17th-century England, when Mothering Sunday began.

Father's Day
Third Sunday in June
This U.S. holiday honoring fathers began in 1910 in Spokane, Washington.

Halloween
October 31
Halloween is celebrated with jack-o-lanterns, costumes and the telling of ghost stories.

TFK Puzzles & Games

Straight from the Heart
Cross out all the letters that appear five times. The remaining letters spell out a secret Valentine's Day message.

(See Answer Key that begins on page 340.)

Kwanzaa
December 26 through January 1
Kwanzaa, an African-American holiday, honors the values of ancient African cultures.

The Chinese Calendar
In the Chinese calendar, each year is named after one of 12 animals. **The Chinese New Year** is celebrated at the second new moon after the winter solstice and falls between January 21 and February 19 on the western calendar.
Chinese New Year Dates
2005 (Year of the Rooster) February 9
2006 (Year of the Dog) January 29

Christian Holidays
2005

Ash Wednesday
February 2
The first day of Lent

Easter
March 27
The resurrection of Jesus

Pentecost
May 15
The feast of the Holy Spirit

First Sunday in Advent
November 27
The start of the Christmas season

Christmas Day
December 25
The birth of Jesus

Homework TIP

Be sure to finish homework assignments on time. That way, if you are late handing in your assignment one day, your teacher may be more understanding.

All Jewish and Muslim holidays begin at sundown the day before they are listed here.

Jewish Holidays
2005

Purim
March 25
The feast of lots

Yom Kippur
October 13
The day of atonement

Passover
April 24
The feast of unleavened bread

Sukkot
October 18
The feast of the tabernacles

Shavuot
June 13
The feast of first fruits

Simchat Torah
October 26
The rejoicing of the law

Rosh Hashanah
October 4
The Jewish New Year

Hanukkah
December 25
The festival of lights

Muslim Holidays
2005

Eid al-Adha
January 21
The festival of sacrifice

Muharram
February 10
The Muslim New Year

Mawlid al-Nabi
April 21
The prophet Muhammad's birthday

Ramadan
begins October 4
The month of fasting

Eid al-Fitr
November 3
Ramadan ends

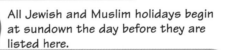

Festivals Around the World

Carnival

Brazil's most popular and festive holiday is **Carnival**. In fact, many people consider Carnival one of the world's biggest celebrations. Each spring, on the Saturday before Ash Wednesday, the streets of Brazil's largest city, Rio de Janeiro, come alive with wild parties, festivals and glamorous balls.

The **Samba School Parade** is the highlight of the four-day event. About 3,000 performers, clad in ornate costumes covered with feathers, beads and thousands of sequins, dance down the parade route alongside dazzling floats and into the Sambadrome—a dance stadium built for the event. Judges award a prize to the most spectacular group of dancers.

In Rio de Janeiro, Brazil, people wear dazzling costumes during Carnival.

Çocuk Bayrami

Each April 23, Turkey celebrates Çocuk Bayrami, or **Children's Day**. Turkish leader Mustafa Kemal Atatürk declared the holiday in 1920, as Turkey was becoming an independent nation after the fall of the Ottoman Empire. He did it to illustrate that children were the future of the new nation.

Children all over Turkey dress up in special outfits or the national costume for Çocuk Bayrami. Boys who dress in the national costume usually wear baggy silk pants, a colorful vest, a white shirt and a sequined hat called a *tepelik*. Girls wear a long colorful gown called a kaftan and an ornate veil. Many children perform in plays or musicals. The centerpiece of Çocuk Bayrami takes place in Turkey's capital, Ankara, where children from all over the world sing and dance in a spectacular pageant.

Trung Thu

Vietnamese children look forward to the 15th day of the eighth lunar month, when they celebrate Trung Thu. This mid-fall festival commemorates the moon at its brightest and most beautiful. Traditionally, the festival also marked the end of harvest, and parents who had been hard at work in the fields enjoyed spending extra time with their children and giving them gifts.

The children wear colorful masks and dance in the streets with lanterns that are illuminated by candles. The lanterns, which are made out of bamboo and plastic, represent the moon.

The children also feast on moon cakes. Shaped like fish or flowers, the sweet cakes are filled with sugar and meat or eggs.

During Trung Thu, Vietnamese also remember relatives who have died. They light incense and burn fake money as tributes to them.

Holi

Holi is literally one of the most colorful festivals in the world. Hindus celebrate the festival in early March, when wheat is harvested. Holi commemorates spring and the mythological stories of the god Krishna and Prahlad, the son of the king. In Hindu legend, during Holi, Krishna covered Radha and her friends with colored water and stole off with their clothes as they bathed.

In the other story, Prahlad, the son of the king, refused his father's demand that he worship him rather than god. God saved Prahlad from death twice, first when the king ordered him killed and again when the king's evil sister, Holika, led Prahlad into a huge bonfire.

On the eve of Holi, Hindus dress in their finest clothes and watch a bonfire. A large tree branch, representing Prahlad, is placed in the middle of the fire. The branch is removed, recreating Prahlad's rescue. The next morning, people put on old clothes and dust each other with colored powders. It's the one day that parents let their children get filthy!

St. Lucia

On December 13, one of the longest and darkest nights of the winter, Swedes celebrate the festival of St. Lucia, the patron saint of light. In many homes, a girl gets up early in the morning and puts on a long white dress, with a red sash at the waist, and a laurel crown decorated with four candles. She serves her family warm *lussekatt* buns for breakfast. The buns, shaped like the number 8, are usually flavored with saffron and topped with raisins or nuts. Boys, called star boys, wear long white shirts and pointed hats. They help serve the buns. Children often go to school dressed in the costumes and serve the buns to their teachers.

TFK Top 5 New Year's Resolutions

Did you make New Year's resolutions? Almost 8,000 kids from all around the country voted in a New Year's poll. Here are the resolutions that got the most votes. Is yours on this list?

1. Get better grades
2,121 votes

2. Be nicer to my brother or sister
877

3. Eat less junk food
869

4. Get more sleep
868

5. Get more exercise
811

MEASURING YEARS

The calendar most Americans use is called the Gregorian calendar. In an ordinary year this calendar has 365 days, which is about the amount of time it takes Earth to make one trip around the Sun.

Earth's journey actually takes slightly more than a year. It takes 365 days, 5 hours, 48 minutes and 46 seconds. Every fourth year these extra hours, minutes and seconds are added up to make another day. When this happens, the year has 366 days and is called a **leap year.**

GROUPS OF YEARS

- Olympiad: 4 years
- Decade: 10 years
- Century: 100 years
- Millennium: 1,000 years

Seasons

In the Northern Hemisphere, the year is divided into four seasons. **Each season begins at a solstice or an equinox.**

In the Southern Hemisphere, the dates (and the seasons) are reversed. The summer solstice (still the longest day of the year) falls around December 21, and the winter solstice is around June 21. So when it's summer in North America, it's winter in South America (and vice versa).

- The spring equinox brings the start of spring, around March 21. At the equinox, day and night are of about equal length.

- Fall begins at the fall equinox, around September 21. Day and night are of about equal length.

- The summer solstice, which happens around June 21, has the longest daylight time. It's also the first day of summer.

- The winter solstice, around December 21, has the shortest daylight time and officially kicks off winter.

MONTHS

Months are based roughly on the cycles of the moon. A lunar (moon) month is 29½ days, or the time from one new moon to the next.

But 12 lunar months add up to just 354 days—11 days fewer than in our calendar year. To even things out, these days are added to months during the year. As a result, most months have 30 or 31 days.

To figure out how many days are in a month, **remember:** "30 days have September, April, June and November. All the rest have 31, except February, which has 28."

THE NAMES OF THE MONTHS

- January was named after Janus, protector of the gateway to heaven.
- February was named after Februalia, a time period when sacrifices were made to atone for sins.
- March was named after Mars, the god of war, signifying that fighting interrupted by the winter could be resumed.
- April is from aperire, Latin for "to open" (buds).
- May was named after Maia, the goddess of growth of plants.
- June is from Junius, Latin for the goddess Juno.
- July was named after Julius Caesar.
- August was named after Augustus, the first Roman Emperor.
- September is from septem, Latin for seven.
- October is from octo, Latin for eight.
- November is from novem, Latin for nine.
- December is from decem, Latin for ten.

BIRTHSTONES

MONTH	STONE
JANUARY	GARNET
FEBRUARY	AMETHYST
MARCH	AQUAMARINE or BLOODSTONE
APRIL	DIAMOND
MAY	EMERALD
JUNE	PEARL, ALEXANDRITE or MOONSTONE
JULY	RUBY or STAR RUBY
AUGUST	PERIDOT or SARDONYX
SEPTEMBER	SAPPHIRE or STAR SAPPHIRE
OCTOBER	OPAL or TOURMALINE
NOVEMBER	TOPAZ or CITRINE
DECEMBER	TURQUOISE, LAPIS LAZULI, BLUE ZIRCON or BLUE TOPAZ

Days

A day is measured by how long it takes Earth to rotate once—24 hours. The names of the days are based on seven celestial bodies—the Sun (Sunday), the Moon (Monday), Mars (Tuesday), Mercury (Wednesday), Jupiter (Thursday), Venus (Friday) and Saturn (Saturday). The ancient Romans believed these bodies revolved around Earth and influenced its events.

TFK Mystery Person

CLUE 1: I was born in Webster, West Virginia, on May 1, 1864.
CLUE 2: I grew up wanting to create a special day to honor my mother. So in 1907, I started a letter-writing campaign to create a national holiday for mothers in the U.S.
CLUE 3: Mother's Day has since become an international holiday. It is celebrated in 152 countries.

WHO AM I?

(See Answer Key that begins on page 340.)

go Test Your holiday smarts at
www.timeforkids.com/holidays/trivia

53

Messaging Mania

BY KATHRYN R. SATTERFIELD

THINK FAST! Translate this conversation into formal English: "Wass^?" "N2M, U?" "JC." "G2G. BFN." Stumped? The dictionary won't help you, but our handy guide will (*see below*).

If you figured it out right away, you are probably among the 60% of kids online who use instant messaging, or IM. Yahoo, MSN and AOL offer software that allows users to have real-time conversations in pop-up text windows online. Instant messages are typed so fast that users don't slow down to capitalize, add periods and commas or spell out words. As a result, new word abbreviations and IM slang are being invented faster than a high-speed Internet modem.

A typical instant-messaging session usually lasts more than half an hour, involves three or more buddies and often includes friends from different areas. More than one in three IM users say they use it every day, according to the Pew Internet and American Life Project. Nearly half of all online teens believe that the Internet has improved their friendships. It's a quick, easy way to keep in touch.

Steven Mintz, 13, prefers messaging to the phone "because I can talk to more people at once." Chatting online is also a good way to keep up with friends who live far away. Kids don't have to worry about running up the phone bill.

Instant messaging is not always a friendship builder. Sometimes, kids use it to air angry or hurt feelings. Such kids aren't necessarily trying to be mean. Often it's just easier to say something online than in person. Oliver Davies, 11, of Palo Alto, California, says that with IM, "I can express my emotions more easily, without having the guilt of saying it face-to-face."

I.M. NOT SO BAD

Many parents and teachers think kids' instant messaging habits are taking away from more important things. Julia Long of Bellingham, Washington, says that when her son, Taylor, 13, "is waiting for a beep, it's hard (for him) to stay focused on homework or any kind of family activity."

Teachers get upset when Internet slang and emoticons, such as "u," "r" and "wuz," show up in kids' writing.

Kids' safety is also a concern. Staying connected is fine, but an online friendship with a stranger is not. Many parents monitor IM'ing, either by limiting time online or by keeping the computer in a common area.

GET THE MESSAGE!

Here are some abbreviations and slang kids often use while IM'ing with friends.

bfn: bye for now
brb: be right back
g2g: got to go
jc: just chillin'
l8r: later
lol: laugh out loud

CAN YOU BELIEVE JENNY DIDN'T INVITE ME TO HER PARTY!!!!????

Shhh, don't tell her I'm here.

she only invited 3 people, katie... her mom wouldn't let anyone else come.

but i've invited her to all my parties! so bummed! y wuzn't i invited?!!

maybe you should ask jenny

SupaStar2003

y should i??? if she doesn't want me at her party I'm not speaking to her!

Signed Off at 7:56:08 PM

GoodGirl109

Researchers who study kids and the Internet say instant messaging isn't getting in the way of real life. They note that new technology often triggers old, exaggerated fears. "It's similar to what was said in the 1980s about video games and in the '60s about television," says Nalini Kotamraju, an expert on how kids use technology to communicate. "There was this worry that kids would do nothing else."

Even parents and teachers who don't like IM have to admit that at least kids are writing. And their typing skills are improving. Is it at the expense of proper English? Not so long as kids learn the difference between formal and conversational English, says Naomi Baron, professor of linguistics at American University in Washington, D.C.

"Language has always changed, and it always will," Baron said. "It must change as the things we do and the things we encounter change."

Wat a relief! G2G. L8R.

nm: not much
n2m: not too much
oic: Oh, I see
pos: parents over shoulder
rly: really
rofl: rolling on the floor laughing
sry: sorry
sup, wass^: What's up?
ur: your
wat: what
wuz: was

Excellent Emoticons

:-)	happy
:-(	sad
:-I	no feelings
:-D	very happy
:-P	tongue out
:-&	tongue twisted
;-)	wink
:-$	mouth shut, "not tellin'"
:'(	crying
:-o	surprised

Did You Know?

About 74 million U.S. households have at least one computer. That's 69% of the population. More than 50% of the U.S. population has Internet access at home.

COMPUTER, INTERNET

1945 >The computer age begins with the debut of ENIAC (Electronic Numerical Integrator and Calculator). It is the first multipurpose computer.

1969 >The Internet era begins. Four universities in the U.S. are connected in a communications network created by the Advanced Research Project Agency (ARPA). It is called ARPANET.

1972 >Electronic mail is introduced.
>Magnavox's Odyssey debuts as the first home video-game system. It offers only one game.

1975 >Bill Gates and Paul Allen establish Microsoft.

1976 >Queen Elizabeth sends her first e-mail. She's the first state leader to do so.
>Steven Jobs and Stephen Wozniak start Apple Computer.

1977 >Apple Computer unveils the Apple II computer.
>Atari 2600 is introduced. It's the first multi-game system. Hits include Donkey Kong and Space Invaders.

1978 >Floppy disks replace older data cassettes.

1981 >IBM introduces a complete desktop PC.

1982 >The word *Internet* is used for the first time.

1983 >TIME magazine names the PC "Man of the Year."

1984 >Writer William Gibson coins the term cyberspace.
>The Domain Name System (DNS) is established. Network addresses are identified by extensions such as .com, .org and .edu.
>The user-friendly Apple Macintosh goes on sale.

1985 >Quantum Computer Services, which later changes its name to America Online, launches. It offers e-mail, electronic bulletin boards, news and other information.
>The Nintendo Entertainment System arrives in the United States and makes Mario an instant star.
>Microsoft launches Windows.

1988 >A virus called the Internet Worm temporarily shuts down about 10% of the world's Internet servers.

1989 >The World (world.std.com) debuts as the first provider of dial-up Internet access for consumers.
>The handheld Nintendo Game Boy makes portable game-playing possible.
>The Sega Genesis system debuts with impressive graphics.

VIDEO-GAME TIMELINE

&

1991 >The World Wide Web is introduced to the public as a text-only interface. It marks the dawn of the Internet!
>Gopher provides point-and-click navigation on the Internet.

1992 >The Apple PowerBook and IBM ThinkPad debut.

1993 >Mosaic, the first graphics-based web browser, is launched.

1994 >The White House creates a website, www.whitehouse.gov.
>The first shopping sites are established. Companies market their products via e-mail, and the term spamming is introduced.

1995 >Sony PlayStation offers its games on CDs rather than on cartridges.

1996 >Nintendo 64 features cutting-edge 3D graphics.
>Palm releases the PalmPilot, a handheld computer also called a "personal digital assistant."

1997 >The NASA website broadcasts pictures taken by Pathfinder on Mars and smashes Internet traffic records. The broadcast generates 46 million hits in one day.

1999 >College student Shawn Fanning invents Napster, a computer application that allows users to swap music over the Internet.
>The number of Internet users worldwide reaches 150 million.
>Sega Dreamcast comes out with online games and a built-in modem.

2000 >The computer viruses Love Bug and Stages wreak havoc with computers worldwide.

2001 >About 9.8 billion electronic messages are sent each day.
>Nintendo GameCube dazzles with cool graphics and amazing speed.
>Microsoft XBOX sets the gaming bar even higher with a lightning-fast Pentium III processor, tons of memory and ports for modems.

2003 >It's estimated that Internet users illegally download about 2.6 billion music files each month.
>Spam, unsolicited e-mail, becomes a server-clogging menace. It accounts for about half of all e-mails.

go Find out about playing it safe online at www.timeforkids.com/safeweb

57

INTERNET RESOURCE GUIDE

The Internet has become a convenient tool for finding information on just about anything. Here's a list of especially useful and informative sites.

Animals
>**American Zoo and Aquarium Association:** www.aza.org
>**Kid's Planet:** www.kidsplanet.org/
>**National Wildlife Federation:** www.nwf.org/kids/

Art
>**Metropolitan Museum of Art, New York:** www.metmuseum.org/explore/museumkids.html
>**National Gallery of Art for Kids:** www.nga.gov/kids
>**Smithsonian Institution, Washington, D.C.:** www.mnh.si.edu/

Geography
>**Atlapedia Online:** www.atlapedia.com/
>**CIA World Factbook:** www.cia.gov/cia/publications/factbook
>**50 States.com:** www.50states.com

Government and Politics
>**Congress for Kids:** www.congressforkids.net
>**State and Local Governments:** lcweb.loc.gov/global/state/stategov.htm/
>**White House:** www.whitehouse.gov/kids/

News
>**Scholastic News:** www.teacher.scholastic.com/scholasticnews/
>**TIME For Kids:** www.timeforkids.com/TFK

Reference
>**Fact Monster:** www.factmonster.com
>**Internet Public Library:** www.ipl.org
>**Kids Zone:** www.lycoszone.lycos.com/
>**Refdesk:** www.refdesk.com

Science and Math
>**Ask Dr. Math:** mathforum.org/dr.math/
>**Astronomy for Kids:** www.frontiernet.net/~kidpower/astronomy.html
>**Bill Nye the Science Guy:** www.billnye.com
>**Cool Science for Curious Kids:** www.hhmi.org/coolscience/
>**FunBrain:** www.funbrain.com
>**NASA Kids:** kids.msfc.nasa.gov/

Search
>**Ask Jeeves Kids:** ajkids.com
>**Google:** www.google.com
>**Yahooligans!:** www.yahooligans.com

TFK Puzzles & Games

Loopy Lingo
Unscramble the seven computer-related terms below, and write the correct words in the boxes. The letters in the shaded boxes will spell out the answer to this riddle: How did the computer programmer get rid of the blades of grass growing from his circuit boards?

RAHD ERIVD

WOTSFERA

SOUEM

OTOB

ODWSASPR

ROBSWER

GROPTAINE MYSTES

(See Answer Key that begins on page 340.)

Cool Computer Software

Liberty's Kids (The Learning Company) As a reporter for the Philadelphia *Gazette*, you interview the major players in the American Revolution, gather facts and quotes and write your own front-page story. Lots of puzzles to solve and games to play along the way.

Incredible Machine: Even More Contraptions (Sierra On-Line) Design, build and test your own contraptions, using pulleys, conveyor belts, soccer balls and baboons. In addition, you can tackle 250 puzzles on your own or in a race against another player.

Nancy Drew: Ghost Dogs of Moon Lake (Her Interactive) Travel to spooky Moon Lake to help supersleuth Nancy Drew unravel the mystery surrounding a ghostly pack of dogs that may or may not have risen from the dead.

Ultimate Ride Coaster Deluxe (Disney Interactive) Here's a chance to design, build and test-drive your own amusement-park masterpiece. Cool graphics and endless options make this one wild ride.

Zoombinis Island Odyssey (The Learning Company/Riverdeep) The Zoombinis return to Zoombini Isle to find that their once lush homeland has been destroyed and abandoned. Navigating a series of adventurous puzzles, you help them restore the habitat.

TFK Top 5 Countries for Internet Use

If you think Americans lead the world in surfing the Internet, think again! The U.S. is Number 6 after these five nations, all of them wealthy countries with long, cold winters. It seems that when the weather is cold, surf's up on the Web! Experts say that by 2005, there will be more than 1 billion Internet users around the world.

1. SWEDEN
   60.3% of the population

2. ICELAND
   60.2%

3. DENMARK
   59.3%

4. NORWAY
   58.7%

5. CANADA
   57%

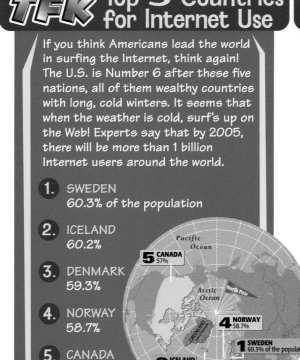

Source: Computer Industry Almanac; www.c-i-a.com

TFK Mystery Person

CLUE 1: I am an engineer. I was born in London, England, in 1955.
CLUE 2: I built my first computer at age 21. I used an old television as a monitor.
CLUE 3: In 1990, working on my own, I created the World Wide Web. It gives a unique address to every spot on the Internet. Soon after, Web surfing was born!

WHO AM I?

(See Answer Key that begins on page 340.)

DANCE
& THEATER

From earliest times people have used dance to entertain, to celebrate, to convey beliefs and feelings, and just for the fun of it.

Almost every culture in the world has used dance as a means of expression. Argentina, for example, is the home of the sultry ballroom dance called the **tango**.

Traditional African dances often form part of religious ceremonies or mark important events. The **square dances** that developed in colonial America became an opportunity for farmers to gather socially with their often far-flung neighbors.

Some of the most common forms of dance performance are **ballet, modern dance** and **Broadway musical dance**.

TYPES OF DANCE

Some Popular Dance Crazes
Boogie-woogie
Cakewalk
Cha-cha
Fandango
Fox-trot
Frug
Funky chicken
Hustle
Jitterbug
Jive
Lindy hop
Macarena
Rumba
Shimmy
Twist

Ballet
was first created in 16th-century Italy. Each position and step in ballet is choreographed. Many ballets convey a feeling of delicate beauty and lightness—ballet dancers' graceful motions seem airy and effortless, and much of the movement is focused upward. Toe (or pointe) shoes allow ballerinas to dance on their toes and appear to defy gravity.

Modern dance
, created in the 20th century, is a rejection of many of the traditions of ballet. It goes against what were viewed as ballet's rigid steps, limited emotional expression and sense of dainty beauty. Modern-dance steps often seem informal, and modern dancers don't mind if a step looks rough if it expresses the truth.

The waltz
is a romantic ballroom dance in which the couple revolves in circles to a beat of three. The Viennese waltz is the most famous.

Flamenco
is a fiery, emotional dance that originated in Spain and is characterized by hand clapping and fast, rhythmic foot stamping.

Native American dance
is often ceremonial or religious, calling on the spirits for help in farming or hunting or giving them thanks for rain or for victory in war.

Hip-Hop
was developed by teenagers in New York City's South Bronx in the late 1970s. It brings together driving rhythm, athletic moves and urban style.

The Five Ballet Positions

first position   second position   third position   fourth position   fifth position

The five ballet positions have certainly endured the test of time. Pierre Beauchamps developed them around 1670!

Play Day

Do you ever find yourself looking for something to do on a rainy day? Try putting on a play for your family or friends.

Here's a guide to help you create a dazzling drama.

Put on your director's hat

The director has the most important job in a play. A director tells the actors where to stand, advises them on how to act and oversees the creation of the set and the selection of costumes. But a director shouldn't be too bossy or critical.

Choose a script

Decide whether you want to write your own play or act out your favorite story or fairy tale. Either way, you'll need to write a script, which tells the actors what to say, where to stand and what to do.

Cast the play

Decide which person is going to play each character. If you don't have enough people to fill all the roles, actors can play more than one part. If one of your friends is shy, he or she can be the narrator. The narrator tells the audience what is going on in the play.

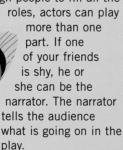

Set the stage

Think about how the actors will enter and exit the stage. Don't have all the characters lumped together in one spot. The person who's talking should appear at the middle of the stage whenever possible. Don't turn your back to the audience while you're talking.

Costumes

The costumes should help define the character each person is playing. Costumes can be as simple as a mask or as elaborate as a jeweled gown. Be creative! A pan could work well as a knight's hat. A towel makes a great cape. Go through your closets; you may be surprised what you can whip together with a little imagination.

Props

What will you need to create an interesting set, one that will make the play seem more realistic? You can probably use household items as props for your play. Props include scenery and the things that actors use on stage. It's easier to practice the play with props in place, so you'll be familiar with the stage when it's time to perform. An old curtain rod can become a wand. A broom could stand in for a horse. Ask your parents if you can paint an old sheet to use as background.

Sound

You may want to have music or other sounds in the background. You can use taped music or perform your own music. In addition, many libraries offer collections of sound effects on CD.

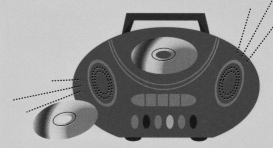

Rehearse

It's important to practice the play several times before you perform in front of other people. At first you can rehearse the play with the script, but you should memorize your lines before you perform in front of an audience.

Set up!

Try to have chairs for the audience. Make tickets, posters and programs for your fans.

Perform

Have fun and ham it up!

Did You Know?

An opera is a drama (a play) in which the parts are sung to music played by an orchestra. The libretto, or words to the opera, can be either serious or comic. Some famous operas include Aïda, La Bohème, Madama Butterfly and Don Giovanni.

TFK Top 5 Plays By Shakespeare

These plays by William Shakespeare are produced most often on Broadway.

	Play	Productions
1.	Hamlet	61
2.	The Merchant of Venice	46
3.	Macbeth	40
4.	Romeo and Juliet	32
5.	Twelfth Night	29

Source: The League of American Theaters and Producers

TFK Mystery Person

CLUE 1: I've been a professional dancer since age 12, when I starred in *The Tap Dance Kid* on Broadway.
CLUE 2: I have appeared on *Sesame Street* and in the movies *Tap* and *Bamboozled*.
CLUE 3: In 1996, I won a Tony award for my dancing and choreography in the Broadway hit *Bring in 'Da Noize, Bring in 'Da Funk.*

WHO AM I?

(See Answer Key that begins on page 340.)

DINOSAURS

Ichthyosaurus

JURASSIC 208 to 146 million years ago

- The supercontinent Pangaea continued to break apart.
- Dinosaurs ruled the land and flourished during the period.
- Herbivores and carnivores increased in size; some of the largest dinosaurs emerged during the Jurassic Period.
- Birdlike dinosaurs first appeared.
- Flowering plants began to appear late in the period.
- The Jurassic Period also ended with an extinction, but it was not as extensive as the one in the Triassic Period. Only a few types of dinosaurs died out.

Jurassic dinosaurs include:

Allosaurus "different lizard"

Apatosaurus (formerly called *Brontosaurus*) "deceptive lizard"

Archaeopteryx "ancient wing"

Compsognathus "pretty jaw"

Diplodocus "double-beamed"

Mamenchisaurus "Mamenchin lizard"

Stegosaurus "plated lizard"

Camptosaurus "bent lizard"

Tyrannosaurus rex

Triceratops

When Did Dinosaurs Live?

Dinosaurs lived throughout the **MESOZOIC ERA**, which began 245 million years ago and lasted for 180 million years. It is sometimes called the Age of Reptiles. The era is divided into **three periods**, the Triassic, the Jurassic and the Cretaceous, shown here.

TRIASSIC 245 to 208 million years ago

- During the Triassic Period, all land on Earth existed as one enormous mass. It was called Pangaea. The supercontinent slowly began to break up during the Triassic Period.
- Some reptiles, frogs, turtles and crocodiles existed earlier, but dinosaurs didn't appear until late in the Triassic Period.
- The period marked the rise of small, lightly built dinosaurs.
- The first mammals evolved during the Triassic Period.
- Most of the plants that existed were ever-greens.

- The period ended with a mass extinction that wiped out most animals and reptiles. The dinosaurs that survived flourished in the next period, the Jurassic.

Triassic dinosaurs include:
Coelophysis "hollow form"
Desmatosuchus "link crocodile"
Eoraptor "dawn thief"
Ichthyosaurus "fish lizard"
Iguanodon "iguana teeth"
Plateosaurus "flat lizard"
Saltopus "leaping foot"

Apatosaurus

Stegosaurus

CRETACEOUS 146 to 65 million years ago

- Pangaea continued to separate into smaller continents.
- A wide variety of dinosaurs roamed the land.
- Birds flourished and spread all over the globe.
- Flowering plants developed.
- Mammals thrived.
- Dinosaurs became extinct by the end of the period. The extinction, the second largest of all time, marked the end of the Age of Reptiles and the beginning of the Age of Mammals.

Cretaceous dinosaurs include:
Ankylosaurus "crooked lizard"
Hadrosaurus "bulky lizard"
Megaraptor "huge robber"
Ornithomimus "bird mimic"
Seismosaurus "seismic lizard"
Triceratops "three-horned face"
Troodon "wounding tooth"
Tyrannosaurus rex "tyrant lizard"

FOSSILS

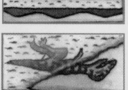

Fossils are the remains or imprints of prehistoric plants or animals. They are found in sedimentary rock (rock formed from sand and mud), coal, tar, volcanic ash or fossilized tree sap. Usually only the hard parts of plants and animals, like their bones and teeth, become fossils.

How Fossils Form

Most animals that became fossils either lived in water or were washed into a body of water. After an animal died, its soft parts, such as its fur, skin, muscles and organs, decomposed. The hard parts that remained were buried under moist layers of mud or sand, where there was no oxygen or bacteria to cause them to decay. Over time, many of these bodies of water dried up. The sediment that covered the bones eventually turned into solid rock. Over millions of years, minerals in the surrounding rock partly or completely replaced the original animal material, forming a fossil.

Sometimes, water seeped into the rocks and dissolved the animal remains. When this happened, the outline of the animal remained intact between the layers of rock, leaving a fossil in the form of a natural mold.

Paleontologists, or scientists who study fossils, use fossils to learn about the creatures who roamed Earth millions of years ago.

TEK NEWS

A Fantastic Fossil Find

By Jennifer Marino

Five years ago, Miguel Avelas, then age 12, gave paleontologists in Patagonia, Argentina, a huge surprise. He led them to a place where they found hundreds of 90 million-year-old fossils of lizardlike reptiles called *sphenodontians*. Scientists had thought that the reptiles had disappeared 120 million years ago. The discovery was recently published in the science journal *Nature*.

"It was fantastic," says paleontologist Sebastian Apesteguia. "We had no idea that *sphenodontians* could possibly be found there."

Several of the fossilized skeletons were nearly complete and up to three feet long. The sharp-toothed reptiles lived alongside dinosaurs and crocodiles.

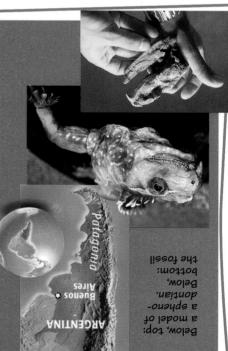

Below, top: a model of a spheno-dontian. Below, bottom: the fossil

ARGENTINA
Buenos Aires
Patagonia

HOW ARE DINOSAURS CLASSIFIED?

The word **DINOSAUR** comes from *Dinosauria*, which means "terrible lizards." Dinosaurs belong to a group of reptiles called *Archosauria* (ruling reptiles). They are classified based on the shape of their pelvises (hip areas) into **two orders**.

Saurischian (lizard hipped)

All Saurischian dinosaurs had lizardlike pelvises. In a lizard pelvis, an arch in the front points forward, which makes the animal's rear end very stable.

Saurischians included both carnivores and herbivores. Neither chewed their food much. Saurischian carnivores gulped down meat in chunks, and herbivores swallowed plant material in a wad called a bolus.

Saurischians included *Allosaurus*, *Apatosaurus* and *Tyrannosaurus*.

Ornithischian (bird hipped)

All Ornithischian dinosaurs had pelvises similar to those of modern birds. In a bird pelvis, an arch in the front points backward, which allows room for a longer digestive tract that makes digestion easier. Ornithischians were herbivores. They chewed their food well. Most of them had cheeks, just as a cow or a human does, which would help them to chew their food neatly.

Ornithischians included *Iguanodon*, *Hadrosaur*, *Stegosaurus* and *Triceratops*.

Did You Know?

A massive extinction of dinosaurs took place 65-million years ago, at the end of the Cretaceous Period. Many scientists believe that a meteorite impact was at least partially to blame for this extinction. Other factors may be volcanic gases, climatic cooling, sea-level change, low reproduction rates, poison gases from a comet or changes in Earth's orbit or magnetic field.

For more on dinosaur discoveries, www.FACTMONSTER.COM

TFK Mystery Person

CLUE 1: I searched the world for rare animals for the American Museum of Natural History.
CLUE 2: I led several fossil-hunting expeditions to the Gobi Desert in the 1920s. My team was the first to discover dinosaur eggs.
CLUE 3: Some people think the film character Indiana Jones was based on me.

WHO AM I?
(See Answer Key that begins on page 340.)

CALIFORNIA'S WILDFIRES

A fire crew faces a fireball north of Los Angeles.

California

San Gabriel Mountains
San Bernardino Mountains
Los Angeles
San Diego
Pacific Ocean
MEXICO
Nevada
Arizona

In smoke-clouded Valley Center, California, residents sprayed water on their rooftops. They were trying to prevent a nearby wall of wildfire from burning down their homes. Some packed their things and prepared to flee. Suddenly, flames leaped up from Hell Hole Canyon with a mighty roar and little warning. Valley Center residents had to drop their hoses and belongings and scram. Like thousands of other Californians who fled the fires, they knew they would probably never see their homes again.

Wildfires raged across Southern California in late October 2003, causing heartbreaking losses. More than 20 people, including a firefighter, died. Nearly 3,500 homes were burned. An area of about 1,130 square miles—bigger than the state of Rhode Island—was blackened. About 13,000 firefighters worked to protect homes and contain the fire.

"This is some of the most stressful fire fighting I've done," said Damien Sanchez, 25, who has been a firefighter for seven years. "We just didn't have any time because of the winds."

What caused the firestorm? Sadly, it seems that at least a few fires were set on purpose. At least one fire appeared to have been set accidentally by a lost hunter. Fire experts said that no matter what sparked the flames, a long list of risky conditions caused them to blaze out of control. The main culprits were:

DROUGHT Low rainfall and hot weather have combined to cause water shortages across the West for about five years. Dried-up grasses, shrubs and trees catch fire easily.

PINE BARK BEETLES The beetles feasted on, and killed, millions of pine trees. The dead wood piled up and dried out—the perfect fuel to spark a wildfire.

UNDERBRUSH The area had not had a big fire for nearly 50 years. This allowed a tangle of dry underbrush (low grasses and shrubs) to collect.

SANTA ANA WINDS These hot winds blast westward from the desert and down the mountains every autumn. When the Santa Anas hit the fires, they created a natural blowtorch.

PACIFIC WINDS When the Santa Anas died down, moister winds from the Pacific Ocean blew in the opposite direction, driving fires in new directions.

BY MARTHA PICKERILL

To the Rescue

When disasters occur in the U.S., the Federal Emergency Management Agency (FEMA) steps in to help victims find a place to live if their homes are damaged or destroyed. FEMA also helps to repair homes and public buildings that have been damaged. The agency is part of the Executive Branch of the government.

FEMA also teaches people how to prepare for natural calamities and offers tips for people to make their homes as safe and as disaster-resistant as possible. Here are some ways to make disasters less disastrous.

Assemble a Disaster Kit

According to the American Red Cross, your disaster kit should include:

★ First-aid kit and essential medications
★ Canned food and a can opener
★ At least three gallons of water for each person in the house
★ Warm clothing, rainwear and bedding or sleeping bags
★ A battery-powered radio, a flashlight and extra batteries
★ Special items for babies, the elderly or disabled family members
★ Written instructions for how to turn off the electricity, gas and water in your home
★ Several places to meet if told to evacuate.

Be Prepared for a Fire

★ Install a smoke alarm outside each bedroom and on each level of your home. Test the batteries monthly and replace them twice a year.
★ Make sure you have at least one fire extinguisher in your home.
★ Plan two ways to escape from each room.
★ Choose a place for family members to meet outside.
★ Practice "stop, drop and roll"—which you do if your clothing catches fire.

... Or an Earthquake

★ Choose a safe place in every room—under a sturdy table or desk or against an inside wall where nothing can fall on you—where you will go during an earthquake.
★ Practice "drop, cover and hold on" at least twice a year. Drop under a sturdy desk or table, cover your eyes by pressing your face against your arm and hold on. If there's no table or desk nearby, sit on the floor against an inside wall away from windows, bookcases or tall furniture.
★ Have an adult strap your gas water heater to a nearby wall. This will keep it from falling on someone or starting a fire from a broken gas main.
★ Have an adult bolt or strap cupboards and bookcases to the walls.

DISASTERS near and FAR

Disasters can be natural occurrences, such as floods; human mistakes, such as shipwrecks; or acts of violence, such as terrorism. Here's a look at some of the world's worst disasters.

Destructive Avalanches

An avalanche is any quick movement of snow, ice, mud or rock down a mountain or slope. An avalanche might be triggered by an earthquake, a human disturbance or heavy rain.

- Where: **Washington State**
- When: **1910**
- **The worst snowslide in U.S. history occurred in the Cascade Mountains in Wellington, Washington, when 118 people were trapped in a snowbound train. An avalanche then swept them to their deaths.**

- Where: **Peru**
- When: **1962**
- **Nearly 4,000 people died when tons of snow slid down Huascaran Peak in the Andes Mountains. It was the world's worst avalanche.**

TFK Top 5 Worst Floods

WHERE (WHEN)	PEOPLE KILLED
1. Huang He (Yellow) River, China (August 1931)	3.7 million
2. Huang He (Yellow) River, China (March 1887)	1.5 million
3. Netherlands (November 1530)	400,000
4. Kaifong, China (1642)	300,000
5. Henan, China (September - November 1939)	200,000+

Droughts and Famines

- Where: **Many states in the U.S.**
- When: **1930s**
- **About 80% of the population was affected by drought. An enormous "dust bowl" covered about 50 million acres of the Great Plains. During 1934, dry areas stretched from New York to the California coast.**

- Where: **Northern China**
- When: **1959–1961**
- **The world's deadliest famine killed about 30 million people in China.**

The dust bowl was the worst drought in U.S. history.

Epidemics

An epidemic occurs when a disease affects a large number of people in one area or when a disease spreads to areas that are not usually associated with the disease.

- What: **Bubonic plague, also called Black Death**
- Where: **Europe**
- When: **1347–1351**
- **The disease spread rapidly throughout Europe. About 25 million people, or about one-quarter of Europe's population, died of bubonic plague.**

- What: **Spanish influenza**
- Where: **United States and other countries**
- When: **March–November 1918**
- **An outbreak of Spanish influenza killed more than 500,000 people. It was the single worst U.S. epidemic. The outbreak was considered a pandemic because it also struck throughout the world.**

For more on disasters of all kinds, www.FACTMONSTER.COM

Earthquakes and Tidal Waves

An earthquake is a trembling movement of Earth's crust. The movement causes vibrations to pass through and around Earth in waves, just as ripples are created when a pebble is dropped into water. Volcanic eruptions, landslides and explosions can also cause the ground to tremble.

A tidal wave is a huge sea wave that follows an earthquake or volcanic eruption. Tsunami is the Japanese word for a tidal wave caused by an undersea earthquake.

Worst EARTHQUAKE IN HISTORY

Where: Near East & Mediterranean Sea
When: 1201
This powerful earthquake killed an estimated 1 million people. Hardest hit were the areas in and around Egypt and Syria.

A Monster Wave WALLOPS JAPAN

- **Where:** Honshu, Japan
- **When:** 1933
- A deadly tsunami killed 3,000 people on the island of Honshu. The tidal wave, caused by an earthquake, sank 8,000 ships and destroyed 9,000 homes.

VOLCANOES

A volcanic eruption occurs when molten rock, ash and steam pour through a vent in Earth's crust. Volcanoes can be active (erupting), dormant (not erupting at the present time) or extinct (no longer able to erupt).

KRAKATAU
Indonesia 1883
The greatest explosion in modern times occurred when Krakatau erupted. The roar of the explosion was heard over one-thirteenth of the surface of Earth. The eruption wiped out 163 villages, killing 36,380 people.

Did You Know?
Moment magnitude, not the Richter scale, as many people believe, is the most widely used scale to measure earthquake intensity.

The Volcano of Fire in Mexico erupted in 2002.

Disastrous Events
THAT MADE HISTORY

The Chicago Fire •••••••▶
October 8, 1871
The legendary fire consumed 17,450 buildings, killed 250 people and caused $196 million in damage.

The Chicago fire burned down 2,000 acres of the city.

A *Titanic* Disaster
April 15, 1912
They called it "unsinkable." But on its maiden voyage, the British luxury steamship *Titanic* collided with a massive iceberg southeast of Newfoundland. The ship began to fill with icy water. Less than three hours later, the 883-foot-long *Titanic* turned on end and then slipped into the ocean. More than 1,500 people died.
••••••••••••••••••▶

The *Titanic* was considered unsinkable.

The Fall of the *Hindenburg*
May 6, 1937
The German blimp, or airship, *Hindenburg* burst into flames 200 feet over its intended landing spot at New Jersey's Lakehurst Naval Air Station. Thirty-five people on board the flight were killed, along with one crewman on the ground. The majestic ship turned into a ball of flames on the ground in only 34 seconds.

The *Hindenburg* was 804 feet long.

Homework TIP
Use a calendar to plan long-term assignments and projects.

Nuclear Disaster at Chernobyl

April 26, 1986

In the worst nuclear disaster in history, a reactor blew at a nuclear power plant in Chernobyl, Ukraine. The explosion released eight tons of radioactive material over part of the Soviet Union, Eastern Europe, Scandinavia and later Western Europe. Total casualties are unknown, but estimates run into the thousands.

The *Exxon Valdez* Oil Spill

March 24, 1989

The *Exxon Valdez* oil tanker hit an undersea reef and tore open, spilling 11.2 million gallons of crude oil into Alaska's Prince William Sound. The worst oil spill in U.S. history, it killed millions of birds, fish and other wildlife. Cleanup efforts began late and ended up costing billions of dollars.

Terrorist Attack Against the U.S.

September 11, 2001 •••••••••••➤

One of the worst disasters of all time was the September 11, 2001, terrorist attack against the U.S. Hijackers who were members of the al-Qaeda terrorist group crashed two commercial jets into the Twin Towers of the World Trade Center in New York City. Another hijacked plane crashed into the Pentagon in Washington, D.C., and a fourth in a field in rural Pennsylvania. The total number of people who died in the attacks reached 2,995, including the hijackers. That's more than the number of people who died in the Japanese attack on Pearl Harbor in 1941.

Space Shuttle Tragedies

February 1, 2003 and January 28, 1986

The *Columbia* space shuttle broke up as it was preparing to land at the Kennedy Space Center in Florida in February 2003. All seven astronauts aboard the shuttle died, including six Americans and Israel's first astronaut. As the shuttle was reentering Earth's atmosphere, hot gases entered the wing, leading to the destruction of the spacecraft.

The tragedy occurred 17 years after the *Challenger* exploded 73 seconds after liftoff. All seven people aboard the shuttle died, including six NASA astronauts and Christa McAuliffe, a schoolteacher who was to be the first civilian in space. A booster fuel leak had ignited, causing the explosion.

Terrorists brought down the Twin Towers.

DISASTERS

TFK Mystery Person

CLUE 1: I served as the Governor of Pennsylvania from 1995 to 2001.
CLUE 2: After the terrible events of September 11, 2001, I was chosen by President George W. Bush to be the first Secretary of the Office of Homeland Security.
CLUE 3: My job is to protect the U.S. from terrorist threats.
WHO AM I?
(See Answer Key that begins on page 340.)

Look back at space-shuttle history at www.timeforkids.com/columbia

The Power of OIL

BY MARTHA PICKERILL

Deep beneath the Earth's surface, nature's most powerful substance lies in shiny, sticky pools. Oil began forming hundreds of millions of years ago as plants and animal remains were covered with layers of rock. Over the ages, those remains decayed to form the mighty black brew from which we make gasoline and other fossil fuels. Oil's energy powers our cars, trucks, trains, planes, automobiles, factories and electrical plants. Oil is used to make tires, crayons, even bubblegum.

Oil can also make trouble. Some nations sit atop vast underground lakes of oil. Other places—Japan and most European nations, for example—have little, if any, oil of their own. The nations that need oil must buy it from oil-rich countries that control the oil market. This imbalance of power can make relations between nations tricky, says energy expert Robert Ebel of the Center for Strategic and International Studies.

"Four countries—Saudi Arabia, Iraq, Iran and Russia—control almost 70% of world oil reserves," says Ebel. "The greater our dependence on foreign oil, the greater the risk that events in oil-producing countries will interfere with our supply."

That risk has grown clearer. A strike in Venezuela, the fifth biggest oil producer, caused oil prices to jump. The war in Iraq also caused oil prices to spike. The United States produces oil, but it also

Middle East nations, including Iraq (shown here), provide only 14% of U.S. oil.

imports about 59% of what it needs. So when foreign oil prices rise, we pay more.

The U.S. uses more oil than any other nation. Most is pumped into our 200 million cars in the form of gasoline. On average, an American burns through 25 barrels of oil a year. Compare this with 15 barrels for a citizen of Japan or 12 for a French person.

OIL IS A STICKY PROBLEM

High costs and sticky foreign relations are not the only drawbacks of our oil habit. Oil is also one messy fuel. When fossil fuels burn, they release carbon dioxide and other polluting gases. The gases are bad for our health and our planet. They can trap heat near the Earth's surface, contributing to the rise in temperatures known as global warming. In addition,

MOST AND LEAST FUEL-EFFICIENT VEHICLES

There's no doubt Lamborghinis are cool cars, but it's not so cool that they only get 9 miles per gallon. Here's a look at the vehicles that get the best and worst gas mileage.

MOST FUEL EFFICIENT

	M.P.G.* City	Highway
Overall: Honda Insight	60	66
Station wagon: Volkswagen Jetta Wagon (diesel)	36	47
Pickup truck (tie): Ford Ranger Pickup 2WD and Mazda B2300 2WD	24	29
Sport-utility vehicle (SUV): Toyota Rav4 2WD	24	30
Minivan (tie): Chrysler Voyager/Town & Country 2WD and Dodge Caravan 2WD	20	26

LEAST FUEL EFFICIENT

	M.P.G.* City	Highway
Overall: Lamborghini L-147 Murcielago	9	13
Station wagon: Audi S4 Avant 4WD	15	21
Pickup truck: Ford F150 Pickup	12	16
Sport-utility vehicle (tie): Land Rover Discovery Series II and Range Rover	12	16
Minivan: Kia Sedona	16	22

*miles per gallon
Source: Fueleconomy.com

ships carrying oil have accidentally spilled millions of gallons, polluting our oceans and killing sea life.

If oil is so bad, why do we depend on it? For starters, nearly all of our cars and factories are designed to use oil and gas. Changing them to use other fuels would be very costly. Besides, oil does its job. "We continue to look for a practical oil replacement," says Ebel. "We just haven't found one."

Still, it's possible to be less wasteful. In fact, we've done it before. In 1973, a few oil-producing nations got angry at the U.S. and tripled oil prices in just a few months. Gasoline was in short supply, and there were long lines at gas stations. U.S. leaders vowed to cut our reliance on foreign oil. New rules forced auto companies to build cars that use less gas. In 1975, the average car could go just 12 miles on a gallon of gas. By 1990, some got more than 30 miles per gallon.

But in recent years, with low oil prices, Americans have gone back to buying big gas-guzzlers. About one of every four cars now sold is a sport-utility vehicle (SUV), which gets as little as 10 or 11 miles per gallon.

"Right now, consumers don't value efficiency," says Eron Shosteck of the Alliance of Automobile Manufacturers.

NEW CAR TO THE RESCUE?

President Bush recently called for a $1.2 billion program to develop a pollution-free, hydrogen-powered car. Such a car would solve many problems, but it's at least 20 years away.

Other options are available right now. Hybrid cars that run on both electricity and a little gas, like the Honda Insight, are already on the market. If world events keep driving up the price of oil, Americans may once again rethink what they're driving.

ENERGY and the EARTH

Energy is the power we use for transportation, for heat and light in our homes and for the manufacture of all kinds of products. Energy comes in two types of sources: nonrenewable and renewable.

Nonrenewable Sources of Energy

Most of the energy we use comes from fossil fuels, such as coal, natural gas and petroleum. Once these natural resources are used up, they are gone forever. Uranium, a metallic chemical element, is another nonrenewable source, but it is not a fossil fuel. Uranium is converted to a fuel and used in nuclear power plants.

The process of gathering these fuels can be harmful to the environment. Fossil fuels are put through a process called combustion in order to produce energy. Combustion releases pollution, such as carbon monoxide and sulfur dioxide, and may contribute to acid rain and global warming.

Renewable Sources of Energy

Renewable sources of energy can be used over and over again. Renewable resources include solar energy, wind, geothermal energy, biomass and hydropower. They generate much less pollution—both in gathering and production—than nonrenewable sources.

Solar panels provide power to a building in Kyoto, Japan.

- **Solar energy** comes from the Sun. Some people use solar panels on their homes to convert sunlight into electricity.

- **Wind turbines,** which look like giant windmills, generate electricity.

- **Geothermal energy** comes from the Earth's core. Engineers extract steam or very hot water from the Earth's crust and use the steam to generate electricity.

- **Biomass** includes natural products such as wood, manure and corn. These materials are burned and used for heat.

- Dams and rivers generate **hydropower.** When water flows through a dam, it activates a turbine, which runs an electric generator.

U.S. ENERGY SOURCES

Here's a breakdown of the sources of energy in the United States:

Source	Percentage
OIL	39%
NATURAL GAS	24%
COAL	23%
NUCLEAR	8%
HYDROPOWER	3%
OTHER	3%

■ nonrenewable fossil fuels
■ renewable sources
■ neither

Source: The New York *Times*, November 2003

Energy Producers and Consumers

The United States, Russia and China are the world's leading energy producers and energy consumers. In 2001 these countries produced 38% and consumed 41% of the world's total energy. Here's a look at the top 10 energy consumers and producers.

Top Energy Consumers	Top Energy Producers
● United States	● United States
● China	● Russia
● Russia	● China
● Japan	● Saudi Arabia
● Germany	● Canada
● India	● United Kingdom
● Canada	● Iran
● France	● Norway
● United Kingdom	● Australia
● Brazil	● Mexico

Source: Energy Information Administration, U.S. Dept. of Energy

Did You Know?

Fossil fuels are called fossil fuels because over many millions of years, heat from the Earth's core and pressure from rock and soil have reacted with the fossils (or remains) of dead plants and animals to form fuel.

Most Polluted Cities in the U.S.

Are you breathing dirty air? The American Lung Association compiled this list of the most polluted cities in the United States.

1. Los Angeles and the surrounding area
2. Bakersfield, Calif.
3. Fresno, Calif.
4. Visalia, Calif., and the surrounding area
5. Houston area
6. Atlanta, Ga.
7. Washington, D.C., and the surrounding area
8. Charlotte, N.C., and the surrounding area
9. Knoxville, Tenn.
10. Philadelphia and the surrounding area

TFK Top 5 Smoggiest Cities in the World

Smog is one of Earth's nastiest problems. A hazy blend of smoke and fog, it causes breathing problems in industrial areas. These five cities—the world's smoggiest—need to clean up their act!

1. Mexico City, Mexico
2. São Paulo, Brazil
3. Cairo, Egypt
4. New Delhi, India
5. Shanghai, China

A smoggy day in Mexico City

Source: Environmental News Network

Environmental DANGERS

Human-caused pollution is making the world a warmer place, a process called GLOBAL WARMING. Scientists think pollution could contribute to a rise in the Earth's surface temperature over the next 100 years. A warmer world could mean big trouble. Hotter temperatures are causing some ice at the North and South Poles to melt and oceans to rise. The warmer climate is also changing our weather patterns and could result in dangerous tornadoes or droughts.

The Earth stays warm the same way a greenhouse does. Gases in the atmosphere, such as carbon dioxide, methane and nitrogen, act like the glass of a greenhouse: they let in the Sun's light and warmth, but they keep the Earth's heat from escaping. This is known as the GREENHOUSE EFFECT. Scientists think that if too many of these greenhouse gases are released into the atmosphere, from pollution, for example, the gases can trap too much heat, causing temperatures to rise.

The OZONE LAYER, a thin sheet of an invisible gas called ozone, surrounds Earth about 15 miles above its surface. Ozone protects us from the Sun's harmful rays. In recent years, the amount of ozone in the atmosphere has decreased, probably due to man-made gases called chlorofluorocarbons (CFCs) and certain chemicals. As the ozone level decreases, the Sun's rays become more dangerous to humans.

POLLUTION is the contamination of air or water by harmful substances. One source of pollution is HAZARDOUS WASTE—anything thrown away that could be dangerous to the environment, such as paint, oven cleaner, furniture polish and pesticides. These materials can seep into water supplies and contaminate them.

Another source of pollution is ACID RAIN, which occurs when rainwater is contaminated with pollutants such as sulfur dioxide and nitrogen oxide. These gases come from fuels being burned at high temperatures, as in car exhausts. When acid rain falls, it can damage wildlife and erode buildings.

R U Helping?

Recycling is great way to conserve resources and help the environment. Remember the three Rs:

REDUCE: Reducing waste is the best way to help the environment. Buy large containers of food whenever possible. For example, buy a 32-ounce container of yogurt rather than four 8-ounce cups.

REUSE: Instead of throwing things away, find new ways to use them again. Use food containers for paint cups or to store toys or art supplies. Cut old clothes into smaller pieces and use them for rags.

RECYCLE: Recycled items are new products made out of the materials from old ones. Recycle all of your tin, plastic and glass containers and your used paper.

RECYCLE THESE FACTS!

- Recycling 1 ton of paper saves 17 trees and 7,000 gallons of water.
- Recycling one aluminum can saves enough electricity to run a TV for three hours.
- Recycling one glass bottle or jar saves enough electricity to light a 100-watt bulb for four hours.
- More than 30 million trees are cut down to produce a year's supply of newspapers.
- Recycling 1 ton of plastic saves the equivalent of 1,000–2,000 gallons of gasoline.

 See how you can help the environment without leaving home at *www.timeforkids.com/house*

Change Those Wasteful Ways

It often takes monumental events for us to think about our wasteful ways. For example, after the power blackout in the northeast and midwest in August 2003, we were urged to conserve electricity. In the same way, the 2002 drought taught us that water is a precious resource that needs to be used wisely.

Here are some tips to conserve our natural resources:

- Turn off the lights and television when you leave a room.
- Set your computer to the "sleep mode." It darkens the screen when it's not in use.
- Turn off or turn down the heat or air conditioner when you go to bed or when you leave your home for a long time.
- Fix drafty windows and doors.
- Encourage your parents to buy appliances that have an Energy Star label. The label has the word *energy* and a picture of a star with a rainbow.
- Walk or ride your bike rather than having your parents drive you places.
- Turn off the water while brushing your teeth and lathering up.
- Run dishwashers only when they are fully loaded. The light-wash feature uses less water.
- Fix dripping faucets. One drop per second wastes 540 gallons of water per year!
- Don't use water toys that require a constant flow of water.
- Don't water your lawn too much. Grass only needs to be watered about once a week in the summer. Lawns can go two weeks without water after a heavy rain.

TFK Puzzles & Games

It's Your Turn to Clean Up!

This playground is a mess! Pick up the trash and put each piece in the correct recycling bin. Circle the plastic trash in green. Circle the metal trash in blue. Circle the items made of paper in yellow. Which bin has the fewest items?

(See Answer Key that begins on page 340.)

Major BIOMES of the WORLD

Have you visited any biomes lately? A biome is a large community of plants and animals that is supported by a certain type of climate.

Arctic Tundra

Where: The Arctic tundra is a cold, treeless area of low, swampy plains in the far north around the Arctic Ocean.

Special features: This is Earth's coldest biome. The Arctic tundra's frozen subsoil, called permafrost, makes it impossible for trees to grow.

What lives there? Animals that live in this biome include **polar bears**, Arctic foxes, caribou and gray wolves. Plants that you might find include small shrubs and the lichen that covers the tundra's many rocks.

The Arctic is home to polar bears.

Coniferous Forest

Where: The coniferous-forest biome is south of the Arctic tundra. It stretches from Alaska across North America and across Europe and Asia.

Special features: These forests consist mainly of cone-bearing trees such as spruce, hemlock and fir. The soil is not very fertile, because there are no leaves to decompose and enrich it.

What lives there? Some animals that thrive in this biome are ermine, moose, red fox, snowshoe rabbits and great horned owls.

Desert

Where: About one-fifth of Earth's land surface is desert. Deserts are found on every continent except Europe. There are two kinds: hot and dry (such as the Sahara) and cold and dry (such as Antarctica).

Special features: Lack of water and intense heat or cold make this biome unfriendly for most life forms.

What lives there? Most of the plants you'll see in the hot desert are types of cactuses. A few animals—mainly reptiles, such as snakes and lizards, and amphibians, such as frogs and toads—are adapted to the hot desert. Another famous hot-desert animal is the camel. Emperor penguins are well-known animals that live at the edge of the Antarctic desert.

Deciduous Forest

Where: This biome is in the mild-temperate zone of the Northern Hemisphere. Major regions are found in eastern North America, Europe and eastern Asia.

Special features: Deciduous trees lose their leaves in fall. The natural decaying of the fallen leaves enriches the soil and supports all kinds of plant and animal life.

What lives there? Oak, beech, ash and maple trees are typical, and many types of insect and animal life abound. In the U.S., the deciduous forest is a home for many animals including deer, American gray squirrels, rabbits, raccoons, and woodpeckers.

Did You Know?

An ecosystem is a community of plants and animals in an environment that supplies them with the raw materials they need, such as nutrients and water. An ecosystem may be as small as a puddle or as large as a forest.

Grasslands

Where: Grasslands are known throughout the world by different names. In the U.S. they are called prairies.

Special features: Grasslands are places with hot, dry climates that are perfect for growing food. This inland biome includes vast areas of grassy fields. It receives so little rain that very few trees can grow.

What lives there? The U.S. prairies are used to graze cattle and to raise cereal crops. There is little variety of animal life. Today, common grassland animals include the prairie dog and the mule deer in North America, the giraffe and the zebra in Africa and the lion in Africa and Asia.

Mountains

Where: Mountains exist on all the continents. Many of the world's mountains lie in two great belts. The Circum-Pacific chain runs from the west coast of the Americas through New Zealand and Australia, and through the Philippines to Japan. The Alpine-Himalayan system stretches from the Pyrenees in Spain and France through the Alps, and on to the Himalayas before ending in Indonesia.

Special features: A mountain biome is very cold and windy. The higher the mountain, the colder and windier the environment. There is also less oxygen at high elevations.

What lives there? Mountain animals that have adapted to the cold, the lack of oxygen and the rugged landscape include the **mountain goat,** sheep and puma. Lower elevations are commonly covered by forests, while very high elevations are usually treeless.

Mountain goats thrive in Colorado.

Rain Forests

Where: Tropical rain forests are found in Asia, Africa, South America, Central America and on many of the Pacific islands. Almost half the total area is in Brazil.

Special features: Tropical rain forests receive at least 70 inches of rain each year and have more species of plants and animals than any other biome. The thick vegetation absorbs moisture, which then evaporates and falls as rain.

A rain forest grows in three levels. The canopy, or tallest level, has trees between 100 and 200 feet tall. The second level, or understory, contains a mix of small trees, vines and palms, as well as shrubs and ferns. The third and lowest level is the forest floor, where herbs, mosses and fungi grow.

What lives there? The combination of heat and moisture makes the tropical rain forest the perfect environment for more than 15 million types of plants and animals. Some of the animals of the tropical rain forest are the anteater, jaguar, lemur, orangutan, macaw, sloth and toucan. Among the many plant species are bamboo, banana trees and rubber trees.

TFK Mystery Person

CLUE 1: I founded the Sierra Club in 1892. It was the first environmental group in the U.S.
CLUE 2: I worked to preserve forests and wildlife areas, including Yosemite, California.
CLUE 3: I convinced President Theodore Roosevelt to protect huge areas of natural land and to create many national parks.

WHO AM I?

(See Answer Key that begins on page 340.)

go For more about famous biomes, www.FACTMONSTER.com

FASHION
Clothes Encounters
Fashion Through the Decades

1900s

- corsets for tiny waists
- tight collars
- lots of lace
- long, lightweight "duster" coats
- upswept hair
- narrow shoes for both men and women
- straw "boater" hats for men
- feathered hats for women

1930s

- hats worn at an angle
- patterned sweaters
- one-piece wool bathing suits
- long, flowing gowns
- sandals
- fox-fur collars
- wide overcoats for men
- rectangular wrist-watches

1940s

- matching skirts and sweaters
- fur muffs
- rolled-up blue jeans
- narrow "drainpipe" trousers
- the "pompadour" hairstyle
- sleek evening dresses
- cork-soled "wedgie" shoes
- baggy pull-on sweaters
- Hawaiian shirts for men

1910s

- bathing costumes
- lace-up boots
- decorated stockings
- narrow "hobble" skirts
- trenchcoats
- beaded handbags
- Middle Eastern patterns
- V-neck sweaters

1950s

- white T-shirts
- motorcycle jackets
- pedal pushers (Capri pants)
- Bermuda shorts
- poodle skirts
- saddle shoes
- full skirts with petticoats
- strapless evening gowns
- jeans

1920s

- drop-waist flapper dresses
- cloches (close-fitting hats) for women
- baggy flannel trousers for men
- long, wide coats
- costume jewelry
- T-strap shoes
- sheer stockings
- bobbed hair

1960s

- bell-bottoms
- miniskirts
- T-shirts with messages
- pale lipstick and dark eyeliner
- longer hair for men and women
- white vinyl "go-go" boots
- peace signs
- paisley and Indian prints

1970s

- Western boots
- lots of lip gloss and blusher
- T-shirts with logos
- denim, denim, denim
- leg warmers
- pantsuits
- earth tones
- leotards with wraparound skirts

Did You Know?

Jeans were called waist overalls until the 1950s. The pants became a big hit with teenagers after movie idol James Dean wore them in the 1955 film *Rebel Without a Cause*.

1980s

- big hair with lots of mousse
- fingerless lace gloves
- frills on collars and hems
- bright vests and shirts for men
- "power suits" with big shoulder pads for women
- long fake-pearl necklaces
- tunics over leggings
- Levis 501 jeans

TFK Mystery Person

CLUE 1: I was a design director at Ralph Lauren.
CLUE 2: I designed ice-skating outfits, one of which Nancy Kerrigan wore at the 1994 Winter Olympics.
CLUE 3: I design evening wear but am most famous for my wedding dresses. My many famous clients include Halle Berry, Sharon Stone and Tyra Banks

WHO AM I?
(See Answer Key that begins on page 340.)

1990s

- designer athletic shoes
- puffy jackets
- chain wallets
- baggy pants
- small eyeglasses
- hooded sweatshirts
- mehndi (henna tattoos)

2000s

- low-rise pants
- bare midriffs
- bell-bottoms
- graphic T-shirts

 Go back in time for fashion inspiration at www.timeforkids.com/fashionflashback

GEOGRAPHY

A Golden Discovery

By Elizabeth Winchester

This bell came from the Republic.

After 12 years of searching for buried treasure, sea explorers finally struck gold in 2003. The team of marine archaeologists found 80 loose gold coins. They also spotted at least two wooden crates that may prove to be packed with hundreds of coins.

The team from Odyssey Marine Exploration, a company that investigates shipwrecks, discovered the gold along with the remains of the *Republic*. The shipwreck lies deep below the surface of the Atlantic Ocean, about 100 miles off the coast of Florida and Georgia.

In 1865, the steamship left New York City for New Orleans, Louisiana. According to old newspaper reports, the ship carried between 59 and 81 passengers. It held at least 20,000 gold coins. It is likely that bankers and other business people in the North had shipped the coins to New Orleans to help the southern city rebuild after the Civil War. When a violent hurricane struck, the *Republic* sank. Most of the passengers survived. The gold coins went down with the ship.

"It could be a very valuable find," says Laura Lionetti Barton, who is a spokesperson for Odyssey. Valuable, indeed! Experts say the coins could be worth more than $120 million.

Odyssey's team is still searching for more coins and artifacts from the ship. Barton expects almost all of the treasures to become the property of Odyssey. The company plans to sell most of them. The others, says Barton, will be exhibited in museums. Then the public will learn the story behind what was lost, and found, at sea.

EARTH ON THE MOVE

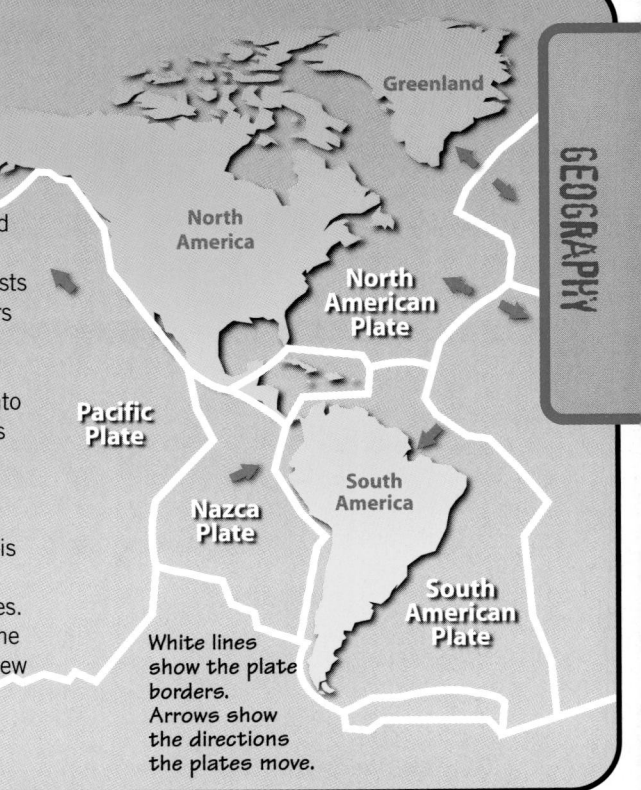

If you look at a map of the world, you'll see that the continents look as if they are pieces of a big puzzle. If you pushed South America and Africa into each other, they would fit together as one land mass. Many scientists believe that until about 200 million years ago, the world was made up of a single supercontinent called Pangaea. It eventually separated and drifted apart into the seven continents we have today. This movement is called **continental drift**.

According to the theory of **plate tectonics**, the Earth's lithosphere—the crust and the outer part of the mantle—is not one giant piece of rock. Instead, it's broken into several moving slabs or plates. These plates slide above a hot layer of the mantle. The plates move as much as a few inches every year. The oceans and the continents sit on top of the plates and move with them.

Greenland

North America

North American Plate

Pacific Plate

Nazca Plate

South America

South American Plate

White lines show the plate borders. Arrows show the directions the plates move.

IMPORTANT EXPLORERS

1000 Leif Eriksson (Viking) explored Labrador and Newfoundland in Canada.

1271 MARCO POLO (Italian) explored China.

1325–1349 Ibn Batuta (Arab) explored Africa, Middle East, Europe, parts of Asia

1488 Bartolomeu Dias (Portuguese) rounded South Africa's Cape of Good Hope.

1492 Christopher Columbus (Italian) arrived in the West Indies.

1498 Vasco da Gama (Portuguese) explored the coast of India.

1513 PONCE DE LEÓN (Spanish) reached Florida.

1519–1521 Hernando Cortés (Spanish) conquered Mexico.

1519–1522 The expedition led by Ferdinand Magellan (Portuguese) circled the globe.

1532–1533 Francisco Pizarro (Spanish) conquered Peru.

1535–1536 Jacques Cartier (French) sailed up Canada's St. Lawrence River.

1539–1542 Hernando de Soto (Spanish) explored the southeastern U.S.

1607 John Smith (British) settled Jamestown, Virginia.

1609–1610 Henry Hudson (British) explored the river, strait and bay that bear his name.

1769 James Cook (British) explored New Zealand.

1804–1806 MERIWETHER LEWIS and **WILLIAM CLARK** (American) explored the northwest U.S.

1909 Robert E. Peary (American) reached the North Pole.

1911 Roald Amundsen (Norwegian) reached the South Pole.

The Seven Continents

CONTINENT	APPROX. AREA	HIGHEST POINT	LOWEST POINT
Africa	11,608,000 square miles (30,065,000 sq km)	Mount Kilimanjaro, Tanzania, 19,340 feet (5,895 m)	Lake Assal, Djibouti, 512 feet (156 m) below sea level
Antarctica	5,100,000 square miles (13,209,000 sq km)	Vinson Massif, 16,066 feet (4,897 m)	Ice covered 8,327 feet (2,538 m) below sea level
Asia (includes the Middle East)	17,212,000 square miles (44,579,000 sq km)	Mount Everest, Tibet/Nepal, 29,035 feet (8,850 m)	Dead Sea, Israel/Jordan, 1,349 feet (411 m) below sea level
Australia (includes Oceania)	3,132,000 square miles (8,112,000 sq km)	Mount Kosciusko, Australia, 7,316 feet (2,228 m)	Lake Eyre, Australia, 52 feet (16 m) below sea level
Europe (Ural Mountains divide Europe from Asia)	3,837,000 square miles (9,938,000 sq km)	Mount Elbrus, Russia/Georgia, 18,510 feet (5,642 m)	Caspian Sea, Russia/Kazakhstan, 92 feet (28 m) below sea level
North America (includes Central America and the Caribbean)	9,449,000 square miles (24,474,000 sq km)	Mount McKinley, Alaska, U.S., 20,320 feet (6,194 m)	Death Valley, California, U.S., 282 feet (86 m) below sea level
South America	6,879,000 square miles (17,819,000 sq km)	Mount Aconcagua, Argentina, 22,834 feet (6,960 m)	Valdes Peninsula, Argentina, 131 feet (40 m) below sea level

Source: WorldAtlas.com

THE FIVE OCEANS

In spring 2000, the International Hydrographic Organization delimited (marked the boundaries of) a fifth ocean. The new ocean, called the Southern Ocean, surrounds Antarctica and extends north to 60 degrees south latitude. It is the fourth largest ocean, bigger only than the Arctic Ocean.

OCEAN	AREA	AVERAGE DEPTH
Pacific Ocean	60,060,700 square miles (155,557,000 sq km)	13,215 feet (4,028 m)
Atlantic Ocean	29,637,900 square miles (76,762,000 sq km)	12,880 feet (3,926 m)
Indian Ocean	26,469,500 square miles (68,556,000 sq km)	13,002 feet (3,963 m)
Southern Ocean	7,848,300 square miles (20,327,000 sq km)	13,100–16,400 feet* (4,000–5,000 m)
Arctic Ocean	5,427,000 square miles (14,056,000 sq km)	3,953 feet (1,205 m)

*Official depths of the Southern Ocean are in dispute.

The Andes cover parts of Venezuela, Colombia, Ecuador, Peru, Bolivia, Chile and Argentina.

Record Breakers

LARGEST CONTINENT
Asia: 17,212,000 square miles (44,579,000 sq km)

SMALLEST CONTINENT
Australia: 3,132,000 square miles (8,112,000 sq km)

HIGHEST MOUNTAIN
Mount Everest: Himalayan Mountains, Nepal/Tibet, 29,035 feet (8,850 m) above sea level

LOWEST POINT ON LAND
The Dead Sea: Israel/Jordan, 1,349 feet (411 m) below sea level

LARGEST LAKE
Caspian Sea: 152,239 square miles (394,299 sq km)

DEEPEST LAKE
Lake Baikal: Russia, 5,315 feet (1,620 m)

DEEPEST OCEAN
Pacific Ocean: average depth, 13,215 feet (4,028 m); deepest point, 36,198 feet (11,033 m)

LARGEST OCEAN
Pacific Ocean: 60,060,700 square miles (155,557,000 sq km)

SMALLEST OCEAN
Arctic Ocean: 5,427,000 square miles (14,056,000 sq km)

LARGEST ISLAND
Greenland: 839,999 square miles (2,175,600 sq km)

LONGEST MOUNTAIN RANGE
The Andes: South America, more than 5,000 miles (8,000 km)

SHORTEST RIVER
The Roe: Montana, U.S., 201 feet (61 m)

HIGHEST WATERFALL
Angel (Salto Angel): Venezuela, 3,212 feet (979 m) high

The Lines on a Map

The equator divides Earth into halves, or **hemispheres**. The Northern Hemisphere is the half of Earth between the North Pole and the equator. The Southern Hemisphere is the half between the South Pole and the equator.

Earth can also be divided into the Eastern and Western Hemispheres. The Western Hemisphere includes North and South America. The Eastern Hemisphere includes Asia, Africa, Australia and Europe.

Latitude measures distance from the equator. Latitude is measured in degrees and shown on a map by lines that run east and west. Lines of latitude are also called parallels.

Longitude measures distance from the prime meridian, an imaginary line on a map that runs through Greenwich, England. It is measured in degrees and shown on a map by lines that run north and south. Lines of longitude are also called meridians.

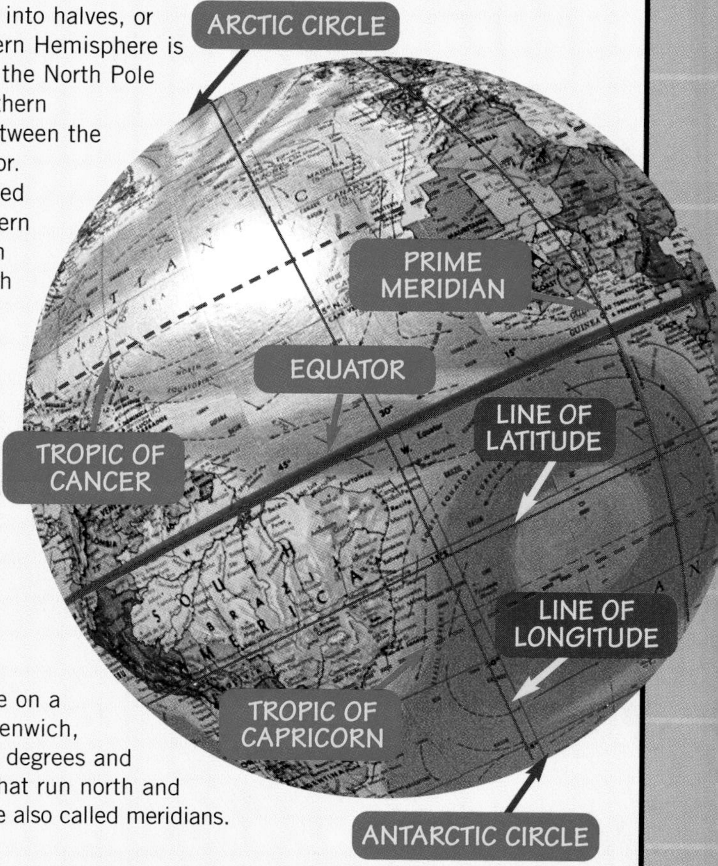

ARCTIC CIRCLE

PRIME MERIDIAN

EQUATOR

LINE OF LATITUDE

TROPIC OF CANCER

LINE OF LONGITUDE

TROPIC OF CAPRICORN

ANTARCTIC CIRCLE

TFK Puzzles & Games

Follow That Map!

Winnie's new in town and can't find her way home. Use the directions and compass rose on the map to guide Winnie from school to her house.

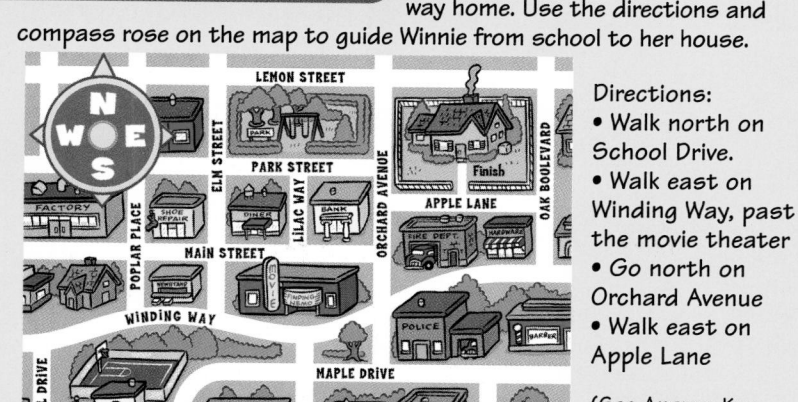

Directions:
• Walk north on School Drive.
• Walk east on Winding Way, past the movie theater
• Go north on Orchard Avenue
• Walk east on Apple Lane

(See Answer Key that begins on page 340.)

Types of Maps

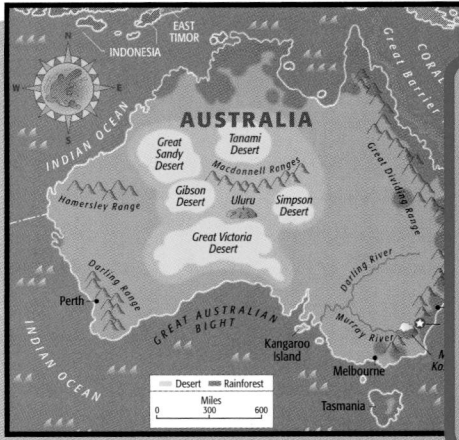

There are several types of maps. Each one serves a different purpose. Most maps include a compass rose, which indicates which way is north, south, east and west.

They also include a scale so you can estimate distances. Here's a look at some different types of maps.

Climate maps give general information about the climate and precipitation (rain and snow) of a region. Cartographers, or mapmakers, use colors to show different climate or precipitation zones.

Economic or resource maps feature the type of natural resources or economic activity that dominates an area. Cartographers use symbols to show the locations of natural resources or economic activities. For example, oranges on a map of Florida tell you that oranges are grown there.

Physical maps illustrate the physical features of an area, such as mountains, rivers and lakes. The water is usually shown in blue. Colors are used to show relief—differences in land elevations. Green is typically used at lower elevations, and orange or brown indicates higher elevations.

Political maps do not show physical features. Instead, they indicate state and national boundaries and capital and major cities. A capital city is usually marked with a star within a circle.

Road maps show major—and some minor—highways and roads, airports, railroad tracks, cities and other points of interest in an area. People use road maps to plan trips and for driving directions.

Topographic maps include contour lines to show the shape and elevation of an area. Lines that are close together indicate steep terrain, and lines that are far apart denote flat terrain.

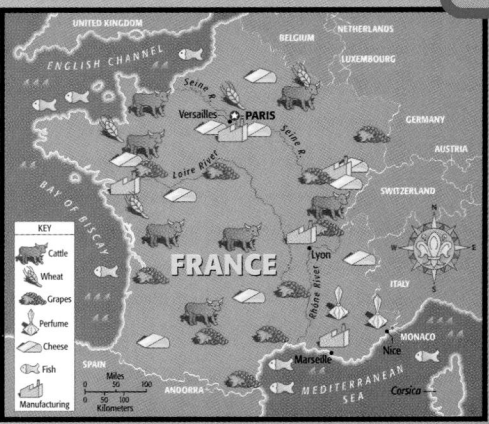

Physical map

Economic Map

Mystery Person

CLUE 1: My father, Erik the Red, discovered Greenland.
CLUE 2: I was a Viking who sailed across uncharted seas in the 10th century.
CLUE 3: Many say I was the first European to set foot in North America. I discovered a land rich with wheat and grapes, so I called it Vineland.

WHO AM I?
(See Answer Key that begins on page 340.)

89

GOVERNMENT

The Constitution

★ ★ ★ ★ ★ ★

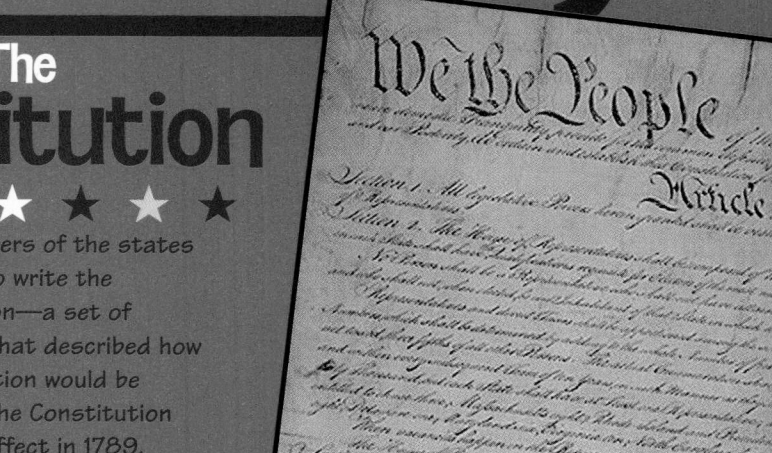

In 1787 leaders of the states gathered to write the Constitution—a set of principles that described how the new nation would be governed. The Constitution went into effect in 1789.

The Constitution begins with a famous section called the preamble. The preamble says that the U.S. government was created by the people and for the benefit of the people:

We the people of the United States, in order to form a more perfect Union, establish justice, insure domestic tranquility, provide for the common defense, promote the general welfare and secure the blessings of liberty to ourselves and our posterity, do ordain and establish this Constitution for the United States of America.

The leaders of the states wanted a strong and fair national government. But they also wanted to protect individual freedoms and prevent the government from abusing its power. They believed they could do this by having three separate branches of government: the Executive, the Legislative and the Judicial. This separation is described in the first three articles, or sections, of the Constitution.

The Constitution was originally made up of seven articles.

ARTICLE I Creates the Legislative Branch—the House of Representatives and the Senate—and describes its powers and responsibilities.

ARTICLE II Creates the Executive Branch, which is led by the President, and describes its powers and responsibilities.

ARTICLE III Creates the Judicial Branch, which is led by the Supreme Court, and describes its powers and responsibilities.

ARTICLE IV Describes the rights and powers of the states.

ARTICLE V Explains how amendments (changes or additions) can be made to the Constitution.

ARTICLE VI Says the Constitution is "the supreme law of the land."

ARTICLE VII Tells how the Constitution would be ratified (approved and made official) by the states.

The Bill of Rights

As Article V shows, the authors of the Constitution expected from the beginning that amendments would be made to it. There are now **27 amendments.**

The first 10 Amendments are known as the Bill of Rights. They list individual freedoms promised by the new government. The Bill of Rights was approved in 1791.

AMENDMENT I Guarantees freedom of religion, speech and the press.

AMENDMENT II Guarantees the right of the people to have firearms.

AMENDMENT III Says that soldiers may not stay in a house without the owner's permission.

AMENDMENT IV Says that the government cannot search people and their homes without a strong reason.

AMENDMENT V Says that every person has the right to a trial and to protection of his or her rights while waiting for a trial. Also, private property cannot be taken without payment.

AMENDMENT VI Says that every person shall have the right to "a speedy and public trial."

AMENDMENT VII Guarantees the right to a trial in various types of legal cases.

AMENDMENT VIII Outlaws all "cruel and unusual punishment."

AMENDMENT IX Says that people have rights in addition to those listed in the Constitution.

AMENDMENT X Says that the powers the Constitution does not give to the national government belong to the states and to the people.

Other Notable Amendments

AMENDMENT XIII (approved 1865) Declares slavery illegal.

AMENDMENT XV (approved 1870) Says the right to vote cannot be denied because of race.

AMENDMENT XVI (approved 1913) Gives Congress the power to tax incomes.

AMENDMENT XIX (approved 1920) Grants women the right to vote.

AMENDMENT XXII (approved 1951) Says that a President may serve no more than two four-year terms.

AMENDMENT XXIV (approved 1964) Forbids poll taxes—money paid for the right to vote—in national elections.

AMENDMENT XXV (approved 1967) Says the Vice President becomes President if the President leaves office early.

AMENDMENT XXVI (approved 1971) Lowers the voting age to 18.

go. For the complete Constitution, including all the amendments, WWW.FACT MONSTER.COM

The Constitution was signed in Philadelphia by the nation's leaders.

The Legislative Branch

★ ★ ★ ★ ★ ★ ★ ★

The Legislative Branch is made up of the two houses of Congress—the **Senate** and the **House of Representatives.** The most important duty of the Legislative Branch is to make laws. Laws are written, discussed and voted on in Congress.

There are **100 Senators** in the Senate, two from each state. Senators are elected by their states and serve six-year terms. The Vice President of the U.S. is considered the head of the Senate but does not vote in the Senate unless there is a tie. The President Pro Tempore of the Senate presides over the chamber in the absence of the Vice President. The Senator in the majority party who has served the longest is usually elected to the position.

The Senate approves nominations made by the President to the Cabinet, the Supreme Court, federal courts and other posts. The Senate must ratify all treaties by a two-thirds vote.

There are **435 Representatives** in the House of Representatives. The number of Representatives each state gets is based on its population. For example, California has many more Representatives than Montana has. When Census figures determine that the population of a state has changed significantly, the number of Representatives in that state may shift proportionately. Representatives are elected by their states and serve two-year terms. The Speaker of the House, elected by the Representatives, is considered the head of the House.

Both parties in the Senate and the House of Representatives elect leaders. The leader of the party that controls the house is called the Majority Leader. The other party leader is called the Minority Leader.

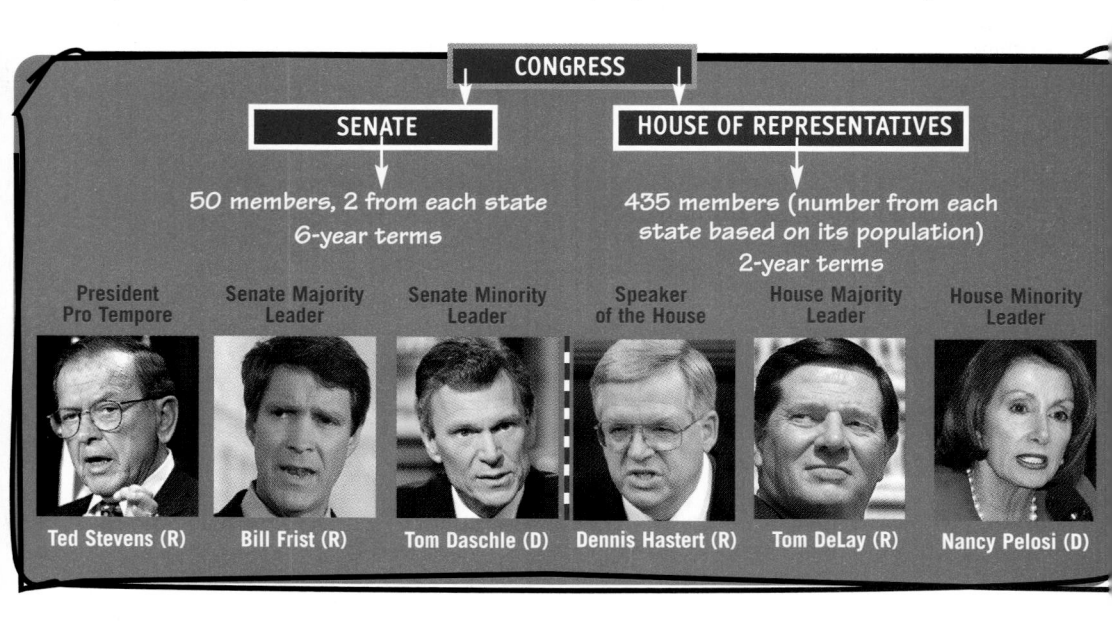

CONGRESS

SENATE	HOUSE OF REPRESENTATIVES
50 members, 2 from each state 6-year terms	435 members (number from each state based on its population) 2-year terms

President Pro Tempore	Senate Majority Leader	Senate Minority Leader	Speaker of the House	House Majority Leader	House Minority Leader
Ted Stevens (R)	Bill Frist (R)	Tom Daschle (D)	Dennis Hastert (R)	Tom DeLay (R)	Nancy Pelosi (D)

go ➤ Find and contact your Representative and Senator in Congress at *www.timeforkids.com/congress*

The Executive Branch

★ ★ ★ ★ ★ ★ ★ ★ ★

The President is the head of the Executive Branch, which makes laws official. The President is elected by the entire country and serves a four-year term. The President cannot serve more than two four-year terms. He or she approves and carries out laws passed by the Legislative Branch, appoints or removes Cabinet members and officials, negotiates treaties and acts as head of state and Commander-in-Chief of the armed forces.

The Executive Branch also includes the **Vice President** and other officials, such as members of the **Cabinet.** The Cabinet is made up of the heads of the 15 major departments of the government.

The Cabinet gives advice to the President about important matters.

THE PRESIDENT

GEORGE W. BUSH

THE VICE PRESIDENT

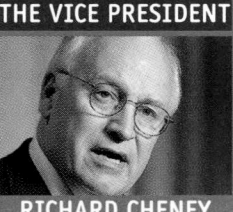

RICHARD CHENEY

THE CABINET

Secretary of Agriculture	Secretary of Commerce	Secretary of Defense	Secretary of Education	Secretary of Energy

Ann Veneman	**Donald Evans**	**Donald Rumsfeld**	**Rod Paige**	**Spencer Abraham**
Secretary of Health and Human Services	Secretary of Housing and Urban Development	Secretary of the Interior	Attorney General	Secretary of Labor

Tommy Thompson	**Alphonso Jackson**	**Gale Norton**	**John Ashcroft**	**Elaine Chao**
Secretary of State	Secretary of Transportation	Secretary of the Treasury	Secretary of Veterans Affairs	Secretary of Homeland Security

Colin Powell	**Norman Mineta**	**John W. Snow**	**Anthony Principi**	**Tom Ridge**

The
Judicial Branch

★ ★ ★ ★ ★ ★ ★ ★ ★

The Judicial Branch oversees the court system of the U.S. Through court cases, the Judicial Branch explains the meaning of the Constitution and laws passed by Congress. **The Supreme Court** is the head of the Judicial Branch. Unlike a criminal court, the Supreme Court rules whether something is constitutional or unconstitutional—whether or not it is permitted under the Constitution.

On the Supreme Court there are **nine Justices,** or judges: eight associate Justices and one Chief Justice. The judges are nominated by the President and approved by the Senate. They have no term limits.

The Supreme Court is the highest court in the land. Its decisions are final, and no other court can overrule those decisions. Decisions of the Supreme Court set precedents—new ways of interpreting the law.

Justices of the Supreme Court, from left: Antonin Scalia, Ruth Bader Ginsburg, John Paul Stevens, David Souter, Chief Justice William Rehnquist, Clarence Thomas, Sandra Day O'Connor, Stephen Breyer and Anthony Kennedy.

Significant Supreme Court Decisions

1803 *Marbury v. Madison*
The first time a law passed by Congress was declared unconstitutional

1857 *Dred Scott v. Sanford*
Declared that a slave was not a citizen, and that Congress could not outlaw slavery in U.S. territories

1896 *Plessy v. Ferguson*
Said that racial segregation was legal

1954 *Brown v. Board of Education*
Made racial segregation in schools illegal

1966 *Miranda v. Arizona*
Stated that criminal suspects must be informed of their rights before being questioned by police

2003 *Grutter v. Bollinger* and *Gratz v. Bollinger*
Ruled that colleges can, under certain conditions, consider race and ethnicity in admissions

Checks and Balances

★ ★ ★ ★ ★ ★ ★ ★

The system of checks and balances is an important part of the Constitution. With checks and balances, each of the three branches of government can limit the powers of the others. This way, no one branch becomes too powerful. Each branch "checks" the power of the other branches to make sure that the power is balanced among them. How does this system of checks and balances work?

The process of making laws (see following page) is a good example of checks and balances in action. First, the **Legislative Branch** introduces and votes on a bill. If the bill passes, it then goes to the **Executive Branch,** where the President decides whether the bill is good for the country. If so, the the bill is signed and becomes a law.

If the President does not believe the bill is good for the country, it does not get signed. This is called a veto. But the Legislative Branch gets another chance. With enough votes, the Legislative Branch can override the Executive Branch's veto, and the bill becomes a law.

Once a law is in place, the people of the country can test it through the court system, which is under the control of the **Judicial Branch.** If someone believes a law is unfair, a lawsuit can be filed. Lawyers then make arguments for and against the case, and a judge decides which side has presented the most convincing arguments.

The side that loses can choose to appeal to a higher court, and the case may eventually reach the highest court of all, the Supreme Court. If the Legislative Branch does not agree with the way in which the Judicial Branch has interpreted the law, it can introduce a new piece of legislation, and the process starts all over again.

Homework TIP

Do the assignments that you find most difficult first, when you are more alert and energetic.

How a
Bill Becomes a Law
★ ★ ★ ★ ★ ★ ★ ★

1. A member of Congress introduces the bill.

When a Senator or Representative introduces a bill, it is sent to the clerk of the Senate or House, who gives it a number and title. Next, the bill goes to the appropriate committee.

2. Committees review and vote on the bill.

Committees specialize in different areas, such as foreign relations or agriculture, and are made up of small groups of Senators or Representatives.

The committee may reject the bill and "table" it, meaning it is never discussed again. Or the committee may hold hearings to listen to facts and opinions, make changes in the bill and cast votes. If most committee members vote in favor of the bill, it is sent back to the Senate and the House for debate.

3. The Senate and the House debate and vote on the bill.

Separately, the Senate and the House debate the bill, offer amendments and cast votes. If the bill is defeated in either the Senate or the House, the bill dies.

Sometimes, the House and the Senate pass the same bill, but with different amendments. In these cases, the bill goes to a conference committee made up of members of both houses of Congress. The conference committee works out differences between the two versions of the bill.

Then the bill goes before all of Congress for a vote. If a majority of both the Senate and the House votes for the bill, it goes to the President for approval.

You're Grounded

The President, the Vice President and other U.S. officials can be impeached—that is, formally charged with "high crimes and misdemeanors," which include bribery, perjury, treason and abuse of power.

Under the Constitution, only the House of Representatives has the power to impeach a federal official. If a majority of the House votes for impeachment, then the Senate holds a trial and votes on whether to convict the official. If two-thirds of the Senate votes for conviction, the official will be removed from office.

Only two Presidents have been impeached: Andrew Johnson and Bill Clinton. However, neither was convicted by the Senate.

4. The President signs the bill–or not.

If the President approves the bill and signs it, the bill becomes a law. However, if the President disapproves, he or she can veto the bill by refusing to sign it.

Congress can try to overrule a veto. If both the Senate and the House pass the bill by a two-thirds majority, the President's veto is overruled and the bill becomes a law.

Division of Powers

★ ★ ★ ★ ★ ★ ★ ★

any of the powers the Constitution granted to the Federal Government are **exclusive powers**—only the national level of government can use them. State governments also have some powers that are theirs alone. Both levels of government, however, share some powers; these are called **concurrent powers.**

Powers of the Government

Federal Government

★ Print money
★ Regulate interstate (between states) and international trade
★ Make treaties
★ Conduct foreign policy
★ Provide and maintain armed forces
★ Declare war
★ Govern U.S. territories and admit new states
★ Establish post offices

State Government

★ Issue licenses
★ Regulate intrastate (within the state) businesses
★ Conduct elections
★ Establish local governments
★ Ratify amendments to the Constitution
★ Take measures for public health and safety
★ Create public schools

Concurrent Powers

In addition to having unique powers, both the Federal Government and state governments can:

★ Collect taxes
★ Build roads
★ Borrow money
★ Establish courts
★ Make and enforce laws
★ Charter banks and corporations
★ Spend money for the good of the people
★ Take private property for public use, with fair payment

Who Can Vote?
Anyone who is
1. 18 years of age.
2. a citizen of the U.S. and meets the residency requirements of his or her state.

Who Can Be a Senator?
Anyone who is
1. at least 30 years old.
2. a U.S. citizen for at least nine years.
3. a resident of the state where he or she is elected.

Who Can Be a Representative?
Anyone who is
1. at least 25 years old.
2. a U.S. citizen for at least seven years.
3. a resident of the state where he or she is elected.

Who Can Be President?
Anyone who is
1. a natural-born citizen of the U.S.
2. at least 35 years of age.
3. a resident of the U.S. for at least 14 years.

How The
President Gets Elected

★ ★ ★ ★ ★ ★ ★ ★

Step by Step on the Campaign Trail

1. Candidate announces plan to run for office.

This announcement launches the candidate's official campaign. Speeches, debates and baby kissing begin.

2. Candidate campaigns to win delegate support.

The first stage of a presidential campaign is the nomination campaign. At this time the candidate is competing with other candidates in the same party, hoping to get the party's nomination. The candidate works to win delegates—representatives who pledge to support the candidate's nomination at the national party convention—and to persuade potential voters in general.

3. Caucuses and primary elections take place in the states.

Caucuses and primaries are ways for the general public to take part in nominating presidential candidates.

At a caucus, local party members gather to nominate a candidate. A caucus is a lively event at which party leaders and activists debate issues and consider candidates. The rules governing caucus procedures vary by party and by state.

A primary is more like a general election. Voters go to the polls to cast their votes for a presidential candidate (or delegates who will represent that candidate at the party convention). A primary election is the main way voters choose a nominee.

4. Nominee for President is announced at national party convention.

There are two primary political parties in the U.S.—the Democratic Party and the Republican Party. The main goal of a national party convention is to unify party members. Thousands of delegates gather to rally support for the party's ideas and to formally nominate party candidates for President and Vice President.

After the convention, the second stage of the presidential campaign begins: the election campaign. In this stage, candidates from different parties compete against each other as they try to get elected President.

5. Citizens cast their votes.

Presidential elections are held every four years on the Tuesday after the first Monday of November.

Many Americans think that when they cast their ballot, they are voting for their chosen candidate. Actually, they are selecting groups of electors in the Electoral College.

Get the facts on the 2004 Presidential election at *www.timeforkids.com/electionconnection*

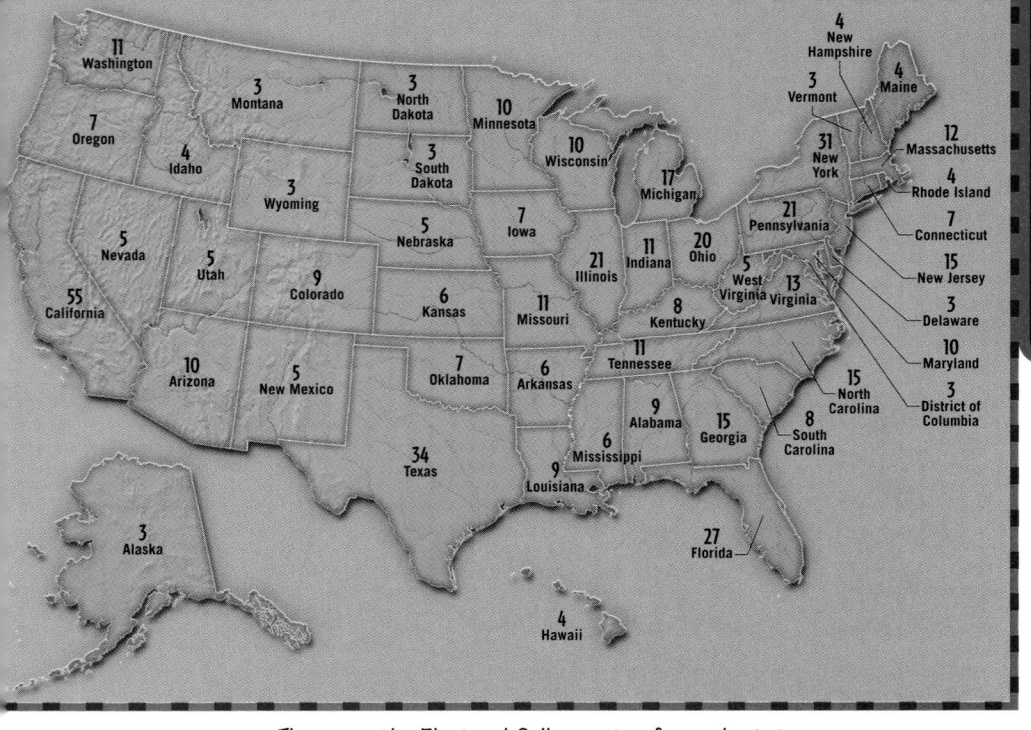

These are the Electoral College votes for each state.

6. The Electoral College casts its votes.

Some of the Founding Fathers wanted Congress to elect the President. Others wanted the President to be elected by popular vote. The Electoral College represents a compromise between these ideas.

Every state has a number of electors equal to its number of Senators and Representatives. In addition, there are three electors for the District of Columbia. Laws vary by state, but electors are usually chosen by popular vote. An elector may not be a Senator, Representative or other person holding a national office.

In most cases, the electoral votes from a particular state go to the candidate who leads the popular vote in that state. (Only Maine and Nebraska divide electoral votes among candidates.)

This "winner takes all" system can produce surprising results; in the elections of 1824, 1876, 1888 and 2000, the candidate who had the greatest popular vote did not win the greatest Electoral College vote and so lost the presidency.

On the first Monday after the second Wednesday in December, the electors cast their ballots. At least 270 electoral votes are required to elect a President. If this majority is not reached, the House of Representatives chooses the President.

7. The President is inaugurated.

On January 20, the President enters office in a ceremony that is known as the Inauguration and takes the presidential oath: "I do solemnly swear (or affirm) that I will faithfully execute the office of President of the United States, and will to the best of my ability, preserve, protect, and defend the Constitution of the United States."

Party Animals

★ ★ ★ ★ ★ ★ ★

The **DEMOCRATIC DONKEY** was first associated with Democrat Andrew Jackson's 1828 presidential campaign. His opponents called him a jackass (a donkey), and Jackson decided to use the image of the strong-willed animal on his campaign posters. Later, cartoonist Thomas Nast used the Democratic donkey in newspaper cartoons and made the symbol famous.

Nast invented another famous symbol—the **REPUBLICAN ELEPHANT.** After the

A Thomas Nast cartoon from 1879

Republicans lost the White House to the Democrats in 1877, Nast drew a cartoon of an elephant walking into a trap set by a donkey. He chose the elephant to represent the Republicans because elephants are intelligent but easily controlled.

Democrats today say that the donkey is smart and brave, while Republicans say that the elephant is strong and dignified.

POLITICAL MAVERICKS

Democrats and Republicans typically control national and state politics. But minor parties also play an important role in elections, often taking away votes from major candidates. Some minor parties include the Green Party, the Libertarian Party, the Natural Law Party and the Reform Party. Here's a look at minor-party candidates who fared well in presidential elections.

Year	Candidate	Party	Votes earned
1880	James B. Weaver	Greenback	308,578
1888	Clinton B. Fisk	Prohibition	249,506
1892	James B. Weaver	Populist	1,041,028
	John Bidwell	Prohibition	264,133
1904	Eugene V. Debs	Socialist	402,400
1908	Eugene V. Debs	Socialist	402,820
1912	Eugene V. Debs	Socialist	897,011
1916	A. L. Benson	Socialist	585,113
1920	Eugene V. Debs	Socialist	917,799
1924	Robert M. LaFollette	Progressive	4,822,856
1928	Norman Thomas	Socialist	267,420
1932	Norman Thomas	Socialist	884,781
1948	Strom Thurmond	States' Rights	1,176,125
	Henry A. Wallace	Progressive	1,157,326
1968	George C. Wallace	American Independent	9,906,473
1996	Ross Perot	Reform	8,085,402
2000	Ralph Nader	Green	2,882,897

TFK Puzzles & Games

Run for Office!

So you want to be elected President of the U.S.? Just solve this maze and you'll be calling the White House home sweet home!

WIN PRIMARIES

NOMINATED AT CONVENTION

WIN ELECTION

VOTE

(See Answer Key that begins on page 340.)

The Presidential Succession

Who would take over if the President died, resigned or was removed from office? The list of who's next in line is known as **presidential succession**.

★ The Vice President
★ Speaker of the House
★ President Pro Tempore of the Senate
★ Secretary of State
★ Secretary of the Treasury
★ Secretary of Defense
★ Attorney General
★ Secretary of the Interior
★ Secretary of Agriculture
★ Secretary of Commerce
★ Secretary of Labor
★ Secretary of Health and Human Services
★ Secretary of Housing and Urban Development
★ Secretary of Transportation
★ Secretary of Energy
★ Secretary of Education
★ Secretary of Veterans Affairs
★ Secretary of Homeland Security

Can you name which member of the current Cabinet cannot become President because she was not born in the U.S.?

(See Answer Key that begins on page 340.)

TFK Mystery Person

CLUE 1: I was born in 1930 and grew up on a cattle ranch in Arizona.
CLUE 2: In 1952, law firms wouldn't hire a female lawyer, so after graduating from law school, I turned to public service.
CLUE 3: In 1981, President Ronald Reagan appointed me to the U.S. Supreme Court. I was the first woman ever to serve on our country's highest court.

WHO AM I?

(See Answer Key that begins on page 340.)

We Can Eat Smarter

By Kathryn R. Satterfield

America has a supersize problem. The Centers for Disease Control and Prevention (CDC) estimates that about 64% of adults are overweight or obese, which means excessively overweight. Over the past 20 years, the rate of adult obesity in the United States has more than doubled, going from 15% in 1980 to 31% in 2000.

These numbers reflect a troubling upward trend—and not just for grownups. Over the same 20 years, the percentage of obese kids ages 6 to 19 has tripled to 15% of that population. About 9 million children are excessively overweight.

Obesity can lead to serious health problems, including heart disease, stroke, diabetes, cancer and high blood pressure. The occurrence of type 2 diabetes, once considered an adult disease, has increased dramatically in young people.

How did so many people get so big so fast? Health experts point to junk foods, huge portion sizes and less activity. The U.S. Department of Health and Human Services (HHS) says that nearly half of all American children do not get enough vigorous physical activity.

An occasional order of fries won't harm anyone, but most fast foods are too high in calories, fat and artery-clogging cholesterol to eat every day. The trend toward supersizing is also contributing to the big fat problem. In 1957, the average fast-food burger weighed about one ounce. Today, the typical hamburger weighs a whopping six ounces.

The bad news has prompted some companies to shape up their menus. Experts say that such changes are good, but more must be done.

Many families have taken notice of the obesity crisis. They are already making changes to their lifestyles and eating habits. Most important is having the right attitude, says Dr. Naomi Neufeld of the KidShape Foundation, in California. "Eating healthily and exercising is not done to conform to some image of the perfect body," she says. "It's to treat yourself better, because you deserve it."

Fries and burgers are high in fat and low in nutrients.

THE RIGHT STUFF

Nutritionist Jeffrey S. Hampl of Arizona State University has these tips for eating smart:

Encourage your family to keep fresh vegetables and dried fruits on hand. Baby carrots, dried apricots and apples make great snacks, and they're loaded with vitamins.

Go nuts! Peanuts and almonds are easy to eat on the run. They are high in fat, but some of the fat is actually good for you!

Got calcium? Milk is a great source of calcium. Cheese, yogurt and orange juice with calcium added are also good choices.

Most fast food is fattening. If you eat at a fast-food place, don't load up on greasy stuff. Order a salad or some frozen yogurt instead of fries. Try to choose the smallest burger. Don't supersize!

Watch how much soda you drink. It's full of sugar and has no calcium or vitamins. If you drink more than a can a day, try bubbly or flavored water instead.

Exercise—It's Good for You

Not only is exercise fun, but it also helps your mind, body and overall well-being. Kids who exercise regularly often do better in school, sleep better, are less likely to be overweight or obese and are stronger than less-active kids. Exercise can also relieve stress and improve your mood.

There are two types of exercise, **aerobic** and **anaerobic**. When you do aerobic exercises, such as running, swimming, biking and playing soccer, you increase your heart rate and the flow of oxygen-rich blood to your muscles. Aerobic exercise also builds endurance and burns fat and calories. Anaerobic exercise, such as weight lifting, involves short bursts of effort. It helps to build strength and muscle mass.

Here are some tips to help you stay fit:

- Exercise every day. Try new and varied activities so you work different muscles.
- Start slowly. Do one of your daily physical activities for at least 10 minutes at a time. Increase the amount of time as you get stronger.
- Don't spend more than two hours a day at the computer or watching TV.
- You can still exercise when the weather's not great. Try dancing, jumping rope, running up and down the stairs or setting up an obstacle course in your home.
- Partner up. Invite a friend or family member to join you the next time you're ready for active play.

The Doctor's In

Fact Monster asked pediatrician Dr. Brian Orr to answer some questions kids frequently ask about their bodies. Dr. Orr, whose office is in Gloucester, Massachusetts, has practiced medicine for more than 22 years. A father of three kids, Dr. Orr is also a writer.

Why do we sneeze?
We sneeze to clear our breathing passages. We all have a natural reflex to sneeze whenever a small foreign substance enters our airways. So don't hold back your sneezes—let 'em rip!

What happens when my foot falls asleep?
Feet don't really sleep. They just feel tingly when an adequate blood supply to our nerves is cut off. This usually happens when you stay in one position too long—like sitting with your legs crossed. It just goes to show that it's good to keep your body moving.

Why does my nose run?
The nose serves as one of the body's first barriers against infection. Your nose makes more mucus when a foreign substance, such as a virus, enters the body. The increased mucus, combined with increased blood flow to the nose due to the infection, causes your nose to "run" with excess liquid. And it keeps tissue companies in business!

Why do we shiver?
When we shiver, our bodies are doing the opposite of sweating. Sweating cools the body by putting a layer of liquid on the skin. Shivering tightens the skin and shakes the muscles, a process that conserves and generates heat. You can stop your shivering by bundling up—just like your mother says.

Why does a bruise turn colors?
A bruise is actually a pocket of blood under the skin caused by a broken blood vessel. It changes color and fades as the body reabsorbs the blood from the bruise.

Why do our temperatures rise when we are sick?
Temperatures rise in our bodies to fight infections. Fevers create an enviornment that, we hope, is too warm for the invading organisms. Turning up the heat makes viruses and bacteria feel unwelcome.

How does a scab form?
Scabs patch up holes in the skin. Certain cells in our bloodstream recognize when our skin has been broken. These cells, called platelets, start patching the break in the skin and call in other blood components to help complete the process. They do an amazing job. Don't make your platelets work overtime by picking your scabs!

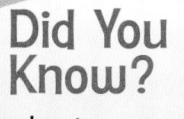

go Take a quiz about the science behind staying healthy at *www.timeforkids.com/health*

The Food Pyramid: Healthy or Not?

The food pyramid, created by the U.S. Department of Agriculture (USDA), debuted in 1992. It recommends the number of servings from each food group a person should eat a day to stay healthy. The food groups include: grains, fruits, vegetables, meat, dairy and fats and oils.

But in recent years, doctors and scientists have begun to question just how helpful—and healthful—the guidelines really are. In fact, the USDA itself is reevaluating the food pyramid.

The pyramid indicates that people should eat between 6 and 11 servings of grains a day. Grains include bread, pasta and cereals. One serving equals one slice of bread or one-half cup of cooked rice or pasta. By recommending so many bread products, which are usually low in fat, the USDA has been promoting a low-fat diet.

But many experts now believe that a low-fat diet that's high in sugar (most processed

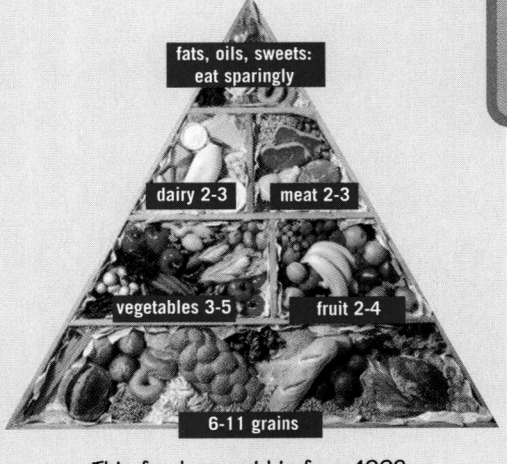

fats, oils, sweets: eat sparingly

dairy 2-3   meat 2-3

vegetables 3-5   fruit 2-4

6-11 grains

This food pyramid is from 1992.

grains, such as white flour, are made out of forms of sugar like glucose and fructose) has actually led to an increase in obesity and heart problems.

Some doctors now contend that a diet higher in fat—with the fat coming from nuts, cheeses, some oils (such as olive oil), poultry, eggs and some lean red meat—will keep people trimmer and healthier than a high-carbohydrate, low-fat diet.

So what should you eat? Eat a variety of foods from all of the food groups. But when eating grains, try to avoid white bread and pasta. Instead eat whole-grain foods, such as whole-wheat bread. They contain more natural nutrients.

Try to eat less red meat, such as hamburgers and steak, and more fish, nuts and cheese. You won't go wrong eating lots of fruits and vegetables. No one questions their nutritional value.

Finally, avoid junk foods, such as soda, candy and potato chips. They provide little or no nutritional value. Instead, choose healthful snacks, such as fruit, nuts and yogurt.

TFK Top 5 Fruits

Here are Americans' favorite fruits and the average amount each person eats in a year.

1. **Bananas** 27 pounds
2. **Apples** 16 pounds
3. **Watermelons** 15 pounds
4. **Oranges** 12 pounds
5. **Cantaloupes** 11 pounds

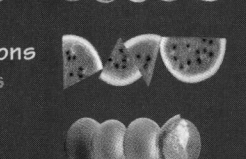

Source: Produce Marketing Association, 2002 U.S. sales figures for fresh fruit

Your Body

If you could peek inside your own body, what would you see? Hundreds of bones, miles of blood vessels and trillions of cells, all of which are constantly working together.

Skin

MAIN JOB: To protect your internal organs from drying up and to prevent harmful bacteria from getting inside your body

HOW MUCH: The average person has about six pounds of skin.

MAIN LAYERS:
- **Epidermis:** Outer layer of skin cells, hair, nails and sweat glands
- **Dermis:** Inner layer of living tissue, containing nerves and blood vessels

Ligaments

MAIN JOB: To hold joints together. These bands of tough tissue are strong and flexible.

Joints

MAIN JOB: To allow bones to move in different directions

DID YOU KNOW? Bones don't bend. Joints allow two bones next to each other to move.

Cells

MAIN JOB: To perform the many jobs necessary to stay alive, such as moving oxygen around your body, taking care of the fuel supply and waste removal

DID YOU KNOW? There are 26 billion cells in a newborn baby and 50 trillion cells in an adult.

SOME DIFFERENT CELLS
- **Bone cells** help to build your skeleton by producing the fibers and minerals from which bone is made.
- **Fat cells** contain fat, which is burned to create energy.
- **Muscle cells** are organized into muscles, which move body parts.
- **Nerve cells** pass nerve messages around your body.
- **Red blood cells** carry oxygen around your body.

Muscles

MAIN JOB: To make body movement possible

HOW MANY: Your body has more than 650 muscles.

KINDS OF MUSCLES
- **Skeletal muscles** help the body move. You have about 400 skeletal muscles.
- **Smooth muscles** are located inside organs, like the stomach.
- **Cardiac muscle** is found only in the heart.

Bones

MAIN JOB: To give shape and support to your body
HOW MANY: At birth you had more than 300 bones in your body. As an adult you'll have 206, because some bones fuse together.
DID YOU KNOW? The largest bone in the body is the femur, or thighbone. In a 6-foot-tall person, it is 20 inches long. The smallest is the stirrup bone, in the ear. It is one-tenth of an inch long.

KINDS OF BONES
- **Long bones** are thin; they are found in your legs, arms and fingers.
- **Short bones** are wide and chunky; they are found in your feet and wrists.
- **Flat bones** are flat and smooth, like your shoulder blades.
- **Irregular bones**, like the bones in your inner ear and the vertebrae in your spine, come in many different shapes.

Glands

MAIN JOB: To manufacture substances that help your body to function

KINDS OF GLANDS
- **Endocrine glands** make hormones, which tell the different parts of your body when to work.
- **Oil glands** keep your skin from drying out.
- **Salivary glands** make saliva, which helps to digest and swallow food.
- **Sweat glands** make perspiration, which regulates your body temperature.

Viscera

This term refers to the organs that fill your body's chest and abdominal cavity.
MAIN JOB: To provide your body with food and oxygen and to remove waste
HOW MANY: The viscera include the trachea (windpipe), lungs, liver, kidneys, gallbladder, spleen, stomach, large intestine, small intestine and bladder.

Tendons

MAIN JOB: To hold your muscles to your bones
DID YOU KNOW? Tendons look like rubber bands.

Body Count

- Your body contains eight pints of blood.
- You use 14 muscles to smile and 43 to frown.
- Kids have 20 first teeth. Adults have 32 teeth.
- Most people shed 40 pounds of skin in a lifetime.
- Your body is 70% water.
- You blink your eyes about 20,000 times a day.
- Your heart beats about 100,000 times a day.
- When you sneeze, air rushes through your nose at a rate of 100 miles per hour.
- Humans breathe 20 times per minute, more than 10 million times per year and about 700 million times in a lifetime.
- You have about 100,000 hairs on your head.
- Your tongue has four taste zones: bitter (back), sour (back sides), salty (front sides) and sweet (front).

Your Body's Systems

Circulatory System

The circulatory system transports blood throughout the body. The heart pumps the blood and the **arteries** and **veins** transport it. Blood is carried away from the heart by arteries. The biggest artery, called the **aorta,** branches from the left side of the heart into smaller **arteries,** which then branch into even smaller vessels that travel all over the body. When blood enters the smallest of these vessels, which are called **capillaries,** it gives nutrients and oxygen to cells and takes in carbon dioxide, water and waste. The blood then returns to the heart through **veins.** Veins carry waste products away from cells and bring blood back to the heart, which pumps it to the lungs to pick up oxygen and eliminate waste carbon dioxide.

Digestive System

The digestive system breaks down food into protein, vitamins, minerals, carbohydrates and fats, which the body needs for energy, growth and repair. After food is chewed and swallowed, it goes down a tube called the **esophagus** and enters the **stomach,** where it is broken down by powerful acids. From the stomach the food travels into the **small intestine,** where it is broken down into nutrients. The food that the body doesn't need or can't digest is turned into waste and eliminated from the body through the **large intestine.**

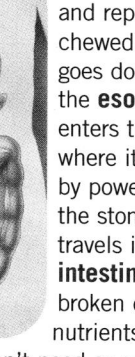

Endocrine System

The endocrine system is made up of glands that produce **hormones,** the body's long-distance messengers. Hormones are chemicals that control body functions, such as metabolism and growth. The **glands,** which include the pituitary gland, thyroid gland, adrenal glands, pancreas, ovaries and testes, release hormones into the bloodstream, which then transports the hormones to organs and tissues throughout the body.

Immune System

The immune system is our body's defense system against infections and diseases. It works to respond to dangerous organisms, such as viruses or bacteria, and substances that may enter the body. There are **three** types of response systems in the immune system.

- **The anatomic response physically prevents dangerous substances from entering your body. The anatomic system includes the skin and the mucous membranes.**
- **The inflammatory system eliminates the invaders from your body. Sneezing and fever are examples of the inflammatory system at work.**
- **The immune response is made up of white blood cells, which fight infection by gobbling up toxins, bacteria and other threats.**

Muscular System

The muscular system is made up of fibrous tissues that work with the skeletal system to control movement of the body. Some muscles—like the ones in your arms, legs, mouth and tongue—are **voluntary,** meaning that you decide when to move them. Other muscles, like the ones in your stomach, heart, blood vessels and intestines, are **involuntary.** This means that they're controlled by the nervous system and hormones, and you often don't even realize they're at work.

Respiratory System

The respiratory system brings air into the body and removes carbon dioxide. It includes the nose, trachea (windpipe) and lungs. When you inhale, air enters your **nose** and goes down the **trachea.** The trachea branches into two bronchial tubes, which go to the **lungs.** These tubes branch off into even smaller bronchial tubes, which end in air sacs. Oxygen follows this path and passes through the air sacs and blood vessels and enters the blood stream. At the same time, carbon dioxide passes into the lungs and is exhaled.

Skeletal System

The skeletal system is made up of **bones, ligaments** and **tendons.** It shapes the body and protects organs. The skeletal system works with the muscular system to help the body move.

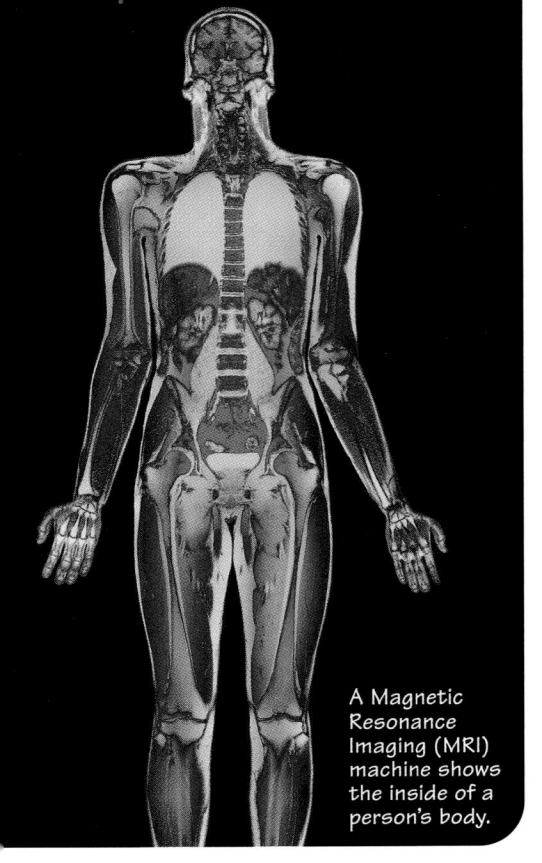

A Magnetic Resonance Imaging (MRI) machine shows the inside of a person's body.

Nervous System

The nervous system is made up of the brain, the spinal cord and nerves. The nervous system sends and receives nerve impulses that tell your muscles and organs what to do. There are three parts of your nervous system that work together.

- **The central nervous system consists of the brain and spinal cord. It sends out nerve impulses and receives sensory information, which tells your brain about things you see, hear, smell, taste and feel.**
- **The peripheral nervous system includes the nerves that branch off from the brain and the spinal cord. It carries the nerve impulses from the central nervous system to the muscles and glands.**
- **The autonomic nervous system regulates involuntary action, such as heartbeat and digestion.**

TFK Mystery Person

CLUE 1: Fighting the AIDS virus has been the focus of my ground-breaking research.
CLUE 2: During the 1980s, as a molecular biologist, I uncovered many secrets of HIV.
CLUE 3: In 1995, I discovered that a combination of drugs could work successfully against the disease. For my AIDS research, I was named TIME Person of the Year in 1996.

WHO AM I?
(See Answer Key that begins on page 340.)

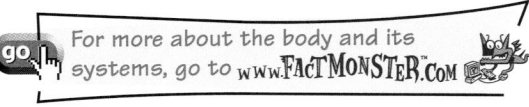 For more about the body and its systems, go to www.FACTMONSTER.COM

HISTORY

Heroes of the Civil Rights Movement

Rosa Parks (right) refused to give up her seat because she didn't want to be treated unfairly.

The year 2005 marks the 50th anniversary of the Montgomery bus boycott. The boycott launched the civil rights movement, which challenged racism in America and made the country a more just society. Martin Luther King Jr. is famous for his inspiring leadership in the movement. Below are a few of the many other civil rights heroes.

Rosa Parks

On December 1, 1955, in Montgomery, Alabama, **Rosa Parks,** an African-American seamstress, was ordered to give up her seat to a white passenger on a bus. Montgomery's buses were segregated, with the seats in the front reserved "for whites only." Blacks had to sit at the back of the bus. If the bus was crowded, black people were expected to give their seats to a white person. Rosa refused to give up her seat. "I felt I had a right to stay where I was," she said. The bus driver had her arrested.

Martin Luther King Jr. heard about Parks's brave defiance and launched a boycott of Montgomery buses. The 17,000 black residents of Montgomery pulled together and refused to ride on public buses for more than a year. Finally, the Supreme Court declared segregation on buses to be unconstitutional. Rosa Parks became known as "the mother of the civil rights movement."

Thurgood Marshall

Thurgood Marshall was a courageous civil-rights lawyer during a period when racial segregation was the law of the land. Between 1938 and 1961, Marshall presented more than 30 civil rights cases before the Supreme Court. He won 29 of them.

Marshall's most important case was *Brown v. Board of Education of Topeka, Kansas* (1954). By law, black and white students had to attend separate public schools. As long as schools were "separate but equal"—providing equal education for all races—segregation was considered legal. In reality, Marshall argued, segregated schools were unequal: white schools were far more privileged than black schools, which were largely poor and overcrowded. The Supreme Court agreed, ruling that "separate educational facilities are inherently unequal." Marshall went on to become the first African-American Supreme Court Justice in American history.

The Little Rock Nine

The Little Rock Nine, as they later came to be called, were the first black teenagers to attend all-white Central High School in Little Rock, Arkansas, in 1957.

Although *Brown v. Board of Education* outlawed segregation in schools, many school systems defied the law by intimidating and threatening black students. Central High School

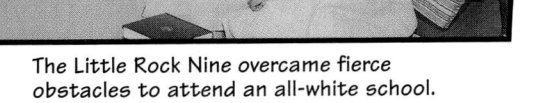

The Little Rock Nine overcame fierce obstacles to attend an all-white school.

was a notorious example. The Little Rock Nine were determined to attend the school and receive the same education offered to white students. Things grew frightening right away. On the first day of school, the Governor of Arkansas ordered the state's National Guard to block the black students from entering the school. President Eisenhower sent in federal troops to protect the students. Still, every morning on their way to school, angry crowds of whites taunted and insulted the Little Rock Nine. As scared as they were, the students didn't give up, and several went on to graduate from Central High.

TFK Mystery Person

CLUE 1: Born Malcolm Little in 1925, I became a leading member of a religious group called the Black Muslims.
CLUE 2: I preached the need for education, self help and self defense for African Americans.
CLUE 3: Spike Lee directed a movie based on my life story.

WHO AM I?

(See Answer Key that begins on page 340.)

TFK Puzzles & Games

Words to Live By

Hidden in this puzzle are famous words from a 1963 speech by Martin Luther King Jr. Find the six words on the list. Hint: Some run diagonally, and some run backwards. The leftover letters spell out Dr. King's most famous phrase. What is it? Find: ALABAMA, CIVIL, EQUALITY, MARCH, PEACE, RIGHTS

Y	M	A	R	C	H		A
C	T	I		H	A	M	P
I		I	V		A		E
V			L	B	E		A
I	A		A	A			C
L		L	D	R	U	E	E
	A			A	M	Q	
	S	T	H	G	I	R	E

(See Answer Key that begins on page 340.)

 Hear and see famous moments in black history at www.timeforkids.com/bhm

ANCIENT HISTORY

10,000–4000 B.C. In Mesopotamia, settlements develop into cities, and people learn to use the wheel.

4500–4000 B.C. Earliest-known civilization arises in Sumer.

3000–2000 B.C. The rule of the pharaohs begins in Egypt. King Khufu completes construction of the Great Pyramid at Giza (ca.* 2680 B.C.), and King Khafre builds the Great Sphinx of Giza (ca. 2540 B.C.).

3000–1500 B.C. The Indus Valley civilization flourishes in what is today Pakistan. In Britain, Stonehenge is erected.

1500–1000 B.C. Moses leads the Israelites out of Egypt and delivers the Ten Commandments. Chinese civilization develops under the Shang Dynasty.

1000–900 B.C. Hebrew elders begin to write the books of the Hebrew Bible.

900–800 B.C. Phoenicians establish Carthage (ca. 810 B.C.). The Iliad and the Odyssey are composed, probably by the Greek poet Homer.

800–700 B.C. The first-recorded Olympic games (776 B.C.) take place.

700–600 B.C. Lao-tse, Chinese philosopher and founder of Taoism, is born around 604 B.C.

600–500 B.C. Confucius (551–479 B.C.) develops his philosophy in China. Buddha (ca. 563–ca. 483 B.C.) founds Buddhism in India.

500–400 B.C. Greek culture flourishes during the Age of Pericles (450–400 B.C.). The Parthenon is built in Athens as a temple of the goddess Athena (447–432 B.C.).

400–300 B.C. Alexander the Great (356–323 B.C.) destroys Thebes (335 B.C.), conquers Tyre and Jerusalem (332 B.C.), occupies Babylon (330 B.C.) and invades India.

300–250 B.C. The Temple of the Sun is built at Teotihuacán, Mexico (ca. 300 B.C.).

250–200 B.C. The Great Wall of China is built (ca. 215 B.C.).

100–31 B.C. Julius Caesar (100–44 B.C.) invades Britain (55 B.C.) and conquers Gaul (France) (ca. 50 B.C.). Cleopatra rules Egypt (51–31 B.C.).

44 B.C. Julius Caesar is murdered.

*"ca." is an abbreviation for "circa," which means "around."

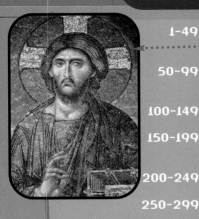

1-49 — Life of Jesus Christ (ca. 1-30). Emperor Kuang Wu Ti founds Han dynasty in China. Buddhism introduced to China.

50-99 — Jews revolt against the Romans; Jerusalem destroyed (A.D. 70).

100-149 — The great emperor Hadrian rules Rome (A.D. 117-138).

150-199 — The earliest Mayan temples are built in Central America.

200-249 — Goths invade Asia Minor (ca. A.D. 220).

250-299 — Mayan civilization (A.D. 250-900) has advances in art, architecture and science.

300-349 — Constantine the Great (rules A.D. 312–337) unites eastern and western Roman empires, with new capital at Constantinople (A.D. 330).

350-399 — Huns (Mongols) invade Europe (ca. A.D. 360).

400-449 — St. Patrick returns to Ireland (A.D. 432) and brings Christianity to the island.

450-499 — Vandals destroy Rome (A.D. 455).

500-549 — Arthur, semi-legendary king of the Britons, is killed around 537.

550-599 — After killing about half the European population, plague subsides (594).

600-649 — Muhammad, founder of Islam, flees from Mecca to Medina (the Hegira, 622). Arabs conquer Jerusalem (637) and destroy the Alexandrian library (641).

650-699 — Arabs attack North Africa (670) and destroy Carthage (697).

700-749 — Arab empire extends from Lisbon to China (by 716).

750-799 — City of Machu Picchu flourishes in Peru.

800-849 — Charlemagne is crowned first Holy Roman Emperor in Rome (800).

850-899 — Russian nation is founded by Vikings under Prince Rurik (855-879).

900-949 — Vikings discover Greenland (ca. 900). Arab Spain under Abd al-Rahman III becomes center of learning (912-961).

950-999 — Erik the Red establishes first Viking colony in Greenland (982).

CR. 1000-1300	The Pueblo period of Anasazi culture flourishes; cliff dwellings are built.
CR. 1000	Viking raider Leif Eriksson reaches North America.
CR. 1008	Murasaki Shikibu finishes *The Tale of Genji*, the world's first novel.
1066	William of Normandy invades England, crowned William I ("the Conqueror").
1096	Pope Urban II launches the First Crusade, one of at least eight European military campaigns between 1095 and 1291 to take the Holy Land from the Muslims.
CR. 1150	The temple complex of Angkor Wat is completed in Cambodia.
1211	Genghis Khan invades China, captures Peking (1214), conquers Persia (1218) and invades Russia (1223).
1215	Britain's King John is forced by barons to sign the Magna Carta, limiting royal power.
1231	The Inquisition begins as the Catholic Church fights heresy; torture is used.
1251	Kublai Khan governs China.
1271	Marco Polo of Venice travels to China; visits court of Kublai Khan (1275-1292).
1312-1337	The Mali Empire reaches its height in Africa under King Mansa Musa.
CR. 1325	Aztecs establish Tenochtitlán on the site of modern Mexico City.
1337-1453	In the Hundred Years' War, English and French kings fight for control of France.
1347-1351	At least 25 million people die in Europe's Black Death (bubonic plague).
1368	The Ming Dynasty begins in China.
CR. 1387	Geoffrey Chaucer writes *The Canterbury Tales*.
1428	Joan of Arc leads the French against the English.
1438	The Incas rule in Peru.
1450	Florence, Italy, becomes the center of Renaissance art and learning.
1453	The Turks conquer Constantinople, thus beginning the Ottoman Empire.
1455	Johannes Gutenberg invents the printing press.
1462	Ivan the Great rules Russia until 1505 as first czar.
1492	Christopher Columbus reaches the New World.

1501 The first African slaves in America are brought to the Spanish colony of Santo Domingo.

CR. 1503 Leonardo da Vinci paints the *Mona Lisa*.

1509 Henry VIII takes the English throne. Michelangelo begins painting the ceiling of the Sistine Chapel.

1517 Martin Luther protests wrongdoing in the Catholic Church; start of Protestantism.

1519 Hernando Cortés conquers Mexico for Spain.

1520 Suleiman I ("the Magnificent") becomes Sultan of Turkey.

1522 Portuguese explorer Ferdinand Magellan's expedition circumnavigates the globe.

1543 Copernicus publishes his theory that Earth revolves around the Sun.

1547 Ivan IV ("the Terrible") is crowned czar of Russia.

1588 The Spanish Armada is defeated by the English.

1609 Galileo makes the first astronomical observations using a telescope.

1618 Thirty Years' War begins. European Protestants revolt against Catholic oppression.

1620 Pilgrims, after a three-month voyage aboard the Mayflower, land at Plymouth Rock.

1775 The American Revolution begins with the Battle of Lexington and Concord.

1776 The U.S. Declaration of Independence is signed.

1783 The American Revolution ends with the Treaty of Paris.

1789 The French Revolution begins with the storming of the Bastille.

1819 Simón Bolívar leads wars for independence throughout South America.

1824 Mexico becomes a republic, three years after declaring independence from Spain.

1846 Failure of potato crop causes famine in Ireland.

1861 The U.S. Civil War begins as attempts to reach a compromise on slavery fail.

1865 The U.S. Civil War ends.

1884 The Berlin West Africa Conference is held; Europe colonizes the African continent.

1893 New Zealand becomes the first country in the world to give women the right to vote.

1898 The Spanish-American War begins.

1903	The Wright brothers fly the first powered airplane at Kitty Hawk, North Carolina.
1904	The Russo-Japanese War begins as competition for Korea and Manchuria heats up.
1909	U.S. explorers Robert E. Peary and Matthew Henson reach the North Pole. The National Association for the Advancement of Colored People (NAACP) is founded in New York City.
1912	The *Titanic* sinks on its maiden voyage; more than 1,500 drown.
1914	World War I begins.
1917	U.S. enters World War I. Russian Revolution begins.
1918	World War I fighting ends. A worldwide flu epidemic strikes; by 1920, nearly 20 million are dead.
1919	Mahatma Gandhi begins his nonviolent resistance against British rule in India.
1924	Joseph Stalin begins his rule as Soviet dictator, which lasts until his death in 1953.
1929	In the U.S., stock market prices collapse and the Depression begins.
1933	Adolf Hitler is appointed German Chancellor; Nazi oppression begins. Franklin Delano Roosevelt is inaugurated U.S. President; he launches the New Deal.
1937	The Nazis open their first concentration camp (Buchenwald); by 1945, the Nazis had murdered some 6 million Jews in what is now called the Holocaust.
1939	World War II begins.
1941	A Japanese attack on the U.S. fleet at Pearl Harbor in Hawaii (December 7) brings U.S. into World War II. Manhattan Project (atomic bomb research) begins.
1945	War ends in Europe on V-E Day (May 8). The U.S. drops the atomic bomb on Hiroshima, Japan (August 6), and Nagasaki, Japan (August 9). The war ends in the Pacific on V-J day (September 2).
1947	The U.S. Marshall Plan is proposed to help Europe recover from the war. India and Pakistan gain independence from Britain.
1948	The existence of the nation of Israel is proclaimed.
1949	The North Atlantic Treaty Organization (NATO) is founded. Communist People's Republic of China is proclaimed by Chairman Mao Zedong. South Africa sets up apartheid (a policy of discrimination against nonwhites).
1950	Korean War begins when North Korean Communist forces invade South Korea. It lasts three years.

Homework TIP

- Use sticky notes in books to mark down where you stopped reading. Write notes on them summarizing what you've read.

1957	Russians launch *Sputnik I*, the first Earth-orbiting satellite; the Space Race begins.
1963	Martin Luther King Jr. delivers his "I have a dream" speech in Washington, D.C. President Kennedy is shot and killed by a sniper in Dallas.
1965	U.S. planes begin combat missions in Vietnam War.
1967	Israeli and Arab forces battle; Six-Day War ends with Israel occupying Sinai Peninsula, Golan Heights, Gaza Strip and part of the Suez Canal.
1969	Apollo 11 astronauts take man's first walk on the moon.
1973	Vietnam War ends with the signing of peace pacts. The Yom Kippur War begins as Egyptian and Syrian forces attack Israel.
1979	Muslim leader Ayatollah Khomeini takes over Iran; U.S. citizens seized and held hostage.
1981	Scientists identify the AIDS virus.
1989	Thousands rallying for democracy are killed in Tiananmen Square, China. After 28 years, the Berlin Wall that divided Germany is torn down.
1990	South Africa frees Nelson Mandela, who was imprisoned 27 years. Iraqi troops invade Kuwait, setting off nine-month Persian Gulf War.
1991	The Soviet Union breaks up after President Mikhail Gorbachev resigns. In Yugoslavia, Slovenia and Croatia secede; a four-year war with Serbia begins.
1994	South Africa holds first interracial national election; Nelson Mandela is elected President.
2000	Elections in Yugoslavia formally end the brutal rule of Slobodan Milosevic.
2001	Hijackers crash two jetliners into New York City's World Trade Center and another into the Pentagon. A fourth hijacked plane crashes 80 miles outside Pittsburgh, Pennsylvania. In response to the Sept. 11 terrorist attacks, U.S. and British forces launch a bombing campaign against the Taliban government and al-Qaeda terrorist camps in Afghanistan.
2002	U.S. and British troops defeat the Taliban in Afghanistan; Hamid Karzai elected its President.
2003	The U.S. and Britain lead an invasion of Iraq. Troops topple Saddam Hussein's government within weeks. U.S. troops capture the former dictator in December.

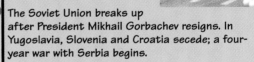

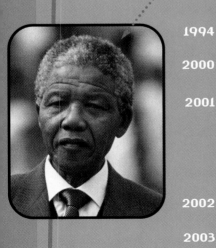

1607   Jamestown, the first permanent English settlement in America, is established in Virginia.

1620   After a three-month voyage aboard the Mayflower, the Pilgrims land at Plymouth in Massachusetts.

1770   In the Boston Massacre, British troops fire into a mob, killing five men.

1773   A group of patriots dump tea into Boston Harbor to protest the British tea tax. It becomes known as the Boston Tea Party.

1775   The American Revolution begins with the Battle of Lexington and Concord.

1776   The Continental Congress adopts the Declaration of Independence; the United States is born.

1783   The American Revolution officially ends with the signing of the Treaty of Paris.

1787   Delegates from 12 of the original 13 colonies meet in Philadelphia to draft the U.S. Constitution.

1789   George Washington is unanimously elected President of the U.S. The U.S. Constitution goes into effect.

1791   The first 10 amendments to the Constitution, known as the Bill of Rights, are ratified.

1803   The U.S. purchases the Louisiana Territory from France; it nearly doubles the size of the U.S.

1804   Meriwether Lewis and William Clark set out from St. Louis, Missouri, to explore the West and to find a route to the Pacific Ocean.

1805   Lewis and Clark reach the Pacific Ocean.

1812   The U.S. declares war on Britain for interfering with American shipping and westward expansion. It becomes known as the War of 1812.

1814   Francis Scott Key writes the "Star-Spangled Banner." The Treaty of Ghent ends the War of 1812.

1819   The U.S acquires Florida from Spain.

1823   President Monroe declares in the Monroe Doctrine that the Americas are to be off-limits for further colonization by European powers.

1836 Texas declares its independence from Mexico. The Texan defenders of the Alamo are all killed in a siege by the Mexican Army.

1838 More than 15,000 Cherokee Indians are forced to march from Georgia to Indian Territory in present-day Oklahoma. About 4,000 die from starvation and disease along the "Trail of Tears."

1845 Texas joins the U.S.

1846 The U.S. declares war on Mexico to gain territory in the Southwest.

1848 The Mexican War ends; the U.S. gains territory comprising present-day California, Nevada, Utah, most of New Mexico and Arizona and parts of Colorado and Wyoming.

1849 Gold is discovered at Sutter's Mill in California.

1854 Congress establishes the territories of Kansas and Nebraska. Tensions rise between those who want them to be free states and those who want them to be slave states.

1857 Abolitionist John Brown and 21 followers try to spark a slave revolt by capturing a government arms depot in Harpers Ferry, West Virginia.

1860 Following the election of Abraham Lincoln as President, South Carolina secedes from the U.S.

1861 More Southern states secede from the U.S. and form the Confederate States of America, with Jefferson Davis as President. The Civil War, a conflict between the North (the Union) and the South (the Confederacy) over the expansion of slavery, begins when the Confederates attack Fort Sumter in Charleston, South Carolina.

1863 Lincoln issues the Emancipation Proclamation, freeing slaves in the Confederate states.

1865 The Civil War ends with the surrender of Confederate general Robert E. Lee to Union general Ulysses S. Grant. Lincoln is assassinated by John Wilkes Booth in Washington, D.C. The 13th Amendment to the Constitution is ratified, prohibiting slavery.

1867 The U.S. purchases Alaska from Russia.

1869 The Central Pacific and Union Pacific railroads are joined at Promontory, Utah, creating the first transcontinental (cross-country) railroad.

1890	The last major battle of the Indian Wars occurs at Wounded Knee in South Dakota.
1898	The U.S.S. *Maine* is blown up in Havana harbor, which leads the U.S. to declare war on Spain. As a result of the Spanish-American War, the U.S. acquires Puerto Rico, Guam and the Philippines.
1917	The U.S. enters World War I by declaring war on Germany and Austria-Hungary.
1919	The 19th Amendment to the Constitution is ratified, giving women the right to vote.
1929	The U.S. stock market crashes, and the Great Depression begins.
1933	President Franklin Roosevelt's economic recovery measures, known as the New Deal, are enacted by Congress.
1941	Japan attacks the U.S. naval base at Pearl Harbor, Hawaii, leading to the U.S.'s entry into World War II.
1945	Germany surrenders, marking the end of World War II in Europe. The U.S. drops two atomic bombs on Japan. Japan surrenders, and World War II ends in the Pacific.
1950	The Korean War begins as the U.S. sends troops to defend South Korea against communist North Korea.
1953	The Korean War ends.
1954	The Supreme Court decision Brown v. Board of Education of Topeka, Kansas, declares that racial segregation of schools is unconstitutional.
1955	Rosa Parks refuses to sit at the back of the bus. Martin Luther King Jr. leads a black boycott of the Montgomery, Alabama, bus system.
1963	President Kennedy is assassinated in Dallas, Texas.
1965	The first U.S. combat troops arrive in South Vietnam.
1968	Martin Luther King Jr. is assassinated in Memphis, Tennessee.

 go For a year-by-year guide from 1900 onward, www.FACTMONSTER.COM

1969	Astronauts Neil Armstrong and Edwin Aldrin Jr. become the first men to land on the Moon.
1973	The U.S., North Vietnam, South Vietnam and the National Liberation Front (Viet Cong) sign peace pacts in Paris. The U.S. withdraws from Vietnam.
1974	President Nixon resigns as a result of the Watergate scandal.
1979	Iranian students storm the U.S. embassy in Tehran and hold 66 people hostage.
1981	The U.S. hostages held in Iran are released after 444 days in captivity.
1986	The space shuttle Challenger explodes 73 seconds after liftoff.
1991	The U.S. and its allies fight in the first Persian Gulf War, driving the Iraqis out of Kuwait.
1992	President George H.W. Bush and Russian President Boris Yeltsin formally declare an end to the cold war.
1998	The House of Representatives votes to impeach President Clinton.
1999	The Senate acquits Clinton of impeachment charges.
2000	The presidential election contest between George W. Bush and Al Gore is one of the closest in U.S. history. The U.S. Supreme Court determines the outcome, and Bush is declared the winner.
2001	Hijackers crash two jetliners into New York City's World Trade Center and another into the Pentagon. A fourth hijacked plane crashes in rural Pennsylvania. President Bush declares war on terrorism, and U.S. and British forces topple the Taliban government and attack Osama bin Laden's al-Qaeda terrorist camps in Afghanistan.
2002	A wave of corporate accounting scandals rocks the nation's economy as Enron and several other companies are investigated by federal authorities.
2003	Seven astronauts die when the space shuttle Columbia explodes upon re-entry into the Earth's atmosphere. The U.S. and Britain lead a war in Iraq and topple dictator Saddam Hussein. Troops capture Hussein in December.

go For TFK timelines, go to www.timeforkids.com/timelines

HOMEWORK
HELPER

Facing the Blank Page

The staff at *TIME For Kids* magazine goes through the same challenges that you do as you write: finding a topic; researching facts; getting organized; writing a draft; revising; editing and proofreading. Writing is a process, a series of steps that can help you become a better writer. We've shared some of their writing ideas, thoughts and strategies.

Getting Started: Gathering the Facts

Finding good ideas to write about can be difficult. Many writers use a variety of strategies to help them get started. You may be assigned topics to write about. Or you might have to come up with ideas on your own.

EDITOR MARTHA PICKERILL tells how she starts an assignment:
"When I write a story, I begin by gathering every piece of information I think I'll need. As soon as I have gathered all of my interviews, news reports and background information from books and the Internet, I read over every bit of it at least twice. Sometimes I determine that important facts are missing, and I do a bit more research to fill in the gaps. Having all the necessary facts strengthens any writer's work.

"The shape of the story starts to come together in my head as I read over my research. For a short news story, I sort of talk myself through an outline: I'll lead with that great quote, followed by two paragraphs describing exactly what happened. Then I should have room to refer back to the last time such a thing happened, or some other connection to put the story in context. Sometimes, I'll finish with an expert's quote saying why this is important.

"When I cook up my plan, I mentally check off the 5 Ws (WHO, WHAT, WHERE, WHY, WHEN) and H (HOW) to make sure the basic questions will be covered."

Making a Plan

How do you plan and organize a story? Some writers use an outline to organize the facts and details they want to include in a story. WRITER RITU UPADHYAY shares one way of getting organized:

"Once I've done the reporting and research, I write an outline to help me get focused. Planning ahead ensures that I get in all the major points I want to include in my story. Organizing the information into sections gives structure to the story. Of course, the outline can change once I start writing, but it's really helpful to have something to use as a guide when I begin. For example, when I wrote a story about Cleopatra's lost city, I made a quick outline."

I. Introduction
   A. Cleopatra's underwater city
   B. Who is Cleopatra?
   C. Why did the city sink?

II. The city rediscovered
   A. Recovering the artifacts
   B. The city's first complete map
      1. New view of the city
      2. Map might change

III. Other finds from the underwater city
   A. Cleopatra's personal temple
   B. Statues

IV. Recovering artifacts
   A. How it is done
   B. Future expeditions

V. Conclusion

Homework TIP

Set up a quiet, comfortable place to do your homework each day. Avoid places with loud music, television or other noise.

TFK Top 5 Favorite Subjects

Can you guess which school subjects kids like best? (Recess does not count.) Researchers asked 1,016 students ages 10 to 17. More than 1 in 4 picked math. Go figure! Here are the subjects that make the grade:

1. Math—28%

2. Science—21%

3. Art—16%

4. History/Social Studies—15%

5. English—13%

Source: Peter D. Hart Research Associates for National Science Foundation, Bayer

123

Writing a First Draft

You have an idea and a plan. Now you are ready to write the first draft. Your goal is to get all your ideas down on paper.

As RITU UPADHYAY wrote her story (below) on Cleopatra's lost city, she included notes on the side. They will help her to improve the next draft.

Add pronunciation guide

More than 1,600 years ago, a royal court full of treasures was swallowed up by the sea. The island of Antirhodos, home of Cleopatra, the famous Queen of Egypt, sank after the area was hit by a huge earthquake in A.D. 335. Along with the island, part of Alexandria, Egypt's harbor city, also disappeared. For centuries, the palace buildings and statues lay 30 feet underwater, 3.5 miles off the coast of northern Egypt.

Describe how the city was preserved

Put in a quote from Goddio

Add what will happen next now that the map is completed

In 1996, French explorer Franck Goddio rediscovered the fabled city. He and his team of divers have been working on excavating the site ever since. Goddio recently unveiled the first map of the old city.

Add where he made his announcement about the map

Describe Ms. Hendrickson's job

Over the past few years, the group has uncovered many artifacts. "We're looking right at statues from 2,000 years ago that look just as they did back then," says Sue Hendrickson. Along with statues, the team has found buildings and temples that are still standing underwater.

Check if the word is correct

Explain why the divers do this

The marine biologists working in Alexandria are careful not to disturb the city. "We are just mapping it, cleaning it up and leaving it all as we've found it," says Hendrickson. Sometimes the divers bring up a statue to study or photograph, but they always return it to its home underwater. Goddio's team hopes that one day the government of Egypt will allow tourists to dive down and experience the splendor of Cleopatra's palace for themselves.

Change conclusion?

 Read the final, published version of Ritu's story, "Cleopatra's Lost City," at *www.timeforkids.com/cleopatra*

Writing a Paragraph

Words, sentences and paragraphs are the building blocks of writing says ASSOCIATE EDITOR KATHRYN R. SATTERFIELD. A paragraph is made up of one or more sentences that support the subject or idea of the paragraph. Check out the example below.

This is the main idea of the paragraph.

This detail supports the facts.

So what's the big deal if you're a bit tired? Getting too little sleep can affect your mood, your coordination, how well you learn and even your speech. Studies of people who volunteer to go without sleep have shown that they have trouble with memory and can't concentrate well enough to do a task as simple as adding numbers. The biggest change, though, is in your mood. Exhaustion makes you grouchy and depressed.

These facts give more information about the main idea.

This closing sentence ends the paragraph.

Taking the Lead!

Kathryn explains why she works hard at writing a lead, or introduction, to a news story.

"A good introduction should grab the reader's attention by revealing something unique or exciting. When working on an introduction, I ask myself what makes the story interesting. Is there a surprising anecdote or an unusual fact that stands out? If so, introducing the information in the lead will make the reader curious.

"I wrote two introductions for a story about a Native American school. Can you see why I chose the first one to go with my story?"

Introduction 1

The kids at the Akwesane Freedom School in Rooseveltown, New York, start their day the same way lots of other kids around the U.S. do—chatting about the Powerpuff Girls, Britney Spears, the latest Nintendo games and sports. But when class begins, their day takes on a different sound.

This introduction gives a glimpse of the Akwesane school. It shows similarities between the readers and the Akwesane students. The last sentence is a good transition sentence; it sets the tone for some new information.

Introduction 2

The kids at Akwesane Freedom School in Rooseveltown, New York, aren't allowed to speak any English in the classroom. In fact, the students won't speak a word of English until school lets out in the afternoon. Some don't even use it at home. "I never, ever speak it to my mom and dad," says Karonhiakwekon—in perfect English.

This introduction gives too much information, and that information is weaker than the first. The reader isn't yet aware that the student's difficult name is in his native language.

Why Revise?

Revising means making changes. Writers do a lot of revising because first drafts can always be improved. DEPUTY EDITOR NELLIE GONZALEZ CUTLER explains why she revises:

"Revising is one of the most important parts of the writing process. After I've written a first draft of a story, I reread it carefully. Then I mark the areas that need work.

"First, I review the overall structure of the story. Are all the paragraphs arranged in a logical order? Does the first paragraph have an idea and explain it clearly? Do the other paragraphs move the story along? If necessary, I rearrange paragraphs.

"Next, I target specific sentences. I ask myself several questions: Is the writing lively and engaging? Does the story have enough quotes? Do these quotes help tell the story? Does the last paragraph sum up or end the story?

"Finally, I reread the story again, this time circling words that I may have repeated and making sure all the sentences are in the correct tense. I also check to see that words are spelled correctly.

"After making corrections on my first draft, I write a second draft and repeat the entire process. I'll do this as many times as necessary—some stories need only one draft, others need several rewrites! Remember: write, read, revise and repeat!"

Revision Checklist

A checklist can help you remember what to look for when you revise your writing. Use the list as a guide.

Stay Focused on My Topic

❑ Do I have a topic sentence, the main idea of my writing?
❑ Do I stay on my topic throughout my paper?
❑ Does my paper make sense?

Support My Topic

❑ Do I use details, facts or examples to support my main idea?
❑ Do I need to add more details, facts or examples?
❑ Do I say enough about my topic?

Organize My Writing

❑ Do I have an introduction that tells my reader what my story will be about?
❑ Do I use supporting paragraphs to build my story?
❑ Are my ideas in the best order?
❑ Do I have a conclusion that ends my story?
❑ Is my writing easy to follow?

Make Needed Changes

❑ Do I use descriptive words to explain my ideas?
❑ Do I use a variety of words?

Hunting for Errors

In this stage of the writing process, TFK writers rely on copy editors to make sure their writing is free of errors.

COPY EDITOR STEVE LEVINE finds and corrects errors in usage, style and spelling. As he reads a story, he makes sure that:

- *each sentence has a subject and a verb.*
- *each sentence makes sense.*
- *each sentence begins with a capital letter.*
- *each sentence ends with a punctuation mark.*
- *words are correctly capitalized.*
- *commas are used when needed.*
- *quotation marks are used correctly.*
- *the subject and the verb agree.*
- *words are not repeated.*
- *words are spelled correctly.*

Steve reads to make sure there are no fragments or run-on sentences.
FOR EXAMPLE:

Ran away.

This sentence is a fragment. It doesn't have a subject. To correct this fragment, Steve gives it a subject.

The black bear ran away.

A run-on is a sentence that never seems to end.

FOR EXAMPLE:

The black bear ran away from the scientists they had wanted to catch the bear for a study.

To correct this run-on, he splits it into two separate sentences.

The black bear ran away from the scientists. They had wanted to catch the bear for a study.

127

Common Editing Symbols

Editors use symbols to correct writing mistakes. These symbols let writers know what writing changes need to be made.

 Make an uppercase letter

 Add a period

 Make a lowercase letter

 Take out

 Add a comma

 Add a hyphen

 Add quotation marks

 Start a new paragraph

TFK Puzzles & Games

A Reading R + E +
What books and stories will you be reading this year? Solve these rebus puzzles, which combine sounds and letters, to get a few ideas.
BONUS: Name the authors of the three books.

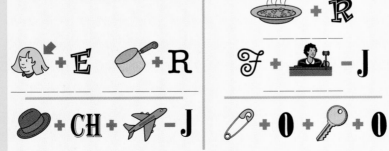

(See Answer Key that begins on page 340.)

Checklist for Expository Writing

The type of writing the editors of *TIME For Kids* do is called expository writing. Expository writing is nonfiction. It gives facts and explanations. Use this checklist to be sure you have done everything you need to do for your writing assignment.

❑ My writing is organized clearly and logically.
❑ I have taken out all details that do not belong in my writing.
❑ I keep a record of all books and other sources of information.
❑ I use a consistent point of view.
❑ I use descriptive language.
❑ I use adjectives and adverbs to make my writing lively.
❑ I use figurative language such as metaphors and similes.
❑ I use original language to create my own style.
❑ I have tried to make this writing interesting for my readers.
❑ I have made the purpose of my writing clear.
❑ I have proofread my writing.
❑ Others have read my writing (classmates or teachers, for example).
❑ I have revised my writing.
❑ My writing is the best that I can make it.

Homework TIP

• Organize your school papers into folders or notebooks by subject.

How to Write a Narrative Essay

The first important thing to remember about a narrative essay is that it tells a story. You may write about:

　❋ An experience or event from your past
　❋ A recent or an ongoing experience or event
　❋ Something that happened to somebody else, such as a parent or a grandparent

> **Learning something new can be a scary experience. One of the hardest things I've ever had to do was to learn how to swim. I was always afraid of the water, but I decided that swimming was an important skill that I should learn.**

The second important thing is that in a narrative essay the story should have a point. In the final paragraph, you should come to a conclusion about the story you told.

> **Learning to swim was not easy for me, but in the end my efforts paid off. Now when I am faced with a new situation I am not so nervous. I may feel uncomfortable at first, but I know that as my skills get better, I will feel more and more comfortable.**

The conclusion is where the author reflects on the larger meaning of the experience described. In this case, the author concludes that learning to swim has helped her to feel more confident about herself in new situations. The idea that self-confidence comes from conquering your fears is something that anyone can relate to. It is the point of this essay.

GET **PERSONAL!**

The writing in an essay should be lively and engaging. Try to keep the reader's interest by adding details or observations. Sharing your thoughts invites the reader into your world and makes the story more personal and more interesting.

Homework TIP

Turn off the TV while you do your homework.

Tackle a Descriptive Essay

The purpose of a descriptive essay is to describe a person, place or thing in such vivid detail that the reader can easily form a mental picture. You may accomplish this by using words that create a mood, making interesting comparisons and describing images that appeal to the senses.

> **I have always been fascinated by carnival rides. My first experience with a carnival ride was a Ferris wheel at a local fair. It was huge, smoky and noisy. Ever since that first impression years ago, these rides have reminded me of mythical beasts carrying off their screaming passengers. Even the droning sound of their engines brings to mind the great roar of a fire-breathing dragon.**

Mood Words The author uses words that create excitement, like "fascinated," "great roar" and "fire-breathing dragon."

Interesting Comparisons One way the author makes his subject interesting is by comparing the Ferris wheel to a mythical beast.

Sensory Details The author uses his senses for details about how the Ferris wheel looks, sounds and feels. The ride is "huge, smoky and noisy" and its engines "drone."

Like any essay, a descriptive essay should be well organized. This essay began with a general statement—that the author has always been fascinated by carnival rides. The body is made of paragraphs that describe the subject. The conclusion restates the main idea—in this case, that the author continues to find carnival rides fascinating.

> **A trip on the Ferris wheel never fails to thrill me. The fascination I have for Ferris wheels comes back with each and every ride.**

 Get writing, research and organizing tips and tools at
www.timeforkids.com/homework helper

How to Write a Persuasive Essay

The purpose of a persuasive essay is to convince the reader to agree with your viewpoint or to accept your recommendation for a course of action. For instance, you might argue that the salaries of professional athletes are too high. Or you might recommend that vending machines be banned from your school cafeteria. A successful persuasive essay will use evidence to support your viewpoint, consider opposing views and present a strong conclusion.

> **Some people worry that adopting a school uniform policy would be too expensive for families. However, there are ways to lessen the cost. For example, in Seattle, Washington, local businesses pay for uniforms at South Shore Middle School. In Long Beach, California, graduating students donate or sell their old uniforms to other students.**

Use evidence to support your viewpoint. Statistics, facts, quotations from experts and examples will help you to build a strong case for your argument. Appeal to the reader's sense of logic by presenting specific and relevant evidence in a well-organized manner.

Consider opposing views. Try to anticipate the concerns and questions that a reader might have about your subject. Responding to these points will give you the chance to explain to the reader why your viewpoint or recommendation is the best one.

Present a strong conclusion. All your evidence and explanations should build toward a strong ending in which you summarize your view in a clear and memorable way. The conclusion in a persuasive essay might include a call to action.

Remember: Use a pleasant, reasonable tone in your essay. Sarcasm and name-calling weaken an argument. Logic and fairness will help to keep it strong.

Homework TIP

Take short breaks when you have a long assignment.

Spelling Tips

This may be the best-known spelling rule:

i **before** *e*, **except after** *c* **(or when sounded like** *ay* **as in** *neighbor* **and** *weigh***)**

Examples: *ie* words: *believe, field*
cei words: *ceiling, deceit*
ei words: *freight, reign*

Silent *e* helps a vowel say its name.

This means that when a word ends with a vowel followed by a consonant and then silent *e*, the vowel has a long sound. For example, the *a* in *rate* has a long *a*. The *a* is short in *rat*. The *i* in *hide* is long. The *i* is short in *hid*.

When two vowels go walking, the first one usually does the talking.

This means that when there are two vowels in a row, the first has a long sound and the second is silent. For example, the *o* in *coat* is long, and the *a* is silent.

Make sure that you are pronouncing words correctly.

This can help you to avoid some common spelling errors, such as *canidate* instead of *candidate*, *jewelery* instead of *jewelry*, and *libary* instead of *library*.

Make up funny memory aids.

For example, do you have trouble remembering which has two *s*'s—*desert* (arid land) or *dessert* (a sweet treat)? Remember that with dessert, you'd like two of them. Similarly, do you have trouble remembering how to spell *separate*? Remember that there's *a rat* in the middle.

Break a word into syllables.

Look for prefixes, suffixes and roots. Practice each short part and then the whole word.

dis-ap-pear-ing
tra-di-tion-al

After you break apart a word, ask yourself: How is this word like other words I know? Spelling the word *traditional* may make you think of spelling *functional* and *national*. Finding patterns among words is one of the best ways to learn spelling.

How to Write a

Book reports are a way to show how well you understood a book and to tell what you think about it. Many teachers have their own rules about what should be in a book report, so be sure to check with your teacher. Here are some general guidelines.

Introduction

The introduction starts your report and captures the reader's attention. It should include:

☞ **The title and author of the book**

☞ **Some information about the book (but don't give away the ending)**

☞ **What kind of story it is—adventure, fantasy, biography, animal, history, science fiction?**

Body

This is where you describe the main parts of the story: theme, plot, setting and characters. Then you can give your opinions about the book.

☞ The **theme** is the most important message in the story. An example might be the importance of friendship. Tell what you think the theme is and why you do. Lessons learned by the main character are often important clues to the theme.

☞ The **plot** is the main story or event in the book. In your book report, you should explain the plot's main event or conflict. What events lead up to it? What happens as a result?

Be careful not to re-tell the whole plot in detail—you will need room in your report to write about other things. Just say enough about the plot so that the rest of your report will make sense. If the plot has a big mystery or a surprise, be careful not to give away the ending.

☞ The **setting** is the time and place of the story. Is it set a long time ago, now or in the future? Does it take place in another country or in an imaginary place?

☞ The **characters** are people, animals and creatures in the book. The main character is called the protagonist. Who are the other characters? Do they help or hinder the protagonist?

Homework TIP

If your home is noisy, use your school or local library to complete assignments.

Book Report

An important part of a book report is giving your opinion or telling what you thought about the book. Some questions you might want to answer are:

☞ Did you like the story? Why or why not?

☞ What was the best part of the book? Why?

☞ How did the story make you feel? Did you feel different emotions at different points?

☞ Would you recommend the book to friends?

☞ Would you read other books by the author?

☞ What new things did you learn from the book?

Conclusion

The conclusion sums up your report. It tells your overall opinion of the book and the most important thing you want readers to know about it.

Mrs. Coverlet's Magicians: A Spellbinding Story

The babysitter has been in bed for weeks, and Toad says it's because he put a spell on her. Could it be true? That's the question that runs through *Mrs. Coverlet's Magicians* by Mary Nash. This hilarious novel tells about the troubles that Toad, his sister Mary and his brother Malcolm get into while the one adult in the house lies asleep.

I loved this book because whenever people said Toad's ideas were silly, he found a surprising way to prove them wrong. For example, when Toad announced that he could find a Christmas tree to chop down, Malcolm and Molly laughed, because there are no woods near their town. But soon afterward, Toad led them into the old marsh and began to make a very strange-looking wand.

How to Write a Research Paper

Writing a research paper involves all of the steps for writing an essay plus some additional ones. To write a research paper you must first do some research; that is, investigate your topic by reading about it in different sources, including books, magazines, newspapers and the Internet. The information you gather is used to support the points you make in your paper.

Writing a research paper also involves documenting your sources of information in footnotes or endnotes. This way, the reader knows where you got your information and can judge if it is reliable.

EIGHT STEPS TO A GREAT RESEARCH PAPER

1. **Find your topic.** Try to pick a topic that's fun and interesting. If your topic genuinely interests you, chances are, you'll enjoy working on it.

2. **Look for sources.** Take a trip to the library. Use the electronic catalog or browse the shelves to look for books on your topic. If you find a book that is useful, check the bibliography (list of sources) in the back of that book for other books or articles on that topic. If you need help finding sources, ask a librarian.

Keep a list of all the sources that you use. Include the title of the source, the author, publisher and place and date of publication.

3. **Read your sources and take notes.** After you've gathered your sources, begin reading and taking notes.

Use 3 x 5 index cards, writing one fact or idea per card. This way related ideas from different sources can be easily grouped together. Be sure to note the source and the page number on each card.

4. **Make an outline.** Organize your index cards by topic, then develop an outline to organize your ideas. An outline shows your main ideas and the order in which you are going to write about them. (See page 123 for a sample outline.)

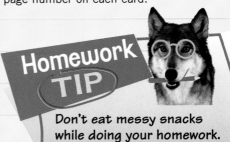

Homework TIP

Don't eat messy snacks while doing your homework.

5. **Write a first draft.** Every essay or paper is made up of three parts: the introduction, the body and the conclusion.

☞ The **introduction** is the first paragraph. It often begins with a general statement about the topic and ends with a more specific statement of your main idea.

☞ The **body** of the paper follows the introduction. It has a number of paragraphs in which you develop your ideas in detail. Limit yourself to one main idea per paragraph, and use examples and quotations to support your ideas.

☞ The **conclusion** is the last paragraph of the paper. Its purpose is to sum up your points—leaving out specific examples—and to restate your main idea.

6. **Use footnotes or endnotes.** These identify the sources of your information. If you are using footnotes, the note will appear on the same page as the information you are documenting, at the bottom (or foot) of the page. If you are using endnotes, the note will appear together with all other notes on a separate page at the end of your report, just before the bibliography.

There are different formats, so be sure to use the one your teacher prefers.

The National Beagle Club held its first show in 1891.[1]

[1] Samantha Lopez, *For the Love of Beagles* (New York: Ribbon Books, 1993), p. 24.

7. **Revise your draft.** After you've completed your first draft, you'll want to make some changes. (See page 126 for general tips.) Also remember that in a research paper, it's important to check that you have footnotes or endnotes wherever they are needed.

8. **Proofread your final draft.** When you are happy with your revision, print it and check spelling, punctuation and grammar. It is good to do this more than once, checking for different kinds of mistakes each time.

Don't Copy This!

Plagiarism means using someone else's work as your own. If you take words or ideas from a source without giving credit, you are plagiarizing. When you copy something directly from a book without putting it in your own words, put quotation marks around it so that you know it is an exact quotation. This will help you avoid plagiarism.

How to Write a Biography

A biography is the story of a life. Biographies can be just a few sentences long, or they can fill an entire book. Biographers (people who write biographies) use primary and secondary sources.

⁑ Primary sources convey first-hand experience. They include letters, diaries, interview tapes and other accounts of personal experience.

⁑ Secondary sources convey second-hand experience. They include articles, textbooks, reference books and other sources of information.

To write a biography, you should:

1. Select a person you find interesting.

2. Find out the basic facts of the person's life. You might want to start by looking in an encyclopedia.

3. Think about what else you would like to know about the person.

⁑ What makes this person special or interesting?

⁑ What kind of effect did he or she have on the world?

⁑ What are the adjectives you would use to describe the person?

⁑ What examples from the person's life show those qualities?

⁑ What events shaped or changed this person's life?

And Furthermore: Transition Words and Phrases

Transition words and phrases help establish clear connections between ideas and ensure that sentences and paragraphs flow together smoothly, making them easier to read. Use the following words and phrases in the circumstances below.

To indicate more information:	To indicate an example:	To indicate a cause or reason:	To indicate a result or an effect:
Besides	For example	As	Accordingly
Furthermore	For instance	Because	Consequently
In addition	In particular	Because of	Finally
In fact	Particularly	Due to	Therefore
Moreover	Specifically	Since	Thus

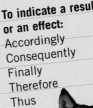

If you are having trouble with homework, ask for help from friends, parents or teachers.

Putting Together a Bibliography

Abibliography is a list of the sources you used to get information for your report. It is included at the end of your report. You will find it easy to prepare your bibliography if you keep track of each source you use as you are reading and taking notes.

When putting together a final bibliography, list your sources (texts, articles, interviews and so on) in alphabetical order by authors' last names. Sources that don't have authors should be alphabetized by title. There are different formats for bibliographies, so be sure to use the one your teacher prefers.

General Guide for Bibliographies

BOOK

Author (last name first). *Title of the book*. City: Publisher, Date of publication.
Dahl, Roald. *The BFG*. New York: Farrar, Straus and Giroux, 1982.

ENCYCLOPEDIA

***Encyclopedia title*, edition, date. Volume number, "Article title," page numbers.**
Encyclopædia Britannica, 1997. Volume 7, "Gorillas," pp. 50-51.

MAGAZINE

Author (last name first), "Article title." *Name of magazine*. Volume number, (Date): page numbers.
Jordan, Jennifer, "Filming at the Top of the World." *Museum of Science Magazine*. Volume 47, No. 1 (Winter 1998): p. 11.

NEWSPAPER

Author (last name first), "Article title." *Name of newspaper*, city, state of publication. (Date): edition if available, section, page number(s).
Powers, Ann, "New Tune for the Material Girl." *The New York Times*, New York, N.Y. (3/1/98): Atlantic Region, Section 2, p. 34.

PERSON

Full name (last name first). Occupation. Date of interview.
Martin, Jayce. Police officer. April 1, 2004.

CD-ROM

***Disc title:* version, date. "Article title," pages if given. Publisher.**
Compton's Multimedia Encyclopedia: Macintosh version, 1995. "Civil rights movement," p. 3. Compton's Newsmedia.

INTERNET

Author (last name first) (date). "Article title." Date work retrieved, name and URL of website.
Brunner, Borgna (2001). "Earthquakes!" Retrieved January 27, 2003, from *www.infoplease.com/spot/earthquake1.html*.

How to Study for Tests

Tests are a way for you and your teacher to measure how well you have learned the material covered in class. Think of them as a challenge!

Before the Test

1. If possible, find out what material the test will cover and what type of test it will be (multiple choice, true or false, short answer or essay).

2. Study at a time when you are alert and not hungry or sleepy.

3. Don't wait until the last minute! Short, daily study sessions are better than cramming the night before the test.

4. Set a goal for each study period. If you are being tested on three chapters, set up four study sessions—one for each chapter and one for a review of all three.

5. Repeat, repeat, repeat! Read and reread your notes and the key parts of the textbook.

6. While reviewing your notes, cover them up and summarize them out loud.

Group Study

Working in a group can be a great way to study. Here's one plan for getting the most out of it.

1. First, compare your notes and review old homework.

2. Next, drill each other on facts you need to memorize. For example: What are the four stages of a butterfly's life cycle?

3. Finally, take the time to discuss "why" questions. For example: Why do monarch butterflies migrate?

Remember—be prepared!
A study group is a place to share your understanding of a subject. The other people in the group aren't there to teach you facts you should already know.

Study Tips

● Use your notes to make an outline of the main ideas.

● Make a timeline of important dates.

● Make flashcards for studying key events or vocabulary.

● Have someone test you.

10 Tips for Taking Tests

1. Read the instructions carefully. Never assume you will know what they will say! Ask the teacher if you are unsure about anything.

2. Read the entire test through before starting. Notice the point value of each section. This will help you to pace yourself.

3. Answer the easiest questions first, then the ones with the highest point value. You don't want to spend 20 minutes trying to figure out a two-point problem!

4. Keep busy! If you get stuck on a question, go back to it later. The answer might come to you while you are working on another part of the test.

5. If you aren't sure how to answer a question fully, try to answer at least part of it. You might get partial credit.

6. Need to guess on a multiple-choice test? First, eliminate the answers that you know are wrong. Then take a guess. Because your first guess is most likely to be correct, you shouldn't go back and change an answer later unless you are certain you were wrong.

7. On an essay test, take a moment to plan your writing. First, jot down the important points you want to make. Then number these points in the order you will cover them.

8. Keep it neat! If your teacher can't read your writing, you might lose points.

9. Don't waste time doing things for which you will not receive credit, such as rewriting test questions.

10. Leave time at the end to look over your work. Did you answer every question? Did you proofread for errors? It is easy to make careless mistakes while taking a test.

After the Test

☞ Read the teacher's comments carefully and try to learn from your mistakes.

☞ Save tests to review for end-of-term tests.

Homework TIP

Keep your homework out of reach of pets and younger siblings.

Conducting an Interview

Books, magazines and the Internet aren't the only sources for research. Conducting an interview can be a great way to learn about a subject too! You may learn unexpected things, and you'll feel like a reporter.

Before the Interview

Make a list of questions you plan to ask. What would you like to learn about? Let's say the person you're interviewing survived the wildfires that struck a large area of California in 2003. You could ask the person to explain how she escaped from her house. You could ask her to describe the rescue effort. How did she feel after her house burned down? Does she feel safe living in California?

You should try to avoid asking "yes" or "no" questions. You'll get much more interesting answers if your questions require an explanation. For example, instead of asking, "Were you scared?" ask, "What terrified you most?" or "What was the most frightening part of the experience?"

During the Interview

1. If the person gives you permission, tape-record the interview. Even if you tape the interview, you should take notes so that you'll remember important points.

2. At the beginning of the interview, ask when and where the person was born and ask the person to spell his or her name. This will save you from having to backtrack later to find the information.

3. Don't interrupt or correct the person you are talking to. People sometimes remember things wrong. That's okay—you can check dates and facts later. The important thing is to hear about the person's impressions and feelings.

4. Listen carefully. Something the person says may inspire you to ask a question you hadn't planned. For example, the person might say that she hopes California officials take steps to prevent future wildfires. You could ask what steps should be taken.

After the Interview

Look back over the questions you prepared before the interview. Did the interview help to answer them? If you are going to do an oral report, think about how you will present your information. You might talk about what you had hoped to get out of the interview, and what you learned from it that was unexpected. You could also talk about the difference between reading a book and getting a personal view.

Fact Monster's INTERNET REsearch Guide

The Internet has become a convenient tool for finding information on just about anything. Here are some things to keep in mind when you're doing research on the Internet.

> **Be as specific as possible with search terms.** If, for example, you have heard that scientists discovered that Jupiter has more moons, include all the information you know when doing your search. If you simply search on Jupiter, you'll get too much general information. But if you type in *Jupiter, moon* and *new*, you'll probably find out what you want much more quickly.

> **If you're searching for a specific phrase, put the words in quotes.** The search engine will only look for the exact term. For example, if you want information on the Vietnam War, type *"Vietnam War."*

> **Use the word AND (in uppercase letters) to indicate when you want two or more terms to appear in the search results.** For example, if you're looking for hurricanes that occurred in Bermuda, you'd type *Bermuda AND hurricanes*. Similarly, you can use the word NOT (in uppercase letters) to eliminate a term from the search. For example, by typing *Bermuda NOT shorts*, you'd tell the search engine you're not interested in Bermuda shorts. You can also use the plus sign (+) and minus sign (-) in place of AND and NOT. Don't put a space between the sign and the search term.

> **If you're not having luck with your search term, try using a synonym.** Instead of typing *Revolutionary War*, try *American Revolution*. Or instead of *9/11*, try *September 11*.

> **When searching for a biography, it helps to type the word *biography* after the person's name in the search engine.** That weeds out some irrelevant search results. Biographies on the web are notoriously inaccurate, so it's very important to check dates and other facts against other biographies—in books, say—to make sure they are right.

> **Go directly to a site if you know it will help you.** For example, if you're looking for information on Saturn, you might try NASA's site first. You can type the URL directly in the address bar. If you don't know the URL, you can search for the site using a search engine.

> **Try different search engines if one isn't producing results.** Google, Ask Jeeves and Alta Vista are some search engines.

> **Know your source!** Anybody can put up information on the Internet and claim to be an expert. The information you read on someone's home page may be incorrect. The websites of government sources, schools and magazine and newspaper publishers are more accurate. If you use other sources, verify the information in a book or on another website.

How to Give an Oral Report

In many ways, planning an oral report is similar to planning a written report.

☛ **Choose a subject that is interesting to you.** What do you care about? What would you like to learn more about? Follow your interests, and you'll find your topic.

☛ **Be clear about your purpose.** Do you want to persuade your audience? Inform them about a topic? Or just tell an entertaining story?

An oral report also has the same three basic parts as a written report.

☛ The **introduction** should "hook" your audience. Catch their interest with a question, a dramatic tale or a personal experience that relates to your topic.

☛ The **body** is the main part of your report and will take up most of your time. Make an outline of the body so that you can share information in an organized way.

☛ The **conclusion** is the time to summarize and get across your most important point. What do you want the audience to remember?

1. Research!

It's important to really know your subject and be well organized. If you know your material well, you will be confident and able to answer questions. If your report is well organized, the audience will find it informative and easy to follow.

Think about your audience. If you were listening to a report on your subject, what would you want to know? Too much information can seem overwhelming, and too little can be confusing. Organize your outline around your key points, and focus on getting them across.

Remember—enthusiasm is contagious! If you're interested in your subject, the audience will be interested, too.

2. Rehearse!

Practicing your report is a key to success. At first, some people find it helpful to go through the report alone. You might practice in front of a mirror or in front of your stuffed animals. Then try out your report in front of a practice audience—friends or family. Ask your practice audience:

☛ *Could you follow my presentation?*

☛ *Did I seem knowledgeable about my subject?*

☛ *Was I speaking clearly? Could you hear me? Did I speak too fast or too slowly?*

If you are using visual aids, such as posters or overhead transparencies, practice using them while you rehearse. Also, you might want to time yourself to see how long your report actually takes. The time will probably go by faster than you expect.

3. Report!

Stand up straight. Hold your upper body straight, but not stiff, and keep your chin up. Try not to distract your audience by shifting around or fidgeting.

Make eye contact. You will seem more sure of yourself, and the audience will listen better, if you make eye contact during your report.

Use gestures. Your body language can help you make your points and keep the audience interested. Lean forward at key moments, and use your hands and arms for emphasis.

Use your voice effectively. Vary your tone and speak clearly. If you're nervous, you might speak too fast. If you find yourself hurrying, take a breath and try to slow it down.

Nerves!

Almost everyone is nervous when speaking before a group. Many people say public speaking is their Number 1 fear. Being well prepared is the best way to prevent nerves from getting the better of you. Also, try breathing deeply before you begin your report, and remember to breathe during the report. Being nervous isn't all bad—it can help to keep you on your toes!

One last thing!

Have you prepared and practiced your report? Then go get 'em! Remember: you know your stuff, and your report is interesting and important.

Homework TIP

• Read the questions in an assignment first. Then read to find the answers.

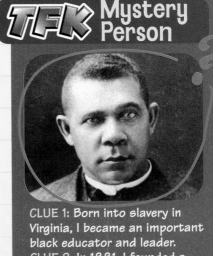

TFK Mystery Person

CLUE 1: Born into slavery in Virginia, I became an important black educator and leader.

CLUE 2: In 1881, I founded a school for African Americans that's now called Tuskegee University.

CLUE 3: I explained the importance of education in my best-selling autobiography, *Up from Slavery*, published in 1901.

WHO AM I?

(See Answer Key that begins on page 340.)

FROM **TFK** MAGAZINE

INVENTIONS

The Year's COOLEST Inventions

A ROBOT WITH SKILLS

It may be little, but it has a lot of talent. Qrio (pronounced "curio") can sing, dance and kick a ball. Cameras behind each of its eyes help Qrio identify the objects in a room. It can learn to recognize up to 10 different faces. It even speaks Japanese.

Here are some of this year's most amazing inventions. Many seem almost magical. Others are tools to make life a little easier or more fun. Take a look at TFK's favorites, from robots to glowing fish.

ROBO-RAPTOR

Built by Walt Disney Imagineering, this friendly fellow goes by the name Lucky. The 9-foot-tall raptor wanders on his own. Lucky can laugh, sneeze, smile and yell. He can even get the hiccups. How does he do it? He has a computerized brain stored in the cart he pulls.

ICY RIDER

ROCKON

This Gibson electric guitar is a lot like a computer. It has microchips—just like the ones in computers—built right into it. The chips help give the instrument a clearer sound.

Doug Stoup has helped create a bike that he can ride in Antarctica. The ice bike has no plastic parts, which would freeze and shatter in the extreme conditions. Its superfat, low-pressure tires provide extraordinary traction on ice, snow and other slippery surfaces. Stoup says he is ready to pedal it to the South Pole!

GLOW FISH

A Taiwanese scientist has made fish glow green in the dark. Professor H.J. Tsai injects cells from glowing jellyfish into the eggs of rice fish. The glowing fish can't have babies. Some people say fish shouldn't be messed with this way.

Watch Out!

Parents can keep track of their kids with the Wherify watch. It finds kids by sending a signal to a satellite in space. Parents can then check a private website to learn their child's location.

WANT TO DISAPPEAR?

A professor in Japan has created an "invisibility" cloak. A video camera records the scenery behind the wearer. A projector flashes that scenery onto the wearer's cloak, which acts like a screen. This lets the wearer blend into the background!

Great Ideas from Great

ca. 3800-3600 B.C.	Wheel
ca. A.D. 100	Paper
1608	Telescope
1709	Piano
1752	Lightning rod
1753	Hot-air balloon
1783	Steamship
1829	Braille
1831	Lawn mower
1839	Rubber
1850	Refrigerator
1867	Dynamite Fluorescent lamp Typewriter
1869	Vacuum cleaner
1870	Chewing gum
1876	Telephone
1877	Phonograph (record player)
1885	Bicycle
1888	Handheld camera Ballpoint pen
1891	Zipper
1893	Motion pictures (movies)
1895	X ray
1899	Aspirin Tape recorder
1901	First transatlantic radio signals
1903	First motorized plane (Wright brothers)
1904	Ice-cream cone
1907	Plastic

MINDS

1908	Model T car
1909	Toaster
1913	Moving assembly line
1927	Television
1928	Penicillin, a cure for infections Animated sound cartoons
1929	"Scotch" tape
1930	Pre-sliced bread
1933	FM radio
1939	Jet airplane
1945	Microwave oven
1949	Silly Putty
1953	Structure of DNA (gene chemical) discovered
1955	Polio vaccine
1957	Sputnik satellite
1963	Home video recorder
1972	Compact disk
1979	Sony Walkman
1980	Rollerblades Post-It Notes
1981	Space shuttle
1983	Cellular telephones
1988	Facsimile (fax) machine
1991	World Wide Web
1995	DVD (digital video disk)
1997	Dolly the sheep, first animal made by cloning adult cells
2000	Human genome map
2003	FluMist (flu vaccine in a nasal spray)

TFK Mystery Person

CLUE 1: Born in 1863, I was a self-taught mechanic from Dearborn, Michigan.
CLUE 2: In 1903, I launched a car company that still bears my name.
CLUE 3: My goal was to make cars more affordable. I came up with the idea of using factory assembly lines to produce lots of cars quickly. By 1927, I had sold 15 million of my model T cars.

WHO AM I?

(See Answer Key that begins on page 340.)

149

LANGUAGE

Saving a Native Language

By Elizabeth Winchester

Lane Smith (right) teaches his big brother, Kristian, the Cherokee word for butterfly.

Walk by the music room at Lost City School, near Hulbert, Oklahoma, and you'll hear unusual sounds. Old MacDonald had a *wa-ga* and a *ka-wo-nu* on his farm, shout the students. Those words mean *cow* and *duck* in Cherokee.

In the building next door, kindergarten kids learn everything from colors to numbers to animal names in Cherokee. Students are called by their American Indian names and speak in Cherokee for most of the day. These kindergartners are in the first Cherokee-immersion class in a U.S. public school.

By teaching kids Cherokee and not just English, Lost City School is working to help save a dying language. Less than 1 of every 100 fluent Cherokee speakers is under age 45. Doug Whalen, of the Endangered Language Fund, says all 170 or so American Indian languages in the United States are at risk of disappearing.

"If we don't learn Cherokee, our grandsons won't know it," says Crystal Braden, a seventh-grader. Crystal is Cherokee, as are 65 of the school's 100 preschool through eighth-grade students. Her seventh-grade class made a video to help teach the Cherokee words for colors to younger students.

Fifth-grader Kristian Smith is learning words from his little brother, Lane, or A-wi, who is in kindergarten. "It's weird," says Kristian. "I'm the one who should be teaching him!"

The Cherokee word *ga-du-gi* best sums up the school's efforts. It means "working together for the benefit of the community."

Puzzles & Games

Anagram Antics

An anagram is a word, phrase or sentence formed by rearranging another word or group of words. For example, an anagram of the word now is won. Can you match each word below to its anagram?

1. angel
2. teacher
3. Clint Eastwood
4. dance
5. senator

a. old west action
b. treason
c. caned
d. glean
e. cheater

(See Answer Key that begins on page 340.)

Languages Spoken Around the World

There are more than 2,700 languages throughout the world. Here are the world's 10 most widely spoken languages.

LANGUAGE	COUNTRIES WHERE SPOKEN	NUMBER OF PEOPLE
1. Chinese (Mandarin)	China	1.1 billion
2. English	U.S., U.K., Canada, Australia, New Zealand	514 million
3. Hindustani	India	496 million
4. Spanish	Spain, Latin America	425 million
5. Russian	Russia	275 million
6. Arabic	Middle East, North Africa	256 million
7. Bengali	Bangladesh	215 million
8. Portuguese	Portugal, parts of Africa and South America	194 million
9. Malay-Indonesian	Malaysia, Indonesia	176 million
10. French	France, Belgium, Switzerland, Canada, parts of Africa	129 million

Source: Ethnologue

Top 5 Languages

More than 300 languages besides English are spoken in the U.S. Here are the five most common.

1. Spanish
2. Chinese
3. French
4. German
5. Tagalog (spoken in the Philippines)

Source: U.S. Census Bureau

151

Latin and Greek Word Elements

LATIN ROOT	BASIC MEANING	EXAMPLES
-dict-	to say	dictate, predict
-ject-	to throw	eject, projectile
-port-	to carry	portable, transport
-scrib-, -script-	to write	scribble, describe
-vert-	to turn	convert, vertical

Many English words and word elements can be traced back to Latin and Greek. A word root is a part of a word. It contains the core meaning of the word, but it cannot stand alone.

LATIN PREFIX	BASIC MEANING	EXAMPLES
co-	together	coordinate, cowrite
inter-	between, among	international, interject
re-	again; back, backward	rebuild, recall
sub-	under	submarine, subway
trans-	across, beyond, through	transatlantic, transport

A prefix is placed at the beginning of a word to change its meaning.

A suffix is placed at the end of a word to change its meaning.

LATIN SUFFIX	BASIC MEANING	EXAMPLES
-able, -ible	capable or worthy of	likable, flexible
-ation	forms nouns form verbs	create, creation; civilize, civilization
-fy, -ify	to make or cause to become	purify, humidify
-ment	forms nouns from verbs	entertain, entertainment; amaze, amazement
-ty, -ity	forms nouns from adjectives	cruel, cruelty; sane, sanity

GREEK ROOT	BASIC MEANING	EXAMPLES
-anthrop-	human	philanthropy, anthropology
-chron-	time	synchronize, chronicle
-dem-	people	democracy, demography
-path-	feeling, suffering	pathetic, sympathy
-phon-	sound	phonograph, cacophony

GREEK PREFIX	BASIC MEANING	EXAMPLES
anti-, ant-	opposite; opposing	antiwar, antagonize
auto-	self, same	autobiography, automatic
bio-, bi-	life, living organism	biology, biopsy
neo-	new, recent	neophyte, neonatal
thermo-, therm-	heat	thermometer, thermal

GREEK SUFFIX	BASIC MEANING	EXAMPLES
-ism	the act, state or theory of	capitalism, criticism
-ist	a person who practices or believes something	cyclist, conformist
-logue, -log	speech, discourse; to speak	dialogue, monologue
-logy	talk, theory, study	dermatology, biology
-meter, -metry	measuring device; measure	kilometer, geometry

Word Relationships:
Analogies

An **analogy** is a type of word problem. It is made up of two word pairs, like this:

BLUE : SKY :: _____ : GRASS

Your goal in solving an **analogy** is to find a word that correctly completes the second pair. Both pairs of words have the same kind of relationship. To solve the analogy you need to find that relationship. Read the analogy like this:

Blue is to sky as "blank" is to grass.

Ask yourself: What is the relationship between **blue** and **sky**? The relationship between the first pair of words is descriptive—one word describes the other word. Therefore, the second pair of words must also have a descriptive relationship. **Green** describes **grass**.

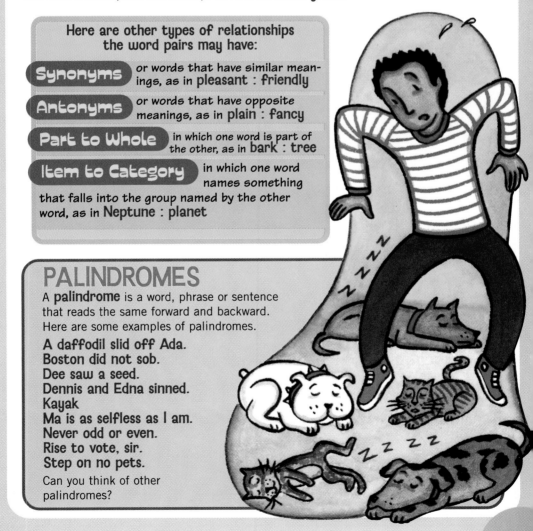

Here are other types of relationships the word pairs may have:

Synonyms or words that have similar meanings, as in **pleasant : friendly**

Antonyms or words that have opposite meanings, as in **plain : fancy**

Part to Whole in which one word is part of the other, as in **bark : tree**

Item to Category in which one word names something that falls into the group named by the other word, as in **Neptune : planet**

PALINDROMES

A **palindrome** is a word, phrase or sentence that reads the same forward and backward. Here are some examples of palindromes.

A daffodil slid off Ada.
Boston did not sob.
Dee saw a seed.
Dennis and Edna sinned.
Kayak
Ma is as selfless as I am.
Never odd or even.
Rise to vote, sir.
Step on no pets.

Can you think of other palindromes?

American Sign Language (ASL) and the American Manual Alphabet

American Sign Language (ASL) was developed at the American School for the Deaf, which was founded in 1817 in Hartford, Connecticut. Teachers at the school created ASL by combining French Sign Language with several American visual languages. It includes signs, gestures, facial expressions and the **American Manual Alphabet** shown below. Today, ASL is the fourth most used language in the U.S.

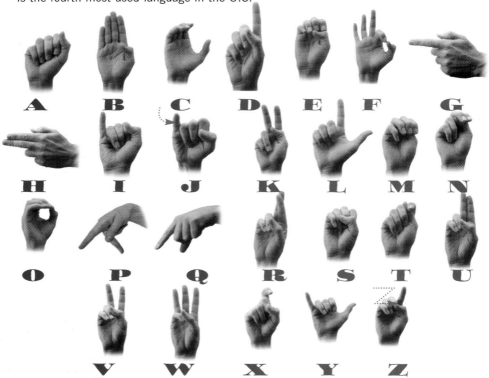

Braille System

In the 1800s **Louis Braille** developed the Braille System to help teach blind children to read and write. Braille, a Frenchman, had himself been blind since an accident at age 3. His system of letters, numbers and punctuation marks is made up of raised points or dots.

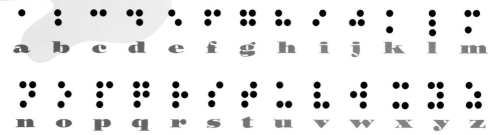

"Onyms"

Acronyms are words or names formed by combining the first letters of words in a phrase. For example, SCUBA comes from Self-Contained Underwater breathing apparatus.

Antonyms are words with opposite meanings. Sweet and bitter are antonyms.

Eponyms are words based on or derived from a person's name. For example, the word diesel was named after Rudolf Diesel, who invented the diesel engine.

Heteronyms are words with identical spellings but different meanings and pronunciations. For example, bow and arrow, and to bow on stage.

Homonyms are words that sound alike (and are sometimes spelled alike) but name different things. Die (to stop living) and dye (color) are homonyms.

Pseudonyms are false names or pen names used by an author. The word comes from the Greek pseud (false) and onym (name). Mark Twain is a pseudonym for Samuel Langhorne Clemens.

Synonyms are words with the same or similar meanings. Cranky and grumpy are synonyms.

Winning Words

Kids have been participating in the National Spell Bee since 1925. In 2003, 13-year-old Sai Gunturi, an eighth-grader from Dallas, took home $12,000 cash, among other prizes, for correctly spelling pococurante. Here are some other winning words that made students into national champions.

1990	fibranne
1991	antipyretic
1992	lyceum
1993	kamikaze
1994	antediluvian
1995	xanthosis
1996	vivisepulture
1997	euonym
1998	chiaroscurist
1999	logorrhea
2000	demarche
2001	succedaneum
2002	prospicience

TFK Mystery Person

CLUE 1: I was born in Hartford, Connecticut, in 1758.
CLUE 2: I wrote the first American dictionary. Completed in 1828, the dictionary took more than 27 years to write.
CLUE 3: Today, my name is linked with American dictionaries.

WHO AM I?
(See Answer Key that begins on page 340.)

155

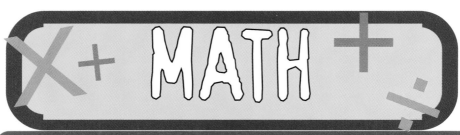

MATH

Numerical Prefixes

A prefix is an element at the beginning of a word. A numerical prefix lets you know how many there are of a particular thing. You can use these prefixes to figure out how many sides a figure has. For example, a hexagon has six sides, and a heptagon has seven.

PREFIX	MEANING	EXAMPLE
uni-	1	unicorn: mythical creature with one horn
mono-	1	monorail: train that runs on one track
bi-	2	bicycle: two-wheeled vehicle
tri-	3	triceratops: three-horned dinosaur
quadr-	4	quadruped: four-footed animal
quint-	5	quintuplets: five babies born at a single birth
penta-	5	pentagon: figure with five sides
hex-	6	hexapod: having six legs—an insect, for example
sex-	6	sextet: group of six musicians
hept-	7	heptathlon: athletic contest with seven events
sept-	7	septuagenarian: a person between ages 70 and 80
octo-	8	octopus: sea creature with eight arms
nove-	9	novena: prayers said over nine days
deka- or deca-	10	decade: a period of 10 years
cent-	100	century: a period of 100 years
hecto-	100	hectogram: 100 grams
milli-	1,000	millennium: a period of 1,000 years
kilo-	1,000	kilogram: 1,000 grams
mega-	1,000,000	megaton: 1 million tons
giga-	1,000,000,000	gigabyte: 1 billion bytes

More Than a MILLION

Numbers don't stop at the millions, billions or trillions. In fact, they go on and on and on. Here's what some really big numbers look like:

10 million 10,000,000
100 million 100,000,000
billion 1,000,000,000
trillion 1,000,000,000,000
quadrillion 1,000,000,000,000,000
quintillon 1,000,000,000,000,000,000
sextillion 1,000,000,000,000,000,000,000
septillion 1,000,000,000,000,000,000,000,000
octillion 1,000,000,000,000,000,000,000,000,000
nonillion 1,000,000,000,000,000,000,000,000,000,000
googol 1 followed by 100 zeroes
centillion 1 followed by 303 zeroes
googolplex 1 followed by a googol of zeroes

Integers

Integers are **whole numbers.** They include positive numbers, negative numbers and zero, but **not** fractions, decimals, percents or exponents. Here are some rules to remember when you add, subtract, multiply and divide integers.

★ **Adding a negative number is the same as subtracting a positive number.**
$$3 + -4 = 3 - 4$$

★ **Subtracting a negative number is the same as adding a positive number. The two negatives cancel out each other.**
$$3 - -4 = 3 + 4$$

★ **If you multiply or divide two positive numbers, the result will be positive.**
$$6 \times 2 = 12$$

★ **If you multiply or divide a positive number with a negative number, the result will be negative.**
$$6 \times -2 = -12$$

★ **If you multiply or divide two negative numbers, the result will be positive—the two negatives cancel out each other.**
$$-6 \times -2 = 12$$

Even and Odd Numbers

Is It Even or Odd?

Even numbers are numbers that can be divided evenly by 2. Odd numbers are numbers that cannot be divided evenly by 2. Zero is considered an even number.

To tell whether a number is even or odd, look at the number in the ones place. That single number will tell you whether the entire number is odd or even.

An even number ends in 0, 2, 4, 6 or 8.

An odd number ends in 1, 3, 5, 7 or 9.

Consider the number 3,842,917. It is an odd number because it ends in 7, an odd number. Likewise, 8,322 is an even number because it ends in 2.

Adding Even and Odd Numbers
even + even = even $4 + 2 = 6$
even + odd = odd $4 + 3 = 7$
odd + odd = even $5 + 3 = 8$

Subtracting Even and Odd Numbers
even − even = even $4 - 2 = 2$
even − odd = odd $4 - 3 = 1$
odd − odd = even $5 - 3 = 2$

Multiplying Even and Odd Numbers
even x even = even $4 \times 2 = 8$
even x odd = even $4 \times 3 = 12$
odd x odd = odd $5 \times 3 = 15$

Division, or The Fraction Problem

When you divide numbers, something tricky can happen—you might be left with a fraction. **Fractions are neither even numbers nor odd numbers,** because they are not whole numbers. They are only parts of numbers and can be written in different ways.

For example, you can't say the fraction $1/3$ is odd because the denominator (the bottom part) is an odd number. You could just as well write that same fraction as $2/6$, in which the denominator is an even number.

The terms **even number** and **odd number** are only used for **whole numbers.**

Prime Numbers

A **prime number** is a number that can be divided, without a remainder, only by itself and by 1. For example, 17 is a prime number. It can be divided only by 17 and by 1.

Some facts:

● **The only even prime number is 2. All** other even numbers can be divided by 2.

● **No prime number greater than 5 ends** in a 5. Any number greater than 5 that ends in a 5 can be divided by 5.

● **Zero and 1 are not considered prime** numbers.

● **Except for 0 and 1, a number is either** a prime number or a composite number. A composite number is any number greater than 1 that is not prime.

To prove whether a number is a prime number, first try dividing it by 2, and see if you get a whole number. If you do, it can't be a prime number. If you don't get a whole number, next try dividing it by 3, then by 5, then by 7 and so on, always dividing by an odd number.

Decimal Places 9.0

One decimal place to the left of the decimal point is the ones place. One decimal place to the right of the decimal place is the tenths place.

Keep your eye on the **9** to see where the decimal places fall.

millions	9,000,000.0
hundred thousands	900,000.0
ten thousands	90,000.0
thousands	9,000.0
hundreds	900.0
tens	90.0
ones	9.0
tenths	0.9
hundredths	0.09
thousandths	0.009
ten-thousandths	0.0009
hundred-thousandths	0.00009
millionths	0.000009

To add or subtract decimals, line up the decimal points and use zeros to fill in the blanks:

$$9 - 2.67 =$$

$$
\begin{array}{r}
9.00 \\
-2.67 \\
\hline
6.33
\end{array}
$$

Did You Know?

✓ It would take about 12 days to count to a million and about 32 years to count to 1 billion, if each count were about 1 second long.

Fractions, Decimals & Percents

How to Reduce a Fraction

Divide the numerator (the top part) and the denominator (the bottom part) by their **greatest common factor** (GCF), which is the largest whole number that can be divided evenly into each of the numbers.

Example: $6/15$ The greatest common factor is 3, so
$(6 \div 3) / (15 \div 3) = 2/5$

Or

Divide the numerator and the denominator by a common **factor**. A factor is any number that divides a number evenly without a remainder. Keep dividing until you can no longer divide either the numerator or the denominator evenly by the common factor.

Example: $8/20$, using 2 as the factor:
$(8 \div 2) / (20 \div 2) = 4/10 =$
$(4 \div 2) / (10 \div 2) = 2/5$

To change

A fraction to a decimal:
Divide the numerator by the denominator.
$1/4 = 1.00 \div 4 = 0.25$

A fraction to a percent:
Multiply the fraction by 100 and reduce it. Then, attach a percent sign.
$1/4 \times 100/1 = 100/4 = 25/1 = 25\%$

A decimal to a fraction:
Starting from the decimal point, count the decimal places. If there is one decimal place, put the number over 10 and reduce. If there are two places, put the number over 100 and reduce.
If there are three places, put it over 1,000 and reduce, and so on.
$0.25 = 25/100 = 1/4$

A decimal to a percent:
Move the decimal point two places to the right. Then, attach a percent sign.
$0.25 = 25\%$

A percent to a decimal:
Move the decimal point two places to the left. Then, drop the percent sign.
$25\% = 0.25$

A percent to a fraction:
Drop the percent sign.
Put the number over 100 and reduce.
$25\% = 25/100 = 1/4$

Homework TIP

Do math assignments in pencil.

Common Fractions with Decimal and Percent Equivalents

Here's a list of some common fractions and what they look like written as decimals and percents.

Fraction	Decimal	Percent
1/3	0.333 . . .	33.333 . . .%
2/3	0.666 . . .	66.666 . . .%
1/4	0.25	25%
1/2	0.5	50%
3/4	0.75	75%
1/5	0.2	20%
2/5	0.4	40%
3/5	0.6	60%
4/5	0.8	80%
1/6	0.1666 . . .	16.666 . . .%
5/6	0.8333 . . .	83.333 . . .%
1/8	0.125	12.5%
3/8	0.375	37.5%
5/8	0.625	62.5%
7/8	0.875	87.5%
1/10	0.1	10%
1/12	0.08333 . . .	8.333 . . .%
1/16	0.0625	6.25%
1/32	0.03125	3.125%

Multiplication Table

To find the answer to a multiplication problem, pick one number from the top of the box and one number from the left side. Follow each row into the center. The place where they meet is the answer.

X	0	1	2	3	4	5	6	7	8	9	10	11	12
0	0	0	0	0	0	0	0	0	0	0	0	0	0
1	0	1	2	3	4	5	6	7	8	9	10	11	12
2	0	2	4	6	8	10	12	14	16	18	20	22	24
3	0	3	6	9	12	15	18	21	24	27	30	33	36
4	0	4	8	12	16	20	24	28	32	36	40	44	48
5	0	5	10	15	20	25	30	35	40	45	50	55	60
6	0	6	12	18	24	30	36	42	48	54	60	66	72
7	0	7	14	21	28	35	42	49	56	63	70	77	84
8	0	8	16	24	32	40	48	56	64	72	80	88	96
9	0	9	18	27	36	45	54	63	72	81	90	99	108
10	0	10	20	30	40	50	60	70	80	90	100	110	120
11	0	11	22	33	44	55	66	77	88	99	110	121	132
12	0	12	24	36	48	60	72	84	96	108	120	132	144

Squares and Square Roots

A square of a number is that number times itself.
So the square of:

4 = 16: 4 x 4 = 16

6 = 36: 6 x 6 = 36

Finding a square root is the **inverse operation** of squaring. Inverse operations are two operations that do the opposite, such as multiplication and division. The square root of 4 is 2, or:

$\sqrt{4}$ is 2: 2 x 2 = 4

$\sqrt{9}$ is 3: 3 x 3 = 9

Here's a table of squares and square roots for numbers between 1 and 20.

Number	Square	Square Root
1	1	1.00
2	4	1.414
3	9	1.732
4	16	2.000
5	25	2.236
6	36	2.449
7	49	2.646
8	64	2.828
9	81	3.000
10	100	3.162
11	121	3.317
12	144	3.464
13	169	3.606
14	196	3.742
15	225	3.873
16	256	4.000
17	289	4.123
18	324	4.243
19	361	4.359
20	400	4.472

The easiest way to find a square root is to use a calculator, but you can do it without one. Here's one way, using 12 as an example of the squared number:

1. Pick a number that when squared comes close to (but is less than) the number whose square root you're finding: **3 x 3 = 9.** This is a better choice than 4: **4 x 4 = 16**

2. Divide the number you're finding the square root of by the square from step 1: 12 ÷ 3 = 4

3. Average the closest square (3) and the answer of step 2 (4): **3 + 4 = 7.** **7 ÷ 2 = 3.5**

4. Square the average to see how close the number is to 12:

3.5 x 3.5 = 12.25—Close, but not close enough!

Repeat steps 2 and 3 until the number squared is very close to 12:

Divide: **12 ÷ 3.5 = 3.43**

Average: **3.5 + 3.43 = 6.93**

6.935 ÷ 2 = 3.465

3.465 x 3.465 + 12.006, close enough!

Did You Know?

$\sqrt{\ }$ A nominal number identifies or names something:
- Jersey number 2
- ZIP code 02116

An ordinal number shows rank—the order of a thing in a set.
- 3rd fastest
- 10th in line

Common Formulas

Finding Area

Area is the amount of surface within fixed lines.

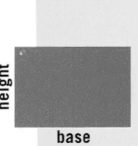

Square
Multiply the length of the side by itself. (For example, if the side is 6 inches long, multiply 6 x 6.)

Rectangle
Multiply the base by the height.

Circle
Multiply the radius by itself, then multiply the result by 3.1416.

Trapezoid
Add the two parallel sides, multiply by the height and divide by 2.

Triangle
If you know the base and the height, multiply them and then divide by 2.

Finding Circumference and Perimeter

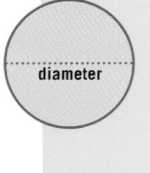

The **circumference** of a circle is the complete distance around it. To find the circumference of a circle, multiply its diameter by 3.1416.

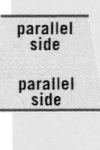

The **perimeter** of a geometrical figure is the complete distance around that figure. To find the perimeter, simply add up the lengths of the figure's sides.

Polygons: How Many Sides?

A geometrical figure with three or more sides is called a **polygon** or a **polyhedron**. Here are the names of some polygons.

Sides	Name	Shape
3	triangle, trigon	
4	quadrilateral, tetragon	
5	pentagon	
6	hexagon	
7	heptagon	
8	octagon	
9	nonagon, enneagon	
10	decagon	

Rounding Numbers

A rounded number has about the same value as the number you start with, but it is less exact. For example, 341 rounded to the nearest hundred is 300. That is because 341 is closer in value to 300 than to 400.

Rules for Rounding

Here's the general rule for rounding:

● If the number you are rounding ends with 5, 6, 7, 8 or 9, round the number up.

Example: 38 rounded to the nearest 10 is 40.

● If the number you are rounding ends with 0, 1, 2, 3 or 4, round the number down.

Example: 33 rounded to the nearest 10 is 30.

What Are You Rounding To?

When rounding a number, ask: What are you rounding it to? Numbers can be rounded to the nearest 10, the nearest 100, the nearest 1,000 and so on.

Consider the number 4,827:

● 4,827 rounded to the nearest 10 is 4,830.

● 4,827 rounded to the nearest 100 is 4,800.

● 4,827 rounded to the nearest 1,000 is 5,000.

Rounding and Decimals

Rounding decimals works exactly the same as rounding whole numbers. The only difference is that you round to tenths, hundredths, thousandths and so on.

● 7.8899 rounded to the nearest tenth is 7.9.

● 1.0621 rounded to the nearest hundredth is 1.06.

● 3.8792 rounded to the nearest thousandth is 3.879.

Did You Know?

When rounding long decimals, look only at the number in the place you are rounding to and the number that follows it. For example, to round 5.3874791 to the nearest hundredth, just look at the number in the hundredths place—8—and the number that follows it—7. Then you can easily round it up to 5.39.

Powers & Exponents

A power is the product of multiplying a number by itself.

Usually, a power is represented with **a base number** and an **exponent**. The **base number** tells **what number is being multiplied.** The exponent, a small number written above and to the right of the base number, tells how many times the base number is being multiplied.

For example, "6 to the 5th power" may be written as 6^5. Here, the base number is 6 and the exponent is 5. This means that 6 is being multiplied by itself 4 times:

6 x 6 x 6 x 6 x 6

6 x 6 x 6 x 6 x 6 = 7,776 or 6^5 = 7,776

BASE NUMBER	2ND POWER	3RD POWER	4TH POWER	5TH POWER
1	1	1	1	1
2	4	8	16	32
3	9	27	81	243
4	16	64	256	1,024
5	25	125	625	3,125
6	36	216	1,296	7,776
7	49	343	2,401	16,807
8	64	512	4,096	32,768
9	81	729	6,561	59,049
10	100	1,000	10,000	100,000
11	121	1,331	14,641	161,051
12	144	1,728	20,736	248,832

I am VIII years old!

Roman Numerals

The ancient Romans gave us this numbering system. The year 2005 in Roman numerals is **MMV**.

One	I
Two	II
Three	III
Four	IV
Five	V
Six	VI
Seven	VII
Eight	VIII
Nine	IX
Ten	X
Eleven	XI
Twelve	XII
Thirteen	XIII
Fourteen	XIV
Fifteen	XV
Sixteen	XVI
Seventeen	XVII
Eighteen	XVIII
Nineteen	XIX
Twenty	XX
Thirty	XXX
Forty	XL
Fifty	L
Sixty	LX
Seventy	LXX
Eighty	LXXX
Ninety	XC
One hundred	C
Five hundred	D
One thousand	M

Rules for Roman numerals

Here are the basic principles for reading and writing Roman numerals:

● A letter repeats its value that many times (XXX = 30, CC = 200). A letter can only be repeated three times.

● If one or more letters are placed after another letter of greater value, add that amount.

VI = 6 (5 + 1 = 6)

LXX = 70 (50 + 10 + 10 = 70)

● If a letter is placed before another letter of greater value, subtract that amount.

IV = 4 (5 – 1 = 4)

XC = 90 (100 – 10 = 90)

● A bar placed on top of a letter or string of letters increases the numeral's value by 1,000 times.

XV = 15, $\overline{XV}$ = 15,000

There are several rules for subtracting amounts from Roman numerals:

● Only subtract powers of 10 (I, X, or C, but not V or L)

**For 95, do NOT write VC (100 – 5).
DO write XCV (XC + V or 90 + 5)**

● Only subtract one number from another.

**For 13, do NOT write IIXV (15 – 1 – 1).
DO write XIII (X + I + I + I or 10 + 3)**

● Do not subtract a number from one that is more than 10 times greater (that is, you can subtract 1 from 10 [IX] but not 1 from 20—there is no such number as IXX.)

**For 99, do NOT write IC
(C – I or 100 – 1).
DO write XCIX (XC + IX or 90 + 9)**

Did You Know?

In ancient times, an inch was the width of a man's thumb. A hand was approximately 5 inches across. Today, a hand is 4 inches across and is used to measure horses (from the ground to the horse's shoulder). Long ago, the foot was 11 ½₂ inches. Today, it is 12 inches.

Puzzles & Games

Roamin' Numerals

This is sum quiz! First, find the image of each item below in the book. Note the page number where each item is located, then add up all the page numbers. Can you convert the answer to Roman numerals?

I. Michelangelo's *David* _____

II. Millard Fillmore _____

III. Matt Groening _____

IV. Gidget Schultz _____

V. A baboon _____

VI. Periodic Table _____

VII. Sir Isaac Newton _____

VIII. Delaware _____

IX. $20 bill _____

X. Food pyramid _____

_____

(See Answer Key that begins on page 340.)

Metric Weights and Measures

Most of the world uses the metric system. The only countries not on this system are the U.S., Myanmar (formerly called Burma) and Liberia.

The metric system is based on **10s**. For example, 10 decimeters make a meter.

Length

UNIT	VALUE
millimeter (mm)	0.001 meter
centimeter (cm)	0.01 meter
decimeter (dm)	0.1 meter
meter (m)	1 meter
dekameter (dam)	10 meters
hectometer (hm)	100 meters
kilometer (km)	1,000 meters

Metric Conversions

MULTIPLY	BY	TO FIND
centimeters	.3937	inch
feet	.3048	meter
gallons	3.7853	liters
grams	.0353	ounce
inches	2.54	centimeters
kilograms	2.2046	pounds
kilometers	.6214	mile
liters	1.0567	quarts
liters	.2642	gallon
meters	3.2808	feet
meters	1.0936	yards
miles	1.6093	kilometers
ounces	28.3495	grams
pounds	.4536	kilogram
quarts	.946	liter
square kilometers	.3861	square mile
square meters	1.196	square yards
square miles	2.59	square kilometers
square yards	.8361	square meter
yards	.9144	meter

Mass & Weight

UNIT	VALUE
milligram (mg)	0.001 gram
centigram (cg)	0.01 gram
decigram (dg)	0.10 gram
gram (g)	1 gram
dekagram (dag)	10 grams
hectogram (hg)	100 grams
kilogram (kg)	1,000 grams
metric ton (t)	1,000,000 grams

Capacity

UNIT	VALUE
milliliter (ml)	0.001 liter
centiliter (cl)	0.01 liter
deciliter (dl)	0.10 liter
liter (l)	1 liter
dekaliter (dal)	10 liters
hectoliter (hl)	100 liters
kiloliter (kl)	1,000 liters

U.S. Weights and Measures

Measuring Length

12 inches = 1 foot	
3 feet = 1 yard	
5$\frac{1}{2}$ yards = 1 rod	
40 rods = 1 furlong	
8 furlongs = 1 mile	

Measuring Area

144 square inches = 1 square foot	
9 square feet = 1 square yard	
30$\frac{1}{4}$ square yards = 1 square rod	
160 square rods = 1 acre	
640 acres = 1 square mile	

Measuring Weight

16 ounces = 1 pound	
2,000 pounds = 1 ton	

Measuring Liquid

2 cups = 1 pint	
2 pints = 1 quart	
4 quarts = 1 gallon	

Cooking Measures

3 teaspoons = 1 tablespoon	
4 tablespoons = $\frac{1}{4}$ cup	
5 tablespoons + 1 teaspoon = $\frac{1}{3}$ cup	
16 tablespoons = 1 cup	

Did You Know?

A **cardinal number** shows quantity—it tells how many.
- 8 puppies
- 10 friends

TFK Mystery Person

CLUE 1: Born in England, 1643, I am considered by many to be the greatest mathematician and physicist in history.

CLUE 2: In 1665, I made important discoveries in math, physics and optics, including the laws of motion and gravity.

CLUE 3: I used math to prove the relationship between colors, solved difficult problems in geometry and invented a type of math called calculus.

WHO AM I?

(See Answer Key that begins on page 340.)

MILITARY

& WAR

AMERICA'S WARS

From the American Revolution to the war in Iraq, the U.S. has fought in 12 major conflicts. Do you know their names, where they were fought and why, and who won? Here's a quick look.

American colonists fought the British in the Battle of Lexington in 1775.

The American Revolution
1775–1783

CAUSE: Great Britain forced its 13 American colonies to pay taxes but did not give them any representation in the British Parliament. "Taxation without representation" and other injustices led the colonies to seek independence.

OUTCOME: The U.S. declared its independence on July 4, 1776. It achieved independence when the Treaty of Paris was signed with Britain in 1783.

At the Battle of Bunker Hill, colonial officer William Prescott ordered, "Do not fire until you see the whites of their eyes!" His troops had the courage and discipline to hold their fire until the enemy was near, an early sign that the ragtag American army had a chance at defeating the well-trained, well-armed British troops.

The War of 1812
1812–1815

CAUSE: The British obstructed American trade overseas and forced American sailors to serve on British ships. Some members of Congress, called "war hawks," encouraged the war because they hoped to gain some of Britain's territory in North America.

OUTCOME: Trade issues between the two countries remained unresolved, but Britain gave up claims to some of its land on the continent.

The American victory at Fort McHenry near Baltimore inspired Francis Scott Key to write our national anthem, "The Star-Spangled Banner."

During the War of 1812, the British set fire to Washington, D.C.

The Mexican War
1846–1848

CAUSE: Mexico was angered by the U.S.'s annexation of Texas, which formerly belonged to Mexico. The U.S. wanted to gain more of Mexico's land, especially California.

OUTCOME: Mexico was forced to give up two-fifths of its territory and received $15 million from the U.S. in damages. This land eventually became the states of California, Nevada, Arizona, New Mexico and Utah.

The war was fought in the name of "manifest destiny," the belief that the U. S. should possess the entire continent from the Atlantic Ocean to the Pacific Ocean.

Nearly 215,000 soldiers died in battle during the Civil War.

The Civil War
1861–1865

CAUSE: The northern states (the Union) and the southern states (the Confederacy) fought over slavery and states' rights. Eleven states seceded from the Union (South Carolina, Mississippi, Florida, Alabama, Georgia, Louisiana, Texas, Arkansas, North Carolina, Virginia and Tennessee) to form a separate nation called the Confederate States of America.

OUTCOME: The Union victory led to the reunification of the country and ended slavery.

More than 180,000 black soldiers fought in the Union Army. By the end of the war, they made up 10% of the Union troops. Both free African Americans and runaway slaves volunteered as soldiers.

The Spanish-American War
1898

CAUSE: The U.S. supported Cuba's desire for independence from Spanish rule. It saw the war as an opportunity to expand its power in other parts of the world.

OUTCOME: Cuba was freed from Spanish rule, and the U.S. gained several former Spanish territories: Puerto Rico, Guam and the Philippines

Before the war began, an explosion in Havana Harbor sank the U.S. battleship *Maine*, killing 260 crew members. "Remember the Maine!" became the war's most famous slogan.

World War I
1914–1918

CAUSE: Rivalries over power, territory and wealth led to the Great War. The U.S. joined the Allies (Britain, France, Russia, Italy and Japan), who were at war with the Central Powers (Germany, Austria-Hungary, Bulgaria and Turkey), after German submarines began sinking unarmed ships—notably the *Lusitania*.

OUTCOME: About 10 million soldiers died and 20 million were wounded. Germany was forced to declare guilt for the war, pay the other countries for the damage it caused and return territory it claimed during the war.

World War I was characterized by trench warfare. Each army dug protective trenches—long, deep rows of ditches in the ground. The troops slept, ate and fought against the enemy in these trenches.

World War II
1939-1945

CAUSE: The Axis powers—Hitler's Germany, along with the dictatorships of Italy and Japan—attempted to dominate the world. The Allies (the U.S., Britain, France, the U.S.S.R. and others) fought to stop them.

OUTCOME: Germany surrendered in 1945, and Japan surrendered later that same year, after the U.S. dropped atom bombs on the cities of Hiroshima and Nagasaki.

One of the most horrific chapters of the war was the Holocaust, the systematic annihilation of about 6 million Jews as well as millions of others who did not conform to Nazi Germany's racist ideals.

The Korean War
1950-1953

CAUSE: Communist North Korea, supported by China, invaded non-communist South Korea. U.N. forces, mostly made up of U.S. troops, fought to protect South Korea.

Adolf Hitler led Germany into World War II.

OUTCOME: South Korea maintained its independence from North Korea.

The Korean War was the first armed conflict in the global struggle between democracy and communism, called the "cold war."

The Vietnam War
1955-1975

CAUSE: Communist North Vietnam invaded noncommunist South Vietnam in an attempt to unify the country and impose communist rule. The United States fought on the side of South Vietnam to keep it independent.

OUTCOME: The United States withdrew its combat troops in 1973. In 1975, North Vietnam succeeded in taking control of South Vietnam.

Vietnam was the longest conflict the U.S. ever fought and the first war it lost.

More than 500,00 American troops were in Vietnam.

go Watch a BrainPOP movie about the U.S. military at www.timeforkids.com/military

Persian Gulf War
1991

CAUSE: Iraq invaded the country of Kuwait. The U.S., Britain and other countries came to Kuwait's aid.

OUTCOME: Iraq withdrew from Kuwait.

In a brilliant, lightning-fast campaign, U.S. and coalition ground troops defeated President Saddam Hussein's troops in just four days.

Did You Know?

The U.S. has also fought in smaller conflicts, including ones involving the countries of Grenada, Panama, Somalia, Haiti and Yugoslavia.

Afghanistan War
2002

CAUSE: Afghanistan's Taliban government harbored Osama bin Laden and members of the al-Qaeda terrorist group, who were responsible for the Sept. 11, 2001, attacks on the U.S. After they refused to turn over bin Laden, the U.S. and U.N. coalition forces attacked.

OUTCOME: The Taliban government was ousted and many terrorist camps in Afghanistan were destroyed.

The Taliban surrendered within two months, much earlier than expected.

U.S. troops remain a presence in Afghanistan.

Iraq War
2003

CAUSE: Dictator Saddam Hussein's alleged possession of illegal weapons of mass destruction and Iraq's suspected ties to terrorism prompted the U.S. and Britain to invade and topple his government.

OUTCOME: Iraq was defeated and Saddam Hussein removed from power.

In December 2003, U.S. troops captured Saddam Hussein. They found him hiding in an eight-foot hole on a farm near his hometown of Tikrit. He had been on the run for nearly nine months.

AMERICA'S WARS

TFK NEWS

Life for the Troops

The U.S.-led troops in Iraq are far from the comforts of home. When they are on the move, they live in make-shift camps without running water or beds. They eat premade meals from a pouch and sleep when they can.

Temperatures in Iraq can often exceed 100°F, making protective suits, armor and helmets seem even heavier. Sandstorms make it hard to see or breathe.

Life on the front lines is a struggle. Many soldiers draw inner strength from thoughts of home and family. Sergeant William Mitchell has photos of his wife and 10-year-old son strapped to his arm. He doesn't know how long he'll be away. Says Mitchell: "All I know is, home is after Baghdad."

The U.S. military offers 24 kinds of instant meals (above). A soldier's backpack and gear (left) weigh as much as 120 pounds.

Weapons That Changed Warfare

★ Invented by the Greeks in 400 B.C., **catapults** were used in ancient and medieval times to hurl stones, spears and other objects at fortifications.

★ The discovery of gunpowder led to the development of **cannons** in the 1300s. Cannons could demolish castle walls and blast through wooden ships.

★ **Machine guns** allowed for rapid, continuous fire, which eliminated frequent reloading. The first was the Gatling gun, used in the American Civil War.

★ The **tank,** an armored combat vehicle equipped with a cannon and machine guns, emerged as a symbol of modern war. Tanks were first used at the end of World War I.

★ **Combat aircraft**, both **bombers** and **fighter planes,** changed the nature of war during World War II. Air superiority became critical to victory. The British Spitfire, American Mustang and the German Messerschmitt were among the most famous fighter planes of the war.

Label on box: MEAL, READY-TO-EAT, INDIVIDUAL / DO NOT ROUGH HANDLE WHEN FROZEN / (0 degrees Fahrenheit or below)

A Who's Who of Warriors

AMAZONS Mythical female warriors known for their stature and strength

BUFFALO SOLDIERS Members of African-American army regiments who patrolled the Wild West after the Civil War

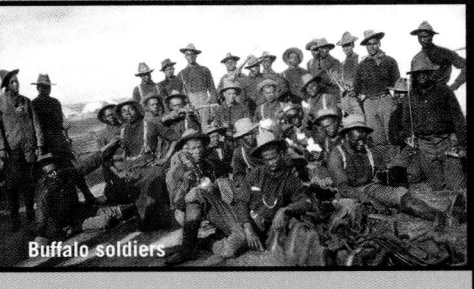
Buffalo soldiers

COMMANDOS Elite, highly trained soldiers. In the U.S. military, these special forces include the Navy Seals, the Army Rangers, the Green Berets and Delta Force.

CONQUISTADORS Spanish soldiers who conquered the people of the Americas in the 1500s

CRUSADERS Soldiers from Europe who tried to recover the Holy Land (Palestine) from the Muslims. Eight crusades took place between 1095 and 1291.

FOREIGN LEGION French mercenary (paid) army, mostly made up of foreigners. Founded in the 1800s, now it's made up of about 8,000 soldiers.

GUERRILLAS Irregular soldiers (those not part of the official military) who ambush and attack their enemies

GURKHAS Fighters from the nation of Nepal who have served in the British army since the 1800s. They carry 18-inch curved knives, and their motto is "Better to die than be a coward."

KAMIKAZES World War II Japanese airplane pilots who fought to the death, diving their planes into aircraft carriers

SAMURAI Warriors from Japan (1100–1800) who carried two swords

SPARTANS The ancient Greek city-state of Sparta was known for its extraordinary military superiority. The word Spartan has come to mean very disciplined and able to live without comfort, just as these ancient troops were.

VIKINGS Warriors from Scandinavia (700–1000) who raided and plundered the coast of Europe

All Spartan boys trained to be soldiers.

TFK Mystery Person

CLUE 1: A four-star general, I was appointed Chairman of the Joint Chiefs of Staff in 1989—the top military position in the U.S.
CLUE 2: I commanded the armed forces during the 1991 Persian Gulf War.
CLUE 3: I served as Secretary of State for President George W. Bush, becoming the first African American to hold that position.

WHO AM I?

(See Answer Key that begins on page 340.)

MONEY
& ECONOMY

Making Changes

Blue, peach and yellow money is nothing new to anyone who has ever played Monopoly. But since October 2003, these colors now appear on real $20 bills. The change marked the first time in 95 years that the U.S. bill had been printed in colors other than black and green.

The government alters our currency every seven to 10 years. The changes, says U.S. Treasury Secretary John W. Snow, help prevent counterfeiters from printing fake money. Next up for a makeover is the $50 bill.

Unlike the old bill, the new $20 bill doesn't include the oval around President Andrew Jackson's face. Two more American eagles appear on the front of the bill. Little 20s and the phrase "Twenty USA" were also added.

The nickel is also going through changes—and they make a lot of cents! The U.S. Mint, which makes American coins, is changing the design of the nickel.

The image of Thomas Jefferson remains on the front of the coin. As President in 1803, Jefferson made a deal for the U.S. to buy from France a huge area of land. The back of one new nickel honors that deal, known as the Louisiana Purchase. Jefferson later sent Meriwether Lewis and William Clark to explore the land. In fall 2004, the back of a second nickel will honor the 200th anniversary of their trip.

Before this new coin, the nickel hadn't changed in 65 years. Henrietta Holsman Fore is the director of the U.S. Mint. "This is a historic moment for the nation," she says.

By Elizabeth Winchester

174

U.S. Paper Money

BILL*	PORTRAIT	DESIGN ON BACK
$1	Washington	ONE between images of the front and back of the Great Seal of the U.S.
$2 (1998)	Jefferson	The signing of the Declaration of Independence
$5 (2000)	Lincoln	Lincoln Memorial
$10 (2000)	Hamilton	U.S. Treasury Building
$20 (2003)	Jackson	White House
$50 (1997)	Grant	U.S. Capitol
$100 (1996)	Franklin	Independence Hall in Philadelphia, Pennsylvania

*Date in parentheses indicates when new versions of the bills were introduced.

- The Treasury first printed paper money in 1862, during a coin shortage. The bills were issued in denominations of $1, $5, $25 and 50¢.

- The $100 bill is the largest that is now in circulation.

- Bills that get worn out from everyday use are taken out of circulation and replaced.

- A $1 bill usually lasts 18 months; $5 bill, two years; $10 bill, three years; $20 bill, four years; and $50 and $100 bills, nine years. Circulating coins last about 25 years.

- About 1% of $5 and $10 bills are counterfeited each week.

U.S. Coins

COIN	PORTRAIT	DESIGN ON BACK
Cent	Lincoln	Lincoln Memorial
Nickel	Jefferson	Commemoration of the Louisiana Purchase
Dime	F.D. Roosevelt	Torch, olive branch, oak branch
Quarter	Washington	Eagle*
Half-dollar	J.F. Kennedy	Presidential coat of arms
Dollar	Sacagawea and her infant son	Eagle in flight

* The 50 State Quarters Program features new quarters with unique designs on the back. Five coins have debuted each year since 1999, and five new quarters will be released every year until 2008.

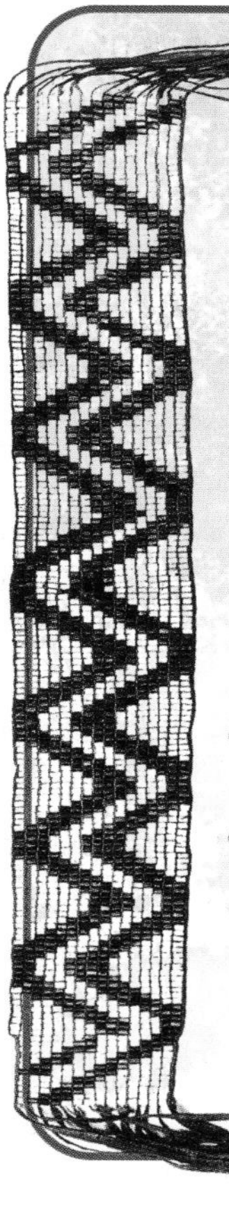

Old Money

- Before coins existed, the ancient Greeks used iron nails as money, the ancient Britons used sword blades and the ancient Chinese used swords and knives. The Hercules coin was introduced by Alexander the Great in 325 B.C.

- **Cowrie shells** have been used as money in many cultures.

- Some American colonists used **wampum** as money. Wampum was beautiful strands of beads made by Native Americans for ceremonial purposes.

- Chinese coins had holes in the center so they could be strung together like beads, which made carrying them easier.

- A Roman coin shows the double-faced god **Janus**. It dates from 240–220 B.C.

- People used banks even before they used paper money and coins! In ancient Mesopotamia, grains and other valuable trade goods were stored in palaces and temples for safekeeping.

Thrill Bill
Can you find five things wrong with this five-dollar bill?

(See Answer Key that begins on page 340.)

Learn more fun facts about money at, www.FACTMONSTER.COM

Word Bank

This glossary of economic terms will help you make sense of the bulls and bears, the recessions and the depressions.

Bear market A time when stock prices have been generally falling

Bull market A period when stock prices are mostly rising

Depression A long period of time when business, the employment rate and stock-market values decline sharply and stay at low levels

Economy The system a country uses to manage money and resources to produce goods (things to buy) and services (work done for others)

Federal Reserve The central bank of the United States

Inflation A continuous increase in the price of goods and services. As prices increase, the value of money decreases.

Interest The fee paid to use borrowed money, or, the money earned when you deposit money in a bank or other similar institution

Mutual fund A fund that pools money from many investors and buys a variety of stocks and bonds

NASDAQ The National Association of Securities Dealers' Automated Quotation marketplace. Companies traded on the NASDAQ include many small-to-medium-size firms and many technology companies. NASDAQ shares are traded electronically.

New York Stock Exchange The oldest stock exchange in the U.S. Companies traded on the N.Y.S.E. are typically the largest in the U.S.

Recession A period of time when people and companies are spending less and unemployment rises. A recession can turn into a depression if it continues for an extended period of time.

Stock Shares, or pieces, of a company that are sold to the public

Unemployment rate The percentage of workers who don't have jobs and are actively seeking employment. For example, if 5 out of every 100 workers need a job, the unemployment rate is 5%.

MONEY & ECONOMY

The Stock Market

Who owns companies like Disney, McDonald's and Wal-Mart? Ordinary people do. In fact, about half of all Americans own stock. People buy stock in companies hoping that they can make money by selling it later for a higher price. A stock's price depends on how many people want to buy it. If the demand for a stock is strong (maybe the company has a hot new product), then the price goes up. If only a few people want to buy it, the price drops. Shares of companies are bought and sold in a marketplace called the **stock market**.

The stock market goes through cycles. When stock prices are on the rise, it's usually a sign of a healthy economy. Prices tend to fall when the economy is in a slump.

The New York Stock Exchange is full of activity.

177

Budget Keeping

A **budget** is a tool used by people, businesses and governments to predict how much money will come in and how much will be spent over a period of time, usually a year. If you spend more money than you receive, you will experience a "budget deficit."

A **household budget** lists all the sources of money for that household, such as income from a job, loans or rent, and all the ways that money will be spent, usually on things like housing, school, clothes, food, cars and other bills.

The **government's budget** shows how much money it expects to take in from taxes and where it will spend that money—on such things as defense, education, roads, energy and health care. The U.S. Government often spends more than it receives. Today the national debt is about $5.8 trillion.

2003 Federal Budget

In 2003 the government took in about $2 trillion in taxes and spent about $2.1 trillion. As you can see, the government experienced a deficit. Here's a look at how the money was spent.

Defense 18%

Social Security 26%

Interest on the public debt 9%

Other expenses, including education, science and technology, transportation, social services and veterans' benefits 29%

Medicare and Medicaid 18%

Make Your Own Budget

Grownups aren't the only ones who have to worry about making ends meet. Say you'd like to buy a new video game, but you don't have any money saved. Make a budget to see if you can afford to put a few dollars a week toward the new game. You may be surprised to see how you spend your money.

Here's how to make your own budget: write down every single item you spend money on each week and how much it costs. Your list may include movies, CDs and food. Now add up how much you earn each week from an allowance, baby-sitting or a paper route. Subtract the money you spend from the money you earn. You have a budget surplus if there's money left over. You have a deficit if there's no money left or you come up with a negative number. In that case, look at each item on your "spend" list to see if there's anything that you can cut.

To manage your own budget, try www.timeforkids.com/budget

TEEN WORK

Have you ever thought about what type of job you'd like to have to earn spending money or to save for college? These are the types of businesses that employ the most teenagers.

TYPES OF BUSINESSES	PERCENT OF ALL YOUTHS WHO WORK
MALE	
EATING AND DRINKING PLACES	31.3%
GROCERY STORES	13.6
ENTERTAINMENT AND RECREATION SERVICES	4.5
AGRICULTURE	3.6
CONSTRUCTION	3.6
DEPARTMENT STORES	3.1
FEMALE	
EATING AND DRINKING PLACES	32.6%
GROCERY STORES	9.9
PRIVATE HOUSEHOLDS	5.7
DEPARTMENT STORES	4.4
ENTERTAINMENT AND RECREATION SERVICES	4.0

Source: U.S. Department of Labor

MONEY & ECONOMY

TFK Top 5 Most Dangerous Jobs

JOB	DEATH RATE (PER 100,000 U.S. WORKERS)
1. Timber cutters	117.8
2. Fishers	71.1
3. Pilots and navigators	69.8
4. Structural metal workers	58.2
5. Driver-sales workers*	58.2

*For example, pizza deliverers and vending-machine fillers
Source: CNN

Cutting timber is not a safe job.

TFK Mystery Person

CLUE 1: I was a delegate from New York at the Constitutional Convention in 1787.
CLUE 2: George Washington picked me to serve as the first Secretary of the Treasury. In that job, I helped strengthen the economy of the young nation.
CLUE 3: My face is on the $10 bill.

WHO AM I?

(See Answer Key that begins on page 340.)

179

MOVIES & TV

MOVIE MILESTONES

1889	William Dickson, hired by Thomas Edison, builds the first movie camera and names it the Kinetograph.
1894	The Edison Corporation opens the first motion-picture studio. The first Kinetoscope parlor opens in New York City, where people can see films for 25¢.
1895	In France, the Lumière brothers hold the first public screening of a film.
1905	The first movie theater opens in Pittsburgh, Pennsylvania.
1914	Winsor McCay unleashes *Gertie the Dinosaur*, the first animated cartoon.
1923	German shepherd Rin Tin Tin becomes Hollywood's first dog star.
1924	Walt Disney creates his first cartoon, *Alice's Wonderland*.
1927	Al Jolson performs his nightclub act in *The Jazz Singer*, the first feature-length talkie.
1928	Walt Disney introduces the first cartoons with sound. The Academy Awards are handed out for the first time. *Wings* wins best picture.
1937	Walt Disney's first full-length animated feature, *Snow White and the Seven Dwarfs*, hits theaters.
1968	The movie rating system debuts with G, PG, R and X.
1977	*Star Wars* opens in theaters.
1998	*Titanic* becomes the highest-grossing film of all time.
1999	*Star Wars: Episode One—The Phantom Menace* opens and breaks a string of box-office records.
2001	The first *Harry Potter* movie premieres.
2003	*Finding Nemo* replaces *The Lion King* as the highest-grossing animated film of all time.

1927 — Philo Farnsworth transmits the first all-electronic television image.

1928 — GE introduces a TV set with a 3 in. to 4 in. screen.

1931 — There are nearly 40,000 television sets in the U.S.; 9,000 of them are in New York City alone.

1947 — The Yankees beat the Dodgers in the first televised World Series.
Meet the Press debuts on NBC. The first news show will become TV's longest-running program.

1949 — The first Emmy Awards are handed out.
These Are My Children, a live, 15-minute show, premieres on NBC. It is the first soap opera.

1950 — Saturday-morning children's programming begins.

1951 — Color television is introduced in the U.S.
For the first time, a nationwide program airs: Edward R. Murrow's *See It Now* series.

1952 — Television's first magazine-style program, the *Today* show, debuts on NBC.

1960 — Seventy million people watch the presidential debate between John F. Kennedy and Richard Nixon.
Ninety percent of U.S. homes have a TV set.

1966 — The first *Star Trek* episode is broadcast.

1967 — Congress creates the Public Broadcasting System (PBS).

1968 — *60 Minutes* airs on CBS, beginning its reign as the longest-running prime-time newsmagazine.

1969 — Children's Television Workshop introduces *Sesame Street*.

1973 — *An American Family* debuts on PBS. The show follows the real-life Loud family and marks the beginning of reality TV.

1980 — Ted Turner launches CNN, the first all-news network.

1988 — Ninety-eight percent of U.S. homes have at least one television set.

1990 — *The Simpsons* debuts on Fox. It goes on to be TV's longest-running comedy.

2003 — A study reveals that kids age 6 and under spend as much time in front of the TV or computer screen as they do playing outside.

Classics to Catch on Video

Check out these classic films the next time you're at the video store.

The Absent-Minded Professor

Professor Brainard can't seem to get to the church on time for his own wedding, but he's certainly no slouch. He invented flying rubber—or flubber, as he calls it. This 1961 classic was remade into the 1997 movie *Flubber*.

Babe

It doesn't take long for **Babe**, a pig, to realize his destiny at Hoggett farm. Desperate to save himself from becoming Christmas dinner, the crafty swine devises a plan to prove his worth.

Chitty Chitty Bang Bang

At the urging of his children, eccentric inventor Caractacus Potts transforms a dilapidated race car into a sleek vehicle his kids name Chitty Chitty Bang Bang. Chitty takes the family on a magical adventure.

E.T.—The Extra-Terrestrial

When a spaceship leaves behind one of its passengers, a young boy shelters the alien and tries to help it return home.

Toy Story and Toy Story 2

With the help of Mr. Potato Head, Slinky and Etch-a-Sketch, cowboy Woody battles astronaut Buzz Lightyear for top position on Andy's pillow. **Toy Story 2** introduced a toybox full of new characters and adventures.

The Wizard of Oz

Dorothy gets her wish to travel over the rainbow, but she soon longs to be back home in Kansas. She takes a trip down the Yellow Brick Road with the Scarecrow, the Tin Man and the Cowardly Lion in search of the Wizard of Oz, who she hopes can help her.

TOP-RATED Kid Shows*

Kids 6 to 11
Network Shows
1. *American Idol* (Fox)
2. *The Simpsons* (Fox)
3. *Survivor: Thailand* (CBS)
4. *Yu-Gi-Oh* (WB)
5. *The Wonderful World of Disney* (ABC)

Cable Shows
1. *All Grown Up* (Nickelodeon)
2. *Jimmy Neutron* (Nickelodeon)
3. *Fairly Odd Parents* (Nickelodeon)
4. *Hocus Pocus* (Disney Channel)
5. *SpongeBob SquarePants* (Nickelodeon)

Kids 12 to 17
Network Shows
1. *American Idol* (Fox)
2. *Joe Millionaire* (Fox)
3. *The Simpsons* (Fox)
4. *Malcolm in the Middle* (Fox)
5. *Oliver Beene* (Fox)

Cable Shows
1. *Hocus Pocus* (Disney Channel)
2. *World Wrestling Entertainment* (Spike TV)
3. *Smart Guy* (Disney Channel)
4. *Family Guy* (Cartoon Network)
5. *Lizzie McGuire* (Disney Channel)

*September 2002 – September 2003
Source: Nielson Media Research

TFK Top 5 Highest Grossing Kids Movies of 2003

MOVIE	MONEY EARNED IN THE U.S.
1. *Finding Nemo*	$339,714,367
2. *Elf*	$170,837,644
3. *Spy Kids 3D: Game Over*	$111,678,621
4. *Freaky Friday*	$110,180,505
5. *Daddy Day Care*	$104,148,781

Source: Exhibitor Relations. *Through Jan. 4, 2004

TFK Mystery Person

CLUE 1: I had two big interests when I was growing up in Portland, Oregon: watching television and drawing cartoons.
CLUE 2: In 1987, I was asked to create a cartoon for *The Tracey Ullman Show*, which developed into *The Simpsons*, one of TV's most popular shows.
CLUE 3: I created another funny animated TV series, *Futurama*.

WHO AM I?
(See Answer Key that begins on page 340.)

go! Read an interview with Dory from *Finding Nemo* at *www.timeforkids.com/dory*

MUSIC

Downloaders Face the Music

By Kathryn R. Satterfield

Listen up, music lovers! In late 2003, the Recording Industry Association of America (RIAA) filed lawsuits against 261 people, including 12-year-old Brianna Torres. The message: Swapping songs free of charge over the Internet is illegal.

The RIAA represents U.S. record companies. It says that the music industry is losing money to downloading freeloaders—people who illegally trade songs online. Its lawsuits target anyone who has shared more than 1,000 music files.

About 60 million Americans use Internet file-sharing networks (KaZaA is a popular one). The networks let users locate and download almost any song and copy it onto a CD without paying. This breaks U.S. copyright laws, which protect artists' words or images and the artists' right to earn a profit from them.

Brianna's mother paid $2,000 to settle the lawsuit. Like many downloaders, Brianna didn't know that what she did was wrong. Buying and owning file-sharing software is legal. Using it to take copyrighted music is not. Critics argue that lawsuits are not the way to teach fans to respect artists' rights or boost sales. "CDs are far too expensive," singer Sarah McLachlan told TFK. "Kids wouldn't be so interested in downloading if CDs were reasonably priced!"

Universal Music lowered its CD prices. McLachlan hopes for a harmonious ending: "We can find a way to make the Internet work for everybody."

Apple Computer has made downloading music both affordable and legal. Its iTunes Music Store lets people burn songs to CDs and onto Apple's iPod music player for 99¢ per tune.

Should record companies sue downloaders?

Gary Sherman, president of the RIAA

YES! It's no different than shoplifting a CD from a store. That's against the law, and the penalties for breaking the law can be stiff. Our group has been forced to go to court to charge some major violators who were illegally sharing a lot of computer music files with millions of computer users.

John Snyder, a Grammy-winning producer

NO! Sales of CDs and company profits are down. But not just because people are sharing music files online. CDs are too expensive. The record business has released fewer CDs and raised prices as competition has increased from DVDs and video games. Downloading is illegal, so don't do it for now. But laws can be changed. Old copyright laws shouldn't apply to new technology.

Good Vibrations:
Families of Instruments

Musical instruments are grouped into families based on how they make sounds. In an orchestra, musicians sit together in these family groupings. But not every instrument fits neatly into a group. For example, the piano has strings that vibrate and hammers that strike. Is it a stringed instrument or a percussion instrument? Some say it is both!

Brass

Brass instruments are made of brass or some other metal and make sounds when air is blown inside. The musician's lips must buzz, as though making a "raspberry" noise against the mouthpiece. Air then vibrates inside the instrument, which produces a sound.

Brass instruments include the trumpet, trombone, tuba, French horn, cornet and bugle.

Strings

Yes, the sounds of string instruments come from their strings. The strings may be plucked, as with a guitar or harp; bowed, as with a cello or a violin; or struck, as with a hammer dulcimer. This creates a vibration that causes a unique sound.

Stringed instruments include the violin, viola, cello, bass, harp and dulcimer.

Percussion

Most percussion instruments, such as drums and tambourines, make sounds when they are hit. Others are shaken, like maracas, and still others may be rubbed, scratched or whatever else makes the instrument vibrate and produce a sound.

Percussion instruments include drums, cymbals, triangles, chimes, bells and xylophones.

Woodwinds

Woodwind instruments produce sound when air (wind) is blown inside. Air might be blown across an edge, as with a flute; between a reed and a surface, as with a clarinet; or between two reeds, as with a bassoon. The sound happens when the air vibrates inside.

Woodwind instruments include the flute, piccolo, clarinet, recorder, bassoon and oboe.

TFK Puzzles & Games

The Sound of Music?

The members of the TFK band brought their uniforms but forgot their instruments! Draw a line from each instrument to the correct musician.

(See Answer Key that begins on page 340.)
(See Answer Key that begins on page 340.)

music Genres

blues A style of music that evolved from southern African-American work songs and secular (non-religious) songs. Blues influenced the development of rock, rhythm-and-blues and country music. Some blues musicians include Bessie Smith, Muddy Waters, Robert Johnson and Sonny Boy Williamson.

classical Classical music is usually more sophisticated and complex than other styles of music. Many classical compositions are instrumentals, which means there are no words in the songs. Classical music has its roots in Europe. It includes symphonies, chamber music, sonatas and ballets. Some important classical-music composers are Wolfgang Amadeus Mozart, Ludwig Van Beethoven and Johann Sebastian Bach. Philip Glass and John Williams are modern classical composers.

country-and-western music A form of American music that originated in the Southwest and the Southeast in the 1920s. Early country songs often told stories of poor people facing difficult lives. Recent country music is often hard to tell apart from pop music. Johnny Cash, Tammy Wynette, Willie Nelson, Faith Hill and Dolly Parton are popular country-music singers.

folk A style of music that has been passed down orally within cultures or regions. It is known for its simple melodies and the use of acoustic instruments. Modern folk music is based on traditional folk music

and often contains political lyrics. Bob Dylan, Pete Seeger, Woody Guthrie and the group Peter, Paul and Mary are folk performers.

jazz American music born in the early part of the 20th century from African rhythms and slave chants. It has spread from its African-American roots to a worldwide audience. Jazz forms include improvisation (unrehearsed playing), swing, bebop and cool jazz. Ella Fitzgerald, Benny Goodman, Miles Davis and Thelonius Monk are famous jazz musicians.

pop (popular) music Pop covers a wide range of music styles and is often softer than rock and is driven by melody. Pop usually appeals to a broad assortment of listeners. Some famous pop musicians include Frank Sinatra, Avril Lavigne, Justin Timberlake and Beyoncé Knowles.

rap Urban, typically African-American music that features lyrics—usually spoken over sampled sounds or drum loops—often about social or political issues. Hip-hop, a style of music similar to rap, blends rock, jazz and soul with sampled sounds. Jay-Z, Run-D.M.C., Beastie Boys, 50 Cent, Grandmaster Flash and Eminem are rappers.

rock One of the most popular forms of 20th-century music, rock combines African-American rhythms, urban blues, folk and country music. It developed in the early 1950s and has inspired dozens of other styles, such as grunge, ska and heavy metal. Some important rock bands are the Beatles, the Rolling Stones, Led Zeppelin, Nirvana, R.E.M. and U2.

Pivotal Moments in POPULAR MUSIC

Pop music dates back to the late 1800s. In "Tin Pan Alley," an area of New York City, musicians, songwriters and pianists played their tunes for music publishers. People bought sheet music so they could perform popular songs at home. Here are some milestones in popular music.

1896 The rise of ragtime, the earliest form of jazz, marks the birth of American popular music.

1925 Country-and-western music debuts at Nashville's Grand Ole Opry.

1935 Benny Goodman, Glenn Miller and Artie Shaw lead popular dance bands. Goodman helps to popularize jazz.

1955 Elvis Presley becomes the world's first rock star.

1964 The Beatles' song "I Want to Hold Your Hand" is a sensation in the U.S., sparking the "British invasion." The Rolling Stones soon make their mark in the U.S.

1978 Hip-hop is born in New York City. Rap follows shortly after.

1981 MTV hits the airwaves, changing pop music forever.

1982 Michael Jackson releases *Thriller*, one of the top-selling albums of all time.

1983 Madonna's self-titled debut album makes her an instant star. Her success paves the way for future idols like Britney Spears.

1991 Boys II Men release their first album, *Cooleyhighharmony*. Their success inspires dozens of other boy bands, including *N Sync, whose music dominates the charts throughout the 1990s.

TFK Top 5 All-Time Albums

NAME	ARTIST	ALBUMS SOLD
1. *Their Greatest Hits 1971-1975*		
	Eagles	28 million
2. *Thriller*	Michael Jackson	26 million
3. *The Wall*	Pink Floyd	23 million
4. *Led Zeppelin IV*		
	Led Zeppelin	22 million
5. *Greatest Hits Volumes I & II*		
	Billy Joel	21 million

Source: The Recording Industry Association of America

Homework TIP

Take advantage of any help or tutoring a teacher or your school offers.

TFK Mystery Person

CLUE 1: Born in Germany, I was already a concert pianist by age 11.
CLUE 2: I composed many of the world's greatest works of music for piano, string ensembles and orchestra.
CLUE 3: After going deaf, I wrote my last symphony, the *Ninth*, which I conducted on May 7, 1824—my last appearance on stage.

WHO AM I?

(See Answer Key that begins on page 340.)

MYTHOLOGY

Some myths that you know today may have been around for hundreds, or even thousands, of years. Although myths are often entertaining, they did not originate just for entertainment. Unlike folklore or fables, myths were once believed to be true. Myths helped to explain human nature and the mysteries of the world.

THE OLYMPIAN GODS AND GODDESSES

In Greek mythology, 12 gods and goddesses ruled the universe from atop Greece's Mount Olympus. All the Olympians are related to one another. The Romans adopted most of these gods and goddesses, but with new names (given below in parentheses).

The most powerful of all was **ZEUS (Jupiter),** god of the sky and the king of Olympus. His temper affected the weather; he threw thunderbolts when he was unhappy. He was married to Hera.

HERA (Juno) was goddess of marriage and the queen of Olympus. She was Zeus's wife and sister. Many myths tell of how she got back at Zeus for his insults.

POSEIDON (Neptune) was god of the sea. He was the most powerful god after his brother, Zeus. He lived in a beautiful palace under the sea and caused earthquakes when he was in a rage.

HADES (Pluto) was king of the dead. He lived in the underworld, the heavily guarded land where he ruled. He was the husband of Persephone (daughter of the goddess Demeter), whom he kidnapped.

APHRODITE (Venus) was the goddess of love and beauty. Some people believe she was a daughter of Zeus. Others believe she rose from the sea.

APOLLO (same Roman name) was the god of music and healing. He was also an archer and hunted with a silver bow.

ARES (Mars) was the god of war. He was both cruel and a coward. Ares was the son of Zeus and Hera, but neither of his parents liked him.

HEPHAESTUS (Vulcan) was the god of fire and the forge (a furnace in which metal is heated). Although he made armor and weapons for the gods, he loved peace.

ARTEMIS (Diana) was the goddess of the hunt and the protector of women in childbirth. She loved all wild animals.

ATHENA (Minerva) was the goddess of wisdom. She was also skilled in the art of war. Athena sprang full-grown from the forehead of Zeus and became his favorite child.

HESTIA (Vesta) was the goddess of the hearth (a fireplace at the center of the home). She was the oldest Olympian.

HERMES (Mercury) was the messenger god, a trickster and a friend to thieves. He was the son of Zeus. The speediest of all gods, he wore winged sandals and a winged hat.

These Olympians are sometimes included in the list of rulers:

DEMETER (Ceres) was the goddess of the harvest. The word "cereal" comes from her Roman name.

DIONYSUS (Bacchus) was the god of wine. In ancient Greece, he was honored with springtime festivals that centered on theater.

A Greek Family Tree

ZEUS was the son of Cronus and Rhea. These two Titans ruled the universe before being overthrown by their children, the Olympians. Zeus was the king of Olympus, and **HERA** was the queen. Zeus was the father of many gods with his wife, Hera, and with other women. Here's the genealogy, or family tree, of the Greek gods. A plus sign (+) means that the two gods produced children. For example, Zeus + Leto indicates that they were the parents of Apollo.

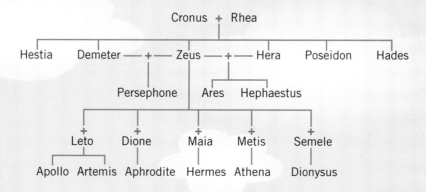

Gods and Goddesses Around the World

AZTEC

COATLICUE was the goddess of the earth and the mother of all the gods. She also gave birth to the moon and stars. The Aztecs carved a gigantic stone statue of her wearing a necklace made of human hearts and hands.

HUITZILOPOCHTLI was the god of the sun and of war. He was the patron god of the Aztec capital of Tenochtitlán, where Mexico City now stands. The Aztecs built a great temple there in his honor and sacrificed many humans to him.

CHICOMECOATL was the goddess of corn and fertility. So important was corn to the Aztecs that she was also known as "the goddess of nourishment."

QUETZALCOATL was the god of learning. A wise god, he helped to create the universe and humankind and later invented agriculture and the calendar. He is often shown as a magnificent feathered serpent.

EGYPTIAN

RA was the supreme god and the god of the sun. The early pharaohs claimed to be descended from him. He sometimes took the form of a hawk or a lion.

NUT represented the heavens and helped to put the world in order. She had the ability to swallow stars and the pharaohs and cause them to be born again. She existed before all else had been created.

OSIRIS was the god of the underworld and the judge of the dead. He was associated with the cycle of life and was often shown wearing mummy wrappings.

ISIS invented agriculture. She was the goddess of law, healing, motherhood and fertility. She came to be seen as a Mother Earth figure.

HORUS was a sky god who loved goodness and light. The son of Osiris and Isis, he was often shown as a young child.

THOTH was the god of wisdom and magic. He was believed to have invented writing, astronomy and other arts, and served as a scribe, or writer, to the gods.

NEPHTHYS was the goddess of the dead. She was a kind friend to the newly dead as well as to those left behind.

MAYAN

HUNAHPU was a god of the sun and the father of the first humans. A great hero, with his brother he defeated the forces of death and went on to rule in the heavens.

HURAKAN was the god of storms and winds. When the first humans made him angry, he swept them away in a violent flood. The word "hurricane" comes from his name.

IXCHEL was the goddess of the moon and the protector of pregnant women. She was often shown as an old woman wearing a full skirt and holding a serpent.

CHAC was the god of agriculture and a great friend to humans. He brought them rain and used his vast tail and fangs to protect planted fields.

ITZAMNA was the official god of the Mayan empire and the founder of its people. Corn, chocolate, writing and calendars were among his many gifts to them.

Native American Myths

American Indian tribes share many myths. If a myth is from a particular tribe, the tribe is given in parentheses.

COYOTE was a popular spirit among western tribes such as the Navajo, Zuni, Sioux and Chinook. A sly trickster, he made life more interesting for people. Coyote was responsible for sorrow and death, but also for the creation of humans and the Milky Way. There are many stories of Coyote's mischievous trickery and his contributions.

RAVEN seemed to have his beak into everything and like Coyote, was a wily god. He could change into a bird, a human or an animal. Raven could bring both good and evil. Always hungry, his search for food often got him into a lot of trouble. Raven was found mainly in tribes of the Pacific Northwest and southeastern Alaska.

SKYWOMAN (Iroquois) fell through a hole in the sky to a dark watery Earth populated only by animals. Birds caught her and put her on the back of a giant turtle. The turtle grew bigger and became the land. The hole Skywoman fell through brought light to the world and the beginning of Earth as we know it.

KACHINAS (Hopi) are spirits that lived in and controlled everything—the sky, water, plants, animals. The kachinas protected humans and brought them good fortune. Today, the Hopi give their children kachina dolls to teach them about different spirits.

TFK Mystery Person

CLUE 1: In Norse mythology, I am known as the god of thunder and the bringer of rain.

CLUE 2: I often used my favorite weapon, a hammer called Mjolnir, to protect humans.

CLUE 3: Not only am I a mighty character in a Marvel comic book, but a day of the week is also named after me.

WHO AM I?

(See Answer Key that begins on page 340.)

PRESIDENTS

1 GEORGE WASHINGTON (SERVED 1789-1797)
Born: Feb. 22, 1732, in Virginia; died: Dec. 14, 1799
Political Party: None
Vice President: John Adams
DID YOU KNOW? Washington was the only President unanimously elected. He received all 69 electoral votes.
"Liberty, when it begins to take root, is a plant of rapid growth."

★

2 JOHN ADAMS (SERVED 1797-1801)
Born: Oct. 30, 1735, in Massachusetts; died: July 4, 1826
Political Party: Federalist
Vice President: Thomas Jefferson
DID YOU KNOW? Adams was the first President to live in the White House.
"The happiness of society is the end of government."

★

3 THOMAS JEFFERSON (SERVED 1801-1809)
Born: April 13, 1743, in Virginia; died: July 4, 1826
Political Party: Democratic-Republican
Vice Presidents: Aaron Burr, George Clinton
DID YOU KNOW? In signing the 1803 Louisiana Purchase, Jefferson nearly doubled the size of the U.S.
"One man with courage is a majority."

★

4 JAMES MADISON (SERVED 1809-1817)
Born: March 16, 1751, in Virginia; died: June 28, 1836
Political Party: Democratic-Republican
Vice Presidents: George Clinton, Elbridge Gerry
DID YOU KNOW? Madison was the only President to have two Vice Presidents die in office. Clinton died in 1812 and Gerry died in 1814.
"The truth is that all men having power ought to be mistrusted."

★

5 JAMES MONROE (SERVED 1817-1825)
Born: April 28, 1758, in Virginia; died: July 4, 1831
Political Party: Democratic-Republican
Vice President: Daniel D. Tompkins
DID YOU KNOW? The Monroe Doctrine forbade foreign countries like Spain and Russia from expanding into North and South America.
"The American continents . . . are henceforth not to be considered as subjects for future colonization by any European powers."

6 JOHN QUINCY ADAMS (SERVED 1825–1829)
Born: July 11, 1767, in Massachusetts; died: Feb. 23, 1848
Political Party: Democratic-Republican
Vice President: John C. Calhoun

DID YOU KNOW? In 1843, Adams became the first President to have his photograph taken.

"Always vote for principle, though you may vote alone, and you may cherish the sweetest reflection that your vote is never lost."

7 ANDREW JACKSON (SERVED 1829–1837)
Born: March 15, 1767, in South Carolina; died: June 8, 1845
Political Party: Democratic
Vice Presidents: John C. Calhoun, Martin Van Buren

DID YOU KNOW? Jackson took several bullets while fighting in duels—an activity for which he was famous.

"I know what I am fit for. I can command a body of men in a rough way; but I am not fit to be President."

8 MARTIN VAN BUREN (SERVED 1837–1841)
Born: Dec. 5, 1782, in New York; died: July 24, 1862
Political Party: Democratic
Vice President: Richard M. Johnson

DID YOU KNOW? Van Buren was the first President born a U.S. citizen rather than a British subject.

"As to the presidency, the two happiest days of my life were those of my entrance upon the office and my surrender of it."

9 WILLIAM HENRY HARRISON (SERVED 1841)
Born: Feb. 9, 1773, in Virginia; died: April 4, 1841
Political Party: Whig
Vice President: John Tyler

DID YOU KNOW? Harrison had the shortest presidency: he died after only a month in office.

"But I contend that the strongest of all governments is that which is most free."

10 JOHN TYLER (SERVED 1841–1845)
Born: March 29. 1790, in Virginia; died: Jan. 18, 1862
Political Party: Whig
Vice President: None

DID YOU KNOW? Tyler was the first President to marry in office. He was also the President with the most children (15).

"Popularity, I have always thought, may aptly be compared to a coquette— the more you woo her, the more apt is she to elude your embrace."

11 JAMES KNOX POLK (SERVED 1845–1849)
Born: Nov. 2, 1795, in North Carolina; died: June 15, 1849
Political Party: Democratic
Vice President: George M. Dallas

DID YOU KNOW? Polk's inauguration was the first one to be reported by telegraph.

"With me it is exceptionally true that the presidency is no bed of roses."

12 ZACHARY TAYLOR (SERVED 1849–1850)

Born: Nov. 24, 1784, in Virginia; died: July 9, 1850
Political Party: Whig
Vice President: Millard Fillmore

DID YOU KNOW? Taylor never voted until he was 62 years old.

"The idea that I should become President . . . has never entered my head, nor is it likely to enter the head of any other person."

13 MILLARD FILLMORE (SERVED 1850–1853)

Born: Jan. 7, 1800, in New York; died: March 8, 1874
Political Party: Whig
Vice President: None

DID YOU KNOW? Fillmore and his first wife, Abigail, started the White House Library.

"An honorable defeat is better than a dishonorable victory."

14 FRANKLIN PIERCE (SERVED 1853–1857)

Born: Nov. 23, 1804, in New Hampshire; died: Oct. 8, 1869
Political Party: Democratic
Vice President: William R. King

DID YOU KNOW? Pierce was the only elected President not re-nominated by his party for a second term.

"The storm of frenzy and faction must inevitably dash itself in vain against the unshaken rock of the Constitution."

15 JAMES BUCHANAN (SERVED 1857–1861)

Born: April 23, 1791, in Pennsylvania; died: June 1, 1868
Political Party: Democratic
Vice President: John C. Breckinridge

DID YOU KNOW? Buchanan was the only President to remain a bachelor—he never married.

"There is nothing stable but heaven and the Constitution."

16 ABRAHAM LINCOLN (SERVED 1861–1865)

Born: Feb. 12, 1809, in Kentucky; died: April 15, 1865
Political Party: Republican
Vice Presidents: Hannibal Hamlin, Andrew Johnson

DID YOU KNOW? Lincoln's Gettysburg Address and Second Inaugural Address are among the greatest presidential speeches.

"If slavery is not wrong, nothing is wrong."

17 ANDREW JOHNSON (SERVED 1865–1869)

Born: Dec. 29, 1808, in North Carolina; died: July 31, 1875
Political Party: Democratic
Vice President: None

DID YOU KNOW? Johnson was the first President to be impeached. The Senate found him not guilty, however, and he remained President.

"Honest conviction is my courage; the Constitution is my guide."

18 ULYSSES S. GRANT (SERVED 1869–1877)
Born: April 27, 1822, in Ohio; died: July 23, 1885
Political Party: Republican
Vice Presidents: Schuyler Colfax, Henry Wilson
DID YOU KNOW? Grant's much praised *Memoirs* has been in print since 1885.
"I have never advocated war except as a means of peace."

19 RUTHERFORD B. HAYES (SERVED 1877–1881)
Born: Oct. 4, 1822, in Ohio; died: Jan. 17, 1893
Political Party: Republican
Vice President: William A. Wheeler
DID YOU KNOW? The first telephone was installed in the White House while Hayes was President.
"Nothing brings out the lower traits of human nature like office seeking."

20 JAMES A. GARFIELD (SERVED 1881)
Born: Nov. 19, 1831, in Ohio; died: Sept. 19, 1881
Political Party: Republican
Vice President: Chester A. Arthur
DID YOU KNOW? Garfield was the first President who campaigned in two languages—English and German.
"I have had many troubles in my life, but the worst of them never came."

21 CHESTER A. ARTHUR (SERVED 1881–1885)
Born: Oct. 5, 1829, in Vermont; died: Nov. 18, 1886
Political Party: Republican
Vice President: None
DID YOU KNOW? A stylish dresser, Arthur was nicknamed "Gentleman Boss" and "Elegant Arthur."
"Good ballplayers make good citizens."

22 GROVER CLEVELAND (SERVED 1885–1889)
Born: March 18, 1837, in New Jersey; died: June 24, 1908
Political Party: Democratic
Vice President: Thomas A. Hendricks
DID YOU KNOW? Cleveland was the only President to be defeated and then re-elected, serving two non-consecutive terms.
"A man is known by the company he keeps, and also by the company from which he is kept out."

23 BENJAMIN HARRISON (SERVED 1889–1893)
Born: Aug. 20, 1833, in Ohio; died: March 13, 1901
Political Party: Republican
Vice President: Levi P. Morton
DID YOU KNOW? Benjamin Harrison was the only President who was a grandson of a President (William Henry Harrison).
"The disfranchisement of a single legal elector by fraud or intimidation is a crime too grave to be regarded lightly."

24 GROVER CLEVELAND (SERVED 1893–1897)

Born: March 18, 1837, in New Jersey; died: June 24, 1908
Political Party: Democratic
Vice President: Adlai E. Stevenson

DID YOU KNOW? Cleveland was the only President to be married in the White House.

"Communism is . . . a menace to peace and organized governments."

★

25 WILLIAM McKINLEY (SERVED 1897–1901)

Born: Jan. 29, 1843, in Ohio; died: Sept. 14, 1901
Political Party: Republican
Vice Presidents: Garret A. Hobart, Theodore Roosevelt

DID YOU KNOW? McKinley was one of four Presidents assassinated in office.

"That's all a man can hope for during his lifetime—to set an example—and when he is dead, to be an inspiration for history."

★

26 THEODORE ROOSEVELT (SERVED 1901–1909)

Born: Oct. 27, 1858, in New York; died: Jan. 6, 1919
Political Party: Republican
Vice President: Charles W. Fairbanks

DID YOU KNOW? Theodore Roosevelt was the first President to ride in an automobile, an airplane and a submarine.

"Speak softly and carry a big stick."

27 WILLIAM H. TAFT (SERVED 1909–1913)

Born: Sept. 15, 1857, in Ohio; died: March 8, 1930
Political Party: Republican
Vice President: James S. Sherman

DID YOU KNOW? Taft was the only President who went on to serve as Chief Justice of the Supreme Court.

"Politics, when I am in it, makes me sick."

★

28 WOODROW WILSON (SERVED 1913–1921)

Born: Dec. 28, 1856, in Virginia; died: Feb. 3, 1924
Political Party: Democratic
Vice President: Thomas R. Marshall

DID YOU KNOW? Wilson was the first President to hold a news conference. About 125 members of the press attended the event on March 15, 1913.

"If you want to make enemies, try to change something."

★

29 WARREN G. HARDING (SERVED 1921–1923)

Born: Nov. 2, 1865, in Ohio; died: Aug. 2, 1923
Political Party: Republican
Vice President: Calvin Coolidge

DID YOU KNOW? Harding was a newspaper publisher before he was President.

"Ambition is a commendable attribute without which no man succeeds. Only inconsiderate ambition imperils."

30 CALVIN COOLIDGE (SERVED 1923–1929)
Born: July 4, 1872, in Vermont; died: Jan. 5, 1933
Political Party: Republican
Vice President: Charles G. Dawes
DID YOU KNOW? **Coolidge was the first President to be sworn in by his father, a justice of the peace.**
"The business of America is business."

31 HERBERT C. HOOVER (SERVED 1929–1933)
Born: Aug. 10, 1874, in Iowa; died: Oct. 20, 1964
Political Party: Republican
Vice President: Charles Curtis
DID YOU KNOW? **An asteroid, Hooveria, was named for Hoover.**
"Peace is not made at the council table or by treaties, but in the hearts of men."

32 FRANKLIN D. ROOSEVELT (SERVED 1933–1945)
Born: Jan. 30, 1882, in New York; died: April 12, 1945
Political Party: Democratic
Vice Presidents: John Garner, Henry Wallace, Harry S. Truman
DID YOU KNOW? **Franklin D. Roosevelt was the only President elected to four terms.**
"The only thing we have to fear is fear itself."

33 HARRY S. TRUMAN (SERVED 1945–1953)
Born: May 8, 1884, in Missouri; died: Dec. 26, 1972
Political Party: Democratic
Vice President: Alben W. Barkley
DID YOU KNOW? **Truman was a farmer, a hatmaker and a judge before entering politics.**
"You cannot stop the spread of an idea by passing a law against it."

34 DWIGHT D. EISENHOWER (SERVED 1953–1961)
Born: Oct. 14, 1890, in Texas; died: March 28, 1969
Political Party: Republican
Vice President: Richard M. Nixon
DID YOU KNOW? **Eisenhower was a five-star general in World War II before becoming President.**
"There is nothing wrong with America that the faith, love of freedom, intelligence and energy of her citizens cannot cure."

35 JOHN F. KENNEDY (SERVED 1961–1963)
Born: May 29, 1917, in Massachusetts; died: Nov. 22, 1963
Political Party: Democratic
Vice President: Lyndon B. Johnson
DID YOU KNOW? **Kennedy was the first Roman Catholic President.**
"Ask not what your country can do for you; ask what you can do for your country."

36 LYNDON B. JOHNSON (SERVED 1963–1969)

Born: Aug. 27, 1908, in Texas; died: Jan. 22, 1973
Political Party: Democratic
Vice President: Hubert H. Humphrey

DID YOU KNOW? Lyndon Johnson was the first person to take
the oath of office on an airplane. It was the presidential jet.

"If government is to serve any purpose, it is to do for others what
they are unable to do for themselves."

★

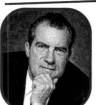

37 RICHARD M. NIXON (SERVED 1969–1974)

Born: Jan. 9, 1913, in California; died April 22, 1994
Political Party: Republican
Vice Presidents: Spiro T. Agnew, Gerald R. Ford

DID YOU KNOW? Nixon was the first President to resign.

"I like the job I have, but if I had to live my life over again, I would
like to have ended up a sportswriter."

★

38 GERALD R. FORD (SERVED 1974–1977)

Born: July 14, 1913, in Nebraska
Political Party: Republican
Vice President: Nelson A. Rockefeller

DID YOU KNOW? After college, Ford was a football coach, a park ranger
and a male model.

"Truth is the glue that holds governments together. Compromise is
the oil that makes governments go."

★

39 JIMMY CARTER (SERVED 1977–1981)

Born: Oct. 1, 1924, in Georgia
Political Party: Democratic
Vice President: Walter F. Mondale

DID YOU KNOW? Carter won the Nobel Peace Prize in October 2002.

"We are of course a nation of differences. Those differences don't
make us weak. They're the source of our strength."

★

40 RONALD W. REAGAN (SERVED 1981–1989)

Born: Feb. 6, 1911, in Illinois
Political Party: Republican
Vice President: George H.W. Bush

DID YOU KNOW? Reagan worked for nearly 30 years as a
Hollywood actor.

"America is too great for small dreams."

★

41 GEORGE H.W. BUSH (SERVED 1989–1993)

Born: June 12, 1924, in Massachusetts
Political Party: Republican
Vice President: J. Danforth Quayle

DID YOU KNOW? Bush was the first President to spend a holiday with
troops overseas—Thanksgiving in Saudi Arabia.

"I want a kinder, gentler nation."

go Read about a reporter who covered nine U.S.
Presidents @ *www.timeforkids.com/presidents*

42 WILLIAM J. CLINTON (SERVED 1993–2001)

Born: Aug. 19, 1946, in Arkansas
Political Party: Democratic
Vice President: Albert Gore Jr.

DID YOU KNOW? **Clinton was the second of two Presidents to be impeached. The Senate acquitted him.**

"There is nothing wrong in America that can't be fixed with what is right in America."

43 GEORGE W. BUSH (SERVED 2001–)

Born: July 6, 1946, in Connecticut
Political Party: Republican
Vice President: Richard B. Cheney

DID YOU KNOW? **George W. Bush was an owner of the Texas Rangers baseball team from the late 1980s until 1998.**

"We will bring the terrorists to justice; or we will bring justice to the terrorists. Either way, justice will be done."

All in the Family

These Presidents were related to one another—some distantly, others very closely.

  George W. Bush (the 43rd President) is the son of George H.W. Bush (the 41st President).

John Quincy Adams (the 6th President) was the son of John Adams (the 2nd President).

  Benjamin Harrison (the 23rd President) was the grandson of William Henry Harrison (the 9th President).

James Madison (the 4th President) and Zachary Taylor (the 12th President) were second cousins.

  Franklin Delano Roosevelt (the 32nd President) was a fifth cousin of Theodore Roosevelt (the 26th President).

Genealogists have determined that F.D.R. was distantly related to a total of 11 U.S. Presidents, 5 by blood and 6 by marriage: Theodore Roosevelt, John Adams, John Quincy Adams, Ulysses Grant, William Henry Harrison, Benjamin Harrison, James Madison, William Taft, Zachary Taylor, Martin Van Buren and George Washington.

Homework TIP

Keep old papers, quizzes and tests. You may need them for future projects or to study for tests.

 For biographies of all the Presidents
WWW.FACTMONSTER.COM

White House Facts

★ The White House has 132 rooms, including 35 bathrooms. The building features 147 windows, 412 doors, 12 chimneys, 8 staircases and 3 elevators.

★ The White House has 6 floors—2 basements, 2 floors for the First Family and 2 floors for offices and visitors.

★ About 6,000 people visit the White House every day.

★ The British burned the White House during the War of 1812. The building was restored, and the smoke-stained, gray stone walls were painted white.

★ President Theodore Roosevelt gave the White House its official name in 1901. It has also been known as the President's Palace, the President's House and the Executive Mansion.

TFK Top 5 Presidential Landslides

What do Bill Clinton and Franklin D. Roosevelt have in common? Both Democratic Presidents were re-elected by defeating Republicans from Kansas. But F.D.R . really stomped his second-term opponent. He won 60.8% of the popular vote to Alfred Landon's 36.5%. Clinton's margin over Robert Dole was much smaller: 49% to 41%. Here are the Presidents who rode into the White House on the biggest waves of popular support.

1. Lyndon B. Johnson (D, 1964) 61.1%
2. Franklin D. Roosevelt (D, 1936) 60.8%
3. Richard M. Nixon (R, 1972) 60.7%
4. Warren G. Harding (R, 1920) 60.3%
5. Ronald W. Reagan (R, 1984) 58.8%

Source: Vital Statistics on American Politics

go Tour a pint-size replica of the nation's most famous home at *www.timeforkids.com/whitehouse*

Words to Remember

During each election season, presidential candidates create catchy slogans to help attract voters. Here's a look at some of the more memorable ones.

★ **"Tippecanoe and Tyler Too"** In 1811, General William Henry Harrison won an important battle against the Indians—the Battle of Tippecanoe, in Indiana. He and vice-presidential candidate John Tyler used the slogan in 1840 to remind voters of his victory.

★ **"Vote Yourself a Farm"** In the 1860 election, **Abraham Lincoln** strongly favored legislation that would give any person settling in the West a free homestead.

★ **"Full Dinner Pail"** William McKinley used the slogan in his 1900 campaign for reelection to recall the prosperity the country experienced during his first term.

★ **"He Kept Us Out of War"** The U.S. had not participated in World War I during Woodrow Wilson's first term (1913–1916). But in 1917, shortly after his reelection, the U.S. did enter the war.

★ **"Return to Normalcy"** In the 1920 election, Warren G. Harding promised that under him, life would return to normal following the dark days of World War I.

★ **"A Chicken in Every Pot and a Car in Every Garage"** During the 1928 election, Herbert Hoover told voters that they would be well off economically if he were President. Little did he know that he would soon face the worst depression in the country's history.

★ **"I Like Ike"** Dwight Eisenhower drew on his nickname and his personal appeal for his short but memorable 1952 slogan. For his reelection campaign in 1956, he used the slogan "Peace, Prosperity, Progress," calling for peace and a strong economy in the years after the U.S. fought in the Korean War.

Did You Know?

In addition to serving one term as President, John Quincy Adams also served as a Senator, a Congressman and as Secretary of State.

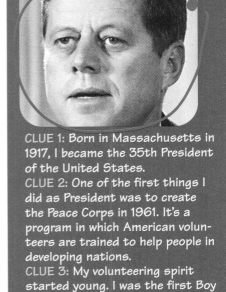

TFK Mystery Person

CLUE 1: Born in Massachusetts in 1917, I became the 35th President of the United States.
CLUE 2: One of the first things I did as President was to create the Peace Corps in 1961. It's a program in which American volunteers are trained to help people in developing nations.
CLUE 3: My volunteering spirit started young. I was the first Boy Scout to become President.

WHO AM I?

(See Answer Key that begins on page 340.)

RELIGION

	JUDAISM	CHRISTIANITY
FOUNDER	The Hebrew leader **Abraham** founded Judaism around 2000 B.C. **Moses** gave the Jews the Torah around 1250 B.C.	**Jesus Christ**, who was crucified around A.D. 30 in Jerusalem
HOW MANY GODS	One	One
HOLY WRITINGS	The most important are the **Torah**, or the five books of Moses. Others include Judaism's oral tradition, which is known as the **Talmud** when it is written down.	The **Bible** is the main sacred text of Christianity.
BELIEFS	Jews believe in the laws of God and the words of the prophets. In Judaism, however, actions are more important than beliefs.	Jesus taught love of God and neighbor and a concern for justice. 
TYPES	The three main types are **Orthodox, Conservative** and **Reform.** Orthodox Jews strictly follow the traditions of Judaism. Conservative Jews follow most traditional practices, but less strictly than the Orthodox. Reform Jews are the least traditional.	In 1054 Christians separated into the Eastern Orthodox Church and the Roman Catholic Church. In the early 1500s the **major Protestant groups** (Lutheran, Presbyterian and Episcopalian) came into being. A variety of other groups have since developed.
WHERE	There are large Jewish populations in **Israel** and the **U.S.**	Through its missionary activity Christianity has spread to most parts of the globe.

FIVE MAJOR FAITHS

Monotheism

Monotheism is the belief that there is only one god. **Judaism, Christianity** and **Islam** are all monotheistic faiths.

ISLAM	HINDUISM	BUDDHISM
Muhammad, who was born in A.D. 570 at Mecca, in Saudi Arabia	Hinduism has no founder. The oldest religion, it may date to prehistoric times.	Siddhartha Gautama, called the Buddha, in the 4th or 5th century B.C. in India
One	Many	None, but there are enlightened beings (Buddhas)
The Koran is the sacred book of Islam. 	The most ancient are the four Vedas.	The most important are the Tripitaka, the Mahayana Sutras, Tantra and Zen texts.
The Five Pillars, or main duties, are: profession of faith; prayer; charitable giving; fasting during the month of Ramadan; and pilgrimage to Mecca at least once.	Reincarnation is the belief that all living things are caught in a cycle of death and rebirth. Life is ruled by the laws of karma, in which rebirth depends on moral behavior.	The Four Noble Truths: (1) all beings suffer; (2) desire—for possessions, power and so on—causes suffering; (3) desire can be overcome; and (4) the path that leads away from desire is the Eight-fold Path (the Middle Way).
Almost 90% of Muslims are Sunnis. Shiites are the second-largest group. The Shiites split from the Sunnis in 632, when Muhammad died.	No single belief system unites Hindus. A Hindu can believe in only one god, in many or in none.	Theravada (Way of the Elders) and Mahayana (Greater Vehicle) are the two main types. 
Islam is the main religion of the Middle East, Asia and the north of Africa.	Hinduism is practiced by more than 80% of India's population.	Buddhism is the main religion in many Asian countries.

The Legacy of Pope John Paul II

The Pope's failing health did not stop him from traveling more than any other Pope in history.

In October 2003, thousands of Roman Catholics helped Pope John Paul II celebrate his 25th anniversary as the leader of the world's 1 billion Roman Catholics.

John Paul, who was born in Poland, was the first non-Italian Pope elected in more than 400 years. He traveled to more than 125 countries to promote peace. "He is truly the global Pope," said Christoph Cardinal Schoenborn of Vienna, Austria.

The Pope's accomplishments are numerous. Many say he helped end communist rule in Eastern Europe by supporting a labor union that brought down the Polish communist government. He also worked to heal divisions between Christians and Jews. He was the first Pope to make an official visit to a synagogue and a mosque. However, the Pope's conservative views troubled many Catholics, especially his opposition to letting women enter the priesthood and allowing priests to marry.

Hierarchy of the Roman Catholic Church

Sean Patrick O'Malley, the Archbishop of Boston

POPE The head of the church, the Pope is based in the Vatican in Italy. He defines the church's views on faith and morals.

CARDINAL Appointed by the Pope, 224 cardinals make up the College of the Cardinals. The international group advises the Pope and chooses a new one when the Pope dies.

ARCHBISHOP The leader of a group of churches, which is called a diocese or an archdiocese. A cardinal can also be an archbishop.

BISHOP A bishop, like a priest, is ordained to the position. He is a teacher of church doctrine, a priest of sacred worship and a minister of church government.

PRIEST An ordained minister who can give most of the sacraments, including the Eucharist, baptism and marriage.

DEACON A transitional deacon is a seminarian (student) studying for the priesthood. A permanent deacon can be married and helps a priest by performing some of the sacraments.

TOP 10

Organized Religions in the World

RELIGION	MEMBERS
1. CHRISTIANITY	1.9 BILLION
2. ISLAM	1.1 BILLION
3. HINDUISM	781 MILLION
4. BUDDHISM	324 MILLION
5. SIKHISM	19 MILLION
6. JUDAISM	14 MILLION
7. BAHA'ISM	6.1 MILLION
8. CONFUCIANISM	5.3 MILLION
9. JAINISM	4.9 MILLION
10. SHINTOISM	2.8 MILLION

Sources: Encyclopedia Britannica and *www.Adherents.com*

Top Religious Groups in the United States

About 140 million Americans belong to a religious group. Here's a breakdown:

Religious Body	Adherents
1. PROTESTANT	66 MILLION
2. CATHOLIC	62 MILLION
3. JEWISH	6 MILLION
4. MORMON	4 MILLION
5. MUSLIM	1.6 MILLION

Source: Religious Congregation and Membership

TFK Top 5 Muslim Nations

People who practice Islam are called Muslims. These countries have the most Muslims.

1. INDONESIA
2. PAKISTAN
3. INDIA
4. BANGLADESH
5. TURKEY

Source: TIME magazine

TFK Mystery Person

CLUE 1: I was born in Germany in 1483. In my early years I was a devout Catholic.

CLUE 2: Over time, I began to disagree with some practices of the church. In 1517, I wrote my disagreements in 95 theses, or arguments.

CLUE 3: My attempts to reform the church led to the start of a new Christian religion called Protestantism.

WHO AM I?

(See Answer Key that begins on page 340.)

SCIENCE

The Code Breaker

AN INTERVIEW WITH SCIENTIST JAMES WATSON

On February 28, 1953, James Watson of the United States and Francis Crick of England made one of the greatest scientific discoveries in history. "We have found the secret of life," Crick announced, according to Watson. What the two scientists had actually found is the structure of DNA, the chemical that carries the recipe for every living thing. In 1962, they were awarded the Nobel Prize for this work. Fifty years after Watson helped unravel DNA, TIME For Kids asked him a few questions.

Q: Fifty years ago, you and Francis Crick solved the structure of DNA before anyone else did. What special talents or qualities allowed you to do that?

A: We were probably more interested in DNA than anyone else was. It was the only scientific problem I wanted to think about.

TFK reporter Noah Sneider interviews James Watson in California.

Q: Has progress in DNA study been faster or slower than you expected?

A: Much faster. I didn't expect we would know the complete sequence of human DNA. This is 3 billion letters long!

Q: What advances in DNA do you think will help the world most?

A: My own particular ambition is to understand the genetic changes that give rise to cancer and to see this information used to treat cancer.

Q: Will scientists be able to alter genes so that we live forever? And would that be a good thing?

A: No, no. I think you always want new people, because you hope that maybe in the future, people will be better than the people of today.

Homework TIP

Be organized! Keep near you a box containing supplies such as paper, pens, pencils, rulers, a calculator and a dictionary.

Q: What advice would you give to kids who are interested in being scientists and making a discovery that could change the world?

A: Read a great deal. You don't get anywhere by merely being bright. You have to know facts. Go to the best school you can get to and take courses by the best teachers. My advice is, have friends who are bright and don't have them because they're popular. Have friends who you can learn from.

The Code of Life

The recipe for making a human or a tulip or a flea is carried in a chemical called DNA. Our genes are made of it. DNA is shaped like a twisted ladder, or double helix. The rings are made of four chemicals, abbreviated as A, C, G and T. They are arranged in a unique pattern in every kind of living thing.

Adenine

Thymine

Guanine

Cytosine

In 1953, Watson (left) and Crick posed with a DNA model in their lab in England.

Science FAQs

Have you ever wondered what makes popcorn pop or lightning flash? Here are some science questions kids frequently ask.

What causes a rainbow?

Although light looks colorless, it's made up of many colors—red, orange, yellow, green, blue, indigo and violet. These colors are known as the spectrum. When light shines into water, the rays of light refract, or bend, at different angles. Different colors bend at different angles—red bends the least and violet the most. When light passes through a raindrop at a certain angle, the rays separate into the colors of the spectrum—and you see a beautiful rainbow.

Why do some objects, such as doors and windows, get bigger and smaller?

Have you noticed that closet doors don't close as easily in the summer as they do in the winter? The reason is they expand in the heat of the summer and contract during the cold winter. Everything on earth is made up of tiny particles called molecules, which are in constant motion. When molecules heat up, they move even faster, pulling apart from one another. As they move farther apart, they take up more space, causing even solid objects to grow slightly larger. Molecules slow down as they cool, and they take up less room. This causes objects to shrink a little bit. (Water is an exception. When it freezes, its molecules line up in such a way that the ice takes up more space.) Try the experiment on page 209 to see what happens when air molecules are heated and cooled.

What makes popcorn pop?

A popcorn kernel is actually a seed. At its center is a tiny plant embryo, a life form in its earliest phase. The embryo is surrounded by soft, starchy material that contains water. Surrounding the embryo is a hard shell. When the kernel is heated to about 400° Fahrenheit, the water in the starch turns to steam. The pressure from the steam causes the kernel's shell to explode and the starch to spill out. You have to add the butter!

Why do cats always land on their feet?

Cats owe some of their nine lives to their unique skeletal structure and agility. Cats don't have a collarbone, and the bones in their spine are more flexible than those of other animals. This makes it easier for them to bend and rotate their bodies during a short fall. A fall of two or more floors, however, can seriously injure a cat. A cat's feet and legs usually can't absorb the impact of a fall from that distance or higher.

What causes lightning?

When air rises and falls within a thunderstorm, positive and negative charges form in the cloud. The bottom of the thundercloud has a negative charge, and the top has a positive charge. A flash of lightning happens when a negative charge becomes so strong that the air can't stop it from jumping from the cloud to the ground, which has a positive charge. Lightning can also form inside the cloud, moving between its positively and negatively charged areas. The average flash of lightning could light up a 100-watt light bulb for more than three months. The air near a lightning strike is hotter than the surface of the sun.

Why do I feel dizzy when I spin?

There are tubes inside your ears that are filled with liquid. The liquid moves when you move, telling your brain what position your body is in. When you spin, the liquid also spins. The liquid continues to spin after you stop. Your brain thinks you're still spinning, so you continue to feel that everything is going in circles—until the liquid stops moving.

Your Turn   Look, no Hands!

Blow up a balloon without using your mouth or your hands.

Materials
- Glass bottle, preferably one with a short neck
- Small to medium-size balloon, with the neck cut off just below the opening
- Large bowl
- Water

What To Do
1. Fill the glass bottle with warm-to-hot water. Let it sit for about three minutes, until the bottle warms up.
2. Pour cold water into the bowl until it's about 3/4 full.
3. Pour the warm water out of the bottle and into a sink.
4. Stretch the balloon over the mouth of the bottle.
5. Put the bottle into the bowl of water.

What Happened
As the air in the bottle cooled, it contracted and took up less space in the bottle. Air from outside the bottle rushed in to fill the space, and it inflated the balloon.

The Branches of Science

THE PHYSICAL SCIENCES	**Physics** The study of matter and energy and the interactions between them. Physicists study such subjects as gravity, light and time. Albert Einstein, a famous physicist, developed the Theory of Relativity.
	Chemistry The science that deals with the composition, properties, reactions and the structure of matter. The chemist Louis Pasteur, for example, discovered that heating liquids, such as milk and orange juice, kills harmful germs. This process is known as pasteurization.
	Astronomy The study of the universe beyond the Earth's atmosphere

THE EARTH SCIENCES	**Geology** The science of the origin, history and structure of the Earth, and the physical, chemical and biological changes that it has experienced or is experiencing
	Oceanography The exploration and study of the oceans
	Paleontology The science of the forms of life that existed in prehistoric or geologic periods as known from fossil remains
	Meteorology The science that deals with the atmosphere and its phenomena, such as weather and climate

THE LIFE SCIENCES (Biology)	**Botany** The study of plants
	Zoology The science that covers animals and animal life
	Genetics The study of heredity
	Medicine The science of diagnosing, treating and preventing illness, disease and injury

Did You Know?

The air we breathe is made up of several gases. Here's a breakdown:
- nitrogen 78%
- oxygen 20%
- carbon dioxide about 1%
- inert gases, called "noble gases," about 1%

The Food Chain

Plants, animals and people need each other to survive. They are linked together by their dependence on food. In a food chain, one creature is eaten by another, which in turn feeds another, and so on. Food chains exist both on land and in water. Here's an example of the food chain at work:

| Grass eaten by grasshoppers | grasshoppers eaten by frogs | frogs eaten by snakes | snakes eaten by eagles |

Earth's Timeline

Life on Earth began about 2 billion years ago, but there are no good fossils from before the Cambrian Period, which began 550–510 million years ago. The largely unknown past before then is called the Precambrian. It is divided into the Lower (older) and Upper (younger) Precambrian—also called the Archeozoic and Proterozoic Eras.

The history of Earth since the Cambrian Period began is divided into three giant chunks of time, or eras, each of which includes a number of shorter periods.

PALEOZOIC ERA

This era began 550 million years ago and lasted for 305 million years. It is sometimes called Early Life.

Period	Millions of Years Ago	Creatures That Appeared
CAMBRIAN	550-510	INVERTEBRATE SEA LIFE
ORDOVICIAN	510-439	FIRST FISH
SILURIAN	439-409	GIGANTIC SEA SCORPIONS
DEVONIAN	409-363	MORE FISH AND SEA LIFE
CARBONIFEROUS	363-290	EARLY INSECTS AND AMPHIBIANS
PERMIAN	290-245	EARLIEST TURTLES

MESOZOIC ERA

This era began 245 million years ago and lasted for 180 million years. It is sometimes called Middle Life or the Age of Reptiles.

Period	Millions of Years Ago	Creatures That Appeared
TRIASSIC	245-208	EARLY REPTILES AND MAMMALS
JURASSIC	208-146	EARLY DINOSAURS; FIRST BIRDS
CRETACEOUS	146-65	MORE DINOSAURS, BIRDS; FIRST MARSUPIALS

CENOZOIC ERA

This era began 64 million years ago and includes the geological present. It is sometimes called Recent Life or the Age of Mammals.

Period	Millions of Years Ago	Creatures That Appeared
TERTIARY	64-2	LARGER MAMMALS; MANY INSECTS; BATS
QUATERNARY	2-present	EARLY HUMANS TO MODERN HUMANS

The Elements

Elements are the building blocks of nature. Water, for example, is built from two basic ingredients: hydrogen elements and oxygen elements. Each element is a pure substance and cannot be split up into any simpler pure substances.

The smallest part of an element is an **atom.** An atom, however, is made up of even smaller particles. These are known as subatomic particles. The most important are:

- **protons,** which have positive electrical charges
- **electrons,** which have negative electrical charges
- **neutrons,** which are electrically neutral

The atomic number of an element is the number of protons in one atom of the element. Each element has a different atomic number. For example, the atomic number of hydrogen is 1, and the atomic number of oxygen is 8.

	1
H	
Hydrogen	

	6
C	
Carbon	

	7
N	
Nitrogen	

	16
S	
Sulfur	

	26
Fe	
Iron	

	53
I	
Iodine	

	79
Au	
Gold	

	92
U	
Uranium	

Types of Elements

As of 2004, scientists have discovered at least 112 different elements.

- Elements with atomic numbers 1 (hydrogen) to 92 (uranium) are found naturally on Earth.

- Those with atomic numbers 94 (plutonium) or greater are artificial elements. They have to be synthesized—that is, created by scientists in a high-tech laboratory.

- Elements with atomic numbers 101 and up are known as the transfermium elements. They are also known as heavy elements because their atoms have very large masses compared with atoms of hydrogen, the lightest of all elements.

How the Elements Are Named

Names for new elements are approved by the International Union of Pure and Applied Chemistry (IUPAC) in Geneva, Switzerland. They are often named for scientists, places or Greek or Latin words. For example, krypton (atomic number 36) is from the Greek word *kryptos,* meaning hidden, because it is colorless and odorless.

go For more informatin on all the elements, www.FACTMONSTER.COM

PERIODIC TABLE of elements

Key: NUMBER 1 · PERIOD 1 · GROUP 1 · SYMBOL H · NAME Hydrogen · WEIGHT 1.00794

Period	1	2	3	4	5	6	7	8	9	10	11	12	13	14	15	16	17	18
1	1 H Hydrogen 1.00794																	2 He Helium 4.002602
2	3 Li Lithium 6.941	4 Be Beryllium 9.012182											5 B Boron 10.811	6 C Carbon 12.0107	7 N Nitrogen 14.0067	8 O Oxygen 15.9994	9 F Flourine 18.9984032	10 Ne Neon 20.1797
3	11 Na Sodium 22.98977	12 Mg Magnesium 24.305											13 Al Aluminum 26.981538	14 Si Silicon 28.0855	15 P Phosphorus 30.973761	16 S Sulfur 32.065	17 Cl Chlorine 35.453	18 Ar Argon 39.948
4	19 K Potassium 39.0983	20 Ca Calcium 40.078	21 Sc Scandium 44.95591	22 Ti Titanium 47.867	23 V Vanadium 50.9415	24 Cr Chromium 51.9961	25 Mn Manganese 54.938049	26 Fe Iron 55.845	27 Co Cobalt 58.9332	28 Ni Nickel 58.6934	29 Cu Copper 63.546	30 Zn Zinc 65.39	31 Ga Gallium 69.723	32 Ge Germanium 72.64	33 As Arsenic 74.9216	34 Se Selenium 78.96	35 Br Bromine 79.904	36 Kr Krypton 83.8
5	37 Rb Rubidium 85.4678	38 Sr Strontium 87.62	39 Y Yttrium 88.90585	40 Zr Zirconium 91.224	41 Nb Niobium 92.90638	42 Mo Molybdenum 95.94	43 Tc Technetium 98[1]	44 Ru Ruthenium 101.07	45 Rh Rhodium 102.9055	46 Pd Palladium 106.42	47 Ag Silver 107.8682	48 Cd Cadmium 112.411	49 In Indium 114.818	50 Sn Tin 118.71	51 Sb Antimony 121.76	52 Te Tellurium 127.60	53 I Iodine 126.90447	54 Xe Xenon 131.293
6	55 Cs Cesium 132.90545	56 Ba Barium 137.327	★	72 Hf Hafnium 178.49	73 Ta Tantalum 180.9479	74 W Tungsten 183.84	75 Re Rhenium 186.207	76 Os Osmium 190.23	77 Ir Iridium 192.217	78 Pt Platinum 195.078	79 Au Gold 196.96655	80 Hg Mercury 200.59	81 Tl Thallium 204.3833	82 Pb Lead 207.2	83 Bi Bismuth 208.98038	84 Po Polonium 209[1]	85 At Astatine 210[1]	86 Rn Radon 222[1]
7	87 Fr Francium 223	88 Ra Radium 226	★★	104 Rf Rutherfordium 261[1]	105 Db Dubnium 262[1]	106 Sg Seaborgium 266[1]	107 Bh Bohrium 264[1]	108 Hs Hassium 277[1]	109 Mt Meitnerium 268[1]	110 Uun Ununnilium 281[1]	111 Uuu Unununium 272[1]	112 Uub Ununbium 285[1]	113 – (–)	114 Uuq Ununquadium 289[1]	115 – (–)	116 – (–)	117 – (–)	118 – (–)

Series															
★ Lanthanide Series 6	57 La Lanthanum 138.9055	58 Ce Cerium 140.116	59 Pr Praseodymium 140.90765	60 Nd Neodymium 144.24	61 Pm Promethium 145[1]	62 Sm Samarium 150.36	63 Eu Europium 151.964	64 Gd Gadolinium 157.25	65 Tb Terbium 158.92534	66 Dy Dysprosium 162.5	67 Ho Holmium 164.93032	68 Er Erbium 167.259	69 Tm Thulium 168.93421	70 Yb Ytterbium 173.04	71 Lu Lutetium 174.967
★★ Actinide Series 7	89 Ac Actinium 227[1]	90 Th Thorium 232.0381	91 Pa Protactinium 231.03588	92 U Uranium 238.02891	93 Np Neptunium 237[1]	94 Pu Plutonium 244[1]	95 Am Americium 243[1]	96 Cm Curium 247[1]	97 Bk Berkelium 247[1]	98 Cf Californium 251[1]	99 Es Einsteinium 252[1]	100 Fm Fermium 257[1]	101 Md Mendelevium 258[1]	102 No Nobelium 259[1]	103 Lr Lawrencium 262[1]

☐ Alkali Metals ☐ Alkaline Earth Metals ☐ Transition Metals ☐ Other Metals ☐ Non-Metals ☐ Noble Gases

Notes: Elements 110, 111, 112 and 114 are under review. A temporary system of naming recommended by J. Chatt has been used above. 1. Mass number of the longest-lived isotope that is known.
Source: International Union of Pure and Applied Chemistry (IUPAC).

Plants

Without plants, nearly all life on Earth would end. Plants provide oxygen for humans and animals to breathe, and they provide food for many animals. There are about 260,000 plant species in the world today. They are found on land, in oceans and in fresh water. They were the first living things on Earth.

Like animals, plants are organisms, or living things. These three features distinguish plants from animals: plants have chlorophyll, a green pigment necessary for photosynthesis; they are fixed in one place (they don't move); and their cell walls are made sturdy by a material called cellulose.

Plants are broadly divided into two groups: flower- and fruit-producing plants and those that do not produce flowers or fruits. Flowering and fruit plants include all garden flowers, agricultural crops, grasses, shrubs and most leaf trees. Non-flowering plants include pines, ferns, mosses and conifers (evergreen trees or shrubs that produce cones).

Photosynthesis

Photosynthesis is a process in which green plants (and some bacteria) use **energy** from the Sun, **carbon dioxide** from the air and **water** from the ground to make **oxygen** and **glucose**. Glucose is a sugar that plants use for energy and growth.

Chlorophyll is what makes the process of photosynthesis work. Chlorophyll, a green pigment, traps the energy from the Sun and helps to change it into glucose.

Photosynthesis is one example of how people and plants depend on each other. It provides us with most of the oxygen we need in order to breathe. We, in turn, exhale the carbon dioxide needed by plants.

TFK Top 5 Garden Flowers

These are the flowers grown in the most U.S. gardens.

1. Sunflowers
2. Zinnias
3. Impatiens
4. Marigolds
5. Petunias

Source: Burpee seed company

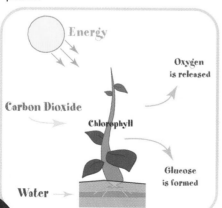

Energy

Oxygen is released

Carbon Dioxide

Chlorophyll

Glucose is formed

Water

ROCKS

Rocks are classified in **three** types based on how they are formed.

Igneous rocks are formed when molten rock (magma) from within the Earth cools and solidifies. There are two kinds: Intrusive igneous rocks solidify beneath the Earth's surface; Extrusive igneous rocks solidify at the surface.
Examples: granite, basalt, obsidian

Sedimentary rocks are formed when sediment (bits of rock plus material such as shells and sand) gets packed together. They can take millions of years to form. Most rocks that you see on the ground are sedimentary.
Examples: limestone, sandstone, shale

Metamorphic rocks are sedimentary or igneous rocks that have been transformed by heat, pressure or both. Metamorphic rocks are usually formed deep within the Earth, during a process such as mountain building.
Examples: schist, marble, slate

Minerals and Gems

Minerals are solid, inorganic (not living) substances that are found in and on Earth. Most are chemical compounds, which means they are made up of two or more elements. For example, the mineral sapphire is made up of aluminum and oxygen. A few minerals, such as gold, silver and copper, are made from a single element. Minerals are considered the building blocks of rocks. Rocks can be made up of as many as six minerals.

Many minerals, such as gold and silver, are very valuable because they are beautiful and rare. Limestone, clay and quartz are other examples of minerals. Quartz is the most common mineral.

Gems are minerals that have been cut and polished. Pearls are also gems, but they're not minerals. They are used as ornaments, like jewelry. Precious stones are the most valuable gems. They include diamonds, rubies and emeralds.

TFK Mystery Person

CLUE 1: Born in 1849, I grew up on a farm in Massachusetts.
CLUE 2: As a horticulturist in California, I bred plants to help the world's food supply. I created 800 varieties of flowers, fruits and vegetables, including new kinds of plums, peaches, lilies— and the Idaho potato.
CLUE 3: A town in California is named for me.

WHO AM I?
(See Answer Key that begins on page 340.)

Did You Know?

Most of the ocean floor is made of basalt. This igneous rock continues to flow out of the Earth from chains of underwater volcanoes known as "mid-ocean ridges."

SPACE

Our Solar System

The Sun

The solar system is made up of the **Sun** (*solar* means Sun) at its center, nine planets and the various moons, asteroids, comets and meteors controlled primarily by the Sun's gravitational pull.

Our closest star, the **Sun,** is thought to be about 4.6 billion years old. This fiery ball is 870,000 miles (1,392,000 km) across and is estimated to be more than 27,000,000°F (15,000,000°C) at its core. Did you know that more than a million Earth-size planets could fit inside the **Sun?** The Sun's great mass exerts a powerful gravitational pull on everything in our solar system, including Earth.

The Planets

Our solar system has nine planets: **Mercury, Venus, Earth, Mars, Jupiter, Saturn, Uranus, Neptune** and **Pluto.** The planets travel around the Sun in an oval-shaped path called an **orbit.** One journey around the Sun is called a **revolution.** As the planets orbit the Sun, they also spin on their axes.

Galaxies

Astronomers think that the universe could contain 40 to 50 billion galaxies—huge systems with billions of stars. Our own galaxy is the **Milky Way.** It contains about 200 billion stars.

MERCURY

VENUS

EARTH

MARS

JUPITER

SATURN

NEPTUNE

URANUS

PLUTO

The Moon

The Moon travels around Earth in an oval orbit at 22,900 miles (36,800 km) per hour. Temperatures range from -299°F (-184°C) during its night to 417°F (214°C) during its day, except at the poles, where the temperature is a constant -141°F (-96°C). The Moon's gravity affects our planet's ocean tides. The closer the Moon is to Earth, the greater the effect. The time between high tides is about 12 hours 25 minutes.

New Moon

Crescent Moon

First Quarter

Full Moon

Last Quarter

Crescent Moon

New Moon

The Planets

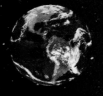

MERCURY

Named for a Roman god, a winged messenger, this planet zooms around the Sun at 30 miles per second!

Size

Two-fifths the size of Earth

Diameter

3,032.4 miles (4,880 km)

Surface

Covered by a dusty layer of minerals, the surface is made up of plains, cliffs and craters.

Atmosphere

A thin mixture of helium (95%) and hydrogen

Temperature

The sunlit side can reach 950°F (510°C). The dark side can drop to -346°F (-210°C).

Mean Distance from the Sun

36 million miles (57.9 million km)

Revolution Time
(in Earth days or years)

88 Earth days

Moons: 0
Rings: 0

VENUS

Named after the Roman goddess of love and beauty, Venus is also known as the "morning star" and "evening star" since it is visible at these times.

Size

Slightly smaller than Earth

Diameter

7,519 miles (12,100 km)

Surface

A rocky, dusty expanse of mountains, canyons and plains, with a 200-mile river of hardened lava

Atmosphere

Carbon dioxide (95%), nitrogen, sulfuric acid and traces of other elements

Temperature

Ranges from 55°F (13°C) to 396°F (202°C) at the surface

Mean Distance from the Sun

67.24 million miles (108.2 million km)

Revolution Time
(in Earth days or years)

243.1 Earth days

Moons: 0
Rings: 0

EARTH

Our planet is not perfectly round. It bulges at the equator and is flatter at the poles.

Size

Four planets in our solar system are larger and four are smaller than Earth.

Diameter

7,926.2 miles (12,756 km)

Surface

Earth is made up of water (70%), air and solid ground.

Atmosphere

Nitrogen (78%), oxygen (20%), other gases

Temperature

Averages 59°F (15°C) at sea level

Mean Distance from the Sun

92.9 million miles (149.6 million km)

Revolution Time
(in Earth days or years)

365 days, 5 hours, 46 seconds

Moons: 1
Rings: 0

THE GREAT RED SPOT

Jupiter's "Great Red Spot" is a raging storm of gases, mainly red phosphorus. The storm is larger in size than Earth and has continued for centuries with no sign of dying down.

MARS

Because of its blood-red color (which comes from iron-rich dust), this planet was named for the Roman god of war.

Size
About one-quarter the size of Earth

Diameter
,194 miles (6,794 km)

Surface
Canyons, dunes, volcanoes and polar caps of water ice and carbon dioxide ice

Atmosphere
Carbon dioxide (95%)

Temperature
As low as -305°F (-187°C)

Mean Distance from the Sun
41.71 million miles 227.9 million km)

Revolution Time
(in Earth days or years)
687 Earth days

Moons: 2

JUPITER

The largest planet in our solar system was named for the most important Roman god.

Size
11 times the diameter of Earth

Diameter
88,736 miles (142,800 km)

Surface
A hot ball of gas and liquid

Atmosphere
Whirling clouds of colored dust, hydrogen, helium, methane, water and ammonia

Temperature
-234°F (-148°C) average

Mean Distance from the Sun
483.88 million miles (778.3 million km)

Revolution Time
(in Earth days or years)
11.9 Earth years

Moons: 63
Rings: 4

SATURN

Named for the Roman god of farming, the second-largest planet has many majestic rings surrounding it.

Size
About 10 times larger than Earth

Diameter
74,97.8 miles (120,660 km)

Surface
Liquid and gas

Atmosphere
Hydrogen and helium

Temperature
-288°F (-178°C) average

Mean Distance from the Sun
887.14 million miles (1,427 million km)

Revolution Time
(in Earth days or years)
29.5 Earth years

Moons: 31
Rings: 1,000?

Planets Continued

URANUS

This greenish-blue planet is named for an ancient Greek sky god.

Size
About four times larger than Earth

Diameter
32,193 miles (51,810 km)

Surface
Little is known.

Atmosphere
Hydrogen, helium and methane

Temperature
Uniform temperature of 353°F (-214°C)

Mean Distance from the Sun
1,783,980,000 miles (2,870,000,000 km)

Revolution Time
(in Earth days or years)
84 Earth years

Moons: 27
Rings: 11

NEPTUNE

This stormy blue planet is named for an ancient Roman sea god.

Size
About four times the size of Earth

Diameter
30,775 miles (49,528 km)

Surface
A liquid layer covered with thick clouds and raging storms

Atmosphere
Hydrogen, helium, methane and ammonia

Temperature
-353°F (-214°C)

Mean Distance from the Sun
2,796,460,000 miles (4,497,000,000 km)

Revolution Time
(in Earth days or years)
164.8 Earth years

Moons: 13

PLUTO

Named for the Roman god of the underworld, Pluto is the coldest and smallest planet. Some astronomers think it is actually a large comet orbiting the Sun.

Size
Less than one-fifth the size of Earth

Diameter
1,423 miles? (2,290 km?)

Surface
A giant snowball of methane and water mixed with rock

Atmosphere
Methane

Temperature
Between -369° and -387°F (-223° and -233°C)

Mean Distance from the Sun
3,666,000,000 miles (5,900,000,000 km)

Revolution Time
(in Earth days or years)
248.5 Earth years

Moons: 1
Rings: ?

The Constellations

For more than 5,000 years, people have looked into the night sky and seen the same stars we see today. They noticed groups of stars and connected them with imaginary lines. These groups are known as **constellations.** They help astronomers quickly locate other objects in the sky. There are 88 recognized constellations. The constellations on this page appear in the sky in North America during the summer.

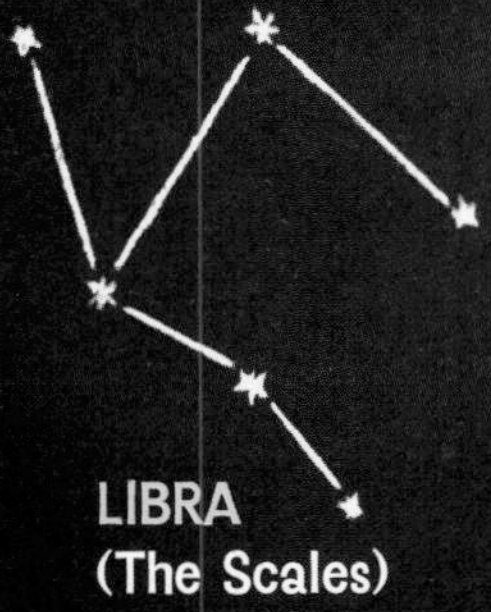

LIBRA
(The Scales)

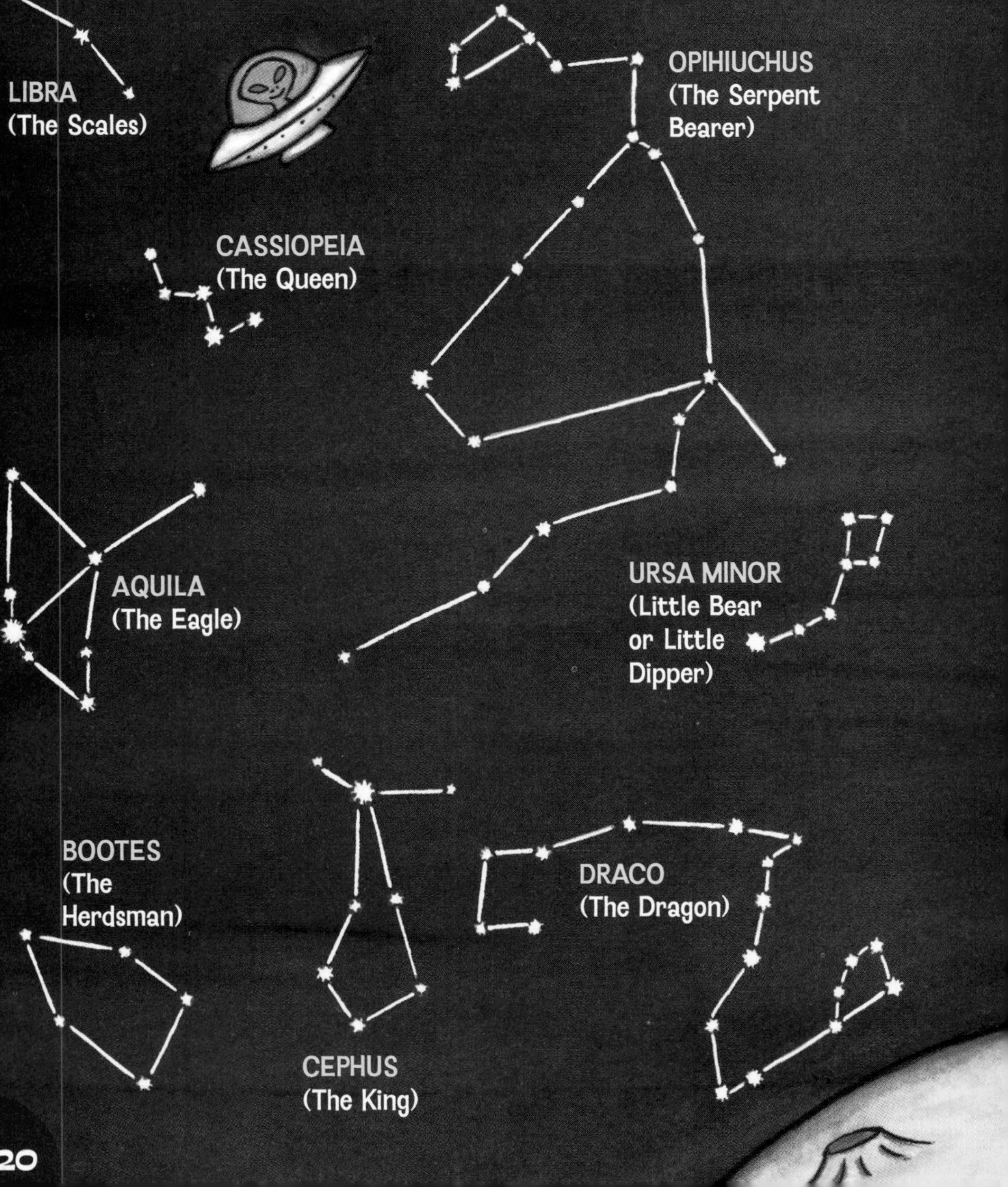

OPIHIUCHUS
(The Serpent Bearer)

CASSIOPEIA
(The Queen)

AQUILA
(The Eagle)

URSA MINOR
(Little Bear
or Little
Dipper)

BOOTES
(The
Herdsman)

DRACO
(The Dragon)

CEPHUS
(The King)

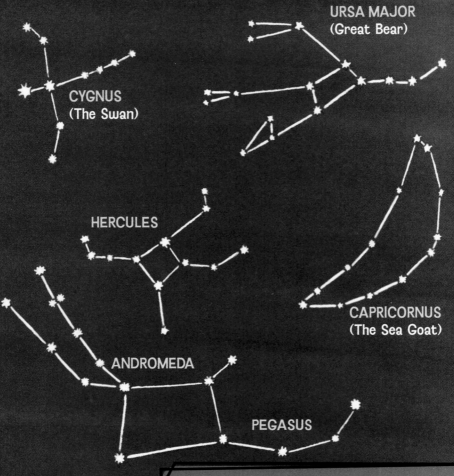

CYGNUS
(The Swan)

URSA MAJOR
(Great Bear)

HERCULES

CAPRICORNUS
(The Sea Goat)

ANDROMEDA

PEGASUS

THE ZODIAC	Twelve constellations, together called "the Zodiac," form a circle around Earth.	
AQUARIUS	Water Bearer	JAN. 20 – FEB. 19
PISCES	Fish	FEB. 20 – MARCH 20
ARIES	Ram	MARCH 21 – APRIL 19
TAURUS	Bull	APRIL 20 – MAY 20
GEMINI	Twins	MAY 21 – JUNE 20
CANCER	Crab	JUNE 21 – JULY 22
LEO	Lion	JULY 23 – AUG. 22
VIRGO	Virgin	AUG. 23 – SEPT. 22
LIBRA	Scales	SEPT. 23 – OCT. 22
SCORPIO	Scorpion	OCT. 23 – NOV. 21
SAGITTARIUS	Archer	NOV. 22 – DEC. 21
CAPRICORN	Sea Goat	DEC. 22 – JAN. 19

China's Big Launch
By Jill Eagan

With a bright flash and a mighty blast, China launched its first human into space in October 2003. Yang Liwei, 38, traveled alone inside the *Shenzou 5* (*shun-joe*) capsule.

"I'm feeling very good," he told his wife, Zhang Yumei, and 8-year-old son as he zoomed through space. Yang returned safely, landing in the grasslands of northern China after 21 hours in orbit.

"I saw our planet," he said after landing. "It's so beautiful."

Until now, only American, Russian or Soviet programs had launched a person into space. The first taikonaut (*tie-ko-not*) kicks off an ambitious space quest. The Chinese also aim to land a robot explorer on the moon, build a space station and "establish a base on the moon," said Ouyang Ziyuan of China's lunar-expedition program.

A rocket carried China's first "taikonaut," Yang Liwei (left). *Taikon* is the Chinese word for "space."

TFK Puzzles & Games

Spaced Out!
All these familiar-looking images are really out of this world. Can you figure out what heavenly body each object suggests?

(See Answer Key that begins on page 340.)

1957 The Soviet Union launches **Sputnik**, the first satellite.

1961 Soviet Yuri Gagarin is the first space traveler. Less than a month later, Alan Shepard Jr. becomes the first American in space.

1962 **John Glenn** is the first American to orbit Earth.

1963 Soviet Valentina Tereshkova becomes the first woman in space.

1965 Soviet cosmonaut Alexei Leonov makes the first space walk.

1969 Apollo 11 astronaut Neil Armstrong becomes the first human to walk on the moon.

1971 The Soviet Union launches the world's first space station, *Salyut 1.*

1973 The United States sends its first space station, *Skylab,* into orbit.

1976 *Viking I* is the first spacecraft to land on Mars.

1981 U.S. space shuttle **Columbia**, the world's first reusable spacecraft, is launched.

1986 The space shuttle *Challenger* explodes 73 seconds after liftoff. Six astronauts and civilian Christa McAuliffe die.

1990 The Hubble Space Telescope is put into orbit.

1998 The Russian *Proton* rocket makes the first flight to the International Space Station. The U.S. space shuttle *Endeavor* follows.

2000 The first crew reaches the **International Space Station.**

2003 The space shuttle *Columbia* breaks up over Texas during re-entry; seven astronauts die. An image taken by a powerful satellite confirms the universe is 13.7 billion years old and supports the theory that the universe formed in a giant burst of energy called the Big Bang.

2004 The Mars rovers *Spirit* and *Opportunity* send detailed, color images of the surface of Mars back to Earth. President George W. Bush unveils plans to send astronauts on missions to the Moon and Mars.

Eclipses

A **SOLAR ECLIPSE** occurs when the Moon is in its new phase and it moves between the Sun and the Earth, blocking the Sun's light from a small part of the Earth. In a **TOTAL SOLAR ECLIPSE,** the Moon completely obscures the Sun.

During an **ANNULAR ECLIPSE** (annular means "ring"), the Moon blocks out most of the Sun's disk, leaving just a ring of light that is still visible around the edge. In a **LUNAR ECLIPSE,** the Earth blocks the Sun's light from the Moon.

Mark Your Calendar!

Here are the dates for lunar and solar eclipses in 2004 and 2005. Check the newspaper to see if the upcoming eclipses are visible where you live.

2004

April 19 Partial eclipse of the Sun
May 4 Total eclipse of the Moon
Oct. 14 Partial eclipse of the Sun
Oct. 28 Total eclipse of the Moon

2005

April 8 Annular eclipse of the Sun
October 3 Annular eclipse of the Sun
October 17 Partial eclipse of the Moon

Your Turn

Lights Out: Make Your Own Solar Eclipse

Materials

▶ Flashlight ▶ Orange ▶ Ball of clay, about one-third the size of the orange ▶ Ruler

What To Do

1. Put the orange and the clay in a line on a table, about eight inches apart.
2. Stand about two feet away from the table. Hold the flashlight at the same level as the clay and orange, then shine the light from behind the clay ball.
3. Check out the shadow on the orange!

What Happened

In the experiment, the clay represents the Moon, the flashlight is the Sun and the orange is the Earth. When the Moon blocks the Sun's light from the Earth, it casts a shadow on Earth. The darker, middle part of the shadow is called the umbra. The lighter shadow on the outer rim is called the penumbra.

Astronomical Terms

Between the orbits of Mars and Jupiter are an estimated 30,000 pieces of rocky debris, known collectively as the asteroids, or planetoids (small planets). Ceres, the largest asteroid, measures about 600 miles across. It was the first asteroid discovered, on New Year's night in 1801.

A black hole is a mysterious, dense object with a gravity so strong that even light cannot escape from it. That's why black holes are almost impossible to see.

A comet is an enormous "snowball" of frozen gases (mostly carbon dioxide, methane and water vapor). Comets originate in the outer solar system. As comets move toward the Sun, heat from the Sun turns some of the snow into gas, which begins to glow and is seen as the comet's tail. Halley's comet was discovered more than 2,000 years ago. It appears every 76 years.

A galaxy is a collection of gas and millions of stars held together by gravity. Almost everything you see in the sky belongs to our galaxy, the Milky Way. This system is about 100,000 light-years in diameter and about 10,000 light-years in thickness.

Gravity is the force that draws objects to each other. On Earth, gravity pulls things down, toward the center of the planet. That's why things fall down.

A light year is the distance light travels in one year. It equals 5.88 trillion miles.

A meteor is a small piece of cosmic matter. When a meteor enters our atmosphere, it is called a meteoroid. It is also known as a shooting star, because it burns while passing through the air. Larger meteoroids that survive the journey through the atmosphere and land on Earth are called meteorites.

The asteroid Galileo

TFK Top 5 Largest Moons

NAME	PLANET	DIAMETER (MI)
1. GANYMEDE	Jupiter	3,274
2. TITAN	Saturn	3,200
3. CALLISTO	Jupiter	2,400
4. IO	Jupiter	2,262
5. MOON	Earth	2,160

TFK Mystery Person

CLUE 1: Growing up in the Bronx, New York, I was interested in the night sky and learned as much as I could about astronomy.
CLUE 2: After graduating from Harvard, I became an astro-physicist.
CLUE 3: In 1996, I was appointed Director of the Hayden Planetarium in New York City.

WHO AM I?
(See Answer Key that begins on page 340.)

A spiraling galaxy

For more on space, go www.FACTMONSTER.COM

SPORTS

OLYMPIC GLORY IN GREECE

For centuries, the world's best athletes have competed in the Olympic Games. In 2004, history's most amazing sports spectacle returns to Greece, the birthplace of the ancient Olympics. A total of 10,500 athletes from all over the world are competing in the Summer Olympics in Athens, the capital of Greece and host to the first modern Olympic Games in 1896.

Birth of the Games

The Games began more than 2,700 years ago. They were called the Olympics because they were first held on the plains of Olympia. In ancient times, the Games were based on Greek myths. They took place every four years with sports competitions and a religious festival that honored Greek gods. The competitions began with short foot races and grew to include distance running, jumping and discus throwing.

About 300 athletes from 13 countries participated in the first modern Olympics in Athens in 1896. They competed in nine different sports: track and field, swimming, cycling, fencing, gymnastics, shooting, lawn tennis, wrestling and weight lifting. The Games were a huge success, and for the next 108 years, the Olympics traveled to countries all over the world.

Return to Athens

The 28th Olympic Games feature competitions in 28 sports. The opening of the games is marked by torchbearers passing the Olympic flame from ancient Olympia to Athens. The Games span 16 days, from August 13 to 29, and include 301 medal ceremonies.

An incredible 21,500 journalists cover the competition in 35 locations. Security is a priority. About 45,000 people (including police

BY DINA EL NABLI

Countries with the Most All-Time Medals

Summer	Gold	Silver	Bronze	Total
1. U.S.A.	872	658	586	2,116
2. U.S.S.R.* (1952-88)	395	319	296	1,010
3. Great Britain	180	233	225	638

Winter	Gold	Silver	Bronze	Total
1. Norway	94	94	75	263
2. U.S.S.R.* (1956-88)	78	57	59	194
3. U.S.A.	69	72	52	193

*In 1991 the U.S.S.R. (Union of Soviet Socialist Republics) broke up into several countries, including Russia.

Upcoming Olympic Games

2006	(WINTER)	Turin, Italy
2008	(SUMMER)	Beijing, China
2010	(WINTER)	Vancouver, B.C., Canada

officers, members of the military and volunteers) are on hand to keep Olympic Village safe.

As usual, the Paralympic Games immediately follow the Olympic games. Second only to the Olympics in size, the Paralympics feature competitions between the world's best athletes with physical disabilities.

Hosting the Olympics is a chance for the historic city of Athens to stand proud. In the end, the Olympics aren't just about winning. The real thrill comes from competing against the best athletes in the world. And for many, watching the competition proves to be the greatest show on earth.

go How much do you know about the Olympics? Find out at www.timeforkids.com/olympicmeet

BASEBALL

Many people believe that baseball was invented in 1839 by Abner Doubleday at Cooperstown, New York, the site of the Hall of Fame and National Museum of Baseball. But research has proved that a game called "base ball" was played in the U.S. and in England before 1839.

The first baseball game as we know it was played at Elysian Fields, Hoboken, New Jersey, on June 19, 1846, between the Knickerbockers and the New York Nine.

The Little League World Series

The Little League World Series—the sport's annual world-championship tournament—has been played in Williamsport, Pennsylvania, every year since 1947. Tokyo, Japan, grabbed the 2003 crown with a 10–1 win over East Boynton Beach, Florida. Taiwan has won 16 times, more than any other foreign country.

Teams representing towns in the U.S. have won 27 times. California has five championship wins; Connecticut, New Jersey and Pennsylvania each have four wins, and New York and Texas have two each.

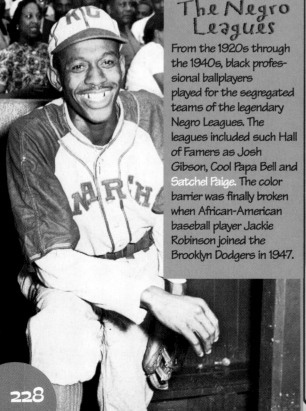

2003 World Series

The **Florida Marlins** beat the New York Yankees 2–0 in game 6 to win their second world championship. Quite a feat, considering the team is only 11 years old. The Yankees, however, have won an astonishing 26 World Series in 38 appearances.

The Negro Leagues

From the 1920s through the 1940s, black professional ballplayers played for the segregated teams of the legendary Negro Leagues. The leagues included such Hall of Famers as Josh Gibson, Cool Papa Bell and Satchel Paige. The color barrier was finally broken when African-American baseball player Jackie Robinson joined the Brooklyn Dodgers in 1947.

Top Players of 2003

Most Valuable Player
A.L.—Alex Rodriguez, Texas Rangers
N.L.—Barry Bonds, San Francisco Giants

Cy Young Award (Best Pitcher)
A.L.—Roy Halladay, Toronto Blue Jays
N.L.—Eric Gagne, Los Angeles Dodgers

Rookie of the Year
A.L.—Angel Berroa, Kansas City Royals
N.L.—Dontrelle Willis, Florida Marlins

Home-Run Champions
A.L.—Alex Rodriguez, Texas Rangers, 47 home runs

N.L.—Jim Thome, Philadelphia Phillies, 47 home runs

Batting Champions
A.L.—Bill Mueller, Boston Red Sox , .326 batting average

N.L.—Albert Pujols, St. Louis Cardinals, .359 batting average

Basketball

In 1891, Dr. James Naismith invented basketball in Springfield, Massachusetts. The game was originally played with a soccer ball and two peach bushel baskets, which is how the game got its name. Twelve of the 13 rules Naismith created are still part of the game. One thing has changed—originally there were nine players on each team. Now there are only five. The Basketball Hall of Fame is named in Naismith's honor.

TOP 5 CAREER NBA SCORERS	AVERAGE POINTS PER GAME
MICHAEL JORDAN	31.0
WILT CHAMBERLAIN	30.1
SHAQUILLE O'NEAL	27.6
ELGIN BAYLOR	27.4
ALLEN IVERSON	27.0

2003 Basketball Championships

NBA (National Basketball Association)
The San Antonio Spurs beat the New Jersey Nets, 4 games to 2.

WNBA (Women's National Basketball Association)
The Detroit Shock beat the Los Angeles Sparks, 2 games to 1.

WNBA Hot Shots

2003 SCORING LEADERS

PLAYER	GAMES	POINTS	AVERAGE
Lauren Jackson, Seattle	33	698	21.2
Chamique Holdsclaw, Washington	27	554	20.5
Tamika Catchings, Indiana	34	671	19.7

Did You Know?

Wilt Chamberlain of the Philadelphia Warriors scored 100 points in one game. It was against the New York Knicks on March 2, 1962. No other player has repeated the spectacular accomplishment.

FOOTBALL

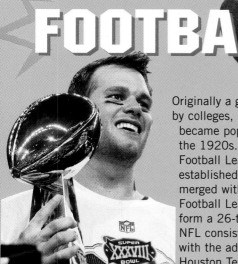

Originally a game played by colleges, professional football became popular in America in the 1920s. The National Football League (NFL) was established in 1922 and merged with the American Football League in 1970 to form a 26-team league. The NFL consists of 32 teams with the addition of the Houston Texans in 2002.

Super Bowl Déjà Vu

New England Patriots kicker Adam Vinatieri booted a 41-yard field goal with just four seconds on the clock to give the Patriots a 32–29 win over the Carolina Panthers in Super Bowl XXXVIII. The win marks the second time in three years the Patriots have won the Super Bowl. Patriots quarterback **Tom Brady** was named the Super Bowl's Most Valuable Player.

FUTURE SUPER BOWL SITES

2005	Super Bowl XXXIX (39)	Jacksonville, Florida
2006	Super Bowl XL (40)	Detroit, Michigan
2007	Super Bowl XLI (41)	Miami, Florida
2008	Super Bowl XLII (42)	Glendale, Arizona

2003 Top Players

PASSING LEADER
Peyton Manning, Indianapolis Colts (4,267 yards)
RUSHING LEADER
Jamal Lewis, Baltimore Ravens (2,066 yards)
RECEIVING LEADER
Torry Holt, Seattle Seahawks (1,696 yards)
TOUCHDOWNS
Priest Holmes, Kansas City Chiefs (27)
INTERCEPTIONS (TIE)
Brian Russell, Minnesota Vikings (9)
Tony Parrish, San Francisco 49ers (9)
SACKS
Michael Strahan, New York Giants (18.5)

Football Phenomena

MOST POINTS SCORED IN A GAME:
● The Washington Redskins beat the New York Giants, 72–41, on Nov. 27, 1966.
LONGEST FIELD GOAL: 63 yards (tie)
● Tom Dempsey, New Orleans Saints vs. Detroit Lions, Nov. 8, 1970
● Jason Elam, Denver Broncos vs. Jacksonville Jaguars, Oct. 25, 1998

LONGEST TOUCHDOWN RUN: 99 yards
● Tony Dorsett, Dallas Cowboys vs. Minnesota Vikings, Jan. 3, 1983

Puzzles & Games

Find the Captain

One of these football players was just voted captain of the team.
Follow the clues in the box to figure out who it is. What is his number?

CLUES

1. The new captain does NOT have an odd number on his jersey.
2. He has freckles on his face.
3. He is next to a player who isn't wearing a helmet.

(See Answer Key that begins on page 340.)

College Basketball

March Madness

Fans describe the end of college-basketball season as "March Madness." That's because the men's and women's championship tournaments are held in March and feature more than 100 of the best teams in the country. Most of the games are exciting and many have dramatic finishes.

Tennessee holds the most women's titles (six). In 2003, Syracuse University won the men's title, and the University of Connecticut won the women's title.

TFK Top 5 "March Madness" Champions

For college basketball fans, the battle begins March 16, when the first two of the 65 NCAA (National Collegiate Athletic Association) men's teams start competing for the National Championship title. Here are the men's teams that have won the most titles.

1. UCLA	11 wins
2. Kentucky	7 wins
3. Indiana	5 wins
4. Duke	3 wins
5. North Carolina	3 wins

More Than Just Lions, Tigers and Bears

A lot of college sports teams have nicknames like Tigers, Wildcats and Huskies. But some team names are more unconventional. Here is an explanation of how a few teams got their unusual nicknames.

BLUE DEVILS—DUKE UNIVERSITY

Chosen in a contest run by the student paper in 1921, the nickname is borrowed from a legendary group of French World War I mountain soldiers known as "les Diables Bleus."

JAYHAWKS—UNIVERSITY OF KANSAS

Believed to be a combination of two birds—the hawk and the blue jay—the Jayhawk has been associated with the school since 1866. It was once a nickname used for lawless pioneers, but during the Civil War, Kansas's first cavalry was named as the "Independent Mounted Kansas Jayhawks."

TROJANS—UNIVERSITY OF SOUTHERN CALIFORNIA

Los Angeles *Times* sports editor Owen Bird chose the school's nickname in 1912. Bird thought the nickname embodied the school's fighting spirit against often bigger and better-equipped teams. The name Trojans refers to the legendary people of Troy, who were famous for taking on the mighty Greek empire.

HOKIES—VIRGINIA TECH

When the school changed its name to the Virginia Polytechnic Institute in 1896, students submitted ideas for a new school cheer. O.M. Stull's "Hokie Yell" won the contest, and it has been used ever since. Stull said the word had no special meaning. He just wanted something that got people's attention.

College Football

Sweet Success

At the 2004 Nokia Sugar Bowl, the Louisiana State University Tigers beat the Oklahoma University Sooners 21–14. By winning the BCS (Bowl Championship Series), LSU earned a share of the national championship with the University of Southern California. The Trojans of USC beat the University of Michigan in the Rose Bowl and received the No.1 ranking in the AP poll, which is voted on by sportswriters.

Top Dog

The Heisman Trophy is an annual award given since 1935 to the most outstanding college-football player in the country. Several Heisman winners have gone on to success in the NFL and have been elected to the Pro Football Hall of Fame after retiring. Current NFL stars Eddie George (1995), Charles Woodson (1997) and Ricky Williams (1998) are recent winners. In 2003, Oklahoma quarterback **Jason White** won the award.

Other 2004 Bowl Games

Rose Bowl (Pasadena, California)
University of Southern California 28, Michigan 14

Fiesta Bowl (Tempe, Arizona)
Ohio State 35, Kansas State 28

Orange Bowl (Miami, Florida)
Miami 16, Florida State 14

Cotton Bowl (Dallas, Texas)
Mississippi 31, Oklahoma State 28

Outback Bowl (Tampa, Florida)
Iowa State 37, Florida 17

Gator Bowl (Jacksonville, Florida)
Maryland 41, West Virginia 7

TFK NEWS

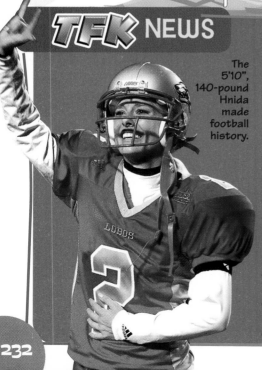

The 5'10", 140-pound Hnida made football history.

Kickin' It in College

On August 31, 2003, University of New Mexico football player **Katie Hnida**, 22, kicked her way into the record books. She became the first woman to score in a Division 1–A football game. That's no small feat—1–A college football is highly competitive. Hnida's two extra-point kicks made the 72-8 blow-out victory of her team, the Lobos, even more impressive. This was not Hnida's first trip into the record books. At a bowl game in 2002, she became the first woman in her college division ever to take the field. Hnida says she would be enjoying herself even if she weren't breaking records: "It's never been about making history. It's just about kicking. I love football so much."

Soccer

Soccer is the world's most popular sport. Known as football throughout the rest of the world, soccer is played by boys, girls, men and women of nearly all ages. Hundreds of millions of people play around the world.

The World Cup

The world's biggest soccer tournament is called the World Cup. It's played every four years by teams made up of each country's best players.

Germany won the women's World Cup in 2003, while Brazil was the winner of the men's World Cup in 2002. The next men's World Cup tournament will be held in 2006 in Germany. China will host the women's World Cup in 2007.

Homework TIP

Ask questions! If you don't understand an assignment, speak up. Chances are, your classmates don't understand it either.

World Cup Champions

Men		Women	
1930	Uruguay	1991	U.S.A.
1934	Italy	1995	Norway
1938	Italy	1999	U.S.A.
1942-1946	not held	2003	Germany
1950	Uruguay		
1954	West Germany		
1958	Brazil		
1962	Brazil		
1966	England		
1970	Brazil		
1974	West Germany		
1978	Argentina		
1982	Italy		
1986	Argentina		
1990	West Germany		
1994	Brazil		
1998	France		
2002	Brazil		

TFK NEWS

Freddy is the highest-paid player in Major League Soccer.

He's Having a Ball

Soccer star **Freddy Adu** has more on his mind than scrimmages and orange slices. At 14, he is already one of the top soccer prospects in the world. Born in Ghana, Africa, Freddy became an American citizen in 2002 after moving with his family to Maryland in 1997.

In late 2003, Freddy signed with D.C. United, a major-league soccer team. He is the youngest person to play in a major U.S. sports league since 1887. That's when 14-year-old Fred Chapman played Major League Baseball.

"If you're good enough, you're old enough," says Freddy.

HOCKEY

Ice hockey, by birth and upbringing a Canadian game, is an offshoot of field hockey. Some historians say that the first ice hockey game was played in Montreal in December 1879 between two teams composed almost exclusively of McGill University students, but others believe that earlier hockey games took place in Kingston, Ontario, or Halifax, Nova Scotia.

In the Montreal game of 1879, there were 15 players on a side. The players used an assortment of sticks to keep the puck in motion. Early rules allowed nine men on a side, but the number was reduced to seven in 1886 and later to six.

In the winter of 1894–1895, a group of college students from the United States visited Canada and saw hockey played. Enthusiastic about the game, they introduced it as a winter sport when they returned home.

NHL All-Time Career Point Scorers

	Goals	Assists	Points
1. WAYNE GRETZKY	894	1,963	2,857
2. GORDIE HOWE	801	1,049	1,850
3. MARK MESSIER	686	1,173	1,859
4. MARCEL DIONNE	731	1,040	1,771
5. RON FRANCIS	541	1,225	1,766

(Through December 14, 2003)

Top Goalies

THESE GOALTENDERS HAVE WON THE MOST GAMES.

	PLAYER	GAMES	WINS	LOSES	TIES
1.	PATRICK ROY	1,029	551	315	131
2.	TERRY SAWCHUK	971	447	330	172
3.	JACQUES PLANTE	837	435	247	146
4.	TONY ESPOSITO	886	423	306	152
5.	GLENN HALL	906	407	326	163

Original Six

Between 1942 and 1967, the NHL consisted of just six teams—Boston Bruins, Chicago Blackhawks, Detroit Red Wings, Montreal Canadiens, New York Rangers and Toronto Maple Leafs. As you might expect, the teams got to know one another pretty well. They had to play each other 14 times during the regular season. Today there are 30 teams in the NHL.

The Stanley Cup

Each player on the team that wins the NHL championship gets his name engraved on the **STANLEY CUP** along with all the previous winners. The original cup was only seven inches high; now it stands about three feet tall. The Montreal Canadiens have won the most titles with 23.

234

Golf

It may be that golf originated in Holland—historians believe it did—but certainly Scotland developed the game and is famous for it. Formal competiton began in 1860 with the British Open championship.

Tiger, Watch Your Tail!

Six-foot-tall golfer **MICHELLE WIE** (Wee), of Hawaii, is head and shoulders above most competitors. In 2003, at 13, she won the U.S. Women's Amateur Public Links Championship, tied for ninth place in the Kraft Nabisco Championship and placed a respectable 39th in the U.S. Women's Open. She's the youngest player ever to finish in the Top 10 at a Ladies Professional Golf Association Tour event. Michelle took up golf at age 4, and at age 12 could drive the ball 300 yards. She began competing with men on the PGA Tour in early 2004 and dreams of playing at the all-male Masters tournament: "It is possible!"

Tee Time

The four major events in men's professional golf (the Grand Slam) are:

> The Masters
> British Open
> U.S. Open
> PGA Championship

The four major events in women's professional golf (the Women's Grand Slam) are:

> LPGA Championship
> U.S. Women's Open
> Nabisco Championship
> Women's British Open

The **Ryder Cup** is the most prestigious team golf event in the world. It is played every two years between a team of American golfers and a team of European golfers.

Cycling

In 2003, **Lance Armstrong** won his fifth consecutive Tour de France, sharing the record with Spanish cyclist Miguel Induráin. His closest competitor finished only 1 minute 1 second behind him, making this Tour the toughest for Armstrong to win. This was amazing because in 1996 Armstrong had been diagnosed with cancer and was given only a 50% chance to live. Armstrong intends to go for the record-breaking sixth race in 2004.

Gymnastics

Gymnastics is one of the world's most physically demanding sports, not to mention one of the most popular sports at the Summer Olympics.

The Fédération Internationale de Gymnastique (FIG) is the organization that oversees gymnastics throughout the world. The FIG recognizes seven gymnastic areas: men's artistic gymnastics, women's artistic gymnastics, rhythmic gymnastics, trampoline, sports aerobics, sports acrobatics and noncompetitive general gymnastics. Artistic, rhythmic and trampoline gymnasts will compete in the 2004 Olympics in Athens.

Here's a look at some of the most popular events.

Artistic Gymnastics
Men and Women
Floor exercise: Gymnasts should use the entire 40-ft. by 40-ft. mat. The men's exercises require strength, flexibility and balance. Women combine dance movements, tumbling and acrobatics and use music in their routines.

Vault: The gymnast runs 82 feet and somersaults over the vaulting table.

Men
Pommel horse: The gymnast performs a series of circular and scissor movements over the "horse." The hands are the only part of the body that should touch the apparatus. He needs great upper-body strength.

Yuri Chechi

Rings: He performs backward and forward swings and holds while keeping the rings as still as possible. Tremendous balance and an acrobatic dismount are important.

Parallel bars: The athlete works along the bars and swings above and below them.

Horizontal (high) bar: He performs several swinging movements and grip changes. It's important that the body does not touch the bar. Spectacular dismounts rate high.

Ashley Postell

Women
Balance beam: Gymnasts do leaps, turns, jumps and more—on a beam 16 feet long and only four inches wide!

Uneven bars: The athletes perform continuous swinging movements in both directions, above and below the bars. Twists, somersaults, high flight and smooth dismounts will help to earn a high score.

Rhythmic Gymnastics
Rhythmic gymnasts combine sport and artistic interpretation. They use ropes, hoops, balls, clubs and ribbons, which must be kept in constant motion.

Gymnastic Stars
Olga Korbut, a Soviet gymnast, inspired many girls to take up gymnastics after she won three gold medals at the 1972 Olympics in Munich. Romanian gymnast **Nadia Comaneci** became the first woman to score a perfect 10, at the 1976 summer games in Montreal, Canada. **Kerri Strug** provided us with one of the most exciting events of the 1996 Olympics—and gymnastics history—when she nailed her vault on an injured ankle to ensure a gold medal for the U.S. team.

Nadia Comaneci

In 2003, the women of Team U.S.A. took home the first ever U.S. team World Championship in gymnastics. The men and women together won a total of five gold medals.

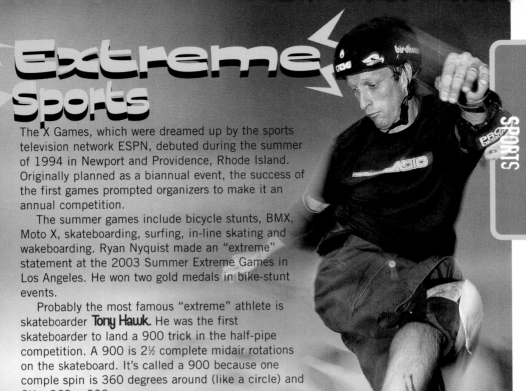

Extreme Sports

The X Games, which were dreamed up by the sports television network ESPN, debuted during the summer of 1994 in Newport and Providence, Rhode Island. Originally planned as a biannual event, the success of the first games prompted organizers to make it an annual competition.

The summer games include bicycle stunts, BMX, Moto X, skateboarding, surfing, in-line skating and wakeboarding. Ryan Nyquist made an "extreme" statement at the 2003 Summer Extreme Games in Los Angeles. He won two gold medals in bike-stunt events.

Probably the most famous "extreme" athlete is skateboarder **Tony Hawk.** He was the first skateboarder to land a 900 trick in the half-pipe competition. A 900 is 2½ complete midair rotations on the skateboard. It's called a 900 because one comple spin is 360 degrees around (like a circle) and 2½ x 360 = 900.

The winter games include snowboarding, skiing, snowmobiling and Moto X. Americans dominated the 2004 winter games in Aspen, Colorado. Crowd-pleaser Hannah Teter took home gold in the superpipe. Extreme-ly talented Kelly Clark earned a silver medal—the third year in a row she medaled.

Swimming

Style Points

The five swimming areas used in competition are:

- Breaststroke
- Backstroke
- Butterfly
- Freestyle
- Medley (combination of all)

Seven Up

Mark Spitz won a record seven gold medals at the 1972 Olympics in Munich—and he set world records in each event! He has nine Olympic gold medals in all, more than any other swimmer.

Did You Know?

In order to fill an Olympic-size pool (50 meters by 25 yards or meters), it takes anywhere from 700,000 to 850,000 gallons of water.

go | For more on all the sports in this chapter, go to www.FactMonster.com

Tennis

The four tournaments of tennis's Grand Slam are:

Australian Open
French Open
Wimbledon
U.S. Open

Love Means Zero

Learn how to speak and score like a tennis pro.

Love is zero points.

15, 30, 40 are tennis terms for one point, two points and three points.

Game point is the fourth point. The first player to win the fourth point (and lead by two) wins the game.

Deuce is the term for the game being tied 40–40. Play continues until one player wins by 2 points.

Set To win a set a player must win six games and lead by at least two. If each player wins six games there is a seven-point tie-breaker game to decide the winner.

Match The match usually ends when one player wins two out of three sets.

Horse Racing

Animals are a big part of the sports world, and horses in particular play a large role. The history of horse racing can be traced to ancient Egypt as well as Greece, where horse-and-chariot races were part of the Olympic Games. It is often called "the sport of kings" because breeding and racing horses was a popular hobby of the royal family in England during the 12th century.

Triple Crown

Horse racing in the U.S. reaches its peak each spring with the running of the **Triple Crown**. The Triple Crown is a series of three prestigious races starting with the Kentucky Derby, which is held each year on the first Saturday in May at Churchill Downs in Louisville, Kentucky. The next race is the Preakness Stakes, followed by the Belmont Stakes.

Here is a list of the 11 horses that have won the Triple Crown—that is, won all three races in the same year. Notice that it hasn't been done in more than 25 years!

1919 Sir Barton	1946 Assault
1930 Gallant Fox	1948 Citation
1935 Omaha	1973 Secretariat
1937 War Admiral	1977 Seattle Slew
1941 Whirlaway	1978 Affirmed
1943 Count Fleet	

Did You Know?

In the annual Iditarod Trail Sled Dog Race, a team of dogs pulls a large sled and its driver more than 1,100 miles through the snowy Alaskan wilderness. The race from Anchorage to Nome commemorates a life-saving delivery of medicine to the village of Nome by sled dogs in 1925.

Homework TIP

- Pace yourself with large projects by breaking them down into small pieces.

Automobile racing originated in France in 1894 and appeared in the U.S. the next year.

Racing Anyone?

The National Association for Stock Car Racing's **Winston Cup Series** is the most popular auto-racing series in the U.S. The NASCAR season runs from February to November. The biggest Winston Cup race of the year is the **Daytona 500**. Michael Waltrip won the 2003 Daytona 500, and Matt Kenseth was the 2003 NASCAR champion.

World Champions

Germany's **Michael Schumacher** won his sixth Formula One driver's world championship in 2003, moving him into first place on the all-time list. Here are the drivers with the most world titles, listed with their home countries.

6 — Michael Schumacher (Germany)
5 — Juan-Manuel Fangio (Argentina)
4 — Alain Prost (France)
3 — Jack Brabham (Australia)
   Niki Lauda (Austria)
   Nelson Piquet (Brazil)
   Ayrton Senna (Brazil)
   Jackie Stewart (Britain)

What Do the Flags Mean?

Race officials use flags to instruct drivers during a race. Here's what they mean:
Green—Go!
Yellow—Caution. There is a problem on the track, and drivers must go slow and not pass.
Red—Stop. Something has made the track unusable (maybe an accident or bad weather).
White—Last lap
Checkered—Finish. The race is over.

SPORTS

Our Need for Speed

The biggest and oldest race held in the U.S. is the **Indianapolis 500**. It's held every year at the oval-shaped Indianapolis Motor Speedway in Indiana. Gil de Ferran was the 2003 Indy 500 winner.

TFK Mystery Person

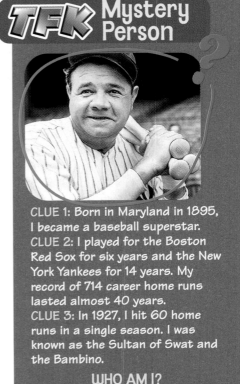

CLUE 1: Born in Maryland in 1895, I became a baseball superstar.
CLUE 2: I played for the Boston Red Sox for six years and the New York Yankees for 14 years. My record of 714 career home runs lasted almost 40 years.
CLUE 3: In 1927, I hit 60 home runs in a single season. I was known as the Sultan of Swat and the Bambino.

WHO AM I?

(See Answer Key that begins on page 340.)

Coming to America

BY JOE McGOWAN

The United States is a nation built by immigrants. In the 1840s, the first wave came from Ireland, England and Germany. From 1890 to 1924, a second wave arrived from countries such as Italy and Russia.

Now, a new wave of immigrants is coming to America. Currently, nearly 30 million immigrants live in the U.S. They make up 11.5% of the population. Like those who came before, these immigrants arrived hoping to build their own version of the American Dream.

Proud, new Americans celebrate after becoming citizens.

Immigrants arrive at Ellis Island in 1920.

Since the terrorist attacks of September 11, 2001, America has been rethinking its immigration policy. New rules were made to keep out foreigners who intend to harm us. Still, some 3.3 million new immigrants have arrived since January 2000.

Once here, immigrants need help. "Family is always the first resource," says Lily Woo, the principal of Public School 130, in Manhattan, where many Chinese newcomers attend school. Extended immigrant families help one another find housing and work. Nearly 25% of today's immigrant households receive government assistance. Some 30% of immigrants have not graduated from high

school, and many have low-paying jobs.

Early immigrants took on all aspects of American culture, says Steven Camarota of the Center for Immigration Studies. "Italian immigrants would claim Thomas Jefferson as an ancestor," Camarota says. With cell phones and the Internet, it's now easier for newcomers to keep in touch with the country they left behind.

"I'm the luckiest kid in the world," says Prudence Simon, 10, who now lives in New York. "I have two homes, Trinidad and the U.S.A."

Only the future will reveal how the new immigrants will build their American Dream. But one thing is certain: They have a rich history on which to lay a foundation.

EXTREME Points of the U.S.

Extreme	Latitude	Longitude	Distance*
Northernmost point: Point Barrow, Alaska	71°23' N	156°29' W	2,507 miles (4,034 km)
Easternmost point: West Quoddy Head, Maine	44°49' N	66°57' W	1,788 miles (2,997 km)
Southernmost point: Ka Lae (South Cape), Hawaii	18°55' N	155°41' W	3,463 miles (5,573 km)
Westernmost point: Cape Wrangell, Alaska (Attu Island)	52°55' N	172°27' E	3,625 miles (5,833 km)

*From the geographic center of the U.S. in Castle Rock, South Dakota

State Regions

Midwest
New England
Middle Atlantic
WA
MT ND MN
OR ID WY SD WI MI
NV NE IA
West CA UT CO KS IL IN OH PA
MO KY WV VA
AZ NM OK AR TN NC
HI TX MS AL GA SC
LA FL
ME
VT NH
NY MA RI
CT NJ DE MD
South
Southwest
AK

Source: The U.S. Department of State

Homework TIP

• Make homework part of your daily schedule.

Did You Know?

Alaska is the largest state. It measures 570,374 square miles. Rhode Island is the smallest. It's a mere 1,045 square miles.

A Look at the U.S. Population*

U.S. Population: 281,421,906

Males: 138,053,563
(49.1% of population)
Females: 143,368,343
(50.9% of population)
Number of kids ages 5 to 9:
20,549,505
Number of kids ages 10 to 14:
20,528,072
**Number of centenarians
(people over age 100):** 50,454
It's estimated that by the year 2050, there
will be about 834,000 Americans over the
age of 100!

Number of families: 71,787,347
Average family size: 3.14 people
Median age of the population: 35.3

Race

75.1% of Americans are white.
12.5% are of Hispanic origin
(they may be of any race).
12.3% are black.
3.6% are Asian, Native Hawaiian or
Pacific Islander.
0.9% are Native American or Alaskan Native.
*Figures based on Census 2000.

Life Expectancy

When the nation was founded, the average
American could expect to live to age 35.
By 1900, life expectancy had increased to
47.3. In 2000, the life expectancy was 74.1
years for men and 79.5 years for women.

Kids at Home

About 71% of kids live with two parents.
About 25% live with one parent.
Nearly 4% live with neither parent.
About 5.5% live in a home maintained
by a grandparent.

A Look Back at the U.S. Population

1790	3,929,214	**1900**	75,994,575
1800	5,308,483	**1920**	105,710,620
1820	9,638,453	**1950**	150,697,361
1850	23,191,876	**1980**	226,545,805
1880	50,155,783	**1990**	248,709,873

Figures do not include armed forces overseas.

Did You Know?

Americans like their pets!
More than 36% of the
households in the U.S. have
at least one dog, and more
than 31% own a cat.

Ancestry of the U.S. Population

The United States is indeed a big melting
pot, made up of people of different
ethnicities and cultures. Here are the top
ancestries of U.S. citizens,
according to the
U.S. Census Bureau.

1. German
2. Irish
3. English
4. African
5. Italian
6. American
7. Mexican
8. French
9. Polish
10. Native American

TFK Top 5 States with the Most Immigrants

There are 28.4 million immigrants living in the U.S., according to the Census Bureau's 2000 Population Survey. That's triple the number counted in 1970 and the most ever recorded. Two-thirds of U.S. immigrants live in these five states:

State	Number of immigrants
1. California	8.8 million
2. New York	3.6 million
3. Florida	2.8 million
4. Texas	2.4 million
5. New Jersey	1.2 million

Source: Center for Immigration Studies

Foreign-Born Americans

The term "foreign born" refers to Americans who were not born in this country. Here's a list of the top 10 places where these Americans were born.

1. Mexico
2. China
3. Philippines
4. India
5. Cuba
6. Vietnam
7. El Salvador
8. Korea
9. Dominican Republic
10. Canada

Source: Immigration and Naturalization Service

Homework TIP

Neatness counts! If your teacher can't read your homework, you might not get the credit you deserve.

TFK Puzzles & Games

They Came to America

People from all over the world have made America home. Some of those countries are in the list below. To find them, search up, down, diagonally, forward and backward. The leftover letters spell the answer to this question:

Since 1886, what has the Statue of Liberty been the symbol of?

_ _ _ _ _ _ _ _ _ _

```
G R U S S I A E
S E P E R U T B
W D R W E H Q R
E A L M I C A A
D H O O A M R Z
E C P E ! N I I
N I L A O S Y L
A A C I A M A J
```

WORD LIST:

Peru	Chad
Ethiopia	Iraq
Laos	Jamaica
Russia	Sweden
Germany	Brazil

(See Answer Key that begins on page 340.)

The Great Seal of the United States

Benjamin Franklin, John Adams and Thomas Jefferson began designing the Great Seal in 1776.

The Great Seal is printed on the back of the $1 bill and is used on certain government documents, such as foreign treaties.

The bald eagle, our national bird, is at the center of the seal. It holds a banner in its beak. The motto says *E pluribus unum*, which is Latin for "out of many, one." This refers to the colonies that united to make a nation. In one claw, the eagle holds an olive branch for peace; in the other claw, it carries arrows for war.

Other Symbols of the United States

The **bald eagle** has been our national bird since 1782. The Founding Fathers had been unable to agree on which native bird should have the honor—Benjamin Franklin strongly preferred the turkey! Besides appearing on the Great Seal, the bald eagle is pictured on coins, the $1 bill, all official U.S. seals and the President's flag.

The image of **Uncle Sam,** with his white hair and top hat, first became famous on World War I recruiting posters. The artist, James Montgomery Flagg, used himself as a model. But the term dates back to the War of 1812, when a meat packer nicknamed Uncle Sam supplied beef to the troops. The initials for his nickname were quite appropriate!

The U.S. Flag

In 1777 the Continental Congress decided that the flag would have 13 alternating red and white stripes, for the 13 colonies, and 13 white stars on a blue background. A new star has been added for every new state. Today the flag has 50 stars.

The Pledge of Allegiance to the Flag

The original pledge was published in the September 8, 1892, issue of *The Youth's Companion* in Boston. For years, there was a dispute over who should get credit for writing the pledge, James B. Upham or Francis Bellamy, both members of the magazine's staff. In 1939, the United States Flag Association decided that Bellamy deserved the credit.

Here's the original version of the pledge.

I pledge allegiance to my Flag and the Republic for which it stands—one nation indivisible—with liberty and justice for all.

AMERICAN Indians

There are more than 550 federally recognized American Indian tribes in the United States, including 223 village groups in Alaska. "Federally recognized" means these tribes and groups have a special legal relationship with the U.S. government.

Largest American Indian Tribes

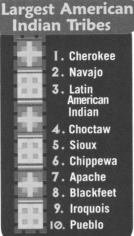

1. Cherokee
2. Navajo
3. Latin American Indian
4. Choctaw
5. Sioux
6. Chippewa
7. Apache
8. Blackfeet
9. Iroquois
10. Pueblo

Source: U.S. Census Bureau

Did You Know?

November is National American Indian Heritage Month. Schools, the government and various organizations sponsor events that honor the history and culture of the first Americans.

INDIAN Reservations

The largest reservation is the Navajo Reservation, which has about 16 million acres of land in Arizona, New Mexico and Utah. Many of the smaller reservations are less than 1,000 acres, with the smallest less than 100 acres.
Here are the reservations with the largest populations:

1. Navajo (Arizona, New Mexico and Utah)
2. Pine Ridge (Nebraska and South Dakota)
3. Fort Apache (Arizona)
4. Gila River (Arizona)
5. Papago (Arizona)
6. Rosebud (South Dakota)
7. San Carlos (Arizona)
8. Zuni Pueblo (Arizona and New Mexico)
9. Hopi (Arizona)
10. Blackfeet (Montana)

AMERICAN INDIAN Population By State

Here are the states with the highest American Indian populations.

	STATE	POPULATION
1.	Oklahoma	252,420
2.	California	242,164
3.	Arizona	203,527
4.	New Mexico	134,355
5.	Washington	81,483
6.	North Carolina	80,155
7.	Texas	65,877
8.	New York	62,651
9.	Michigan	55,638
10.	South Dakota	50,575

Source: U.S. Census Bureau

Most Common First Names in the United States

Is your name Jacob or Michael, Sarah or Olivia? If it is, you have one of the most popular names in the country! Here's a list of the most popular first names.

GIRLS

1. Emily
2. Madison
3. Hannah
4. Emma
5. Alexis
6. Ashley
7. Abigail
8. Sarah
9. Samantha
10. Olivia

BOYS

1. Jacob
2. Michael
3. Joshua
4. Matthew
5. Ethan
6. Joseph
7. Andrew
8. Christopher
9. Daniel
10. Nicholas

Most Common Last Names in the United States

1. Smith
2. Johnson
3. Williams
4. Jones
5. Brown
6. Davis
7. Miller
8. Wilson
9. Moore
10. Taylor

Hello, my name is Emily.

Hi, my name is Jacob.

Largest Cities in the U.S.

RANK	CITY	POPULATION*
1.	New York, New York	8,008,278
2.	Los Angeles, California	3,694,820
3.	Chicago, Illinois	2,896,016
4.	Houston, Texas	1,953,631
5.	Philadelphia, Pennsylvania	1,517,550
6.	Phoenix, Arizona	1,321,045
7.	San Diego, California	1,223,400
8.	Dallas, Texas	1,188,580
9.	San Antonio, Texas	1,144,646
10.	Detroit, Michigan	951,270
11.	San Jose, California	894,943
12.	Indianapolis, Indiana	781,870
13.	San Francisco, California	776,733
14.	Jacksonville, Florida	735,617
15.	Columbus, Ohio	711,470
16.	Austin, Texas	656,562
17.	Baltimore, Maryland	651,154
18.	Memphis, Tennessee	650,100
19.	Milwaukee, Wisconsin	596,974
20.	Boston, Massachusetts	589,141

*Figures based on Census 2000

Homework TIP

Check to see that you have completed all homework assignments. Cross off each one as you finish it.

Great American Claims to Fame

You've probably heard Hollywood called the "movie capital of the world" or Detroit the "automotive capital of the world." But did you know that Alabama boasts the "sock capital of the world"? Here's a look at some of America's most interesting self-proclaimed "capitals of the world."

Beaver

Cow Chip Throwing Capital of the World

Beaver, Oklahoma

Established as a tribute to the unique natural fuel source of the town's early settlers, Beaver has hosted the World Cow Chip Throwing Championship since 1969.

Mont Horeb

Troll Capital of the World

Mount Horeb, Wisconsin

Mount Horeb offers a "Troll Stroll" down the Trollway, site of the country's largest collection of life-sized troll sculptures, which are carved into trees along the town's main drag.

Fort Payne

Sock Capital of the World

Fort Payne, Alabama

According to the Hosiery Association, one out of every eight Americans wears socks made in Fort Payne/DeKalb County.

Cereal Capital of the World

Battle Creek, Michigan

The birthplace of our favorite breakfast food still snaps, crackles and pops with excitement. Today you can visit Kellogg's Cereal City USA, a museum in Battle Creek that honors cereal and its impact on our culture.

Battle Creek

Kennett Square

Mushroom Capital of the World

Kennett Square, Pennsylvania

No U.S. state produces more mushrooms than Pennsylvania. So it makes sense that here, in the heart of mushroom country, one would find the Phillips Mushroom Museum.

Decoy Capital of the World

Havre de Grace, Maryland

Situated on the banks of the Susquehanna River, this Maryland community has been home to the Havre de Grace Decoy Museum since 1986. It features the country's largest collection of wooden duck decoys.

Havre de Grace

Frog Capital of the World

Rayne, Louisiana

More than 30 frog murals adorn buildings throughout Rayne. Frog fans leap into town for its annual Frog Festival.

Rayne

Bratwurst Capital of the World

Sheboygan, Wisconsin

Each year, Sheboygan hosts Bratwurst Days, a two-day festival of music and bratwurst. Sausage lovers come from all over to try some of the newest brats.

Sheboygan

PACIFIC OCEAN

Seattle
Tacoma
Olympia
Portland
Spokane
Great Falls
WASHINGTON
Salem
Eugene
Oregon
Boise
Idaho
Helena
Montana
Billings
Missouri River
Bismarck

Great Falls

ROCKY Mountains

Yellowstone National Park

Wyoming

Rapid City
Pierre

Great Plains

California
Reno
Sacramento
Carson City
Nevada
Great Salt Lake
Salt Lake City
Cheyenne

Santa Rosa
San Francisco
Modesto
San Jose
Fresno
Yosemite National Park
Utah
Denver
Colorado Springs
Colorado
Pueblo

Death Valley
Las Vegas
Grand Canyon
Flagstaff
Santa Fe
Albuquerque
Amarillo

Los Angeles
Escondido
San Diego
Phoenix
Arizona
Tucson
New Mexico
Lubbock
Abilene

El Paso
Texas

Kauai
Oahu
Honolulu
Hawaii
Maui
Hawaii
PACIFIC OCEAN

Laredo
MEXICO

ARCTIC OCEAN

RUSSIA

Alaska

CANADA

BERING SEA

Anchorage

Juneau

Aleutian Islands

0 mi.   300 mi.   600 mi.

0 km   400 km   800 km

PACIFIC OCEAN

248

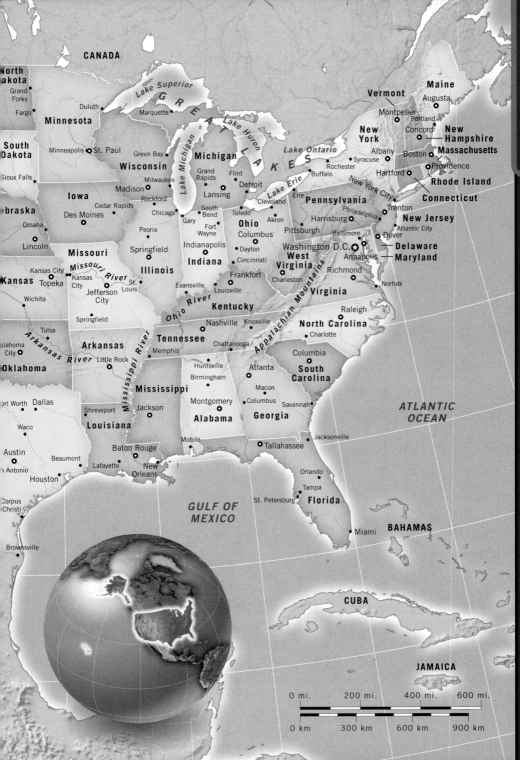

CANADA

North Dakota
Grand Forks
Fargo

Minnesota
Duluth
Marquette

Lake Superior

G R E A T

Lake Huron

Maine
Augusta

Vermont
Montpelier
Portland

New Hampshire
Concord

New York
Albany
Boston
Massachusetts

South Dakota
Sioux Falls

Wisconsin
Green Bay
Milwaukee

Michigan
Grand Rapids
Flint
Detroit
Lansing

Lake Michigan

L A K E S

Lake Ontario
Rochester
Syracuse
Buffalo
Hartford
Providence

Rhode Island

Connecticut

Iowa
Cedar Rapids
Des Moines

Madison
Rockford
Chicago

Gary
South Bend
Fort Wayne

Ohio
Columbus
Akron

Lake Erie
Erie
Cleveland
Toledo

Pennsylvania
Harrisburg
Pittsburgh

New York City

Philadelphia
Trenton

New Jersey
Atlantic City

Minneapolis
St. Paul

braska
Omaha
Lincoln

Missouri

Peoria

Illinois

Springfield

Indianapolis

Indiana

Dayton

Cincinnati

Washington D.C.

West Virginia

Baltimore
Dover

Delaware

Annapolis
Maryland

Missouri River

Kansas City
Topeka

Kansas

Wichita

Kansas City

St. Louis

Jefferson City

Frankfort

Evansville
Louisville

Kentucky

Charleston

Richmond

Virginia

Norfolk

Springfield

Ohio River

Nashville
Knoxville

Raleigh

North Carolina

Tulsa

Arkansas River

Arkansas

Little Rock

Tennessee
Memphis

Chattanooga

Charlotte

Appalachian Mountains

lahoma City

Oklahoma

Mississippi River

Huntsville
Birmingham

Columbia

South Carolina

ort Worth
Dallas

Waco

Mississippi

Jackson

Montgomery

Macon
Columbus

Savannah

Georgia

ATLANTIC OCEAN

Austin
n Antonio
Houston

Beaumont
Lafayette

Louisiana

Shreveport

Alabama

Mobile

Jacksonville

Baton Rouge
New Orleans

Tallahassee

Corpus Christi

GULF OF MEXICO

Orlando
Tampa

St. Petersburg
Florida

Miami

BAHAMAS

Brownsville

CUBA

JAMAICA

| 0 mi. | 200 mi. | 400 mi. | 600 mi. |

| 0 km | 300 km | 600 km | 900 km |

ALABAMA

Capital: Montgomery
Largest City: Birmingham
Abbreviation: Ala.
Postal Code: AL

Origin of name: May come from a Choctaw word meaning "thicket-clearers"

Entered union (rank): December 14, 1819 (22)

Motto: *Audemus jura nostra defendere* (We dare defend our rights)

Tree: southern longleaf pine

Flower: camellia

Bird: yellowhammer (yellow-shafted flicker)

Other: dance: square dance; nut: pecan

Song: "Alabama"

Nickname: Yellowhammer State

Residents: Alabamian, Alabaman

Land area: 50,750 square miles (131,443 sq km)

Population (2003): 4,500,752

Did You Know? The Confederacy was founded in Montgomery in 1861.

Home of: George Washington Carver, who discovered more than 300 uses for peanuts

ALASKA

Capital: Juneau
Largest City: Anchorage
Abbreviation: Alaska
Postal Code: AK

Origin of name: From an Aleut word meaning "great land" or "that which the sea breaks against"

Entered union (rank): January 3, 1959 (49)

Motto: North to the future

Tree: sitka spruce

Flower: forget-me-not

Bird: willow ptarmigan

Other: fossil: woolly mammoth; sport: dog mushing

Song: "Alaska's Flag"

Nicknames: The Last Frontier and Land of the Midnight Sun

Residents: Alaskan

Land area: 570,374 square miles (1,477,267 sq km)

Population (2003): 648,818

Home of: The longest coastline in the U.S., 6,640 miles, which is greater than that of all other states combined

Did You Know? When it was purchased for about 2¢ an acre in 1867, Alaska was called "Seward's Folly."

ARIZONA

Capital: Phoenix
Largest City: Phoenix

Abbreviation: Ariz.
Postal Code: AZ

Origin of name: From the Native American *Arizonac,* meaning "little spring"

Entered union (rank): February 14, 1912 (48)

Motto: *Ditat deus* (God enriches)

Tree: palo verde

Flower: flower of saguaro cactus

Bird: cactus wren

Other: gemstone: turquoise; neckwear: bola tie

Song: "Arizona"

Nickname: Grand Canyon State

Residents: Arizonan, Arizionian

Land area: 113,642 square miles (296,400 sq km)

Population (2003): 5,580,811

Home of: The most telescopes in the world, in Tucson

Phoenix

Did You Know? London Bridge was shipped to Lake Havasu City and rebuilt there stone-by-stone.

ARKANSAS

Capital: Little Rock
Largest City: Little Rock

Abbreviation: Ark.
Postal Code: AR

Origin of name: From the Quapaw Indians

Entered union (rank): June 15, 1836 (25)

Motto: *Regnat populus* (The people rule)

Tree: pine

Flower: apple blossom

Bird: mockingbird

Other: fruit and vegetable: pink tomato; insect: honeybee

Song: "Arkansas"

Nickname: Land of Opportunity

Residents: Arkansan

Land area: 52,075 square miles (134,874 sq km)

Population (2003): 2,725,714

Home of: The only active diamond mine in the U.S.

Little Rock

Did You Know? Arkansas's Hattie Caraway was the first woman elected to the U.S. Senate.

CALIFORNIA

Capital: Sacramento
Largest City: Los Angeles
Abbreviation: Calif.
Postal Code: CA

Origin of name: From a book, *Las Sergas de Esplandián*, by Garcia Ordóñez de Montalvo, circa 1500

Entered union (rank): September 9, 1850 (31)

Motto: *Eureka* (I have found it)

Tree: California redwood

Flower: golden poppy

Bird: California valley quail

Other: dance: West Coast Swing Dance; prehistoric artifact: chipped-stone bear

Song: "I Love You, California"

Nickname: Golden State

Residents: Californian

Land area: 155,973 square miles (403,970 sq km)

Population (2003): 35,484,453

Home of: "General Sherman," a 2,500-year-old sequoia

Did You Know? More immigrants settle in California than in any other state.

COLORADO

Capital: Denver
Largest City: Denver
Abbreviation: Colo.
Postal Code: CO

Origin of name: From the Spanish, "ruddy" or "red"

Entered union (rank): August 1, 1876 (38)

Motto: *Nil sine numine* (Nothing without providence)

Tree: Colorado blue spruce

Flower: Rocky Mountain columbine

Bird: lark bunting

Other: fossil: *Stegosaurus;* gemstone: aquamarine

Song: "Where the Columbines Grow"

Nickname: Centennial State

Residents: Coloradan, Coloradoan

Land area: 103,730 square miles (268,660 sq km)

Population (2003): 4,550,688

Home of: The world's largest silver nugget (1,840 pounds), found in 1894 near Aspen

Did You Know? There are 54 peaks in the Rocky Mountains that rise above 14,000 feet.

CONNECTICUT

Capital: **Hartford**
Largest City: **Bridgeport**

Abbreviation: **Conn.**
Postal Code: **CT**

Origin of name: From a Quinnehtukqut Indian word meaning "beside the long tidal river"

Entered union (rank): January 9, 1788 (5)

Motto: *Qui transtulit sustinet* (He who transplanted still sustains)

Tree: white oak

Flower: mountain laurel

Bird: American robin

Other: hero: Nathan Hale; heroine: Prudence Crandall

Song: "Yankee Doodle"

Nickname: Nutmeg State

Residents: Nutmegger

Land area: 4,845 square miles (12,550 sq km)

Population (2003): 3,483,372

Home of: The first American cookbook—*American Cookery* by Amelia Simmons—published in Hartford in 1796

Hartford

Bridgeport

Did You Know? The U.S. Constitution was modeled after Connecticut's colonial laws.

DELAWARE

Capital: **Dover**
Largest City: **Wilmington**

Abbreviation: **Del.**
Postal Code: **DE**

Origin of name: From Delaware River and Bay, named for Sir Thomas West, Baron De La Warr

Entered union (rank): December 7, 1787 (1)

Motto: Liberty and independence

Tree: American holly

Flower: peach blossom

Bird: blue hen chicken

Other: colors: colonial blue and buff; insect: ladybug

Song: "Our Delaware"

Nicknames: Diamond State, First State and Small Wonder

Residents: Delawarean

Land area: 1,955 square miles (5,153 sq km)

Population (2003): 817,491

Home of: The first log cabins in North America, built in 1683 by Swedish immigrants

Wilmington

Dover

Did You Know? Delaware was the first of the original 13 colonies to ratify the Constitution.

Show what you know about America's 50 states at *www.timeforkids.com/staterace*

FLORIDA

Capital: Tallahassee
Largest City: Jacksonville
Abbreviation: Fla.
Postal Code: FL

Origin of name: From the Spanish, meaning "feast of flowers"

Entered union (rank): March 3, 1845 (27)

Motto: In God we trust

Tree: sabal palm

Flower: orange blossom

Bird: mockingbird

Other: shell: horse conch; soil: Myakka fine sand

Song: "The Sewanee River"

Nickname: Sunshine State

Residents: Floridian, Floridan

Land area: 54,153 square miles (140,256 sq km)

Population (2003): 17,019,068

Home of: U.S. spacecraft launchings from Cape Canaveral, formerly Cape Kennedy

Tallahassee • Jacksonville

Did You Know? There are two rivers in Florida with the name Withlacoochee.

GEORGIA

Capital: Atlanta
Largest City: Atlanta
Abbreviation: Ga.
Postal Code: GA

Origin of name: In honor of George II of England

Entered union (rank): January 2, 1788 (4)

Motto: Wisdom, justice and moderation

Tree: live oak

Flower: Cherokee rose

Bird: brown thrasher

Other: crop: peanut; fossil: shark tooth

Song: "Georgia on My Mind"

Nicknames: Peach State and Empire State of the South

Residents: Georgian

Land area: 57,919 square miles (150,010 sq km)

Population (2003): 8,684,715

Home of: The Girl Scouts, founded in Savannah by Juliette Gordon Low in 1912

★ Atlanta

Did You Know? During the Civil War, Atlanta was burned and nearly destroyed by Union troops.

HAWAII

Capital: Honolulu (on Oahu) Abbreviation: Hawaii
Largest City: Honolulu Postal Code: HI

Origin of name: Probably from a Polynesian word meaning "ancestral home"

Entered union (rank): August 21, 1959 (50)

Honolulu

Motto: *Ua mau ke ea o ka aina i ka pono* (The life of the land is perpetuated in righteousness)

Tree: kukui (candlenut)

Flower: yellow hibiscus

Bird: nene (Hawaiian goose)

Other: gem: black coral; marine mammal: humpback whale

Song: "Hawaii Ponoi"

Nickname: Aloha State

Residents: Hawaiian

Land area: 6,423 square miles (16,637 sq km)

Population (2003): 1,257,608

Home of: The only royal palace in the U.S. (Iolani)

Did You Know?
Hawaii was formed by undersea volcanoes.

IDAHO

Capital: Boise Abbreviation: Idaho
Largest City: Boise Postal Code: ID

Origin of name: Although popularly believed to be a Native American word, it is an invented name whose meaning is unknown.

Entered union (rank): July 3, 1890 (43)

Motto: *Esto perpetua* (It is forever)

Tree: white pine

Flower: lilac

Bird: mountain bluebird

Other: fish: cutthroat trout; horse: Appaloosa

Song: "Here We Have Idaho"

Nickname: Gem State

Residents: Idahoan

Land area: 82,751 square miles (214,325 sq km)

Population (2003): 1,366,332

Home of: The longest Main Street in America, 33 miles, in Island Park

Boise

Did You Know? Idaho produces about 25% of the country's potato crop.

ILLINOIS

Origin of name: **Algonquian for "tribe of superior men"**

Entered union (rank): **December 3, 1818 (21)**

Motto: **State sovereignty, national union**

Tree: **white oak**

Flower: **violet**

Bird: **cardinal**

Other: **animal: white-tailed deer; prairie grass: big bluestem**

Song: **"Illinois"**

Nickname: **Prairie State**

Residents: **Illinoisan**

Land area: **55,593 square miles (143,987 sq km)**

Population (2003): **12,653,544**

Home of: **The tallest building in the country, Sears Tower, in Chicago**

Did You Know? The country's first skyscraper was built in Chicago in 1885.

INDIANA

Origin of name: **Means "land of Indians"**

Entered union (rank): **December 11, 1816 (19)**

Motto: **The crossroads of America**

Tree: **tulip tree**

Flower: **peony**

Bird: **cardinal**

Other: **river: Wabash; stone: limestone**

Song: **"On the Banks of the Wabash, Far Away"**

Nickname: **Hoosier State**

Residents: **Indianan, Indianian**

Land area: **35,870 sq miles (92,904 sq km)**

Population (2003): **6,195,643**

Home of: **The famous car race, the Indianapolis 500**

Did You Know? Wabash, Ind., was the first U.S. city to be lighted by electricity.

IOWA

Capital: Des Moines
Largest City: Des Moines
Abbreviation: Iowa
Postal Code: IA

Origin of name: Probably from an Indian word meaning "this is the place"

Entered union (rank): December 28, 1846 (29)

Motto: Our liberties we prize and our rights we will maintain

Tree: oak

Flower: wild rose

Bird: eastern goldfinch

Other: fossil: crinoid; rock: geode

Song: "Song of Iowa"

Nickname: Hawkeye State

Residents: Iowan

Land area: 55,875 square miles (144,716 sq km)

Population (2003): 2,944,062

Home of: The shortest and steepest railroad in the U.S., in Dubuque: 296 feet, 60° incline

Des Moines

Did You Know? The Eskimo Pie, the first chocolate-covered ice cream bar, was invented in Onawa in 1921.

KANSAS

Capital: Topeka
Largest City: Wichita
Abbreviation: Kans.
Postal Code: KS

Origin of name: From a Sioux word meaning "people of the south wind"

Entered union (rank): January 29, 1861 (34)

Motto: *Ad astra per aspera* (To the stars through difficulties)

Tree: cottonwood

Flower: sunflower

Bird: western meadowlark

Other: animal: buffalo; reptile: ornate box turtle

Song: "Home on the Range"

Nicknames: Sunflower State and Jayhawk State

Residents: Kansan

Land area: 81,823 square miles (211,922 sq km)

Population (2003): 2,723,507

Home of: Helium, discovered by scientists in 1905 at the University of Kansas

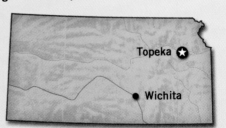
Topeka
Wichita

Did You Know? The world's largest ball of twine is in Cawker City.

KENTUCKY

Capital: Frankfort
Largest City: Louisville
Abbreviation: Ky.
Postal Code: KY

Origin of name: From an Iroquoian word (Kentahten) meaning "land of tomorrow"

Entered union (rank): June 1, 1792 (15)

Motto: United we stand, divided we fall

Tree: tulip poplar

Flower: goldenrod

Bird: Kentucky cardinal

Other: bluegrass song: "Blue Moon of Kentucky"; horse: Thoroughbred

Song: "My Old Kentucky Home"

Nickname: Bluegrass State

Residents: Kentuckian

Land area: 39,732 square miles (102,907 sq km)

Population (2003): 4,117,827

Home of: The largest underground cave in the world, the Mammoth-Flint Cave system, over 300 miles long

Did You Know? "Happy Birthday to You" was written by two Louisville teachers.

LOUISIANA

Capital: Baton Rouge
Largest City: New Orleans
Abbreviation: La.
Postal Code: LA

Origin of name: In honor of Louis XIV of France

Entered union (rank): April 30, 1812 (18)

Motto: Union, justice and confidence

Tree: bald cypress

Flower: magnolia

Bird: eastern brown pelican

Other: crustacean: crawfish; dog: Catahoula leopard hound

Songs: "Give Me Louisiana" and "You Are My Sunshine"

Nickname: Pelican State

Residents: Louisianan, Louisianian

Land area: 43,566 square miles (112,836 sq km)

Population (2003): 4,496,334

Home of: About 98% of the world's crawfish

Did You Know? Tourists have been flocking to New Orleans for Mardi Gras since 1838.

MAINE

Capital: Augusta
Largest City: Portland
Abbreviation: Maine
Postal Code: ME

Augusta ✪

Portland ●

Origin of name: First used to distinguish the mainland from the coastal islands

Entered union (rank): March 15, 1820 (23)

Motto: *Dirigo* (I lead)

Tree: white pine tree

Flower: white pine cone and tassel

Bird: chickadee

Other: animal: moose; cat: Maine coon cat

Song: "State of Maine Song"

Nickname: Pine Tree State

Residents: Mainer

Land area: 30,865 square miles (79,939 sq km)

Population (2003): 1,305,728

Home of: The most easterly point in the U.S., West Quoddy Head

Did You Know? Maine is the world's largest producer of blueberries.

MARYLAND

Capital: Annapolis
Largest City: Baltimore
Abbreviation: Md.
Postal Code: MD

Origin of name: In honor of Henrietta Maria (queen of Charles I of England)

Entered union (rank): April 28, 1788 (7)

Motto: *Fatti maschii, parole femine* (Manly deeds, womanly words)

Tree: white oak

Flower: black-eyed Susan

Bird: Baltimore oriole

Other: crustacean: Maryland blue crab; sport: jousting

Song: "Maryland! My Maryland!"

Nicknames: Free State and Old Line State

Residents: Marylander

Land area: 9,775 square miles (25,316 sq km)

Population (2003): 5,508,909

Home of: The first umbrella factory in the U.S., opened 1928, in Baltimore

Baltimore ●

✪—Annapolis

Did You Know? During the Civil War, Maryland was a slave state but part of the Union.

MASSACHUSETTS

Capital: Boston   **Abbreviation:** Mass.
Largest City: Boston   **Postal Code:** MA

Origin of name: From the Massachusett Indian tribe, meaning "at or about the great hill"

Entered union (rank): February 6, 1788 (6)

Motto: *Ense petit placidam sub libertate quietem* (By the sword we seek peace, but peace only under liberty)

Tree: American elm

Flower: mayflower

Bird: chickadee

Other: beverage: cranberry juice; dessert: Boston cream pie

Song: "All Hail to Massachusetts"

Nicknames: Bay State and Old Colony State

Residents: Bay Stater

Land area: 7,838 square miles (20,300 sq km)

Population (2003): 6,433,422

Home of: The first World Series, played between the Boston Pilgrims and the Pittsburgh Pirates in 1903

Boston ✪

Did You Know? The first basketball game was played in Springfield in 1891.

MICHIGAN

Capital: Lansing   **Abbreviation:** Mich.
Largest City: Detroit   **Postal Code:** MI

Origin of name: From an Indian word (Michigana) meaning "great or large lake"

Entered union (rank): January 26, 1837 (26)

Motto: *Si quaeris peninsulam amoenam circumspice* (If you seek a pleasant peninsula, look around you)

Tree: white pine

Flower: apple blossom

Bird: robin

Other: reptile: painted turtle; wildflower: Dwarf Lake iris

Song: "Michigan, My Michigan"

Nickname: Wolverine State

Residents: Michigander, Michiganite

Land area: 56,809 square miles (147,135 sq km)

Population (2003): 10,079,985

Home of: Battle Creek, "Cereal City," produces most of the breakfast cereal in the U.S.

Lansing ✪

Detroit

Did You Know? Michigan is the country's top producer of automobiles and auto parts.

MINNESOTA

Capital: **St. Paul**
Largest City: **Minneapolis**

Abbreviation: **Minn.**
Postal Code: **MN**

Origin of name: **From a Dakota Indian word meaning "sky-tinted water"**

Entered union (rank): **May 11, 1858 (32)**

Motto: *L'Étoile du nord* **(The north star)**

Tree: **red (or Norway) pine**

Flower: **lady slipper**

Bird: **common loon**

Other: **drink: milk; mushroom: morel**

Song: **"Hail Minnesota"**

Nicknames: **North Star State, Gopher State and Land of 10,000 Lakes**

Residents: **Minnesotan**

Land area: **79,617 square miles (206,207 sq km)**

Population (2003): **5,059,375**

Home of: **One of the world's oldest rocks, 3.8 billion years old**

Minneapolis

St. Paul

Did You Know? Although it's called "Land of 10,000 Lakes," Minnesota has more than 15,000 lakes.

MISSISSIPPI

Capital: **Jackson**
Largest City: **Jackson**

Abbreviation: **Miss.**
Postal Code: **MS**

Origin of name: **From an Indian word meaning "Father of Waters"**

Entered union (rank): **December 10, 1817 (20)**

Motto: *Virtute et armis* **(By valor and arms)**

Tree: **magnolia**

Flower: **magnolia**

Bird: **mockingbird**

Other: **stone: petrified wood; water mammal: bottlenosed dolphin**

Song: **"Go, Mississippi"**

Nickname: **Magnolia State**

Residents: **Mississippian**

Land area: **46,914 square miles (121,506 sq km)**

Population (2003): **2,881,281**

Home of: **Coca-Cola, first bottled in 1894 in Vicksburg**

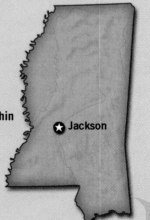

Jackson

Did You Know? Hernando de Soto discovered the Mississippi River in 1540.

MISSOURI

Capital: Jefferson City
Largest City: Kansas City
Abbreviation: Mo.
Postal Code: MO

Origin of name: Named after the Missouri Indian tribe; means "town of the large canoes"

Entered union (rank): August 10, 1821 (24)

Motto: *Salus populi suprema lex esto*
(The welfare of the people shall be the supreme law)

Tree: flowering dogwood

Flower: hawthorn

Bird: bluebird

Other: musical instrument: fiddle; tree nut: eastern black walnut

Song: "Missouri Waltz"

Nickname: Show-Me State

Residents: Missourian

Land area: 68,898 square miles (178,446 sq km)

Population (2003): 5,704,484

Home of: Mark Twain and some of his characters, such as Tom Sawyer and Huckleberry Finn

Did You Know? The strongest earthquake in U.S. history was centered in New Madrid in 1811.

MONTANA

Capital: Helena
Largest City: Billings
Abbreviation: Mont.
Postal Code: MT

Origin of name: The Latin form of a Spanish word meaning "mountainous"

Entered union (rank): November 8, 1889 (41)

Motto: *Oro y plata* (Gold and silver)

Tree: ponderosa pine

Flower: bitterroot

Bird: western meadowlark

Other: animal: grizzly bear; stones: sapphire and agate

Song: "Montana"

Nickname: Treasure State

Residents: Montanan

Land area: 145,556 square miles (376,991 sq km)

Population (2003): 917,621

Home of: Grasshopper Glacier, named for the grasshoppers that can still be seen frozen in ice

Did You Know? Glacier National Park has 60 glaciers, 200 lakes and many streams.

NEBRASKA

Capital: Lincoln
Largest City: Omaha

Abbreviation: Nebr.
Postal Code: NE

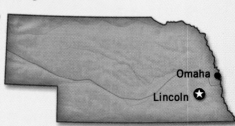

Origin of name: From an Oto Indian word meaning "flat water"

Entered union (rank): March 1, 1867 (37)

Motto: Equality before the law

Tree: cottonwood

Flower: goldenrod

Bird: western meadowlark

Other: ballad: "A Place Like Nebraska";
soft drink: Kool-Aid

Song: "Beautiful Nebraska"

Nicknames: Cornhusker State and Beef State

Residents: Nebraskan

Land area: 76,878 square miles (199,113 sq km)

Population (2003): 1,739,291

Home of: The only roller-skating museum in the world, in Lincoln

Did You Know? A favorite summer drink, Kool-Aid, was invented in Hastings.

NEVADA

Capital: Carson City
Largest City: Las Vegas

Abbreviation: Nev.
Postal Code: NV

Origin of name: From the Spanish, "snowcapped"

Entered union (rank): October 31, 1864 (36)

Motto: All for our country

Trees: single-leaf piñon and bristlecone pine

Flower: sagebrush

Bird: mountain bluebird

Other: metal: silver; reptile: desert tortoise

Song: "Home Means Nevada"

Nicknames: Sagebrush State, Silver State and
Battle Born State

Residents: Nevadan, Nevadian

Land area: 109,806 square miles (284,397 sq km)

Population (2003): 2,241,154

Home of: The Devil's Hole pupfish, found only in
Devil's Hole, an underground pool near Death Valley

Did You Know? Nevada is the driest state in the country, with about seven inches of rainfall each year.

263

NEW HAMPSHIRE

Capital: Concord
Largest City: Manchester
Abbreviation: N.H.
Postal Code: NH

Origin of name: From the English county of Hampshire

Entered union (rank): June 21, 1788 (9)

Motto: Live free or die

Tree: white birch

Flower: purple lilac

Bird: purple finch

Other: amphibian: spotted newt; sport: skiing

Songs: "Old New Hampshire" and "New Hampshire, My New Hampshire"

Nickname: Granite State

Residents: New Hampshirite

Land area: 8,969 square miles (23,231 sq km)

Population (2003): 1,287,687

Home of: Artificial rain, first used near Concord in 1947 to fight a forest fire

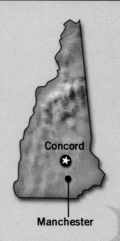

Did You Know? The world's highest wind speed, 231 m.p.h., was recorded on top of Mount Washington.

NEW JERSEY

Capital: Trenton
Largest City: Newark
Abbreviation: N.J.
Postal Code: NJ

Origin of name: From the Isle of Jersey in the English Channel

Entered union (rank): December 18, 1787 (3)

Motto: Liberty and prosperity

Tree: red oak

Flower: purple violet

Bird: eastern goldfinch

Other: folk dance: square dance; shell: knobbed whelk

Song: "I'm from New Jersey"

Nickname: Garden State

Residents: New Jerseyite, New Jerseyan

Land area: 7,419 square miles (19,215 sq km)

Population (2003): 8,638,396

Home of: The world's first drive-in movie theater, built in 1933 near Camden

Did You Know? The street names in the game of Monopoly were named after streets in Atlantic City.

NEW MEXICO

Capital: Santa Fe
Largest City: Albuquerque
Abbreviation: N.M.
Postal Code: NM

Origin of name: From Mexico

Entered union (rank): January 6, 1912 (47)

Motto: *Crescit eundo* (It grows as it goes)

Tree: piñon

Flower: yucca

Bird: roadrunner

Other: cookie: biscochito; vegetables: chili and frijole

Song: "O Fair New Mexico"

Nickname: Land of Enchantment

Residents: New Mexican

Land area: 121,365 square miles (314,334 sq km)

Population (2003): 1,874,614

Home of: Smokey Bear, a cub orphaned by fire in 1950, buried in Smokey Bear Historical State Park in 1976

Santa Fe
Albuquerque

Did You Know? Each night thousands of bats swarm out of Carlsbad Caverns to eat insects.

NEW YORK

Capital: Albany
Largest City: New York
Abbreviation: N.Y.
Postal Code: NY

Origin of name: In honor of the Duke of York

Entered union (rank): July 26, 1788 (11)

Motto: *Excelsior* (Ever upward)

Tree: sugar maple

Flower: rose

Bird: bluebird

Other: animal: beaver; muffin: apple

Song: "I Love New York"

Nickname: Empire State

Residents: New Yorker

Land area: 47,224 square miles (122,310 sq km)

Population (2003): 19,190,115

Home of: The first presidential Inauguration. George Washington took the oath of office in New York City on April 30, 1789.

Albany

New York City

Did You Know? New York City was the nation's first capital. Congress met there from 1785 to 1790.

NORTH CAROLINA

Capital: **Raleigh**
Largest City: **Charlotte**
Abbreviation: **N.C.**
Postal Code: **NC**

Origin of name: **In honor of Charles I of England**

Entered union (rank): **November 21, 1789 (12)**

Motto: *Esse quam videri* **(To be rather than to seem)**

Tree: **pine**

Flower: **dogwood**

Bird: **cardinal**

Other: **dog: plott hound; historic boat: shad boat**

Song: **"The Old North State"**

Nickname: **Tar Heel State**

Residents: **North Carolinian**

Land area: **48,718 square miles (126,180 sq km)**

Population (2003): **8,407,248**

Home of: **Virginia Dare, the first English child born in America, on Roanoke Island around 1587**

Did You Know? Although the state was pro-Union and antislavery, it joined the Confederacy.

NORTH DAKOTA

Capital: **Bismarck**
Largest City: **Fargo**
Abbreviation: **N.D.**
Postal Code: **ND**

Origin of name: **From the Sioux tribe, meaning "allies"**

Entered union (rank): **November 2, 1889 (39)**

Motto: **Liberty and union, now and forever: one and inseparable**

Tree: **American elm**

Flower: **wild prairie rose**

Bird: **western meadowlark**

Other: **equine: Nokota horse; grass: western wheatgrass**

Song: **"North Dakota Hymn"**

Nicknames: **Sioux State, Flickertail State, Peace Garden State and Rough Rider State**

Residents: **North Dakotan**

Land area: **70,704 square miles (183,123 sq km)**

Population (2003): **633,837**

Home of: **The "World's Largest Buffalo," a 26-foot-high, 60-ton concrete monument**

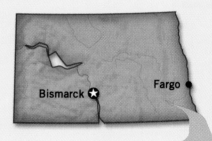

Did You Know? Farms cover more than 90% of North Dakota's land.

OHIO

Capital: **Columbus**
Largest City: **Columbus**

Abbreviation: **Ohio**
Postal Code: **OH**

Columbus

Origin of name: From an Iroquoian word meaning "great river"

Entered union (rank): March 1, 1803 (17)

Motto: With God all things are possible

Tree: buckeye

Flower: scarlet carnation

Bird: cardinal

Other: beverage: tomato juice; fossil: trilobite

Song: "Beautiful Ohio"

Nickname: Buckeye State

Residents: Ohioan

Land area: 40,953 square miles (106,067 sq km)

Population (2003): 11,435,798

Home of: The first electric traffic lights, invented and installed in Cleveland in 1914

Did You Know? The Cincinnati Reds were the world's first professional baseball team.

OKLAHOMA

Capital: **Oklahoma City**
Largest City: **Oklahoma City**

Abbreviation: **Okla.**
Postal Code: **OK**

Origin of name: From two Choctaw Indian words meaning "red people"

Entered union (rank): November 16, 1907 (46)

Motto: *Labor omnia vincit*
(Labor conquers all things)

Tree: redbud

Flower: mistletoe

Bird: scissor-tailed flycatcher

Other: furbearer: raccoon; waltz: "Oklahoma Wind"

Song: "Oklahoma!"

Nickname: Sooner State

Residents: Oklahoman

Land area: 68,679 square miles (177,880 sq km)

Population (2003): 3,511,532

Home of: The first parking meter, installed in Oklahoma City in 1935

Oklahoma City

Did You Know? Oklahoma's state capitol building is the only capitol in the world with an oil well under it.

OREGON

Capital: Salem
Largest City: Portland
Abbreviation: Ore.
Postal Code: OR

Origin of name: **Unknown**

Entered union (rank): **February 14, 1859 (33)**

Motto: *Alis volat propriis* **(She flies with her own wings)**

Tree: **Douglas fir**

Flower: **Oregon grape**

Bird: **western meadowlark**

Other: **fish: Chinook salmon; nut: hazelnut**

Song: **"Oregon, My Oregon"**

Nickname: **Beaver State**

Residents: **Oregonian**

Land area: **96,003 square miles (248,647 sq km)**

Population (2003): **3,559,596**

Home of: **The world's smallest park, totaling 452 square inches, created in Portland on St. Patrick's Day in 1948 for leprechauns and snail races**

Did You Know? Oregon's state flag is the only one with designs on both sides.

PENNSYLVANIA

Capital: Harrisburg
Largest City: Philadelphia
Abbreviation: Pa.
Postal Code: PA

Origin of name: **In honor of Sir William Penn, father of state founder William Penn. It means "Penn's Woodland."**

Entered union (rank): **December 12, 1787 (2)**

Motto: **Virtue, liberty and independence**

Tree: **hemlock**

Flower: **mountain laurel**

Bird: **ruffed grouse**

Other: **dog: Great Dane; insect: firefly**

Song: **"Pennsylvania"**

Nickname: **Keystone State**

Residents: **Pennsylvanian**

Land area: **44,820 square miles (116,083 sq km)**

Population (2003): **12,365,455**

Home of: **The first magazine in America, the *American Magazine*, published in Philadelphia for three months in 1741**

Did You Know? The first baseball stadium in the U.S., Pittsburgh's Forbes Field, was built in 1909.

RHODE ISLAND

Origin of name: From the Greek Island of Rhodes

Entered union (rank): May 29, 1790 (13)

Motto: Hope

Tree: red maple

Flower: violet

Bird: Rhode Island Red hen

Other: shell: quahog; stone: cumberlandite

Song: "Rhode Island"

Nickname: Ocean State

Residents: Rhode Islander

Land area: 1,045 square miles (2,706 sq km)

Population (2003): 1,076,164

Home of: Rhode Island Red chickens, first bred in 1854; the start of poultry as a major American industry

Providence

Did You Know? Rhode Island is the smallest of the 50 U.S. states.

SOUTH CAROLINA

Capital: Columbia   Abbreviation: S.C.
Largest City: Columbia   Postal Code: SC

Origin of name: In honor of Charles I of England

Entered union (rank): May 23, 1788 (8)

Mottoes: *Animis opibusque parati* (Prepared in mind and resources) and *Dum spiro spero* (While I breathe, I hope)

Tree: palmetto

Flower: yellow jessamine

Bird: Carolina wren

Other: hospitality beverage: tea; music: the spiritual

Song: "Carolina"

Nickname: Palmetto State

Residents: South Carolinian

Land area: 30,111 square miles (77,988 sq km)

Population (2003): 4,147,152

Home of: The first tea farm in the U.S., created in 1890 near Summerville

Columbia

Did You Know? South Carolina was the first state to secede from the Union. The Civil War started here.

UNITED STATES

SOUTH DAKOTA

Capital: Pierre
Largest City: Sioux Falls
Abbreviation: S.D.
Postal Code: SD

Origin of name: From the Sioux tribe, meaning "allies"

Entered union (rank): November 2, 1889 (40)

Motto: Under God the people rule

Tree: black hills spruce

Flower: American pasqueflower

Bird: ring-necked pheasant

Other: dessert: kuchen; jewelry: Black Hills gold

Song: "Hail! South Dakota"

Nicknames: Mount Rushmore State and Coyote State

Residents: South Dakotan

Land area: 75,898 square miles (196,575 sq km)

Population (2003): 764,309

Home of: The world's largest natural indoor warm-water pool, Evans' Plunge, in Hot Springs

Did You Know? It took Gutzon Borglum 14 years to carve Mount Rushmore.

TENNESSEE

Capital: Nashville
Largest City: Memphis
Abbreviation: Tenn.
Postal Code: TN

Origin of name: Of Cherokee origin; the exact meaning is unknown

Entered union (rank): June 1, 1796 (16)

Motto: Agriculture and commerce

Tree: tulip poplar

Flower: iris

Bird: mockingbird

Other: amphibian: Tennessee cave salamander; animal: raccoon

Songs: "Tennessee Waltz," "My Homeland, Tennessee," "When It's Iris Time in Tennessee," "My Tennessee," "Rocky Top" and "Tennessee"

Nickname: Volunteer State

Residents: Tennessean, Tennesseean

Land area: 41,220 square miles (106,759 sq km)

Population (2003): 5,841,748

Home of: Graceland, the estate and grave site of Elvis Presley

Did You Know? Nashville, site of the Grand Ole Opry, is considered the country-music capital of the world.

TEXAS

Capital: Austin
Largest City: Houston
Abbreviation: Tex.
Postal Code: TX

Origin of name: From a Native American word meaning "friends"

Entered union (rank): December 29, 1845 (28)

Motto: Friendship

Tree: pecan

Flower: bluebonnet

Bird: mockingbird

Other: fiber and fabric: cotton; small mammal: armadillo

Song: "Texas, Our Texas"

Nickname: Lone Star State

Residents: Texan

Land area: 261,914 square miles (678,358 sq km)

Population (2003): 22,118,509

Home of: NASA, in Houston, the headquarters for all piloted U.S. space projects

Did You Know? Texans fought the Mexican Army at the Alamo, known now as the "cradle of Texas liberty."

UTAH

Capital: Salt Lake City
Largest City: Salt Lake City
Abbreviation: Utah
Postal Code: UT

Origin of name: From the Ute tribe, meaning "people of the mountains"

Entered union (rank): January 4, 1896 (45)

Motto: Industry

Tree: blue spruce

Flower: sego lily

Bird: California gull

Other: cooking pot: Dutch oven; fruit: cherry

Song: "Utah, We Love Thee"

Nickname: Beehive State

Residents: Utahan, Utahn

Land area: 82,168 square miles (212,816 sq km)

Population (2003): 2,351,467

Home of: Rainbow Bridge, the largest natural stone bridge in the world, 290 feet high, 275 feet across

Did You Know? Driving the "golden spike" at Promontory Point in 1869 completed the transcontinental railroad.

VERMONT

Capital: **Montpelier**
Largest City: **Burlington**
Abbreviation: **Vt.**
Postal Code: **VT**

Origin of name: **From the French *vert mont*, meaning "green mountain"**

Entered union (rank): **March 4, 1791 (14)**

Motto: **Vermont, freedom and unity**

Tree: **sugar maple**

Flower: **red clover**

Bird: **hermit thrush**

Other: **animal: Morgan horse; insect: honeybee**

Song: **"Hail, Vermont!"**

Nickname: **Green Mountain State**

Residents: **Vermonter**

Land area: **9,249 square miles (23,956 sq km)**

Population (2003): **619,107**

Home of: **The largest production of maple syrup in the U.S.**

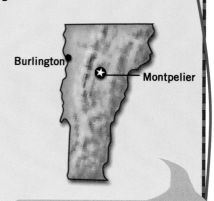

Burlington

Montpelier

Did You Know? Montpelier, with just over 8,000 residents, is the smallest state capital in the United States.

VIRGINIA

Capital: **Richmond**
Largest City: **Virginia Beach**
Abbreviation: **Va.**
Postal Code: **VA**

Origin of name: **In honor of Elizabeth I, "Virgin Queen" of England**

Entered union (rank): **June 25, 1788 (10)**

Motto: ***Sic semper tyrannis* (Thus always to tyrants)**

Tree: **dogwood**

Flower: **American dogwood**

Bird: **cardinal**

Other: **dog: American foxhound; shell: oyster shell**

Song: **"Carry Me Back to Old Virginia"**

Nicknames: **The Old Dominion and Mother of Presidents**

Residents: **Virginian**

Land area: **39,598 square miles (102,558 sq km)**

Population (2003): **7,386,330**

Home of: **The only full-length statue of George Washington**

Richmond

Virginia Beach

Did You Know? Jamestown was the first permanent English settlement in North America.

WASHINGTON

Capital: Olympia
Largest City: Seattle
Abbreviation: Wash.
Postal Code: WA

Seattle

Olympia

Origin of name: In honor of George Washington

Entered union (rank): November 11, 1889 (42)

Motto: *Al-ki* (Indian word meaning "by and by")

Tree: western hemlock

Flower: coast rhododendron

Bird: willow goldfinch

Other: fossil: Columbian mammoth; fruit: apple

Song: "Washington, My Home"

Nickname: Evergreen State

Residents: Washingtonian

Land area: 66,582 square miles (17,447 sq km)

Population (2003): 6,131,445

Home of: The Lunar Rover, the vehicle used by astronauts on the Moon in 1971. Boeing, in Seattle, makes aircraft and spacecraft.

Did You Know? The Grand Coulee dam, on the Columbia River, is the largest concrete structure in the U.S.

WEST VIRGINIA

Capital: Charleston
Largest City: Charleston
Abbreviation: W.Va.
Postal Code: WV

Origin of name: In honor of Elizabeth I, "Virgin Queen" of England

Entered union (rank): June 20, 1863 (35)

Motto: *Montani semper liberi* (Mountaineers are always free)

Tree: sugar maple

Flower: rhododendron

Bird: cardinal

Other: animal: black bear; fruit: golden delicious apple

Charleston

Songs: "West Virginia," "My Home Sweet Home," "The West Virginia Hills" and "This Is My West Virginia"

Nickname: Mountain State

Residents: West Virginian

Land area: 24,087 square miles (62,384 sq km)

Population (2003): 1,810,354

Home of: Marbles. Most of the country's glass marbles are made around Parkersburg.

Did You Know? Mother's Day was first celebrated in Grafton in 1908.

WISCONSIN

Capital: Madison
Largest City: Milwaukee
Abbreviation: Wis.
Postal Code: WI

Origin of name: French corruption of an Indian word whose meaning is disputed

Entered union (rank): May 29, 1848 (30)

Motto: Forward

Tree: sugar maple

Flower: wood violet

Bird: robin

Other: dance: polka; symbol of peace: mourning dove

Song: "On Wisconsin"

Nickname: Badger State

Residents: Wisconsinite

Land area: 54,314 square miles (140,673 sq km)

Population (2003): 5,472,299

Home of: The typewriter, invented in Milwaukee in 1867

Madison
Milwaukee

Did You Know? Wisconsin produced a 17-ton cheddar cheese for the 1964 New York World's Fair.

WYOMING

Capital: Cheyenne
Largest City: Cheyenne
Abbreviation: Wyo.
Postal Code: WY

Origin of name: From a Delaware Indian word meaning "mountains and valleys alternating"

Entered union (rank): July 10, 1890 (44)

Motto: Equal rights

Tree: cottonwood

Flower: Indian paintbrush

Bird: meadowlark

Other: dinosaur: *Triceratops;* gemstone: jade

Song: "Wyoming"

Nickname: Equality State

Residents: Wyomingite

Land area: 97,105 square miles (251,501 sq km)

Population (2003): 501,242

Home of: The Register of the Desert, a huge granite boulder that covers 27 acres and has 5,000 names of early pioneers carved on it

Cheyenne

Did You Know? Wyoming, with fewer than 500,000 people, ranks 50th in state populations.

WASHINGTON, D.C.

The **District of Columbia**, which covers the same area as the city of Washington, is the capital of the United States. It is located between Virginia and Maryland on the Potomac River. The district is named after Columbus. The Federal Government and tourism are the mainstays of its economy. Many unions as well as business, professional and nonprofit organizations have headquarters there.

D.C. history began in 1790 when Congress took charge of organizing a new site for the capital. George Washington chose the spot, midway between the northern and southern states on the Potomac River. The seat of government was transferred from Philadelphia, Pennsylvania, to Washington, D.C., on December 1, 1800, and President John Adams became the first resident of the White House.

A petition asking for the district's admission to the Union as the 51st state was filed in Congress on September 9, 1983. The district is continuing this drive for statehood.

Motto: *Justitia omnibus* (Justice to all)

Flower: American Beauty rose

Tree: scarlet oak

Land area: 68.25 square miles (177 sq km)

Population (2003): 563,384

WASHINGTON, D.C., LANDMARKS

In addition to the **White House,** several architectural masterpieces and symbolic landmarks are found in our nation's capital. Here are some of them.

Capitol Building

This is where Congress meets and conducts business.

Jefferson Memorial

This memorial to Thomas Jefferson is modeled on the Roman Pantheon.

Lincoln Memorial

Lincoln's Gettysburg Address is carved into the walls of the south chamber, and his famous Second Inaugural speech is on the north-chamber wall.

National Archives

The records of the three branches of government are kept here, including the Declaration of Independence.

Smithsonian Institution

The Smithsonian is a network of 14 museums, art galleries and research centers.

U.S. Holocaust Memorial Museum

This is America's national institution for the documentation, study and interpretation of Holocaust history.

Vietnam Veterans Memorial

This V-shaped monument lists the names of the 58,000 veterans who died during the Vietnam War.

Washington Monument

This monument to our first President stands just over 555 feet high. Stones from the 50 states and several foreign countries line the inside walls.

go For fun facts and trivia on all the states, go to www.FACTMONSTER.COM

The U.S. Territories

A territory is a region that belongs to the U.S. but is not one of the 50 states. Although territories govern themselves to a limited extent, they are really governed by the U.S. Territories sometimes become states; Alaska and Hawaii were the last two territories admitted to the Union as states.

The Commonwealth of Puerto Rico

Puerto Rico is located in the Caribbean Sea, about 1,000 miles east-southeast of Miami, Florida. A U.S. possession since 1898, it consists of the island of Puerto Rico plus the adjacent islets of Vieques, Culebra and Mona.

Capital: San Juan
Land area: 3,459 square miles (8,959 sq km)
Population estimate (2003): 3,885,877
Languages: Spanish and English

Guam

Guam, the largest and southernmost island in the Mariana Island chain (see "Northern Mariana Islands," below), became a U.S. territory in 1898.

Capital: Agaña
Land area: 212 square miles (549 sq km)
Population estimate (2003): 163,941
Languages: English and Chamorro; Japanese is also widely spoken

The Commonwealth of the Northern Mariana Islands (CNMI)

The Northern Mariana Islands, east of the Philippines and south of Japan, have been part of the U.S. since 1986. They include the islands of Rota, Saipan, Tinian, Pagan, Guguan, Agrihan and Aguijan.

Capital: Chalan Kanoa (on Saipan)
Total area: 184.17 square miles (477 sq km)
Population estimate (2003): 80,006
Languages: English, Chamorro, Carolinian

The U.S. Virgin Islands

The Virgin Islands consist of nine main islands and some 75 islets. Since 1666, Britain has ruled six of the main islands; the remaining three (St. Croix, St. Thomas and St. John), as well as about 50 of the islets, were acquired by Denmark and then purchased by the U.S in 1917.

Capital: Charlotte Amalie (on St. Thomas)
Land area: 140 square miles (363 sq km): St. Croix, 84 square miles (218 sq km); St. Thomas, 32 square miles (83 sq km); St. John, 20 square miles (52 sq km)
Population estimate (2003): 124,778
Languages: Mostly English, but Spanish and French are also spoken

American Samoa

American Samoa is a group of five volcanic islands and two coral atolls. It is located some 2,600 miles south of Hawaii in the South Pacific. It includes the eastern Samoan islands of Tutuila, Aunu'u and Rose; three islands (Ta'u, Olosega and Ofu) of the Manu'a group; and Swains Island. The territory became part of the U.S. in 1900, except for Swains Island, which was acquired in 1925.

Capital: Pago Pago
Land area: 77 square miles (199 sq km)
Population estimate (2003): 70,260
Languages: Samoan (closely related to Hawaiian) and English

The Midway Islands

The Midway Islands lie about 1,150 miles west-northwest of Hawaii. They became part of the U.S. in 1867.

Total area: 2 square miles (5.2 sq km)
Population estimate (2003): no indigenous inhabitants; about 40 people make up the staff of the U.S. Fish and Wildlife Service.

Wake Island

Wake Island, between Midway and Guam, is an atoll consisting of the three islets of Wilkes, Peale and Wake. It was annexed by Hawaii in 1899.

Total area: 2.5 square miles (6.5 sq km)
Population estimate (2003): no indigenous inhabitants; 200 U.S. military personnel and civilian contractors

Johnston Atoll

Johnston is a coral atoll about 700 miles southwest of Hawaii. It consists of four small islands—Johnston Island, Sand Island, Hikina Island and Akau Island—which lie on a 9-mile-long reef. It was claimed by Hawaii in 1858.

Land area: 1.08 square miles (2.8 sq km)
Population estimate (2003): No indigenous inhabitants; about 800 U.S. military and civilian contractors.

Baker, Howland and Jarvis Islands

These Pacific islands were claimed by the U.S. in 1936. **Baker Island** is an atoll of approximately 1 square mile (2.6 sq km) located about 1,650 miles from Hawaii. **Howland Island,** 36 miles to the northwest, is 1 mile long. Tiny **Jarvis Island** is several hundred miles to the east.

Kingman Reef

Kingman Reef, located about 1,000 miles south of Hawaii, has been a U.S. possession since 1922. Triangular in shape, it is about 9.5 miles long.

Did You Know?

An atoll is a coral island made up of a reef surrounding a lagoon (shallow pool).

Navassa Island

Navassa Island is located in the Caribbean Sea, between Cuba, Haiti and Jamaica. It has an area of 2 square miles (5.2 sq km) and was claimed for the U.S. in 1857.

Palmyra Atoll

Palmyra Atoll has a total area of 4.6 square miles (11.9 sq km) and is located 994 miles (1,600 km) southwest of Honolulu.

TFK Mystery Person

CLUE 1: I was born into slavery in Maryland in 1818.
CLUE 2: When I was 20 years old, I escaped to the North. I became a famous abolitionist and published the antislavery newspaper North Star.
CLUE 3: After the Civil War, I worked to protect the rights of African Americans.

WHO AM I?

(See Answer Key that begins on page 340.)

VOLUNTEERING

Building a Better World

Camille Mahlknecht, 9, and other residents of Agoura Hills, California, plan to pick up trash during their city's annual cleanup. Gathering garbage may not sound like a good time to you—but it does to Camille. "It makes me feel terrific inside to help out and make the community clean," she says.

At the same time, Wissam Raed, 12, will be busy volunteering too. Thousands of miles away in Hasbaya, Lebanon, Wissam plans to help put on a play at an orphanage and bring potted plants to elderly people at a senior-citizens center.

Each April, more than 3 million young Americans and millions of kids from 127 other countries participate in National and Global Youth Service Day, which is run by Youth Service America (YSA) with the Global Youth Action Network. Community service has become hugely popular. *Zoom*, a television show on PBS, conducted a survey of almost 10,000 U.S. kids. Nearly 80% said that they volunteer.

School is a big reason that kids are so involved in volunteer work. According to recent statistics, about two-thirds of all U.S. public schools offer community-service activities. In a third of all schools,

By Elizabeth Winchester

Kids help hang a door at a family center in Washington, D.C., on Youth Service Day.

teachers combine volunteer work with classroom lessons. In many schools and clubs, service work is a requirement.

Almost every student at Oakley Park Elementary School in Walled Lake, Michigan, helps protect children around the world by raising money for "Trick-or-Treat for UNICEF." One year the school collected more than $10,000—more than any other school!

According to a report issued by YSA and a research group called Independent Sector, kids who start volunteering are twice as likely to continue doing good deeds when they are adults. It's never too early to start!

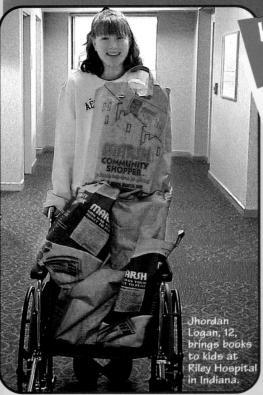

Jhordan Logan, 12, brings books to kids at Riley Hospital in Indiana.

On group projects, make a list of the phone numbers and e-mail addresses of the students with whom you are working.

TIPS for Planning a Service Project

Organizing a service project takes thought and planning. Here are some tips to help you get started.

- Identify a problem that exists in your community.
- Learn more about the problem and think about ways to solve it.
- Set a goal for the project.
- Decide what supplies and help you'll need.
- Get the whole school involved! Encourage other classes to help you with your project. Parents can also lend a helping hand.
- Have fun! Knowing that you are helping to make a difference in your community should bring you enjoyment.

A Little Bit Goes a Long Way

Kids in New York sell treats to raise money for a community garden.

Your service project can be as complex as helping to build a home or as simple as collecting coins for charity. Here are some ways kids can make a difference.

- Visit a local retirement or nursing home. Sing songs, recite poems or read for the elderly people.
- Donate old toys, clothing and toiletries to families in need.
- Have a bake sale. Choose an organization or a cause to support.
- Pick up papers, cans and litter.
- Help the hungry and homeless. Cook or serve a meal at a shelter.
- Help people with special needs. Volunteer to help at a Special Olympics event. Bring books and toys to kids at local hospitals.
- Get involved in government. Find out what you can do to encourage people to register to vote. Identify a local problem and write to officials with your ideas for how to solve it.

go ▸ Find out how to make a difference at *www.timeforkids.com/fixtheworld*

TRICK-OR-TREAT FOR UNICEF

Kids in the United States have been taking part in "Trick-or-Treat for UNICEF" since the program began in 1950. They have raised $115 million! The chart below shows how UNICEF helps the world's children with the money you raise.

Actress Sarah Jessica Parker reads to UNICEF volunteers.

AMOUNT	WHAT IT BUYS
4¢	Two vitamin A capsules to protect a child against blindness
36¢	Penicillin to treat a child's infection
$1.00	Polio vaccine for one child (lifetime protection) or 120 water-purification tablets, each making one gallon of water drinkable
$2.00	40 packets of rehydration salts, used to treat dehydration
$7.00	School supplies for three children, including chalk, a slate, colored pencils and a plastic schoolbag
$20.13	A first-aid kit
$150.00	A hand pump and pipes for a well that will serve 250 people
$220.00	One large cold-storage box to maintain vaccines

TFK SPOTLIGHT

Gidget hopes one day there will be no homeless people in the world.

A Helping Hand

Gidget Schultz, 14, couldn't bear to see kids living on the streets near her Encinitas, California, home. At age 10, she tried to volunteer at homeless shelters but was told she was too young. So she started her own charity! Gidget's Way gives teddy bears, backpacks and school supplies to homeless kids in San Diego County. Each January, Gidget also has an "unbirthday party." Instead of having a bash in her honor, she gives the homeless kids cake, gifts and a party.

"Managing Gidget's Way is a full-time job," says the eighth grader. Sadly, a recent illness left Gidget unable to walk. But she hasn't slowed down. She hopes to expand Gidget's Way nationwide. If you would like to help, go to: www.gidgetswayxoxo.org

Help Wanted

These organizations give kids opportunities to make a difference.

American Society for the Prevention of Cruelty to Animals (ASPCA)
424 E. 92nd St.
New York, NY 10128
212-876-7700
www.aspca.org
Kids can hold fund raisers, and collect blankets, towels and toys for animals in shelters. They can also write letters to lobby for animal welfare.

Do Something
423 W. 55th St.
8th Floor
New York, NY 10019
212-523-1175
http://dosomething.org
Works with kids to identify important issues and create community projects

Habitat for Humanity International
121 Habitat St.
Americus, GA 31709-3498
229-924-6935
www.habitat.org
Kids help build homes for people in need around the world.

Keep America Beautiful
1010 Washington Blvd.
Stamford, CT 06901
302-323-8987
www.kab.org/kids1.cfm
Gives kids ideas on how to clean up their communities

Kids Care Clubs
975 Boston Post Road
Darien, CT 06820
203-656-8052
www.kidscare.org
Gives young people a chance to make a difference by providing monthly service projects

Make-A-Wish Foundation of America
3550 North Central Ave.
Suite 300
Phoenix, AZ 85012-2127
800-722-WISH (9474)
www.wish.org
Kids help raise money to grant the wishes of children with life-threatening illnesses.

National Park Service-Jr. Ranger Programs
1849 C St., NW
Washington, D.C. 20240
202-208-6843
www.nps.gov/learn/grranger zone/ranger.htm
Kids can participate in Jr. Ranger programs to help protect our national parks.

Project Linus
P.O. Box 5621
Bloomington, IL 61702-5621
309-664-7814
www.projectlinus.org
Kids can make blankets for needy children.

Special Olympics
1325 G St., NW
Suite 500
Washington, D.C. 20005
800-700-8585
www.specialolympics.org
Kids can volunteer to help raise money and run the events.

Toys For Tots Marine Toys For Tots Foundation
P.O. Box 1947
Quantico, VA 22134
703-640-9433
www.toysfortots.org
Kids can donate holiday presents to other children.

UNICEF
3 United Nations Plaza
New York, NY 10017
212-326-7000
www.unicef.org/young
Kids can raise money for the Trick-or-Treat for UNICEF campaign each Halloween and all year long.

TFK Mystery Person

CLUE 1: Born in Massachusetts in 1821, I was a nurse and a teacher.
CLUE 2: I worked as a volunteer, caring for wounded soldiers during the Civil War.
CLUE 3: In 1881, I founded the American Red Cross and served as its president for 23 years. Today, the organization helps victims of disasters.

WHO AM I?
(See Answer Key that begins on page 340.)

WEATHER

Hang On to Your Hat! It's a

HURRICANE!

A storm is declared a hurricane when winds reach speeds of 74 miles an hour. Wind speeds can exceed 190 miles per hour in some hurricanes. In the U.S., the official hurricane season lasts from June 1 to November 30, but hurricanes can happen at any time of the year. Cyclones, hurricanes and typhoons are the same kind of tropical storm but are called different names in different parts of the world.

What's Your Name?

Because hurricanes often occur at the same time, officials assign short, distinctive names to the storms to avoid confusion among weather stations, coastal bases and ships at sea. A storm is given a name once its winds reach 40 miles per hour. These are the names that have been chosen for Atlantic storms in 2004 and 2005:

2004: Alex, Bonnie, Charley, Danielle, Earl, Frances, Gaston, Hermine, Ivan, Jeanne, Karl, Lisa, Matthew, Nicole, Otto, Paula, Richard, Shary, Tomas, Virginie and Walter

2005: Arlene, Bret, Cindy, Dennis, Emily, Franklin, Gert, Harvey, Jose, Katrina, Lee, Nate, Ophelia, Philippe, Rita, Stan, Tammy, Vince, Wilma

Did You Know?

When hurricanes are particularly destructive, their names are retired from the list of usable names. A retired name cannot be reused for at least 10 years.

Isabel Hits the Coast
By Dina El Nabli

Isabel pounded the coast of North Carolina.

The hurricane also caused flooding in North Beach, Maryland.

Howling winds roared at 100 miles per hour, downing trees and damaging beachfront homes. Heavy rain fell across hundreds of miles of land. More than 4.5 million people lost power, and over 1,500 airline flights were canceled in the late summer of 2003 as Hurricane Isabel stormed its way ashore, moving into North Carolina and pushing up the East Coast.

Despite its strong winds, Isabel did not do as much damage as weather forecasters had predicted. It did manage to dump as much as four inches of rain in Pennsylvania before moving toward Ohio and Canada. The huge storm was blamed for at least 17 deaths.

National Hurricane Center director Max Mayfield said Isabel posed a threat because of its size, roughly equal to that of Colorado. "This hurricane will not be remembered for how strong it was," Mayfield said. "It will be remembered for how large it was."

Gathering Speed

Tropical wind systems are classified according to their wind speeds. The faster a storm blows, the more destructive it gets.

Tropical Storm
Winds 40 to 73 miles per hour

Category 1 Hurricane
Winds 74 to 95 miles per hour

Category 2 Hurricane
Winds 96 to 110 miles per hour

Category 3 Hurricane
Winds 111 to 130 miles per hour

Category 4 Hurricane
Winds 131 to 155 miles per hour

Category 5 Hurricane
Winds greater than 155 miles per hour

TFK Top 5 Hurricane States

From 1900 to 2002, 166 hurricanes struck the continental United States. The states that hug the Atlantic Ocean and the Gulf of Mexico get hit most often. Here are the states where the most hurricanes have blown ashore.

1. Florida		59 hurricanes
2. Texas		37 hurricanes
3. North Carolina		29 hurricanes
4. Louisiana		25 hurricanes
5. South Carolina		14 hurricanes

Sources: National Hurricane Center and National Climatic Data Center

go Learn how to track weather changes in your area at *www.timeforkids.com/weatherwatch*

THUNDERSTORMS

Nearly 1,800 thunderstorms are happening at any moment around the world. That's 16 million a year!

You can estimate how many miles away a storm is by counting the number of seconds between the flash of lightning and the clap of thunder. Divide the number of seconds by five to get the distance in miles. The lightning is seen before the thunder is heard because light travels faster than sound.

Thunderstorms affect small areas when compared with hurricanes and winter storms. The typical thunderstorm is 15 miles in diameter and lasts an average of 30 minutes.

Did You Know?

Many mythical gods, including Zeus (Greek), Jupiter (Roman), Thor (Germanic), Perun (Slavic) and Chac (Mayan), used the thunderbolt—the ultimate symbol of power.

Safety Zone

During a thunderstorm, avoid open spaces, trees and ball parks. The safest place to be is in a building, preferably one with a lightning rod. The rod offers protection by intercepting lightning—an electrical discharge—and transmitting its current to the ground. The other safe place to be is in a car with the windows rolled up, as long as you don't touch any of the metal parts. Rubber-soled shoes and rubber tires provide NO protection from lightning.

LIGHTNING

TFK Puzzles & Games

Lightning Strikes Twice

These six pictures of a lightning storm look alike, but only two of them are identical. Can you find the matching pair of pictures?

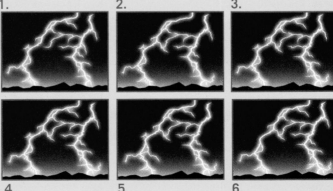

1.
2.
3.
4.
5.
6.

(See Answer Key that begins on page 340.)

EXTREMEs OF CLIMATE

Lowest Recorded Temperatures

Place	Date	°F	°C
World: Vostok, Antarctica	July 21, 1983	–129	–89
U.S.: Prospect Creek, Alaska	January 23, 1971	–80	–62

Highest Recorded Temperatures

Place	Date	°F	°C
World: El Azizia, Libya, Africa	September 13, 1922	136	58
U.S.: Death Valley, California	July 10, 1913	134	57

Greatest Snowfalls in North America

Duration	Place	Date	Inches
24 hours	Silver Lake, Colo.	April 14–15, 1921	76
1 month	Tamarack, Calif.	Jan. 1911	390
1 storm	Mount Shasta Ski Bowl, Calif.	Feb. 13–19, 1959	189
1 season	Mount Baker, Wash.	1998–1999	1,140

BLIZZARD BLITZ

A blizzard is a winter storm with high winds, low temperatures and driving snow. According to the U.S. Weather Bureau's official definition, the winds must exceed 35 miles (56 km) per hour and the temperature must drop to 20°F (-7°C) or lower.

The worst winter storm in U.S. history

The Blizzard of 1888 surprised the northeastern U.S. with as much as five feet of snow in some areas. Two hundred boats sank and more than 400 people died as a result of very powerful winds and frigid temperatures.

Did You Know?

There are six types of snowflakes: needles, columns, plates, columns topped with plates, dendrites and stars.

285

It's a Twister!

A tornado is a dark, funnel-shaped cloud made up of violently churning winds that can reach speeds of up to 300 miles an hour. A tornado can be from a few feet wide to a mile wide, and its track can extend from less than a mile to several hundred miles. Tornadoes generally travel in a northeast direction at speeds ranging from 20 to 60 miles an hour. Tornadoes are most often caused by giant thunderstorms that are called "supercells." These highly powerful storms form when warm, moist air along the ground rushes upward, meeting cooler, drier air. As the rising warm air cools, the moisture it carries condenses, forming a massive thundercloud, sometimes growing to as much as 50,000 feet in height. Winds at different levels of the atmosphere feed the updraft and cause the formation of the tornado's characteristic funnel shape.

The Fujita scale classifies tornadoes according to the damage they cause. Almost half of all tornadoes fall into the F1 or "moderate damage" category. These tornadoes reach speeds of 73 to 112 miles per hour and can overturn automobiles and uproot trees. Only about 1% of tornadoes are classified as F5, causing "incredible damage." With wind speeds in excess of 261 miles per hour, these storms can hurl houses and cars.

Did You Know?

In April 1974, 148 tornadoes hit 11 states, killing 315 people, injuring more than 5,300 and causing more than $600 million in damage. Alabama, Kentucky and Ohio were the states hardest hit. It was the largest known tornado outbreak in U.S. history.

HOW'S THE WEATHER?

Temperature

Air temperature is measured by a mercury thermometer. When the temperature rises, the mercury expands and rises in the thermometer tube. When the temperature falls, the mercury contracts and falls.

In the U.S., the **Fahrenheit** scale is used most often. On this scale, 32° is the freezing point of water, and 212° is the boiling point.

The **Celsius,** or centigrade, scale is used by the World Meteorological Organization and most countries in the world. On this scale, 0° is freezing, and 100° is boiling.

To convert Fahrenheit to Celsius, subtract 32, multiply by 5, and divide the result by 9.
Example: To convert 50°F to °C: 50 − 32 = 18; 18 x 5 = 90; 90 ÷ 9 = 10

To convert Celsius to Fahrenheit, multiply by 9, divide by 5, and add 32.
Example: To convert 10°C to °F: 10 x 9 = 90; 90 ÷ 5 = 18; 18 + 32 = 50

°Celsius	°Fahrenheit
−50	−58
−40	−40
−30	−22
−20	−4
−10	14
0	32
5	41
10	50
15	59
20	68
25	77
30	86
35	95
40	104
45	113
50	122

WEATHER

Did You Know?

Clouds are little drops of water hanging in the atmosphere. When clouds become heavy with humidity, water (precipitation) falls from them. Warm clouds produce rain, cold clouds produce snow and thunderstorm clouds can bring hail.

TFK Mystery Person

CLUE 1: I was born a free African American in 1731. While living on a farm in Maryland, I taught myself math and astronomy.
CLUE 2: I helped in the surveying of Washington, D.C., in 1792.
CLUE 3: I published an almanac from 1792 to 1796. It predicted the yearly weather, as well as sunrises, sunsets and tides.

WHO AM I?

(See Answer Key that begins on page 340.)

WORLD

Stealing Beauty

By Hannah Beech

During the day, the people of Xiaoli, China, sit outside their mud-brick shacks, fanning themselves. Xiaoli is a poor village in China's Henan province. Most people in Xiaoli are farmers, but high taxes have made farming unprofitable. So the farmers have nothing to do but wait for darkness to fall. At night, Xiaoli comes alive. That's when the tomb raiders go to work.

Underneath Xiaoli lie the riches of 5,000 years of Chinese history. The nearby city of Luoyang was the capital of at least nine ruling dynasties, or empires. Xiaoli's fields hold the tombs of emperors and empresses. Many of the tombs contain valuable works of art buried centuries ago. Breaking into tombs and stealing treasure is illegal— and dangerous. But for the poor farmers of Xiaoli, the temptation is great. One major haul of treasure can equal a year's farming income.

Over the past five years, thieves have broken into at least 220,000 tombs, according to China's National Cultural Relics Bureau. "If the looting continues at this pace, we'll soon have nothing left to remind us of our glorious past," says He Shuzhong, the head of Cultural Heritage Watch in Beijing, China's capital.

Wealthy art collectors will pay big bucks for ancient Asian statues, sculptures and vases. In the past year, the desire for the artwork has sparked a lawless gold rush across not just China but all of Asia.

Raiders of the Lost Art

The police in India recently busted a smuggling ring that they claim stripped hundreds of temples and monuments of sculptures. The criminals sent the artworks to collectors in the U.S. and Europe.

Recently, raiders in the Southeast Asian country of Cambodia gouged out the sculpted faces of gods from an 11th-century site. Cambodian police seized several truckloads of sculptures that were also crudely ripped from archaeological sites.

For some poor people in China, India, Cambodia and other

Robbers in Xi'an, China, stole this clay statue from an ancient tomb.

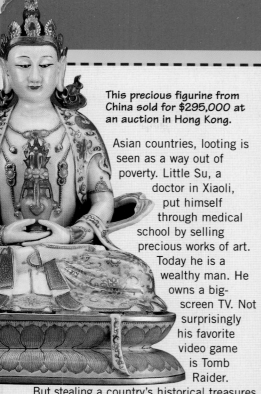

This precious figurine from China sold for $295,000 at an auction in Hong Kong.

Asian countries, looting is seen as a way out of poverty. Little Su, a doctor in Xiaoli, put himself through medical school by selling precious works of art. Today he is a wealthy man. He owns a big-screen TV. Not surprisingly his favorite video game is Tomb Raider.

But stealing a country's historical treasures is no game. Three years ago, tomb raiders broke into the 2,000-year-old tomb of Empress Dou in the city of Xi'an. Looters made off with at least 200 treasures, mostly ceramic statues. Some of the rare statues were valued at up to $80,000. Six of the figurines ended up for sale at an auction in New York City in March 2002. The Chinese government was able to stop the sale just in time.

Bringing Them Home

Now those six figurines, valued at $6,000 to $8,000 each, have been returned to Xi'an. They are on display in a small museum. Li Ku, the vice director of the museum, is overjoyed at their return. "Looking at these figures, I feel like my family has come home at last," he says.

Travel Papers

Your bags are packed and you're ready for a cool vacation abroad (to a foreign country). Do you have all the documents you need?

Passport

A passport is an official document that proves a person's identity and citizenship. U.S. citizens need a passport to leave the country and to enter the U.S. from a foreign country. You also need one to enter most foreign countries.

You can apply for a passport at a passport agency, many federal and state courts, some county and city offices and some post offices. Kids ages 14 and up must apply for a passport in person. For children ages 13 and under, a parent or legal guardian should apply for them.

For more information on what you need to apply for a passport, go to the State Department's website: http://travel.state.gov

Visa

In addition to a passport, some countries require travelers to present a visa before they can enter the country. You must apply for this additional document of identification through the foreign consulate of the country you plan to visit. Most foreign consular representatives have offices in major cities. In most cases, however, you can apply for a visa by mail.

A tourist was stopped from smuggling this Buddha out of Cambodia.

TFK Top 5 Tourist Destinations

International tourists are more likely to visit France than any other country. These are the top vacation spots.

1. France
2. Spain
3. U.S.
4. Italy
5. China

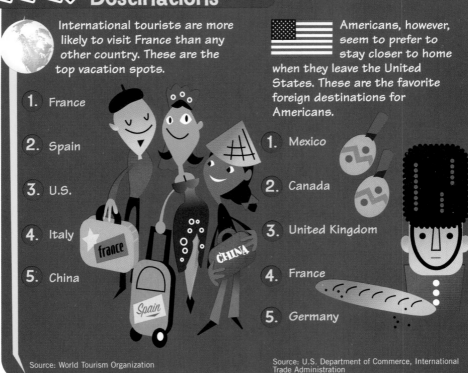

Americans, however, seem to prefer to stay closer to home when they leave the United States. These are the favorite foreign destinations for Americans.

1. Mexico
2. Canada
3. United Kingdom
4. France
5. Germany

Source: World Tourism Organization

Source: U.S. Department of Commerce, International Trade Administration

TFK Puzzles & Games

Wish You Were Here

We got these five snowglobes from a friend who enjoys traveling all around the world. Can you match each cool souvenir to the country it was sent from?

1. Egypt

2. Australia

3 Japan

4. Russia

5. Italy

(See Answer Key that begins on page 340.)

The World's Nations from A to Z

On the following pages you will find information about the world's nations. Here's an example.

If you divide the population by the area, you can find out the population density—how many people there are per square mile.

This tells the main languages and the official languages (if any) spoken in a nation. In this case, most people in the nation speak Icelandic.

This is the type of money used in the nation.

This tells an interesting fact about the country.

Iceland

Where? Europe
Capital: Reykjavik
Area: 39,768 sq mi (103,000 sq km)
Population estimate (2004): 282,151
Government: Constitutional republic
Language: Icelandic
Monetary unit: Icelandic króna
Per capita GDP: $30,200
Literacy rate: 100%
Did You Know? Iceland boasts the world's oldest constitution, drafted around 930.

The per capita GDP is a way to estimate the wealth of a nation. It represents the value of all goods and services produced by a nation in one year, divided by that nation's population.

This tells the percentage of people who can read and write.

Afghanistan

Where? Asia
Capital: Kabul
Area: 251,737 sq mi (647,500 sq km)
Population estimate (2004): 29,547,078
Government: Transitional
Languages: Pushtu, Dari Persian, other Turkic and minor languages
Monetary unit: Afghani
Per capita GDP: $700
Literacy rate: 36%
Did You Know? Islam is Afghanistan's official religion.

Albania

Where? Europe
Capital: Tirana
Area: 11,100 sq mi (28,750 sq km)
Population estimate (2004): 3,544,808
Government: Emerging democracy
Languages: Albanian (Tosk is the official dialect), Greek
Monetary unit: Lek
Per capita GDP: $4,400
Literacy rate: 87%
Did You Know? This former communist country is now a struggling democracy.

Algeria

Where? Africa
Capital: Algiers
Area: 919,590 sq mi (2,381,740 sq km)
Population estimate (2004): 33,357,089
Government: Republic
Languages: Arabic (official), French, Berber dialects
Monetary unit: Dinar
Per capita GDP: $5,400
Literacy rate: 70%
Did You Know? The Sahara Desert covers about 85% of Algeria.

Andorra

Where? Europe
Capital: Andorra la Vella
Area: 181 sq mi (468 sq km)
Population estimate (2004): 69,865
Government: Parliamentary democracy
Languages: Catalán (official), French, Spanish
Monetary units: French franc and Spanish peseta
Per capita GDP: $19,000
Literacy rate: 100%
Did You Know? This country has the world's highest life expectancy.

 Go Places with TFK! Take a country tour, hear the language, explore the history at *www.timeforkids.com/goplaces*

Angola

Where? Africa
Capital: Luanda
Area: 481,350 sq mi
(1,246,700 sq km)
Population estimate (2004):
10,978,552
Government: Republic
Languages: Bantu, Portuguese (official)
Monetary unit: Kwanza
Per capita GDP: $1,700
Literacy rate: 42%
Did You Know? In 2002, Angola ended a decades-long civil war.

Antigua and Barbuda

Where? North America
Capital: St. John's
Area: 171 sq mi
(443 sq km)
Population estimate (2004): 68,320
Government: Constitutional monarchy
Language: English
Monetary unit: East Caribbean dollar
Per capita GDP: $11,000
Literacy rate: 89%
Did You Know? The Bird family has controlled the islands since the 1940s.

Argentina

Where? South America
Capital: Buenos Aires
Area: 1,068,296 sq mi
(2,766,890 sq km)
Population estimate (2004): 39,144,753
Government: Republic
Languages: Spanish (official), English, Italian, German, French
Monetary unit: Peso
Per capita GDP: $10,500
Literacy rate: 96%
Did You Know? Most Argentineans are of Spanish or Italian descent.

Armenia

Where? Asia
Capital: Yerevan
Area: 11,500 sq mi
(29,800 sq km)
Population estimate (2004): 3,325,307
Government: Republic
Language: Armenian
Monetary unit: Dram
Per capita GDP: $3,600
Literacy rate: 99%
Did You Know? About 60% of the world's 8 million Armenians live outside Armenia.

Australia

Where? Pacific Islands
Capital: Canberra
Area: 2,967,893 sq mi
(7,686,850 sq km)
Population estimate (2004): 19,913,144
Government: Democracy
Language: English
Monetary unit: Australian dollar
Per capita GDP: $26,900
Literacy rate: 100%
Did You Know? Australia's Great Barrier Reef is the largest coral reef in the world.

Austria

Where? Europe
Capital: Vienna
Area: 32,375 sq mi
(83,850 sq km)
Population estimate (2004): 8,174,762
Government: Federal Republic
Language: German
Monetary unit: Euro (formerly schilling)
Per capita GDP: $27,900
Literacy rate: 98%
Did You Know? Three-quarters of Austria is covered by the Alps.

Azerbaijan

Where? Asia
Capital: Baku
Area: 33,400 sq mi
(86,600 sq km)
Population estimate (2004): 7,868,385
Government: Republic
Languages: Azerbaijani Turkic, Russian, Armenian
Monetary unit: Manat
Per capita GDP: $3,700
Literacy rate: 97%
Did You Know? Oil recently discovered in Azerbaijan may improve its economy.

Bahamas

Where? North America
Capital: Nassau
Area: 5,380 sq mi
(13,940 sq km)
Population estimate (2004): 299,697
Government: Parliamentary democracy
Language: English
Monetary unit: Bahamian dollar
Per capita GDP: $15,300
Literacy rate: 96%
Did You Know? The Bahamas is made up of more than 700 islands.

Bahrain

Where? Asia
Capital: Manamah
Area: 257 sq mi
(665 sq km)
Population estimate (2004): 667,886
Government: Constitutional monarchy
Languages: Arabic (official), English, Farsi, Urdu
Monetary unit: Bahrain dinar
Per capita GDP: $15,100
Literacy rate: 89%
Did You Know? Bahrain is an archipelago in the Persian Gulf.

Bangladesh

Where? Asia
Capital: Dhaka
Area: 55,598 sq mi
(144,000 sq km)
Population estimate (2004): 141,340,476
Government: Parliamentary democracy
Languages: Bangla (official), English
Monetary unit: Taka
Per capita GDP: $1,800
Literacy rate: 43%
Did You Know? Until 1971, Bangladesh was part of Pakistan.

Barbados

Where? North America
Capital: Bridgetown
Area: 166 sq mi
(431 sq km)
Population estimate (2004): 278,289
Government: Parliamentary democracy
Language: English
Monetary unit: Barbados dollar
Per capita GDP: $15,000
Literacy rate: 97%
Did You Know? Barbados was a British colony before its independence in 1966.

Belarus

Where? Europe
Capital: Minsk
Area: 80,154 sq mi
(207,600 sq km)
Population estimate (2004): 10,310,520
Government: Republic
Language: Belarussian
Monetary unit: Belarussian ruble
Per capita GDP: $8,700
Literacy rate: 100%
Did You Know? Belarus was part of the Soviet Union until it became independent in 1991.

Belgium

Where? Europe
Capital: Brussels
Area: 11,781 sq mi
(30,510 sq km)
Population estimate (2004): 10,348,276
Government: Constitutional monarchy
Languages: Dutch (Flemish), French,
German (all official)
Monetary unit: Euro (formerly Belgian franc)
Per capita GDP: $29,200
Literacy rate: 98%
Did You Know? Nuclear power generates
more than 75% of Belgium's electricity.

Belize

Where? Central America
Capital: Belmopan
Area: 8,865 sq mi
(22,960 sq km)
Population estimate (2004): 272,945
Government: Parliamentary democracy
Languages: English (official), Creole,
Spanish, Garifuna, Mayan
Monetary unit: Belize dollar
Per capita GDP: $4,900
Literacy rate: 94%
Did You Know? Belize is the only English-
speaking country in Central America.

Benin

Where? Africa
Capital: Porto-Novo
Area: 43,483 sq mi
(112,620 sq km)
Population estimate (2004): 7,250,033
Government: Multiparty democracy
Languages: French (official), African
languages
Monetary unit: CFA franc
Per capita GDP: $1,100
Literacy rate: 41%
Did You Know? Benin's pottery, masks
and bronze statues are world renowned.

Bhutan

Where? Asia
Capital: Thimphu
Area: 18,147 sq mi
(47,000 sq km)
Population estimate (2004): 2,185,569
Government: Monarchy
Language: Dzongkha
Monetary unit: Ngultrum
Per capita GDP: $1,300
Literacy rate: 42%
Did You Know? About 75% of
Bhutanese are Buddhists.

Bolivia

Where? South America
Capital: La Paz (seat of
government), Sucre
(legal capital)
Area: 424,162 sq mi (1,098,580 sq km)
Population estimate (2004): 8,724,156
Government: Republic
Languages: Spanish (official), Quechua,
Aymara, Guarani
Monetary unit: Boliviano
Per capita GDP: $2,500
Literacy rate: 87%
Did You Know? Bolivia has had more than
190 revolutions and coups since 1825.

Bosnia and Herzegovina

Where? Europe
Capital: Sarajevo
Area: 19,741 sq mi
(51,129 sq km)
Population estimate (2004): 4,007,608
Government: Emerging democracy
Languages: The language is called
Serbian, Croatian or Bosnian depending
on the speaker.
Monetary unit: Dinar
Per capita GDP: $1,900
Literacy rate: Not available
Did You Know? This country was a part
of Yugoslavia until 1992.

Botswana

Where? Africa
Capital: Gaborone
Area: 231,800 sq mi
(600,370 sq km)
Population estimate (2004): 1,561,973
Government: Parliamentary republic
Languages: English (official), Setswana
Monetary unit: Pula
Per capita GDP: $8,500
Literacy rate: 80%
Did You Know? The Kalahari Desert is located in this southern African country.

Brazil

Where? South America
Capital: Brasília
Area: 3,286,470 sq mi
(8,511,965 sq km)
Population estimate (2004): 184,101,109
Government: Federative republic
Language: Portuguese
Monetary unit: Real
Per capita GDP: $7,600
Literacy rate: 86%
Did You Know? Brazil is the largest country in South America.

Brunei

Where? Asia
Capital: Bandar Seri Begawan
Area: 2,228 sq mi (5,770 sq km)
Population estimate (2004): 365,251
Government: Constitutional sultanate
Languages: Malay (official), Chinese, English
Monetary unit: Brunei dollar
Per capita GDP: $18,600
Literacy rate: 92%
Did You Know? This tiny country is ruled by a sultan who is one of the richest men in the world.

Bulgaria

Where? Europe
Capital: Sofia
Area: 48,822 sq mi
(110,910 sq km)
Population estimate (2004): 7,517,973
Government: Parliamentary democracy
Language: Bulgarian
Monetary unit: Lev
Per capita GDP: $6,500
Literacy rate: 99%
Did You Know? Bulgaria was a communist country until 1991.

Burkina Faso

Where? Africa
Capital: Ouagadougou
Area: 105,870 sq mi
(274,200 sq km)
Population estimate (2004): 13,574,820
Government: Parliamentary republic
Languages: French (official), tribal languages
Monetary unit: CFA franc
Per capita GDP: $1,100
Literacy rate: 27%
Did You Know? This country was formerly named Upper Volta.

Burundi

Where? Africa
Capital: Bujumbura
Area: 10,745 sq mi
(27,830 sq km)
Population estimate (2004): 6,231,221
Government: Republic
Languages: Kirundi and French (both official), Swahili
Monetary unit: Burundi franc
Per capita GDP: $500
Literacy rate: 52%
Did You Know? Burundi was once a German colony.

Cambodia

Where? Asia
Capital: Phnom Penh
Area: 69,900 sq mi
(181,040 sq km)
Population estimate (2004): 13,363,421
Government: Democracy under a
constitutional monarchy
Languages: Khmer (official), French, English
Monetary unit: Riel
Per capita GDP: $1,600
Literacy rate: 70%
Did You Know? Cambodia's Angkor Wat
temple is one of the world's wonders.

Cameroon

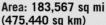

Where? Africa
Capital: Yaoundé
Area: 183,567 sq mi
(475,440 sq km)
Population estimate (2004): 16,063,678
Government: Unitary republic
Languages: French and English
(both official), African languages
Monetary unit: CFA franc
Per capita GDP: $1,700
Literacy rate: 79%
Did You Know? Germany, France and
Britain once controlled Cameroon.

Canada

Where? North America
Capital: Ottawa, Ontario
Area: 3,851,788 sq mi
(9,976,140 sq km)
Population estimate (2004): 32,507,874
Government: Parliamentary democracy
Languages: English and French
(both official)
Monetary unit: Canadian dollar
Per capita GDP: $29,300
Literacy rate: 97%
Did You Know? Canada is the world's
second largest country.

Cape Verde

Where? Africa
Capital: Praia
Area: 1,557 sq mi
(4,033 sq km)
Population estimate (2004): 415,294
Government: Republic
Languages: Portuguese, Crioulo
Monetary unit: Cape Verdean escudo
Per capita GDP: $1,400
Literacy rate: 77%
Did You Know? Off the northwest coast
of Africa, Cape Verde is made up of
10 islands and five islets.

Central African Republic

Where? Africa
Capital: Bangui
Area: 240,534 sq mi
(622,984 sq km)
Population estimate (2004): 3,742,482
Government: Republic
Languages: French (official), Sangho,
Arabic, Hansa, Swahili
Monetary unit: CFA franc
Per capita GDP: $1,200
Literacy rate: 51%
Did You Know? The C.A.R. was called the
Central African Empire from 1976 to 1979.

Chad

Where? Africa
Capital: N'Djamena
Area: 495,752 sq mi
(1,284,000 sq km)
Population estimate (2004): 9,538,544
Government: Republic
Languages: French (official), Sangho,
Arabic, Hansa, Swahili
Monetary unit: CFA franc
Per capita GDP: $1,000
Literacy rate: 48%
Did You Know? The country is named for
its largest lake, Lake Chad.

Chile

Where? South America
Capital: Santiago
Area: 292,258 sq mi
(756,950 sq km)
Population estimate (2004): 15,827,180
Government: Republic
Language: Spanish
Monetary unit: Peso
Per capita GDP: $10,100
Literacy rate: 96%
Did You Know? Chile's Atacama Desert is
the driest place on earth.

China

Where? Asia
Capital: Beijing
Area: 3,705,386 sq mi
(9,596,960 sq km)
Population estimate (2004): 1,294,629,555
Government: Communist state
Languages: Chinese (Mandarin), local
dialects
Monetary unit: Yuan
Per capita GDP: $4,700
Literacy rate: 86%
Did You Know? China is the most
populous country in the world.

Colombia

Where? South America
Capital: Bogotá
Area: 439,733 sq mi
(1,138,910 sq km)
Population estimate (2004):
42,310,775
Government: Republic
Language: Spanish
Monetary unit: Peso
Per capita GDP: $6,100
Literacy rate: 93%
Did You Know? Coffee is Colombia's
major crop.

Comoros

Where? Africa
Capital: Moroni
Area: 838 sq mi
(2,170 sq km)
Population estimate (2004): 651,901
Government: Republic
Languages: French and Arabic (both official),
Shaafi Islam (Swahili dialect), Malagasu
Monetary unit: CFA franc
Per capita GDP: $700
Literacy rate: 57%
Did You Know? Comoros is made up of
three tiny islands off the east African coast.

Congo, Democratic Republic of the

Where? Africa
Capital: Kinshasa
Area: 905,562 sq mi
(2,345,410 sq km)
Population estimate (2004): 58,317,930
Government: Dictatorship
Languages: French (official), Swahili,
Lingala, Ishiluba, Kikongo, others
Monetary unit: Congolese franc
Per capita GDP: $900
Literacy rate: 66%
Did You Know? This country was
formerly named Zaire.

Congo, Republic of the

Where? Africa
Capital: Brazzaville
Area: 132,046 sq mi
(342,000 sq km)
Population estimate (2004): 2,998,040
Government: Dictatorship
Languages: French (official), Lingala,
Kikongo, others
Monetary unit: CFA franc
Per capita GDP: $600
Literacy rate: 84%
Did You Know? Petroleum production
provides 90% of the country's revenues
and exports.

Costa Rica

Where? Central America
Capital: San José
Area: 19,730 sq mi
(51,100 sq km)
Population estimate (2004): 3,956,507
Government: Republic
Language: Spanish
Monetary unit: Colón
Per capita GDP: $8,300
Literacy rate: 96%
Did You Know? This country's name
means "rich coast."

Côte d'Ivoire

Where? Africa
Capital: Yamoussoukro
Area: 124,502 sq mi
(322,460 sq km)
Population estimate (2004): 17,327,724
Government: Republic
Languages: French (official), African
languages
Monetary unit: CFA franc
Per capita GDP: $1,400
Literacy rate: 51%
Did You Know? More than 60 distinct
tribes are represented in Côte d'Ivoire.

Croatia

Where? Europe
Capital: Zagreb
Area: 21,829 sq mi
(56,538 sq km)
Population estimate (2004): 4,435,960
Government: Parliamentary democracy
Language: Croatian
Monetary unit: Kuna
Per capita GDP: $9,800
Literacy rate: 99%
Did You Know? Croatia was part of
Yugoslavia until it declared
independence in 1991.

Cuba

Where? North America
Capital: Havana
Area: 42,803 sq mi
(110,860 sq km)
Population estimate (2004): 11,308,764
Government: Communist state
Language: Spanish
Monetary unit: Peso
Per capita GDP: $2,700
Literacy rate: 97%
Did You Know? Fidel Castro has ruled
Cuba since 1959.

Cyprus

Where? Middle East
Capital: Nicosia
Area: 3,572 sq mi (9,250 sq km)
Population estimate (2004): 775,927
Government: Republic
Languages: Greek, Turkish
Monetary unit: Cypriot pound, Turkish lira
Per capita GDP: Greek Cypriot area:
$15,000; Turkish Cypriot area: $6,000
Literacy rate: 98%
Did You Know? This nation is divided by
a long-standing conflict between its
Greek and Turkish populations.

Czech Republic

Where? Europe
Capital: Prague
Area: 30,450 sq mi
(78,866 sq km)
Population estimate (2004): 10,246,178
Government: Parliamentary democracy
Language: Czech
Monetary unit: Koruna
Per capita GDP: $15,300
Literacy rate: 100%
Did You Know? Until 1993, the country
was part of Czechoslovakia, which now
no longer exists.

Denmark

Where? Europe
Capital: Copenhagen
Area: 16,639 sq mi (43,094 sq km)
Population estimate (2004): 5,413,392
Government: Constitutional monarchy
Languages: Danish, Faeroese, Greenlandic, German
Monetary unit: Krone
Per capita GDP: $28,900
Literacy rate: 100%
Did You Know? One of Denmark's territories, Greenland, is the world's largest island.

Djibouti

Where? Africa
Capital: Djibouti
Area: 8,800 sq mi (23,000 sq km)
Population estimate (2004): 466,900
Government: Republic
Languages: Arabic and French (both official), Afar, Somali
Monetary unit: Djibouti franc
Per capita GDP: $1,300
Literacy rate: 68%
Did You Know? Djibouti's capital is one of Africa's major seaports.

Dominica

Where? North America
Capital: Roseau
Area: 290 sq mi (750 sq km)
Population estimate (2004): 69,278
Government: Parliamentary democracy
Languages: English (official), French patois
Monetary unit: East Caribbean dollar
Per capita GDP: $5,400
Literacy rate: 94%
Did You Know? This mountainous Caribbean island nation was explored by Columbus in 1493.

Dominican Republic

Where? North America
Capital: Santo Domingo
Area: 18,815 sq mi (48,730 sq km)
Population estimate (2004): 8,833,634
Government: Representative democracy
Languages: Spanish
Monetary unit: Peso
Per capita GDP: $6,300
Literacy rate: 85%
Did You Know? This country, along with Haiti, makes up the island of Hispaniola in the Caribbean.

East Timor

Where? Asia
Capital: Dili
Area: 5,814 sq mi (15,057 sq km)
Population estimate (2004): 1,019,252
Government: Republic
Languages: Tetum, Portuguese (official), Bahasa Indonesia, English
Monetary unit: U.S. dollar
Per capita GDP: $500
Literacy rate: 48%
Did You Know? East Timor is the world's newest country, formed in 2002.

Ecuador

Where? South America
Capital: Quito
Area: 109,483 sq mi (283,560 sq km)
Population estimate (2004): 13,971,798
Government: Republic
Languages: Spanish (official), Quechua
Monetary unit: U.S. dollar
Per capita GDP: $3,200
Literacy rate: 93%
Did You Know? The country takes its name from the equator, which runs through it.

Egypt

Where? Africa
Capital: Cairo
Area: 386,660 sq mi
(1,001,450 sq km)
Population estimate (2004): 76,117,421
Government: Republic
Language: Arabic
Monetary unit: Egyptian pound
Per capita GDP: $4,000
Literacy rate: 58%
Did You Know? Almost 95% of Egypt is desert.

El Salvador

Where? Central America
Capital: San Salvador
Area: 8,124 sq mi
(21,040 sq km)
Population estimate (2004): 6,587,541
Government: Republic
Language: Spanish
Monetary unit: U.S. dollar
Per capita GDP: $4,600
Literacy rate: 80%
Did You Know? El Salvador is the smallest country in Central America.

Equatorial Guinea

Where? Africa
Capital: Malabo
Area: 10,830 sq mi
(28,050 sq km)
Population estimate (2004): 523,051
Government: Republic
Languages: Spanish (official), French (second official), pidgin English, Fang, Bubi, Creole
Monetary unit: CFA franc
Per capita GDP: $2,700
Literacy rate: 86%
Did You Know? This is Africa's only Spanish-speaking country.

Eritrea

Where? Africa
Capital: Asmara
Area: 46,842 sq mi
(121,320 sq km)
Population estimate (2004): 4,447,307
Government: Transitional government
Languages: Afar, Bilen, Kunama, Nara, Arabic, Tobedawi, Saho, Tigre, Tigrinya
Monetary unit: Nakfa
Per capita GDP: $700
Literacy rate: 59%
Did You Know? Once a part of Ethiopia, Eritrea became independent in 1993.

Estonia

Where? Europe
Capital: Tallinn
Area: 17,462 sq mi
(45,226 sq km)
Population estimate (2004): 1,401,945
Government: Parliamentary democracy
Languages: Estonian (official), Russian, Finnish, English
Monetary unit: Kroon
Per capita GDP: $11,000
Literacy rate: 100%
Did You Know? Estonia is one of the three Baltic countries.

Ethiopia

Where? Africa
Capital: Addis Ababa
Area: 485,184 sq mi
(1,127,127 sq km)
Population estimate (2004): 67,851,281
Government: Federal republic
Languages: Amharic (official), English, Orominga, Tigrigna, others
Monetary unit: Birr
Per capita GDP: $700
Literacy rate: 43%
Did You Know? Remains of the oldest-known human ancestors have been found in Ethiopia.

Fiji

Where? Oceania
Capital: Suva
Area: 7,054 sq mi
(18,270 sq km)
Population estimate (2004): 880,874
Government: Republic
Languages: Fijian, Hindustani, English
(official)
Monetary unit: Fiji dollar
Per capita GDP: $5,600
Literacy rate: 94%
Did You Know? Fiji is made up of 332
islands in the South Pacific.

Finland

Where? Europe
Capital: Helsinki
Area: 130,127 sq mi
(337,030 sq km)
Population estimate (2004): 5,214,512
Government: Republic
Languages: Finnish and Swedish (both
official)
Monetary unit: Euro (formerly markka)
Per capita GDP: $25,800
Literacy rate: 100%
Did You Know? Laplanders live in the
north of Finland, above the Arctic Circle.

France

Where? Europe
Capital: Paris
Area: 211,208 sq mi
(547,030 sq km)
Population estimate (2004): 60,424,213
Government: Republic
Language: French
Monetary unit: Euro (formerly French
franc)
Per capita GDP: $26,000
Literacy rate: 99%
Did You Know? France is the world's top
travel destination.

Gabon

Where? Africa
Capital: Libreville
Area: 103,347 sq mi
(267,670 sq km)
Population estimate (2004): 1,355,246
Government: Republic
Languages: French (official), Fang, Myene,
Bateke, Bapounou/Eschira, Bandjabi
Monetary unit: CFA franc
Per capita GDP: $6,500
Literacy rate: 63%
Did You Know? Most of Gabon is
covered by a dense tropical forest.

The Gambia

Where? Africa
Capital: Banjul
Area: 4,363 sq mi
(11,300 sq km)
Population estimate (2004): 1,546,848
Government: Republic
Languages: English (official), native
tongues
Monetary unit: Dalasi
Per capita GDP: $1,800
Literacy rate: 40%
Did You Know? Gambia is Africa's
smallest country.

Georgia

Where? Asia
Capital: T'bilisi
Area: 26,911 sq mi
(69,700 sq km)
Population estimate (2004): 4,909,633
Government: Republic
Languages: Georgian (official),
Russian, Armenian, Azerbaijani
Monetary unit: Lari
Per capita GDP: $3,200
Literacy rate: 99%
Did You Know? Georgia was part of the
Soviet Union before its breakup in 1991.

Germany

Where? Europe
Capital: Berlin
Area: 137,846 sq mi
(357,021 sq km)
Population estimate (2004): 82,424,609
Government: Federal republic
Language: German
Monetary unit: Euro (formerly Deutsche mark)
Per capita GDP: $26,200
Literacy rate: 99%
Did You Know? The German name for the country is Deutschland.

Ghana

Where? Africa
Capital: Accra
Area: 92,456 sq mi
(239,460 sq km)
Population estimate (2004): 20,757,032
Government: Constitutional democracy
Languages: English (official), native tongues
Monetary unit: Cedi
Per capita GDP: $2,000
Literacy rate: 75%
Did You Know? Ghana was formerly a British colony called the Gold Coast.

Greece

Where? Europe
Capital: Athens
Area: 50,942 sq mi
(131,940 sq km)
Population estimate (2004): 10,647,529
Government: Parliamentary republic
Language: Greek
Monetary unit: Euro (formerly drachma)
Per capita GDP: $19,100
Literacy rate: 98%
Did You Know? Greece is known for its magnificent ancient temples, particularly the world-renowned Parthenon.

Grenada

Where? North America
Capital: Saint George's
Area: 133 sq mi
(344 sq km)
Population estimate (2004): 89,357
Government: Constitutional monarchy
Language: English
Monetary unit: East Caribbean dollar
Per capita GDP: $5,000
Literacy rate: 90%
Did You Know? This Caribbean island was explored by Columbus in 1498.

Guatemala

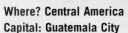

Where? Central America
Capital: Guatemala City
Area: 42,042 sq mi
(108,890 sq km)
Population estimate (2004): 14,280,596
Government: Republic
Languages: Spanish (official), Indian languages
Monetary unit: Quetzal
Per capita GDP: $3,900
Literacy rate: 71%
Did You Know? Most Guatemalans are of Mayan or Spanish descent.

Guinea

Where? Africa
Capital: Conakry
Area: 94,925 sq mi
(245,860 sq km)
Population estimate (2004): 9,246,462
Government: Republic
Languages: French (official), native tongues
Monetary unit: Guinean franc
Per capita GDP: $2,100
Literacy rate: 36%
Did You Know? Guinea's chief exports are agricultural products and minerals, especially bauxite.

Guinea-Bissau

Where? Africa
Capital: Bissau
Area: 13,946 sq mi
(36,120 sq km)
Population estimate (2004): 1,388,363
Government: Republic
Languages: Portuguese (official),
African languages
Monetary unit: CFA franc
Per capita GDP: $700
Literacy rate: 42%
Did You Know? This country was once a
Portuguese colony.

Guyana

Where? South America
Capital: Georgetown
Area: 83,000 sq mi
(214,970 sq km)
Population estimate (2004): 705,803
Government: Republic
Languages: English (official),
Amerindian dialects
Monetary unit: Guyana dollar
Per capita GDP: $3,800
Literacy rate: 99%
Did You Know? Guyana's people
are primarily of East Indian and
African descent.

Haiti

Where? North America
Capital: Port-au-Prince
Area: 10,714 sq mi
(27,750 sq km)
Population estimate (2004): 7,656,166
Government: Elected government
Languages: Creole and French (both
official)
Monetary unit: Gourde
Per capita GDP: $1,400
Literacy rate: 53%
Did You Know? This country, along with
the Dominican Republic, makes up the
island of Hispaniola in the Caribbean.

Honduras

Where? Central America
Capital: Tegucigalpa
Area: 43,278 sq mi
(112,090 sq km)
Population estimate (2004): 6,823,568
Government: Republic
Languages: Spanish, Amerindian
dialects
Monetary unit: Lempira
Per capita GDP: $2,500
Literacy rate: 76%
Did You Know? About 80% of Honduras
is mountainous.

Hungary

Where? Europe
Capital: Budapest
Area: 35,919 sq mi
(93,030 sq km)
Population estimate (2004): 10,032,375
Government: Parliamentary democracy
Language: Magyar (Hungarian)
Monetary unit: Forint
Per capita GDP: $13,300
Literacy rate: 99%
Did You Know? Magyar is the Hungarian
name for the country's people.

Iceland

Where? Europe
Capital: Reykjavik
Area: 39,768 sq mi
(103,000 sq km)
Population estimate (2004): 282,151
Government: Constitutional republic
Language: Icelandic
Monetary unit: Icelandic króna
Per capita GDP: $30,200
Literacy rate: 100%
Did You Know? Iceland boasts the
world's oldest constitution, drafted
around 930.

India

Where? Asia
Capital: New Delhi
Area: 1,269,338 sq mi
(3,287,590 sq km)
Population estimate (2004): 1,065,070,607
Government: Republic
Languages: Hindi (national), English;
24 major languages plus more than 1,600
dialects
Monetary unit: Rupee
Per capita GDP: $2,600
Literacy rate: 60%
Did You Know? India is the world's
second most populous country.

Indonesia

Where? Asia
Capital: Jakarta
Area: 741,096 sq mi
(1,919,440 sq km)
Population estimate (2004): 238,452,952
Government: Republic
Languages: Bahasa Indonesia (official),
Dutch, English; more than 500 languages
and dialects
Monetary unit: Rupiah
Per capita GDP: $3,100
Literacy rate: 89%
Did You Know? Indonesia has the largest
number of active volcanoes in the world.

Iran

Where? Middle East
Capital: Tehran
Area: 636,293 sq mi
(1,648,000 sq km)
Population estimate (2004): 69,018,924
Government: Theocratic republic
Languages: Farsi (Persian), Azari,
Kurdish, Arabic
Monetary unit: Rial
Per capita GDP: $6,800
Literacy rate: 79%
Did You Know? Iran was once known
as Persia.

Iraq

Where? Middle East
Capital: Baghdad
Area: 168,753 sq mi
(437,072 sq km)
Population estimate (2004): 25,374,691
Government: Republic
Languages: Arabic, Kurdish
Monetary unit: Iraqi dinar
Per capita GDP: $2,400
Literacy rate: 40%
Did You Know? The ancient civilization
of Mesopotamia was located in what is
today called Iraq.

Ireland

Where? Europe
Capital: Dublin
Area: 27,136 sq mi
(70,280 sq km)
Population estimate (2004): 3,969,558
Government: Republic
Languages: English, Irish Gaelic
Monetary units: Euro (formerly Irish
pound, or punt)
Per capita GDP: $29,300
Literacy rate: 98%
Did You Know? The name for Ireland in
Gaelic (the Irish language) is Eire.

Israel

Where? Middle East
Capital: Jerusalem
Area: 8,020 sq mi
(20,770 sq km)
Population estimate (2004): 6,199,008
Government: Parliamentary democracy
Languages: Hebrew (official), Arabic,
English
Monetary unit: Shekel
Per capita GDP: $19,500
Literacy rate: 95%
Did You Know? Modern Israel became
a country in 1948.

Italy

Where? Europe
Capital: Rome
Area: 116,305 sq mi
(301,230 sq km)
Population estimate (2004): 58,057,477
Government: Republic
Language: Italian
Monetary unit: Euro (formerly lira)
Per capita GDP: $25,100
Literacy rate: 99%
Did You Know? Italy is known for its magnificent art treasures and architecture.

Jamaica

Where? North America
Capital: Kingston
Area: 4,244 sq mi
(10,991 sq km)
Population estimate (2004): 2,713,130
Government: Parliamentary democracy
Languages: English, patois English
Monetary unit: Jamaican dollar
Per capita GDP: $3,800
Literacy rate: 88%
Did You Know? Jamaica once had a large slave population that worked on sugar-cane plantations.

Japan

Where? Asia
Capital: Tokyo
Area: 145,882 sq mi
(377,835 sq km)
Population estimate (2004): 127,333,002
Government: Constitutional monarchy
Language: Japanese
Monetary unit: Yen
Per capita GDP: $28,700
Literacy rate: 99%
Did You Know? The Japanese name for the country is Nippon.

Jordan

Where? Middle East
Capital: Amman
Area: 34,445 sq mi
(89,213 sq km)
Population estimate (2004): 5,611,202
Government: Constitutional monarchy
Languages: Arabic (official), English
Monetary unit: Jordanian dinar
Per capita GDP: $4,300
Literacy rate: 91%
Did You Know? Jordan is a kingdom ruled by the Hashemite dynasty.

Kazakhstan

Where? Asia
Capital: Astana
Area: 1,049,150 sq mi
(2,717,300 sq km)
Population estimate (2004): 16,798,552
Government: Republic
Languages: Kazak (Qazaq) and Russian (both official)
Monetary unit: Tenge
Per capita GDP: $7,200
Literacy rate: 98%
Did You Know? Oil was discovered in Kazakhstan in 2000. It was the largest oil find in 30 years.

Kenya

Where? Africa
Capital: Nairobi
Area: 224,960 sq mi
(582,650 sq km)
Population estimate (2004): 32,021,856
Government: Republic
Languages: English (official), Swahili, several others
Monetary unit: Kenyan shilling
Per capita GDP: $1,100
Literacy rate: 85%
Did You Know? About 40 different ethnic groups live in Kenya.

305

Kiribati

Where? Pacific Islands
Capital: Tarawa
Area: 313 sq mi (811 sq km)
Population estimate (2004): 100,798
Government: Republic
Languages: English (official), I-Kiribati (Gilbertese)
Monetary unit: Australian dollar
Per capita GDP: $800
Literacy rate: Not available
Did You Know? This nation is made up of three widely separated island groups in the South Pacific.

Korea, North

Where? Asia
Capital: Pyongyang
Area: 46,540 sq mi (120,540 sq km)
Population estimate (2004): 22,697,553
Government: Communist dictatorship
Language: Korean
Monetary unit: Won
Per capita GDP: $1,000
Literacy rate: 99%
Did You Know? North Korea is one of the world's last hard-line communist countries.

Korea, South

Where? Asia
Capital: Seoul
Area: 38,023 sq mi (98,480 sq km)
Population estimate (2004): 48,598,175
Government: Republic
Language: Korean
Monetary unit: Won
Per capita GDP: $19,600
Literacy rate: 98%
Did You Know? About half of South Korea's people are Christian; the other half are Buddhist.

Kuwait

Where? Middle East
Capital: Kuwait
Area: 6,880 sq mi (17,820 sq km)
Population estimate (2004): 2,257,549
Government: Constitutional monarchy
Languages: Arabic (official), English
Monetary unit: Kuwaiti dinar
Per capita GDP: $17,500
Literacy rate: 84%
Did You Know? This small country has the fourth largest oil reserves in the world.

Kyrgyzstan

Where? Asia
Capital: Bishkek
Area: 76,641 sq mi (198,500 sq km)
Population estimate (2004): 4,965,081
Government: Republic
Languages: Kyrgyz (official), Russian
Monetary unit: Som
Per capita GDP: $2,900
Literacy rate: 97%
Did You Know? The Tien Shan mountain range covers about 95% of the country.

Laos

Where? Asia
Capital: Vientiane
Area: 91,429 sq mi (236,800 sq km)
Population estimate (2004): 6,068,117
Government: Communist state
Languages: Lao (official), French, English
Monetary unit: Kip
Per capita GDP: $1,800
Literacy rate: 53%
Did You Know? Laos is one of the 10 poorest countries in the world.

Latvia

Where? Europe
Capital: Riga
Area: 24,938 sq mi
(64,589 sq km)
Population estimate (2004): 2,332,078
Government: Parliamentary democracy
Language: Latvian
Monetary unit: Lats
Per capita GDP: $8,900
Literacy rate: 100%

Did You Know? One of the three Baltic countries, Latvia is located in the far north of Europe.

Lebanon

Where? Middle East
Capital: Beirut
Area: 4,015 sq mi
(10,400 sq km)
Population estimate (2004): 3,777,218
Government: Republic
Languages: Arabic (official), French, English
Monetary unit: Lebanese pound
Per capita GDP: $4,800
Literacy rate: 87%

Did You Know? About 60% of Lebanese are Muslim and 30% are Christian.

Lesotho

Where? Africa
Capital: Maseru
Area: 11,720 sq mi
(30,350 sq km)
Population estimate (2004): 1,865,040
Government: Monarchy
Languages: English and Sesotho (both official), Zulu, Xhosa
Monetary unit: Loti
Per capita GDP: $2,700
Literacy rate: 85%

Did You Know? This small African kingdom is surrounded on all sides by South Africa.

Liberia

Where? Africa
Capital: Monrovia
Area: 43,000 sq mi
(111,370 sq km)
Population estimate (2004): 3,390,635
Government: Republic
Languages: English (official), tribal dialects
Monetary unit: Liberian dollar
Per capita GDP: $1,000
Literacy rate: 58%

Did You Know? Liberia was founded by freed American slaves in 1847.

Libya

Where? Africa
Capital: Tripoli
Area: 679,358 sq mi
(1,759,540 sq km)
Population estimate (2004): 5,631,585
Government: Military dictatorship
Languages: Arabic, Italian, English
Monetary unit: Libyan dinar
Per capita GDP: $6,200
Literacy rate: 83%

Did You Know? The world's highest temperature ever recorded (136°F) was in Al Azizyah, Libya, in 1922.

Liechtenstein

Where? Europe
Capital: Vaduz
Area: 62 sq mi
(160 sq km)
Population estimate (2004): 33,436
Government: Constitutional monarchy
Languages: German (official), Alemmanic dialect
Monetary unit: Swiss franc
Per capita GDP: $25,000
Literacy rate: 100%

Did You Know? This tiny kingdom borders Austria and Switzerland.

Lithuania

Where? Europe
Capital: Vilnius
Area: 25,174 sq mi
(65,200 sq km)
Population estimate (2004): 3,584,836
Government: Parliamentary democracy
Languages: Lithuanian (official), Polish, Russian
Monetary unit: Litas
Per capita GDP: $8,400
Literacy rate: 100%
Did You Know? One of the three Baltic countries, Lithuania is located in northern Europe.

Luxembourg

Where? Europe
Capital: Luxembourg
Area: 999 sq mi
(2,586 sq km)
Population estimate (2004): 462,690
Government: Constitutional monarchy
Languages: Luxembourgian, French, German
Monetary unit: Euro (formerly Luxembourg franc)
Per capita GDP: $48,900
Literacy rate: 100%
Did You Know? This tiny kingdom is located in central Europe.

Macedonia

Where? Europe
Capital: Skopje
Area: 9,781 sq mi
(25,333 sq km)
Population estimate (2004): 2,071,210
Government: Emerging democracy
Languages: Macedonian, Albanian
Monetary unit: Denar
Per capita GDP: $5,100
Literacy rate: Not available
Did You Know? Macedonia was part of Yugoslavia until it declared independence in 1992.

Madagascar

Where? Africa
Capital: Antananarivo
Area: 226,660 sq mi
(587,040 sq km)
Population estimate (2004): 17,501,871
Government: Republic
Languages: Malagasy and French (both official)
Monetary unit: Malagasy franc
Per capita GDP: $800
Literacy rate: 69%
Did You Know? Madagascar is the world's fourth largest island.

Malawi

Where? Africa
Capital: Lilongwe
Area: 45,745 sq mi
(118,480 sq km)
Population estimate (2004): 11,906,855
Government: Multiparty democracy
Languages: English and Chichewa (both official)
Monetary unit: Kwacha
Per capita GDP: $600
Literacy rate: 63%
Did You Know? About 20% of Malawi is made up of a large lake named Nyasa.

Malaysia

Where? Asia
Capital: Kuala Lumpur
Area: 127,316 sq mi
(329,750 sq km)
Population estimate (2004): 23,522,482
Government: Constitutional monarchy
Languages: Malay (official), Chinese, Tamil, English
Monetary unit: Ringgit
Per capita GDP: $8,800
Literacy rate: 89%
Did You Know? Most of Malaysia is located in Southeast Asia; a smaller portion is located on the island of Borneo.

Maldives

Where? Asia
Capital: Malé
Area: 116 sq mi
(300 sq km)
Population estimate (2004): 339,330
Government: Republic
Languages: Dhivehi (official), Arabic, Hindi, English
Monetary unit: Maldivian rufiyaa
Per capita GDP: $3,900
Literacy rate: 97%
Did You Know? This group of islands lies off the southern coast of India.

Mali

Where? Africa
Capital: Bamako
Area: 478,764 sq mi (1,240,000 sq km)
Population estimate (2004): 11,956,788
Government: Republic
Languages: French (official), African languages
Monetary unit: CFA franc
Per capita GDP: $900
Literacy rate: 46%
Did You Know? The famous, ancient city of Timbuktu is located in Mali.

Malta

Where? Europe
Capital: Valletta
Area: 122 sq mi
(316 sq km)
Population estimate (2004): 403,342
Government: Republic
Languages: Maltese and English (both official)
Monetary unit: Maltese lira
Per capita GDP: $17,200
Literacy rate: 93%
Did You Know? The country is made up of five small islands in the Mediterranean.

Marshall Islands

Where? Pacific Islands
Capital: Majuro
Area: 70 sq mi
(181.3 sq km)
Population estimate (2004): 57,738
Government: Constitutional government
Languages: Marshallese and English (both official)
Monetary unit: U.S. dollar
Per capita GDP: $1,600
Literacy rate: 94%
Did You Know? The Marshall Islands were once a dependency of the U.S.

Mauritania

Where? Africa
Capital: Nouakchott
Area: 397,953 sq mi
(1,030,700 sq km)
Population estimate (2004): 2,998,563
Government: Republic
Languages: Arabic (official), French
Monetary unit: Ouguiya
Per capita GDP: $1,700
Literacy rate: 42%
Did You Know? This northern African country is primarily desert.

Mauritius

Where? Africa
Capital: Port Louis
Area: 788 sq mi
(2,040 sq km)
Population estimate (2004): 1,220,481
Government: Parliamentary democracy
Languages: English (official), French, Creole, Hindi, Urdu, Hakka, Bojpoori
Monetary unit: Mauritian rupee
Per capita GDP: $10,100
Literacy rate: 86%
Did You Know? Most of this island's population is of African or Indian descent.

Mexico

Where? **North America**
Capital: **Mexico City**
Area: **761,600 sq mi
(1,972,550 sq km)**
Population estimate (2004): **104,959,594**
Government: **Republic**
Languages: **Spanish, Indian languages**
Monetary unit: **Peso**
Per capita GDP: **$8,900**
Literacy rate: **92%**
Did You Know? Teotihuacán (ca. 300–900) was once the largest city in the Americas.

Micronesia

Where? **Pacific Islands**
Capital: **Palikir**
Area: **271 sq mi
(702 sq km)**
Population estimate (2004): **108,155**
Government: **Constitutional government**
Languages: **English (official), native languages**
Monetary unit: **U.S. dollar**
Per capita GDP: **$2,000**
Literacy rate: **89%**
Did You Know? Four different island groups make up this country.

Moldova

Where? **Europe**
Capital: **Chisinau**
Area: **13,067 sq mi
(33,843 sq km)**
Population estimate (2004): **4,446,455**
Government: **Republic**
Languages: **Moldovan (official), Russian, Gagauz**
Monetary unit: **Moldovan leu**
Per capita GDP: **$2,600**
Literacy rate: **99%**
Did You Know? This eastern European country was once a part of the Soviet Union.

Monaco

Where? **Europe**
Capital: **Monaco**
Area: **0.75 sq mi
(1.95 sq km)**
Population estimate (2004): **32,270**
Government: **Constitutional monarchy**
Languages: **French (official), English, Italian, Monégasque**
Monetary unit: **French franc**
Per capita GDP: **$27,000**
Literacy rate: **99%**
Did You Know? Bordering France, this tiny nation is famous for its casinos.

Mongolia

Where? **Asia**
Capital: **Ulaan Baatar**
Area: **604,250 sq mi
(1,565,000 sq km)**
Population estimate (2004): **2,751,314**
Government: **Parliamentary republic**
Languages: **Mongolian (official), Turkic, Russian, Chinese**
Monetary unit: **Tugrik**
Per capita GDP: **$1,900**
Literacy rate: **99%**
Did You Know? Mongolia is Asia's most sparsely populated country.

Morocco

Where? **Africa**
Capital: **Rabat**
Area: **172,413 sq mi
(446,550 sq km)**
Population estimate (2004): **32,209,101**
Government: **Constitutional monarchy**
Languages: **Arabic (official), French, Berber dialects, Spanish**
Monetary unit: **Dirham**
Per capita GDP: **$3,900**
Literacy rate: **52%**
Did You Know? About 99% of Moroccans are of Arab-Berber descent.

Mozambique

Where? Africa
Capital: Maputo
Area: 309,494 sq mi
(801,590 sq km)
Population estimate (2004): 18,811,731
Government: Republic
Languages: Portuguese (official), Bantu languages
Monetary unit: Metical
Per capita GDP: $1,100
Literacy rate: 48%
Did You Know? In 1992, Mozambique endured a devastating drought.

Myanmar (Burma)

Where? Asia
Capital: Rangoon
Area: 261,969 sq mi
(678,500 sq km)
Population estimate (2004): 42,720,196
Government: Military regime
Languages: Burmese, minority languages
Monetary unit: Kyat
Per capita GDP: $1,700
Literacy rate: 83%
Did You Know? In 1989, the government changed the name of Burma to Myanmar.

Namibia

Where? Africa
Capital: Windhoek
Area: 318,694 sq mi
(825,418 sq km)
Population estimate (2004): 1,954,033
Government: Republic
Languages: Afrikaans, German, English (official), native languages
Monetary unit: Namibian dollar
Per capita GDP: $6,900
Literacy rate: 84%
Did You Know? Namibia achieved independence from South Africa in 1990.

Nauru

Where? Pacific Islands
Capital: Yaren District (unofficial)
Area: 8.2 sq mi (21 sq km)
Population estimate (2004): 12,909
Government: Republic
Languages: Nauruan (official), English
Monetary unit: Australian dollar
Per capita GDP: $5,000
Literacy rate: Not available
Did You Know? Nauru is the smallest island nation in the world.

Nepal

Where? Asia
Capital: Kathmandu
Area: 54,363 sq mi
(140,800 sq km)
Population estimate (2004): 27,070,666
Government: Constitutional monarchy
Languages: Nepali (official), Newari, Bhutia, Maithali
Monetary unit: Nepalese rupee
Per capita GDP: $1,400
Literacy rate: 45%
Did You Know? Nepal's Mount Everest is the world's highest mountain.

The Netherlands

Where? Europe
Capital: Amsterdam
Area: 16,036 sq mi
(41,532 sq km)
Population estimate (2004): 16,318,199
Government: Constitutional monarchy
Language: Dutch
Monetary unit: Euro (formerly guilder)
Per capita GDP: $27,200
Literacy rate: 99%
Did You Know? About 40% of the Netherlands is land reclaimed from the sea.

New Zealand

Where? Pacific Islands
Capital: Wellington
Area: 103,737 sq mi
(268,680 sq km)
Population estimate (2004): 3,993,817
Government: Parliamentary democracy
Languages: English (official), Maori
Monetary unit: New Zealand dollar
Per capita GDP: $20,100
Literacy rate: 99%
Did You Know? In 1893, New Zealand became the world's first country to give women the right to vote.

Nicaragua

Where? Central America
Capital: Managua
Area: 49,998 sq mi
(129,494 sq km)
Population estimate (2004): 5,232,216
Government: Republic
Language: Spanish
Monetary unit: Cordoba
Per capita GDP: $2,200
Literacy rate: 68%
Did You Know? Nicaragua is the largest but most sparsely populated Central American country.

Niger

Where? Africa
Capital: Niamey
Area: 489,189 sq mi
(1,267,000 sq km)
Population estimate (2004): 11,360,538
Government: Republic
Languages: French (official), Hausa, Songhai, Arabic
Monetary unit: CFA franc
Per capita GDP: $800
Literacy rate: 18%
Did You Know? Most of Niger is situated in the Sahara Desert.

Nigeria

Where? Africa
Capital: Abuja
Area: 356,700 sq mi
(923,770 sq km)
Population estimate (2004): 137,253,133
Government: Republic
Languages: English (official), Hausa, Yoruba, Ibo, more than 200 others
Monetary unit: Naira
Per capita GDP: $900
Literacy rate: 68%
Did You Know? Nigeria is Africa's most populous country.

Norway

Where? Europe
Capital: Oslo
Area: 125,181 sq mi
(324,220 sq km)
Population estimate (2004): 4,574,560
Government: Constitutional monarchy
Languages: Two official forms of Norwegian, Bokmål and Nynorsk
Monetary unit: Krone
Per capita GDP: $33,000
Literacy rate: 100%
Did You Know? Norway has won the most winter Olympic medals of any nation.

Oman

Where? Middle East
Capital: Muscat
Area: 82,030 sq mi
(212,460 sq km)
Population estimate (2004): 2,903,165
Government: Monarchy
Languages: Arabic (official), English, Indian languages
Monetary unit: Omani rial
Per capita GDP: $8,300
Literacy rate: 76%
Did You Know? Oman's major product is oil.

Pakistan

Where? Asia
Capital: Islamabad
Area: 310,400 sq mi
(803,940 sq km)
Population estimate (2004): 153,705,278
Government: Republic
Languages: Punjabi, Sindhi, Siraiki,
Pashtu, Urdu (official), others
Monetary unit: Pakistan rupee
Per capita GDP: $2,000
Literacy rate: 46%
Did You Know? Pakistan contains K2, the
world's second highest mountain.

Palau

Where? Pacific Islands
Capital: Koror
Area: 177 sq mi (458 sq km)
Population estimate (2004): 20,016
Government: Constitutional government
Languages: Palauan, English (official)
Monetary unit: U.S. dollar
Per capita GDP: $9,000
Literacy rate: 92%
Did You Know? Palau is made up of
200 islands.

Panama

Where? Central America
Capital: Panama City
Area: 30,193 sq mi
(78,200 sq km)
Population estimate (2004): 3,000,463
Government: Constitutional democracy
Languages: Spanish (official), English
Monetary unit: Balboa
Per capita GDP: $6,200
Literacy rate: 93%
Did You Know? The Panama Canal links
the Atlantic and Pacific oceans and is
one of the world's most vital waterways.

Papua New Guinea

Where? Pacific Islands
Capital: Port Moresby
Area: 178,703 sq mi
(462,840 sq km)
Population estimate (2004): 5,420,280
Government: Constitutional monarchy
Languages: English, Tok Pisin,
Hiri Motu, 717 native languages
Monetary unit: Kina
Per capita GDP: $2,100
Literacy rate: 66%
Did You Know? More languages (800) are
spoken in this country than in any other.

Paraguay

Where? South America
Capital: Asunción
Area: 157,046 sq mi
(406,750 sq km)
Population estimate (2004): 6,191,368
Government: Republic
Languages: Spanish (official), Guaraní
Monetary unit: Guaraní
Per capita GDP: $4,300
Literacy rate: 94%
Did You Know? More than half of
Paraguay's workers are employed in
either agriculture or forestry.

Peru

Where? South America
Capital: Lima
Area: 496,223 sq mi
(1,285,220 sq km)
Population estimate (2004): 28,863,494
Government: Republic
Languages: Spanish and Quechua (both
official), Aymara, other native languages
Monetary unit: Nuevo sol
Per capita GDP: $5,000
Literacy rate: 91%
Did You Know? Peru's Machu Picchu is a
magnificent ancient Incan fortress in the
Andes mountains.

The Philippines

Where? Asia
Capital: Manila
Area: 115,830 sq mi
(300,000 sq km)
Population estimate (2004): 86,241,697
Government: Republic
Languages: Filipino (based on Tagalog) and
English (both official), regional languages
Monetary unit: Peso
Per capita GDP: $4,600
Literacy rate: 96%
Did You Know? The country is made up of
more than 7,000 tropical islands.

Poland

Where? Europe
Capital: Warsaw
Area: 120,727 sq mi
(312,683 sq km)
Population estimate (2004): 38,626,349
Government: Republic
Language: Polish
Monetary unit: Zloty
Per capita GDP: $9,700
Literacy rate: 100%
Did You Know? The Polish name for the
country is Polska.

Portugal

Where? Europe
Capital: Lisbon
Area: 35,672 sq mi
(92,391 sq km)
Population estimate (2004): 10,119,250
Government: Parliamentary democracy
Language: Portuguese
Monetary unit: Euro (formerly escudo)
Per capita GDP: $19,400
Literacy rate: 93%
Did You Know? Many of the world's
famous explorers were Portuguese,
including Magellan and Vasco de Gama.

Qatar

Where? Middle East
Capital: Doha
Area: 4,416 sq mi
(11,439 sq km)
Population estimate (2004): 840,290
Government: Traditional monarchy
Languages: Arabic (official), English
Monetary unit: Qatari riyal
Per capita GDP: $20,100
Literacy rate: 83%
Did You Know? This country is a small
peninsula extending into the Persian Gulf.

Romania

Where? Europe
Capital: Bucharest
Area: 91,700 sq mi
(237,500 sq km)
Population estimate (2004): 22,355,551
Government: Republic
Languages: Romanian (official),
Hungarian, German
Monetary unit: Leu
Per capita GDP: $7,600
Literacy rate: 98%
Did You Know? Romania was once a
Roman province known as Dacia.

Russia

Where?
Europe and Asia
Capital: Moscow
Area: 6,592,735 sq mi
(17,075,200 sq km)
Population estimate (2004): 144,112,353
Government: Federation
Languages: Russian, others
Monetary unit: Ruble
Per capita GDP: $9,700
Literacy rate: 100%
Did You Know? Russia is the world's
largest country.

Rwanda

Where? Africa
Capital: Kigali
Area: 10,169 sq mi
(26,338 sq km)
Population estimate (2004): 7,954,013
Government: Republic
Languages: Kinyarwanda, French, English
(all official)
Monetary unit: Rwandan franc
Per capita GDP: $1,200
Literacy rate: 70%
Did You Know? Ethnic violence led to the
deaths of about 800,000 Rwandans in 1994.

Saint Kitts and Nevis

Where? North America
Capital: Basseterre
Area: 101 sq mi
(261 sq km)
Population estimate (2004): 38,836
Government: Constitutional monarchy
Language: English
Monetary unit: East Caribbean dollar
Per capita GDP: $8,800
Literacy rate: 97%
Did You Know? Nevis is almost entirely
a single mountain, Nevis Peak.

Saint Lucia

Where? North America
Capital: Castries
Area: 239 sq mi
(620 sq km)
Population estimate (2004): 164,213
Government: Parliamentary democracy
Languages: English (official), patois
Monetary unit: East Caribbean dollar
Per capita GDP: $5,400
Literacy rate: 67%
Did You Know? The major crop of this
Caribbean island is bananas.

Saint Vincent and the Grenadines

Where? North America
Capital: Kingstown
Area: 150 sq mi
(389 sq km)
Population estimate (2004): 117,193
Government: Parliamentary democracy
Languages: English (official),
French patois
Monetary unit: East Caribbean dollar
Per capita GDP: $2,900
Literacy rate: 96%
Did You Know? This country's highest
point is the active volcano, Soufrière.

Samoa

Where? Pacific Islands
Capital: Apia
Area: 1,104 sq mi
(2,860 sq km)
Population estimate (2004): 177,714
Government: Constitutional monarchy
Languages: Samoan, English
Monetary unit: Tala
Per capita GDP: $5,600
Literacy rate: 100%
Did You Know? Samoa, now independent,
was once ruled by Germany and
New Zealand.

San Marino

Where? Europe
Capital: San Marino
Area: 24 sq mi
(61 sq km)
Population estimate (2004): 28,503
Government: Republic
Language: Italian
Monetary unit: Italian lira
Per capita GDP: $34,600
Literacy rate: 96%
Did You Know? Tiny San Marino is
part of the Italian peninsula.

São Tomé and Príncipe

Where? Africa
Capital: São Tomé
Area: 386 sq mi
(1,001 sq km)
Population estimate (2004): 181,565
Government: Republic
Language: Portuguese
Monetary unit: Dobra
Per capita GDP: $1,200
Literacy rate: 79%
Did You Know? The recent discovery of oil may bring wealth to this poor nation.

Saudi Arabia

Where? Middle East
Capital: Riyadh
Area: 756,981 sq mi
(1,960,582 sq km)
Population estimate (2004): 25,100,425
Government: Monarchy
Language: Arabic
Monetary unit: Riyal
Per capita GDP: $11,400
Literacy rate: 79%
Did You Know? This country contains two of Islam's holiest cities, Mecca and Medina.

Senegal

Where? Africa
Capital: Dakar
Area: 75,749 sq mi
(196,190 sq km)
Population estimate (2004): 10,852,147
Government: Republic
Languages: French (official), Wolof, Serer, other dialects
Monetary unit: CFA franc
Per capita GDP: $1,500
Literacy rate: 40%
Did You Know? Senegal's capital, Dakar, is the westernmost point of Africa.

Serbia and Montenegro

Where? Europe
Capital: Belgrade
Area: 39,517 sq mi
(102,350 sq km)
Population estimate (2004): 10,663,022
Government: Republic
Languages: Serbian, Albanian
Monetary unit: Yugoslav new dinar
Per capita GDP: $2,200
Literacy rate: 93%
Did You Know? In 2003, the country changed its name from Yugoslavia.

Seychelles

Where? Africa
Capital: Victoria
Area: 176 sq mi
(455 sq km)
Population estimate (2004): 80,832
Government: Republic
Languages: English and French (both official), Seselwa
Monetary unit: Seychelles rupee
Per capita GDP: $7,800
Literacy rate: 58%
Did You Know? This island nation is located in the Indian ocean.

Sierra Leone

Where? Africa
Capital: Freetown
Area: 27,699 sq mi
(71,740 sq km)
Population estimate (2004): 5,883,889
Government: Constitutional democracy
Languages: English (official), Mende, Temne, Krio
Monetary unit: Leone
Per capita GDP: $500
Literacy rate: 31%
Did You Know? This nation is one of the poorest countries in the world.

Singapore

Where? **Asia**
Capital: **Singapore**
Area: **267 sq mi
(692.7 sq km)**
Population estimate (2004): **4,767,974**
Government: **Parliamentary republic**
Languages: **Malay, Chinese (Mandarin),
Tamil, English (all official)**
Monetary unit: **Singapore dollar**
Per capita GDP: **$25,000**
Literacy rate: **93%**
Did You Know? Singapore is the
second most densely populated country
in the world.

Slovakia

Where? **Europe**
Capital: **Bratislava**
Area: **18,859 sq mi
(48,845 sq km)**
Population estimate (2004): **5,423,567**
Government: **Parliamentary democracy**
Languages: **Slovak (official), Hungarian**
Monetary unit: **Koruna**
Per capita GDP: **$12,400**
Literacy rate: **Not available**
Did You Know? Until 1993, the country
was part of Czechoslovakia, which now
no longer exists.

Slovenia

Where? **Europe**
Capital: **Ljubljana**
Area: **7,820 sq mi
(20,253 sq km)**
Population estimate (2004): **1,938,282**
Government: **Parliamentary republic**
Languages: **Slovenian, Serbo-Croatian**
Monetary unit: **Slovenian tolar**
Per capita GDP: **$19,200**
Literacy rate: **100%**
Did You Know? Slovenia was part of
Yugoslavia until declaring
independence in 1991.

Solomon Islands

Where?
Pacific Islands
Capital: **Honiara**
Area: **10,985 sq mi
(28,450 sq km)**
Population estimate (2004): **523,617**
Government: **Parliamentary democracy**
Languages: **English, Solomon pidgin,
more than 60 Melanesian languages**
Monetary unit: **Solomon Islands dollar**
Per capita GDP: **$1,700**
Literacy rate: **Not available**
Did You Know? This island nation was
recently ravaged by civil war.

Somalia

Where? **Africa**
Capital: **Mogadishu**
Area: **246,199 sq mi
(637,657 sq km)**
Population estimate (2004): **8,304,601**
Government: **Transitional government**
Languages: **Somali (official), Arabic,
English, Italian**
Monetary unit: **Somali shilling**
Per capita GDP: **$600**
Literacy rate: **38%**
Did You Know? Between January 1991
and August 2000, Somalia had no
working government.

South Africa

Where? **Africa**
Capital (administrative):
Pretoria
Area: **471,008 sq mi (1,219,912 sq km)**
Population estimate (2004): **42,718,530**
Government: **Republic**
Languages: **11 official languages: Afrikaans,
English, Ndebele, Pedi, Sotho, Swazi,
Tsonga, Tswana, Venda, Xhosa, Zulu**
Monetary unit: **Rand**
Per capita GDP: **$10,000**
Literacy rate: **86%**
Did You Know? South Africa is the
world's largest producer of gold.

Spain

Where? Europe
Capital: Madrid
Area: 194,896 sq mi
(504,782 sq km)
Population estimate (2004): 40,280,780
Government: Parliamentary monarchy
Languages: Castilian Spanish (official),
Catalan, Galician, Basque
Monetary unit: Euro (formerly peseta)
Per capita GDP: $21,200
Literacy rate: 98%
Did You Know? The Spanish name for
this country is España.

Sri Lanka

Where? Asia
Capital: Colombo
Area: 25,332 sq mi
(65,610 sq km)
Population estimate (2004): 19,905,165
Government: Republic
Languages: Sinhala (official), Tamil,
English
Monetary unit: Sri Lankan rupee
Per capita GDP: $3,700
Literacy rate: 92%
Did You Know? Sri Lanka was once
called Ceylon.

Sudan

Where? Africa
Capital: Khartoum
Area: 967,493 sq mi
(2,505,810 sq km)
Population estimate (2004): 39,148,162
Government: Authoritarian regime
Languages: Arabic (official), English,
tribal dialects
Monetary unit: Sudanese dinar
Per capita GDP: $1,400
Literacy rate: 61%
Did You Know? Sudan is Africa's largest
country.

Suriname

Where? South America
Capital: Paramaribo
Area: 63,039 sq mi
(163,270 sq km)
Population estimate (2004): 436,935
Government: Constitutional democracy
Languages: Dutch (official),
Surinamese, English
Monetary unit: Suriname guilder
Per capita GDP: $3,400
Literacy rate: 93%
Did You Know? Suriname is named
after its earliest inhabitants,
the Surinen Indians.

Swaziland

Where? Africa
Capital: Mbabane
Area: 6,704 sq mi
(17,360 sq km)
Population estimate (2004): 1,169,241
Government: Monarchy
Languages: Swazi (official), English
Monetary unit: Lilangeni
Per capita GDP: $4,800
Literacy rate: 82%
Did You Know? The nation's King is one
of the world's last absolute monarchs.

Sweden

Where? Europe
Capital: Stockholm
Area: 173,731 sq mi
(449,964 sq km)
Population estimate (2004): 8,986,400
Government: Constitutional monarchy
Language: Swedish
Monetary unit: Krona
Per capita GDP: $26,000
Literacy rate: 99%
Did You Know? The Nobel Prizes
(except the Peace Prize) are awarded
each year in Sweden.

Switzerland

Where? Europe
Capital: Bern
Area: 15,942 sq mi
(41,290 sq km)
Population estimate (2004): 7,450,867
Government: Federal republic
Languages: German, French, Italian (all official), Romansch
Monetary unit: Swiss franc
Per capita GDP: $32,000
Literacy rate: 99%
Did You Know? Switzerland, in central Europe, is the land of the Alps.

Syria

Where? Middle East
Capital: Damascus
Area: 71,498 sq mi
(185,180 sq km)
Population estimate (2004): 18,016,874
Government: Republic
Languages: Arabic (official), French, English
Monetary unit: Syrian pound
Per capita GDP: $3,700
Literacy rate: 77%
Did You Know? Damascus is considered the oldest capital city in the world.

Taiwan

Where? Asia
Capital: Taipei
Area: 13,892 sq mi
(35,980 sq km)
Population estimate (2004): 22,749,838
Government: Multiparty democracy
Language: Chinese (Mandarin)
Monetary unit: New Taiwan dollar
Per capita GDP: $18,000
Literacy rate: 86%
Did You Know? Taiwan features the world's tallest building, called Taipei 101.

Tajikistan

Where? Asia
Capital: Dushanbe
Area: 55,251 sq mi
(143,100 sq km)
Population estimate (2004): 7,011,556
Government: Republic
Language: Tajik
Monetary unit: Somoni
Per capita GDP: $1,300
Literacy rate: 99%
Did You Know? Once part of the Soviet Union, its name means "Land of the Tajiks."

Tanzania

Where? Africa
Capital: Dar es Salaam
Area: 364,898 sq mi
(945,087 sq km)
Population estimate (2004): 36,588,225
Government: Republic
Languages: Swahili and English (both official), local languages
Monetary unit: Tanzanian shilling
Per capita GDP: $600
Literacy rate: 78%
Did You Know? Mount Kilimanjaro, in Tanzania, is the highest mountain in Africa.

Thailand

Where? Asia
Capital: Bangkok
Area: 198,455 sq mi
(514,000 sq km)
Population estimate (2004): 64,865,523
Government: Constitutional monarchy
Languages: Thai (Siamese), Chinese, English
Monetary unit: Baht
Per capita GDP: $7,000
Literacy rate: 96%
Did You Know? Thailand was once known as Siam.

Togo

Where? Africa
Capital: Lomé
Area: 21,925 sq mi
(56,790 sq km)
Population estimate (2004): 5,556,812
Government: Republic
Languages: French (official), Éwé, Mina,
Kabyé, Cotocoli
Monetary unit: CFA franc
Per capita GDP: $1,400
Literacy rate: 61%
Did You Know? The Danish, Germans,
British and French once ruled Togo.

Tonga

Where?
Pacific Islands
Capital: Nuku'alofa
Area: 290 sq mi
(748 sq km)
Population estimate (2004): 110,237
Government: Constitutional monarchy
Languages: Tongan, English
Monetary unit: Pa'anga
Per capita GDP: $2,200
Literacy rate: 99%
Did You Know? Polynesians have lived
on Tonga for at least 3,000 years.

Trinidad and Tobago

Where? North America
Capital: Port-of-Spain
Area: 1,980 sq mi
(5,130 sq km)
Population estimate (2004): 1,096,585
Government: Parliamentary democracy
Languages: English (official), Hindi,
French, Spanish
Monetary unit: Trinidad and Tobago
dollar
Per capita GDP: $10,000
Literacy rate: 99%
Did You Know? Columbus explored
Trinidad in 1498.

Tunisia

Where? Africa
Capital: Tunis
Area: 63,170 sq mi
(163,610 sq km)
Population estimate (2004): 10,032,050
Government: Republic
Languages: Arabic (official), French
Monetary unit: Tunisian dinar
Per capita GDP: $6,800
Literacy rate: 74%
Did You Know? Bordering the
Mediterranean, Tunisia stretches south
into the Sahara Desert.

Turkey

Where?
Europe and Asia
Capital: Ankara
Area: 301,388 sq mi (780,580 sq km)
Population estimate (2004): 68,893,918
Government: Parliamentary democracy
Language: Turkish
Monetary unit: Turkish lira
Per capita GDP: $7,300
Literacy rate: 87%
Did You Know? Turkey was once the
home of the Byzantine and the
Ottoman empires.

Turkmenistan

Where? Asia
Capital: Ashgabat
Area: 188,455 sq mi
(488,100 sq km)
Population estimate (2004): 4,863,169
Government: Republic
Languages: Turkmen, Russian, Uzbek
Monetary unit: Manat
Per capita GDP: $6,700
Literacy rate: 98%
Did You Know? About nine-tenths of the
country is desert, mainly the Kara-Kum.

Tuvalu

Where? Pacific Islands
Capital: Funafuti
Area: 10 sq mi
(26 sq km)
Population estimate (2004): 11,468
Government: Constitutional monarchy
Languages: Tuvaluan, English
Monetary unit: Tuvaluan dollar
Per capita GDP: $1,100
Literacy rate: Not available
Did You Know? Tuvalu was formerly named the Ellice Islands.

Uganda

Where? Africa
Capital: Kampala
Area: 91,135 sq mi
(236,040 sq km)
Population estimate (2004): 26,404,543
Government: Republic
Languages: English (official), Swahili, Luganda, Ateso, Luo
Monetary unit: Ugandan shilling
Per capita GDP: $1,200
Literacy rate: 70%
Did You Know? Uganda's brutal former dictator, Idi Amin, died in 2003.

Ukraine

Where? Europe
Capital: Kyiv (Kiev)
Area: 233,089 sq mi
(603,700 sq km)
Population estimate (2004): 47,732,079
Government: Republic
Language: Ukrainian
Monetary unit: Hryvnia
Per capita GDP: $4,500
Literacy rate: 100%
Did You Know? In 1986, a nuclear reactor blew at Chernobyl, causing the worst such accident in history.

United Arab Emirates

Where? Middle East
Capital: Abu Dhabi
Area: 32,000 sq mi
(82,880 sq km)
Population estimate (2004): 2,523,915
Government: Federation
Languages: Arabic (official), English
Monetary unit: U.A.E. dirham
Per capita GDP: $22,100
Literacy rate: 78%
Did You Know? This country is made up of seven Gulf states.

United Kingdom

Where? Europe
Capital: London
Area: 94,525 sq mi
(244,820 sq km)
Population estimate (2004): 60,270,708
Government: Constitutional monarchy
Languages: English, Welsh, Scots Gaelic
Monetary unit: British pound
Per capita GDP: $25,500
Literacy rate: 99%
Did You Know? The United Kingdom is made up of England, Wales, Scotland and Northern Ireland.

United States

Where? North America
Capital: Washington, D.C.
Area: 3,717,792 sq mi
(9,629,091 sq km)
Population estimate (2004): 293,027,571
Government: Republic
Languages: English, Spanish (spoken by a sizable minority)
Monetary unit: U.S. dollar
Per capita GDP: $36,300
Literacy rate: 97%
Did You Know? The U.S. is the world's third largest country and the world's third most populous country.

Uruguay

Where? South America
Capital: Montevideo
Area: 68,040 sq mi
(176,220 sq km)
Population estimate (2004): 3,440,205
Government: Republic
Language: Spanish
Monetary unit: Peso
Per capita GDP: $7,900
Literacy rate: 98%
Did You Know? The first inhabitants of Uruguay were a people called the Charrúas.

Uzbekistan

Where? Asia
Capital: Tashkent
Area: 172,741 sq mi
(447,400 sq km)
Population estimate (2004): 26,410,416
Government: Republic
Languages: Uzbek, Russian, Tajik
Monetary unit: Uzbekistani som
Per capita GDP: $2,600
Literacy rate: 99%
Did You Know? In 2001, Uzbekistan gave the U.S. a base to fight the Taliban and al-Qaeda in Afghanistan.

Vanuatu

Where? Pacific Islands
Capital: Port Vila
Area: 5,700 sq mi
(14,760 sq km)
Population estimate (2004): 202,609
Government: Republic
Languages: English and French (both official), Bislama
Monetary unit: Vatu
Per capita GDP: $2,900
Literacy rate: 53%
Did You Know? Vanuatu is an archipelago of 83 islands.

Vatican City (Holy See)

Where? Europe
Capital: none
Area: 0.17 sq mi
(0.44 sq km)
Population estimate (2004): 890
Government: Ecclesiastical
Languages: Latin, Italian, various others
Monetary unit: Italian lira
Per capita GDP: Not available
Literacy rate: 100%
Did You Know? This nation is the world's smallest country.

Venezuela

Where? South America
Capital: Caracas
Area: 352,143 sq mi
(912,050 sq km)
Population estimate (2004): 25,017,387
Government: Republic
Languages: Spanish (official), native languages
Monetary unit: Bolivar
Per capita GDP: $5,400
Literacy rate: 93%
Did You Know? Venezuela's Angel Falls is the world's highest waterfall.

Vietnam

Where? Asia
Capital: Hanoi
Area: 127,243 sq mi
(329,560 sq km)
Population estimate (2004): 82,689,518
Government: Communist state
Languages: Vietnamese (official), French, English, Khmer, Chinese
Monetary unit: Dong
Per capita GDP: $2,300
Literacy rate: 94%
Did You Know? The country was divided into North and South Vietnam in 1954, and reunified in 1976.

Yemen

Where? Middle East
Capital: Sanaa
Area: 203,850 sq mi
(527,970 sq km)
Population estimate (2004): 20,024,867
Government: Republic
Language: Arabic
Monetary unit: Rial
Per capita GDP: $800
Literacy rate: 50%
Did You Know? In 1990, North and South Yemen joined to form the Republic of Yemen.

Zambia

Where? Africa
Capital: Lusaka
Area: 290,584 sq mi
(752,610 sq km)
Population estimate (2004): 10,462,436
Government: Republic
Languages: English (official), local dialects
Monetary unit: Kwacha
Per capita GDP: $800
Literacy rate: 81%
Did You Know? Zambia changed its name from Northern Rhodesia after it gained independence in 1964.

Zimbabwe

Where? Africa
Capital: Harare
Area: 150,803 sq mi
(390,580 sq km)
Population estimate (2004): 12,671,860
Government: Parliamentary democracy
Languages: English (official), Ndebele, Shona
Monetary unit: Zimbabwean dollar
Per capita GDP: $2,100
Literacy rate: 91%
Did You Know? Before independence, this country was called Rhodesia.

The Security Council can send U.N. troops to help settle disputes.

The United Nations

The **United Nations (U.N.)** was created after World War II to provide a meeting place to help develop good relations between countries, promote peace and security around the world and encourage international cooperation in solving problems.

The major organizations of the U.N. are the Secretariat, the Security Council and the General Assembly.

The **Secretariat** is the management center of U.N. operations and is headed by the Secretary-General, who is the director of the U.N.

The **Security Council** is responsible for making and keeping international peace. Its main purpose is to prevent war by settling disputes between nations. The Security Council has 15 members. There are five permanent members: the U.S., the Russian Federation, Britain, France and China. There are also 10 temporary members that serve two-year terms.

The **General Assembly** is the world's forum for discussing matters that affect world peace and security and for making recommendations concerning them. It has no power of its own to enforce decisions. It is made up of the 51 original member nations, and those admitted since, for a total of 191.

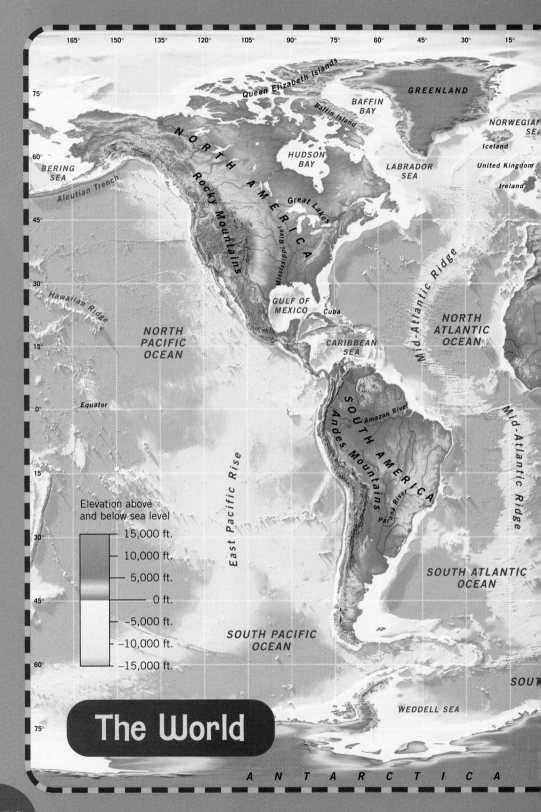

165° 150° 135° 120° 105° 90° 75° 60° 45° 30° 15°

75°

Queen Elizabeth Islands

GREENLAND

BAFFIN
BAY

Baffin Island

NORWEGIAN
SEA

Iceland

60°

BERING
SEA

HUDSON
BAY

LABRADOR
SEA

United Kingdom

Ireland

Aleutian Trench

N O R T H   A M E R I C A

Rocky Mountains

Great Lakes

Mississippi River

Mid-Atlantic Ridge

45°

30°

Hawaiian Ridge

GULF OF
MEXICO

Cuba

NORTH
ATLANTIC
OCEAN

NORTH
PACIFIC
OCEAN

CARIBBEAN
SEA

15°

0°   Equator

Amazon River

S O U T H   A M E R I C A

Andes Mountains

Mid-Atlantic Ridge

15°

East Pacific Rise

Paraná River

Elevation above
and below sea level

15,000 ft.

10,000 ft.

5,000 ft.

0 ft.

−5,000 ft.

−10,000 ft.

−15,000 ft.

30°

SOUTH ATLANTIC
OCEAN

45°

SOUTH PACIFIC
OCEAN

60°

WEDDELL SEA

SOUT

The World

75°

A N T A R C T I C A

324

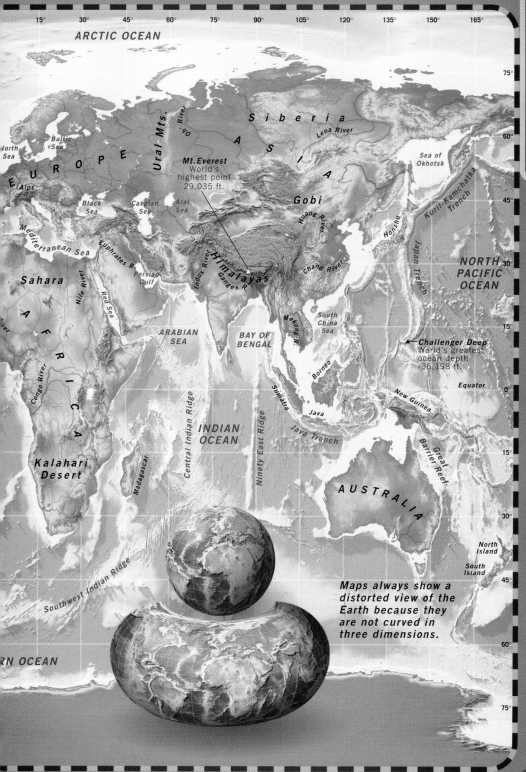

ARCTIC OCEAN

15° 30° 45° 60° 75° 90° 105° 120° 135° 150° 165°

75°

S i b e r i a

E U R O P E

Ural Mts.

Ob River

Lena River

ASIA

60°

North Sea

Baltic Sea

Sea of Okhotsk

Mt. Everest
World's
highest point
29,035 ft.

45°

Alps

Black Sea

Caspian Sea

Aral Sea

Gobi

Huang River

Kuril-Kamchatka Trench

Mediterranean Sea

Euphrates R.

Persian Gulf

Himalayas

Indus River

Ganges R.

Chang River

Honshu

Japan Trench

NORTH
PACIFIC
OCEAN

30°

Sahara

Nile River

Red Sea

ARABIAN
SEA

Mekong R.

South
China
Sea

15°

A F R I C A

Congo River

BAY OF
BENGAL

Borneo

Challenger Deep
World's greatest
ocean depth
-36,198 ft.

Equator

0°

Central Indian Ridge

Sumatra

Java

New Guinea

Great Barrier Reef

INDIAN
OCEAN

Ninety East Ridge

Java Trench

15°

Kalahari
Desert

Madagascar

AUSTRALIA

30°

Southwest Indian Ridge

North
Island

South
Island

45°

Maps always show a
distorted view of the
Earth because they
are not curved in
three dimensions.

RN OCEAN

60°

75°

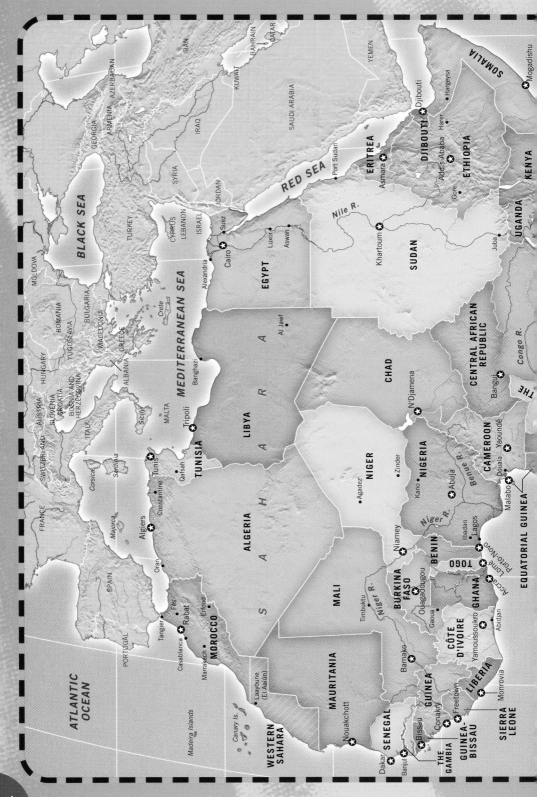

ATLANTIC OCEAN

BLACK SEA

MEDITERRANEAN SEA

RED SEA

MOLDOVA
ROMANIA
BULGARIA
MACEDONIA
YUGOSLAVIA
ALBANIA
GREECE
Crete
HUNGARY
AUSTRIA
SLOVENIA
CROATIA
BOSNIA AND HERZEGOVINA
ITALY
Sicily
MALTA
Sardinia
Corsica
SWITZERLAND
FRANCE
Majorca
SPAIN
PORTUGAL
Madeira Islands
Canary Is.

GEORGIA
ARMENIA
AZERBAIJAN
TURKEY
CYPRUS
LEBANON
ISRAEL
JORDAN
SYRIA
IRAQ
IRAN
KUWAIT
BAHRAIN
QATAR
SAUDI ARABIA
YEMEN

Suez
Cairo ✪
Alexandria
EGYPT
Luxor
Aswan
Al Jawf

S A H A R A

Tunis
Tunis ✪
Qafsah
TUNISIA
Tripoli ✪
Banghazi
LIBYA

Constantine
Algiers ✪
Oran
ALGERIA

Fès
Rabat ✪
Erfoud
Tangier
Casablanca
Marrakech
MOROCCO

Laayoune (El Aaiún)
WESTERN SAHARA

Nouakchott ✪
MAURITANIA

Dakar ✪
SENEGAL
Banjul ✪
THE GAMBIA
Bissau ✪
GUINEA-BISSAU
Conakry ✪
GUINEA
Freetown ✪
SIERRA LEONE
Monrovia ✪
LIBERIA

Timbuktu
MALI
Bamako ✪
Gaoua
Odagadougou
BURKINA FASO
Niamey ✪
NIGER
Agadez
Zinder
Kano
Abuja ✪
NIGERIA
Ibadan
Lagos
Porto-Novo ✪
BENIN
Lomé ✪
TOGO
Accra ✪
GHANA
Yamoussoukro ✪
CÔTE D'IVOIRE
Abidjan

N'Djamena ✪
CHAD

SUDAN
Khartoum ✪
Port Sudan
Nile R.
Juba

ERITREA
Asmara ✪
Addis Ababa ✪
ETHIOPIA
Gore

DJIBOUTI
Djibouti ✪
Harar
Harer

SOMALIA
Hargeysa
Mogadishu ✪

UGANDA
KENYA

CENTRAL AFRICAN REPUBLIC
Bangui ✪
Congo R.
THE

CAMEROON
Yaoundé ✪
Douala
Malabo ✪
EQUATORIAL GUINEA
Benue R.
Niger R.

326

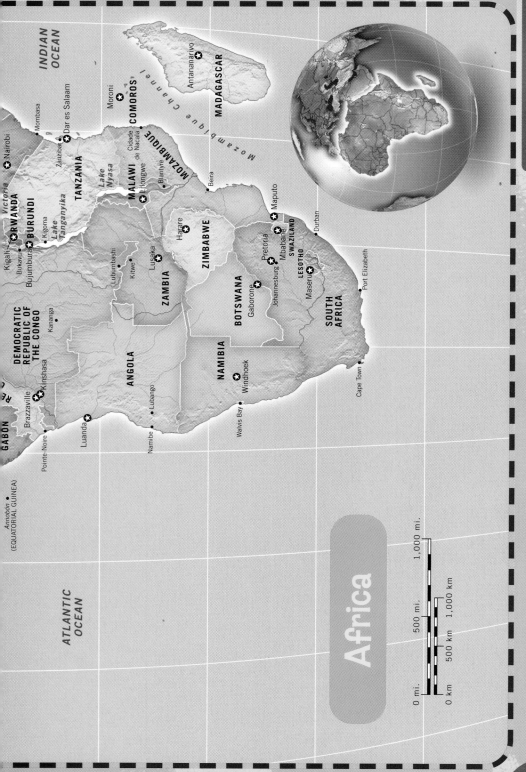

Africa

INDIAN OCEAN

ATLANTIC OCEAN

Mozambique Channel

MADAGASCAR
Antananarivo

COMOROS
Moroni

TANZANIA
Nairobi
Mombasa
Dar es Salaam
Zanzibar

RWANDA
Kigali
Bukavu

BURUNDI
Bujumbura
Kigoma

Lake Victoria
Lake Tanganyika

MALAWI
Lilongwe
Lake Nyasa
Blantyre

MOZAMBIQUE
Cidade de Nacala
Beira
Maputo

DEMOCRATIC REPUBLIC OF THE CONGO
Kinshasa
Lubumbashi
Kananga

RE
Brazzaville
GABON

Pointe-Noire
Luanda

ANGOLA
Lubango
Namibe

Annobón
(EQUATORIAL GUINEA)

ZAMBIA
Lusaka
Kitwe

ZIMBABWE
Harare

BOTSWANA
Gaborone

NAMIBIA
Windhoek
Walvis Bay

SOUTH AFRICA
Pretoria
Johannesburg
Durban
Port Elizabeth
Cape Town

SWAZILAND
Mbabane

LESOTHO
Maseru

0 mi.   500 mi.   1,000 mi.
0 km   500 km   1,000 km

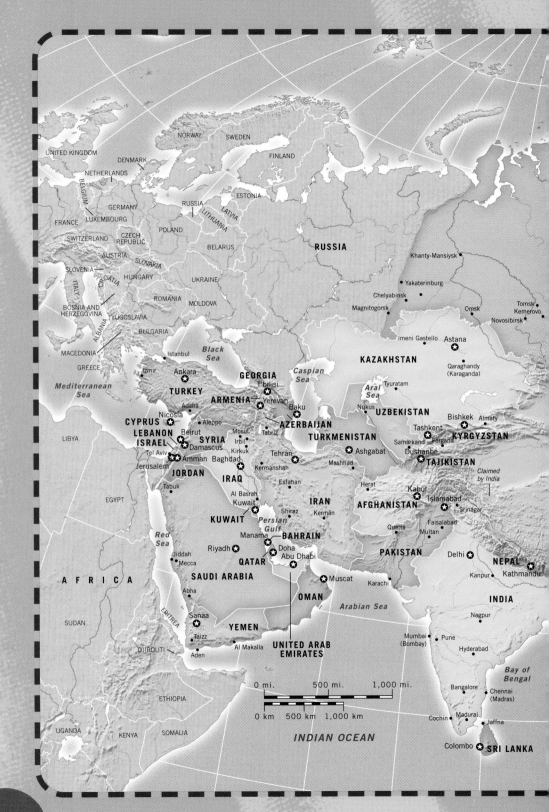

UNITED KINGDOM

NORWAY
SWEDEN
FINLAND

DENMARK
NETHERLANDS
BELGIUM
GERMANY
LUXEMBOURG
FRANCE
SWITZERLAND
CZECH
REPUBLIC
POLAND
AUSTRIA
SLOVAKIA
SLOVENIA
HUNGARY
ITALY
CROATIA
BOSNIA AND
HERZEGOVINA
YUGOSLAVIA
ALBANIA
MACEDONIA
BULGARIA
GREECE

ESTONIA
RUSSIA
LATVIA
LITHUANIA
BELARUS
UKRAINE
MOLDOVA
ROMANIA

RUSSIA

Khanty-Mansiysk
Yakaterinburg
Chelyabinsk
Magnitogorsk
Imeni Gastello
Omsk
Tomsk
Kemerovo
Novosibirsk

Astana

KAZAKHSTAN

Qaraghandy
(Karaganda)

Istanbul
*Black
Sea*

Izmir
Ankara
GEORGIA
T'bilisi

*Caspian
Sea*

*Aral
Sea*

Tyuratam

TURKEY
ARMENIA
Yerevan
Baku

Nukus

UZBEKISTAN
Bishkek
Almaty

Adana
AZERBAIJAN
Tashkent
KYRGYZSTAN

CYPRUS
Nicosia
Aleppo
Tabriz
TURKMENISTAN
Samarkand
Fergana

LEBANON
Beirut
Mosul
Irbil
TAJIKISTAN

ISRAEL
SYRIA
Damascus
Kirkuk
Tehran
Ashgabat
Dushanbe

Tel Aviv
Amman
Baghdad
Mashhad

Jerusalem
JORDAN
Kermanshah
*Claimed
by India*

IRAQ
Esfahan
Herat
Kabul

Tabuk
Al Basrah
IRAN
AFGHANISTAN
Islamabad
Srinagar

EGYPT
Kuwait
Shiraz
Kerman
Quetta
Faisalabad

KUWAIT
*Persian
Gulf*
Multan

*Red
Sea*
Manama
BAHRAIN
PAKISTAN
Delhi

Jiddah
Riyadh
Doha
Abu Dhabi

Mecca
QATAR
Muscat
Karachi
NEPAL
Kathmandu

AFRICA
SAUDI ARABIA
OMAN
Kanpur

Abha
Arabian Sea
INDIA

SUDAN
Sanaa
Nagpur

Taizz
UNITED ARAB
EMIRATES
Mumbai
(Bombay)
Pune

ERITREA
YEMEN
Al Makalla
Hyderabad

DJIBOUTI
Aden

*Mediterranean
Sea*

LIBYA

*Bay of
Bengal*

0 mi.   500 mi.   1,000 mi.

0 km   500 km   1,000 km

ETHIOPIA

Bangalore
Chennai
(Madras)

Cochin
Madurai
Jaffna

INDIAN OCEAN

UGANDA
KENYA
SOMALIA

Colombo
SRI LANKA

Asia and the Middle East

PACIFIC OCEAN

ARCTIC OCEAN

Borneo

Phuket
Songkhla
Phnom Penh
Ho Chi Minh City
CAMBODIA
Bangkok
THAILAND
VIETNAM
Chiang Mai
Da Nang
Rangoon
YANMAR (BURMA)
Vientiane
LAOS
Hanoi
Mandalay
Chittagong
BANGLADESH
Dhaka
BHUTAN
Naba

Cebu
PHILIPPINES
Manila
Quezon City
Baguio
Luzon

Hong Kong
Kao-hsiung
Macau
Guangzhou
Nanning
Liuzhou
Xiamen
Fuzhou
Taipei
TAIWAN
Naha

Chongqing
Chengdu
CHINA
Xi'an
Lanzhou

Shanghai
Hefei
Wuhan
Qingdao
Jinan
Taiyuan
Tianjin
Hohhot
Beijing

Nagasaki
Fukuoka
Hiroshima
S. KOREA
Seoul
Kyoto Osaka
Kobe
Nagoya
Pusan
Taegu
Tokyo
JAPAN
Sapporo

Jinxi
Pyongyang
N. KOREA
Shenyang
Vladivostok
Changchun
Harbin

MONGOLIA
Ulaanbaatar
Gobi

Irkutsk

netsk

snoyarsk

Khabarovsk

S I B E R I A

RUSSIA
Yakutsk

Sakhalin

Sea of Okhotsk
Petropavlovsk-Kamchatskiy
Kamchatka Peninsula
Magadan

Verkhoyansk

Tiksi

Cherskiy

Bering Sea

Asia, Australia and the Pacific Islands

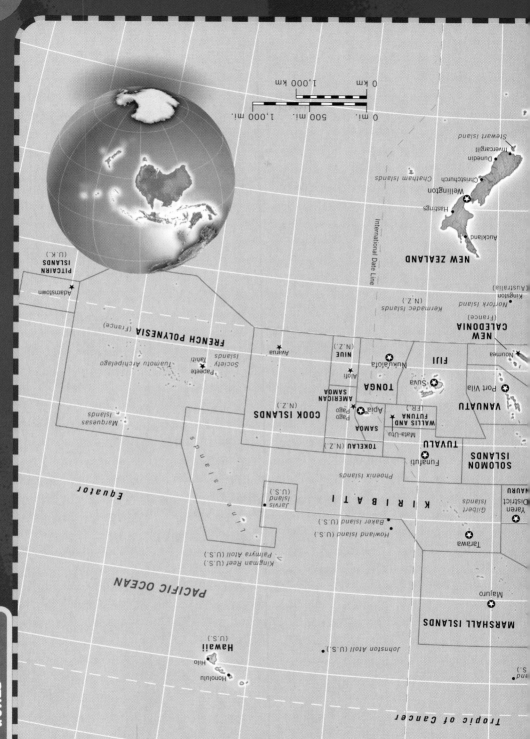

0 km 1,000 km

0 mi. 500 mi. 1,000 mi.

International Date Line

NEW ZEALAND

Stewart Island
Invercargill
Dunedin
Christchurch Chatham Islands
Wellington
Hastings
Auckland

Kingston
(Australia)
Norfolk Island
(N.Z.)
Kermadec Islands
(N.Z.)

NEW
CALEDONIA
(France)

Nouméa

PITCAIRN
ISLANDS
(U.K.)

Adamstown

FRENCH POLYNESIA (France)

Tuamotu Archipelago

Papeete Tahiti
Society
Islands

Avarua

NIUE
(N.Z.)

Nukuʻalofa

FIJI

TONGA

Alofi

Suva

Port Vila

VANUATU

Marquesas
Islands

COOK ISLANDS

AMERICAN
SAMOA
Pago Pago
Apia
SAMOA
WALLIS AND
FUTUNA
(Fr.)
Mata-Utu

TUVALU

SOLOMON
ISLANDS

TOKELAU (N.Z.)

Funafuti

Phoenix Islands

Equator

Line Islands

Jarvis
Island
(U.S.)

Baker Island (U.S.)

Howland Island (U.S.)

Kingman Reef (U.S.)
Palmyra Atoll (U.S.)

K I R I B A T I

Gilbert
Islands

Yaren
District
NAURU

Tarawa

Majuro

PACIFIC OCEAN

Johnston Atoll (U.S.)

Hawaii
(U.S.)

Hilo
Honolulu

MARSHALL ISLANDS

Tropic of Cancer

Europe

0 mi.   300 mi.   600 mi.

0 km   300 km   600 km

ICELAND

Reykjavik

Arctic Circle

FAROE ISLANDS
(Denmark)
Torshavn

SHETLAND ISLANDS

ORKNEY
ISLANDS

HEBRIDES

Trondheim

NORWAY

Bergen

Oslo   Gävle

Stavanger

SWEDEN

Göteborg

DENMARK

Ålborg

Copenhagen

Malmö

Aberdeen

Glasgow

Edinburgh

Belfast

UNITED
KINGDOM

NORTH
SEA

IRELAND

Dublin

Liverpool   Leeds

Manchester

Sheffield

NETHERLANDS

Birmingham

Hamburg

Bremen

Berlin

Poznan

London

Amsterdam
The Hague

GERMANY

Rotterdam

GUERNSEY (U.K.)

JERSEY (U.K.)

Calais   Lille

Antwerp

Essen

Wroclaw

Le Havre

Brussels

Dusseldorf
Cologne

BELGIUM

Bonn   Frankfurt

Prague

LUXEMBOURG

CZECH
REPUBLIC

Brno

Paris

Luxembourg

Stuttgart

Bratislava

Nantes

Strasbourg

Vienna

FRANCE

Dijon

LIECHTENSTEIN

Munich

ATLANTIC OCEAN

Zürich

Vaduz

AUSTRIA

HUNGAR

BAY OF
BISCAY

Bern

Geneva

SWITZERLAND

Ljubljana

SLOVENIA

Bordeaux

Lyon

Trieste

Zagreb

Turin   Milan

Porto

Bilbao

Genoa

CROATIA

Toulouse

SAN
MARINO

BOSNIA AND
HERZEGOVINA

Lisbon

PORTUGAL

Madrid

Andorra
la Vella

Marseille

Sarajevo

MONACO

Bastia

ITALY

Podgo

Barcelona

ANDORRA

Corsica

Vatican
City

Rome

ADRIATIC SEA

SPAIN

Valencia   Majorca

Seville

Sardinia

Naples

Bari

Faro

Palma

Málaga

Kerkira

Gibraltar

MEDITERRANEAN SEA

Cagliari

Palermo   Messina

Sicily

MOROCCO

ALGERIA

AFRICA

TUNISIA

Valletta

MALTA

IRAQ

IRAN

SYRIA

LEBANON

CYPRUS

Crete

TURKEY

izmir

Athens

GREECE

Volos

Thessaloniki

IA

MACEDONIA

Skopje

BULGARIA

Sofia

Nis

MONTENEGRO
AND
RBIA

grade

Craiova

Varna

BLACK SEA

Constanta

Bucharest

ROMANIA

Arad

st

Iasi

Chisinau

MOLDOVA

Odessa

Mykolaiva

Simferopol'

Sevastopol'

Kerch

Grozny

Rostov

Zhdanov

Makeyevka

Gorlovka

Derazhnya

L'viv

IA

UKRAINE

Voroshilovgrad

Kharkiv

Kiev

KAZAKHSTAN

Volgograd

Saratov

Voronezh

Lipetsk

Homyel'

BELARUS

Brest

LAND

aw

Minsk

Smolensk

Samara

Moscow

Vilnius

LITHUANIA

ad

RUS

Riga

LATVIA

Kazan

Nizhniy Novgorod

ESTONIA

Tallinn

Izhevsk

St. Petersburg

olm

Turku

Helsinki

RUSSIA

Tampere

FINLAND

Arkhangel'sk

Oulu

ea

Pechora

ASIA

Murmansk

nso

na

Aleutian Islands

Bering
Sea

RUSSIA

Kodiak

Bethel

Nome

Barrow

Anchorage

Valdez

Fairbanks

Alaska (U.S.)

Prudhoe Bay

Salem
Portland
Olympia
Seattle
Victoria
Vancouver

Boise

Juneau

Whitehorse

Inuvik

Beaufort
Sea

ARCTIC
OCEAN

Helena

Calgary

Edmonton

Yellowknife

Echo Bay

Arctic Circle

Banks Island

Victoria Island

Queen Elizabeth Islands

Bismarck

Regina

Saskatoon

Alert

Winnipeg

Churchill

HUDSON
BAY

Kangiqliniq (Resolute)

Baffin Island

Qaanaaq (Thule)

Baffin Bay

Moosonee

Iqaluit

Davis Strait

Greenland Sea

CANADA

Chisasibi
(Fort George)

Nuuk (Godthab)

GREENLAND
(Denmark)

Happy Valley
Goose Bay

Labrador
Sea

Narsarsuaq

Saint-Pierre

Island of
Newfoundland

St. John's

Tasiilaq
(Ammassalik)

ICELAND

North America and Central America

PACIFIC OCEAN

Tropic of Cancer

Gulf of California

MEXICO

UNITED STATES

GULF OF MEXICO

CARIBBEAN SEA

ATLANTIC OCEAN

Los Angeles
San Diego
Tijuana
La Paz
Puerto Vallarta
Mazatlán
Hermosillo
Phoenix
Ciudad Juárez
El Paso
Santa Fe
Salt Lake City
Denver
Cheyenne
Minneapolis · St. Paul
Acapulco
Guadalajara
León
Monterrey
San Antonio
Austin
Houston
Oklahoma City
Dallas
Little Rock
Topeka
Kansas City
Lincoln
Omaha · Des Moines
Madison
Milwaukee
Oaxaca
Puebla
Mexico City
Veracruz
Tampico
New Orleans
Baton Rouge
Jackson
Montgomery
Memphis
Nashville
Springfield
Saint Louis
Jefferson City
Chicago
Detroit
Toledo
Cleveland
Indianapolis
Frankfort
Cincinnati
Louisville
Charleston
Pittsburgh · Harrisburg
Buffalo
Toronto
Ottawa
Montréal
Concord
Augusta
Halifax
Guatemala City
San Salvador
Managua
San José
Panama City
GUATEMALA
EL SALVADOR
HONDURAS
NICARAGUA
COSTA RICA
PANAMA
Tegucigalpa
Belmopan
Belize City
BELIZE
Mérida
Cancún
CAYMAN ISLANDS
George Town ★
Montego Bay
Kingston
JAMAICA
Havana
Camagüey
CUBA
Guantánamo
Nassau
Freeport
Miami
BAHAMAS
Santiago
Port-au-Prince
HAITI
Santo Domingo
DOMINICAN REPUBLIC
Grand Turk ★
TURKS AND CAICOS ISLANDS (U.K.)
San Juan
PUERTO RICO (U.S.)
VIRGIN ISLANDS (U.S., U.K.)
SAINT MAARTEN/ SAINT MARTIN (Neth. Antilles/Guad.)
ANGUILLA (U.K.)
SAINT BARTHÉLEMY (Guad.)
SAINT KITTS AND NEVIS
MONTSERRAT (U.K.)
ANTIGUA AND BARBUDA
GUADELOUPE (Fr.)
DOMINICA
MARTINIQUE (Fr.)
SAINT LUCIA (Fr.)
SAINT VINCENT AND THE GRENADINES
BARBADOS
GRENADA
NETHERLANDS ANTILLES (Neth.)
ARUBA (Neth.)
TRINIDAD AND TOBAGO
BERMUDA (U.K.)
Hamilton ★
Jacksonville
Tallahassee
Savannah
Columbia
Raleigh
Richmond
Washington, DC
Baltimore
Dover
Philadelphia
New York
Hartford
Providence
Boston
Albany
Montpelier
Norfolk
Atlanta
Birmingham
COLOMBIA
VENEZUELA
GUYANA

0 mi.
0 km
500 km
500 mi.
1,000 km
1,000 mi.
1,000 mi.

Equator

ECUADOR
Esmeraldas
Quito

Guayaquil
Piura
Trujillo
Lima

PERU

Marañón River

Ucayali River

Andes

Cusco

Lake Titicaca

BOLIVIA

Cruzeiro do Sul

Cobija

Riberalta

Porto Velho

BRAZIL

Brasília

Salvador
Maceió
Recife
Natal
Fortaleza

Parnaíba

São Luís

Belém

São Francisco River

Tocantins River

Araguaia River

Xingu River

Santarém

Manaus

Madeira River

AMAZON BASIN

Selvas

Amazon River

Constant
Benjamin

Iquitos

Putumayo River

Negro River

Amazon River

Macapá

Cayenne

FRENCH GUIANA

Paramaribo

SURINAME

Georgetown

GUYANA

Ciudad Guayana

Orinoco River

VENEZUELA

Caracas

Maracaibo

Aruba

Lake Maracaibo

Barranquilla

Cartagena

Medellín

Cali

Bogotá

COLOMBIA

Magdalena River

PANAMA

COSTA RICA

NICARAGUA

HONDURAS

BELIZE

CARIBBEAN SEA

JAMAICA

CUBA

HAITI

DOMINICAN REPUBLIC

Puerto Rico (U.S.)

SAINT KITTS AND NEVIS

ANTIGUA AND BARBUDA

DOMINICA

GUADELOUPE

SAINT LUCIA

BARBADOS

GRENADA SAINT VINCENT AND THE GRENADINES

TRINIDAD AND TOBAGO

ATLANTIC OCEAN

South America

PACIFIC OCEAN

ATLANTIC OCEAN

Scale:
0 km / 0 mi.
500 km / 500 mi.
1,000 km / 1,000 mi.

Andes Mts.

CHILE

ARGENTINA

PARAGUAY

URUGUAY

Puerto Montt

Concepción

Valparaíso

Santiago

Antofagasta

Iquique

Arica

Santa Cruz

Sucre

San Miguel de Tucumán

Córdoba

Rosario

Buenos Aires

Bahía Blanca

Río Gallegos

Punta Arenas

Ushuaia

Comodoro Rivadavia

Mar del Plata

Río de la Plata

Montevideo

Salto

Resistencia

Formosa

Encarnación

Asunción

Ciudad del Este

Paraná River

Paraguay River

Curitiba

Pôrto Alegre

São Paulo

Rio de Janeiro

Belo Horizonte

Brazilian Highlands

Strait of Magellan

Cape Horn

Stanley

Falkland Is. (Islas Malvinas)
(Administered by U.K.; claimed by Argentina)

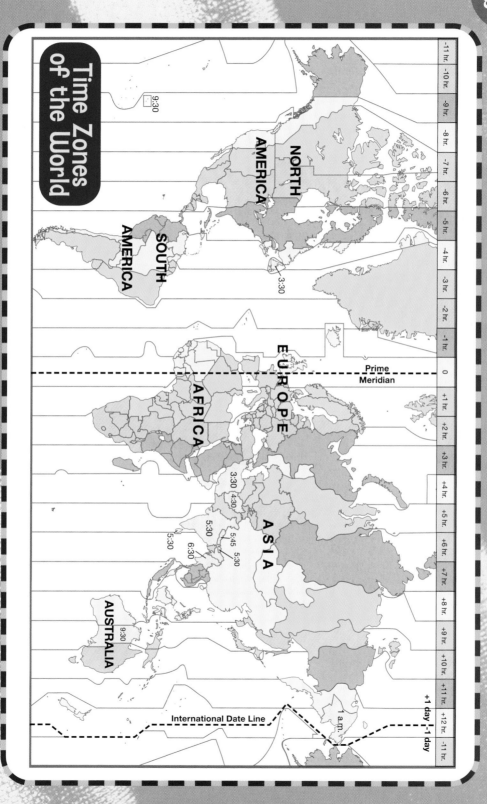

Time Zones of the World

Did You Know?

There are six disputed territories in the world: Antarctica, Gaza Strip, Paracel Islands, Spratly Islands, West Bank and Western Sahara.

Most Populous Countries

	Country	2004 Population
1.	China	1,294,629,555
2.	India	1,065,070,607
3.	United States	293,027,571
4.	Indonesia	238,452,952
5.	Brazil	184,101,109
6.	Pakistan	153,705,278
7.	Russia	144,112,353
8.	Bangladesh	141,340,476
9.	Nigeria	137,253,133
10.	Japan	127,333,002

Source: U.S. Census Bureau, International Database

WORLD POPULATION MILESTONES

1 billion in 1804	
2 billion in 1927	123 years later
3 billion in 1960	33 years later
4 billion in 1974	14 years later
5 billion in 1987	13 years later
6 billion in 1999	12 years later

Sources: United Nations Population Division

Where the World's Refugees Come From

Refugees are people who flee their native lands for safety, usually during war or political upheaval. Here's a list of the regions that people flee from most often.

A Vietnamese refugee seeks safety in Hong Kong.

1. Afghanistan
2. West Bank and Gaza Strip
3. Burma
4. Sudan
5. Angola
6. Congo (Kinshasa)
7. Burundi
8. Vietnam
9. Somalia
10. Iraq

Source: U.N. High Commissioner for Refugees

TFK Mystery Person

CLUE 1: I was born in Russia in 1898.
CLUE 2: I spent much of my childhood in the U.S. and moved to the Middle East on 1906.
CLUE 3: I played a role in the creation of Israel and held many top government jobs. At age 70, I became Israel's fourth Prime Minister.

WHO AM I?

(See Answer Key that begins on page 340.)

ANSWER KEY

ANIMALS
Page 24, A Long Trip

Page 29, Mystery Person: Jane Goodall

ART
Page 33, Mystery Person: Dorothea Lange

BOOKS
Page 39, Puzzling Potter Quiz: 1. a; 2. c; 3. b; 4. c; 5. b
Page 39, Mystery Person: Langston Hughes

BUILDINGS & LANDMARKS
Page 45, Mystery Person: Louis Sullivan

CALENDARS & HOLIDAYS
Page 48, Straight from the Heart: Please be mine
Page 53, Mystery Person: Anna Jarvis

COMPUTERS & THE INTERNET
Page 58, Loopy Lingo: He modem.
Page 59, Mystery Person: Tim Berners-Lee

DANCE & THEATER
Page 63, Mystery Person: Savion Glover

DINOSAURS
Page 67, Mystery Person: Roy Chapman Andrews

DISASTERS
Page 73, Mystery Person: Tom Ridge

ENVIRONMENT & ENERGY
age 79, It's Your Turn to Clean Up: the paper bin
Page 81, Mystery Person: John Muir

FASHION
Page 83, Mystery Person: Vera Wang

GEOGRAPHY
Page 88, Follow That Map!

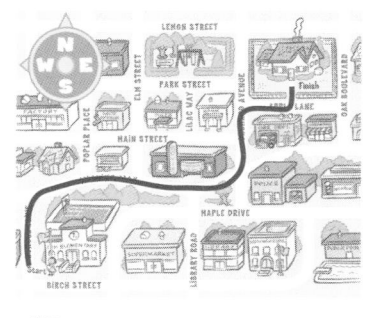

Page 89, Mystery Person: Leif Eriksson

GOVERNMENT
Page 93, Presidential Succession: Elaine Chao
Page 101, Run for Office!

Page 101, Mystery Person: Sandra Day O'Connor

HEALTH & BODY
Page 109, Mystery Person: David Ho

HISTORY
Page 111, Words to Live By: I have a dream
Page 111, Mystery Person: Malcolm X

HOMEWORK HELPER

Page 128, A Reading Rebus: 1. *Harry Potter* (J.K. Rowling); 2. *Hatchet* (Gary Paulsen); 3. *Superfudge* (Judy Blume);
4. *Pinocchio* (Carlo Collodi)
Page 145, Mystery Person: Booker T. Washington

INVENTIONS

Page 149, Mystery Person: Henry Ford

LANGUAGE

Page 151, Anagram Antics: 1. d; 2. e; 3. a; 4. c; 5. b
Page 155, Mystery Person: Noah Webster

MATH

Page 165, Roamin' Numerals: XDCXLII (1,642)
Page 167, Mystery Person: Sir Isaac Newton

MILITARY & WAR

Page 173, Mystery Person: Colin Powell

MONEY & ECONOMY

Page 176, Bill Thrill: 1. George Washington is on the bill instead of Alexander Hamilton; 2. There is a 6 instead of a 5 in the right corner; 3. The Secretary of Defense appears instead of the Secretary of Treasury; 4. The seal of the U.S. Federal Reserve shows a cat instead of an eagle; 5. The Untied States of America appears instead of The United States of America.
Page 179, Mystery Person: Alexander Hamilton

MOVIES & TV

Page 182, Kid Stuff: 1. E (Gertie); 2. B (Harry Potter); 3. D (Kevin McCallister); 4. C (Carmen Cortez); 5. A (young Darth Vader)
Page 183, Mystery Person: Matt Groening

MUSIC

Page 185, The Sound of Music?

Page 187, Mystery Person: Ludwig van

Beethoven

MYTHOLOGY

Page 191, Mystery Person: Thor

PRESIDENTS

Page 201, Mystery Person: John F. Kennedy

RELIGION

Page 205, Mystery Person: Martin Luther

SCIENCE

Page 215, Mystery Person: Luther Burbank

SPACE

Page 122, Spaced Out!: (from left to right) Pluto, Big Dipper, Earth (worms), nova (Scotia), Sun (kist), Mars (bar), Venus (de Milo), Sun (glasses), comet (cleanser), Mercury (thermometer)
Page 225, Mystery Person: Neil de Grasse Tyson

SPORTS

Page 230, Find the Captain: 44
Page 239, Mystery Person: Babe Ruth

UNITED STATES

Page 243, They Came to America: Welcome!
Page 277, Mystery Person: Frederick Douglass

VOLUNTEERING

Page 281, Mystery Person: Clara Barton

WEATHER

Page 284, Lightning Strikes Twice: 3 and 4
Page 287, Mystery Person: Benjamin Banneker

WORLD

Page 290, Wish You Were Here: 1. a; 2. c; 3. d; 4. e; 5. b
Page 339, Mystery Person: Golda Meir

INNER FRONT COVER

Longer (Lounger minus u)
INNER BACK COVER
Slacken (FQBRIGHTOP**SLACKEN**DJM)

INDEX

H

habitat destruction, 25
Hades (Pluto), 188
Hadrian, 113
hair, 107
Haiti, 303
Halloween, 48
hamsters, 24
hand (measurement), 165
Hanging Gardens of Babylon, 45
Hanukkah, 49
Harding, Warren G., 196, 200, 201
Harrison, Benjamin, 195, 199
Harrison, William Henry, 193, 195, 199, 201
Hastert, Dennis, 92
Hawaii, 255, 276, 277
Hawk, Tony, 237
Hayes, Rutherford B., 195
hazardous waste, 78
health, 102–109
    diet and nutrition, 102–103, 105
    exercise, 103
    human body, 106–109
heart, 107
Hebrew Bible, 112
Hegira, 113
Heisman Trophy, 232
helium, 257
hemispheres, 88
Henry VIII, King of England, 115
Hephaestus (Vulcan), 188
Hera (Juno), 188, 189
Hermes (Mercury), 189
Hestia (Vesta), 189
heteronyms, 155
Hindenburg, 72
Hinduism, 203, 205
    Holi festival, 51
hip-hop, 61, 186
Hispaniola, 299, 303
history, 110–121
    ancient-history timeline, 112
    civil rights movement, 110–111
    U.S.-history timeline, 118–121
    world-history timeline, 113–117
Hitler, Adolf, 116, 170
Hobbit, The (Tolkien), 36
hockey, 234
holidays, 47–49
    Christian, 49
    festivals around the world, 50–51
    Jewish, 49
    Muslim, 49
Holi festival, 51
Holocaust, 116, 170
Holy Roman Empire, 113
Homer, 112
homework helper
    conducting interviews, 142
    fact gathering, 122
    Internet research guide, 143
    oral reports, 144–145
    studying for tests, 140–141
    writing papers, 122–139
homonyms, 155
Honduras, 303

Hoover, Herbert C., 197, 201
Hopi, 191
Hopper, Edward, 32
hormones, 108
horse racing, 238
horses, 24, 27
Horus, 190
hot-air balloons, 148
household budgets, 178
House of Representatives, 92, 96, 97, 121
Hudson, Henry, 85
human body, 106–109
    body temperature, 104
    parts of, 106–107
    systems, 108–109
Humphrey, Hubert H., 198
Hundred Years' Way, 114
Hungary, 303
Huns (Mongols), 113
hunting and fishing, 25
hurricanes, 282–283
Hussein, Saddam, 117, 121, 171
hybrid cars, 75
hydropower, 76, 322
hyenas, 26

I

ice hockey, 234
Iceland, 303
    Internet use, 59
Ichthyosaurus, 64
Idaho, 255
idioms, 155
Iditarod Trail Sled Dog Race, 238
igneous rocks, 215
Iliad (Homer), 112
Illinois, 256
immigration, 240, 243, 252
immune system, 108
impeachment, 96, 121, 194
impressionism, 33
Incas, 114
Independence Day, 47
India, 116, 304
Indiana, 256
Indianapolis 500, 239, 256
Indian Ocean, 86
Indonesia, 71, 304
inflammatory system, 108
inflation, 177
influenza
    Spanish, 70
    worldwide epidemic, 116
Inquisition, 114
insects
    endangered and threatened species, 25
    facts about, 22
    groups of, 19
instant messaging, 54–55
integers, 157
interest, 177
Internet
    bibliography form for articles, 139
    emoticons, 55
    instant messaging, 54–55
    research guide, 143
    resource guide, 58

CREDITS

All photos clockwise from top left:
Cover: Motion Picture T.V. Archive (Yu-Gi-Oh);
NASA (rover); Scott Hallerman/Getty
Images/Newscom (Wie); Comstock Images
(computer girl); Dreamworks (Shrek); Disney
Enterprises (Lohan); Gary
Bogdan/Newsport/Corbis (Adu); PD (7).
Back Cover: Peter Arnold (koala); AP
Photo/Brennan Linsley (soldier); AP Photo/Dario
Lopez-Mills (festival boy); Felipe Galindo
(puzzle and illustration); Joe Lertola (map); PD
(3).
Title Page: NASA
Credits Page: Felipe Galindo
Who's News: 8-9: Joe Raedle/Getty Images.
10: NASA (2). **11:** AFP/Newscom. **12:** Siavash
Habibollahi (Iran); EPA/Bernardo Rodriguez
(Spain). **13:** NASA; Martin
Hartley/Eyevine(pole). **14:** Reuters/Ron
Schwane (James); KRT/Newscom. **15:** Theo
Wargo/WireImages.com. **16:** Zuma
Press/Newscom; Disney/Newscom; Disney/Pixar.
17: Joncopaloff/Film Magic (Keisha).
Animals: 18: Courtesy Dr. Joan Silk. **19:** Tim
Davis/Corbis (penguin); Carmela
Leszczynski/Animals Animals (sea horse); M.
Fogden/Animals Animals (frog); Fabio
Columbini Medeiros/Animals Animals (beetle);
Photo Researchers Inc. (bee); Photo
Researchers Inc. (leafhopper). **20:** Image State
(croc); PD; Nicole Duplaix/Getty Images
(platypus). **21:** Stephan Frank/Getty Images
(sponge); George Grall/Getty Images
(anemone); PD. **22:** Art Wolfe/Getty Images
(bat); Gerry Driendl/Getty Images (koala);
23: PD; Art Wolfe/Getty Images (wolf). **24:**
Ronie Magnusson/Getty Images; Jane Shasky
(puzzle). **25:** Art Wolfe/Getty Images (gorilla);
Royalty-Free/Corbis (condor); Ho/Reuters
(crane); Joel W. Rogers/Corbis (salmon); Greg
Vaughn/Getty Images (owl); Corbis (butterfly)
26: Theo Allofs/Corbis (eagle); Setboun/Corbis
(reindeer); Peter Arnold (hyena); Peter Arnold
(llama); Tom Brakefield/Corbis (panda); Peter
Arnold (koala); Joe Lemmonier (globe). **27:**
Carin L. Cain/AP. **28:** Raul Alberto Rodriguez
(dog); Emily Rabin (cat). **29:** Ken Usami/Photo
Disc/Picture Quest (fish); AP Photo/Jose F.
Moreno.
Art: 30: Bettmann/Corbis. **31:** Gianni
Dagliorti/Corbis (da Vinci); Christie's
Images/Corbis (Van Gogh); Geoffrey
Clements/Corbis (Monet); Elio Ciol/Corbis
(mosaic); Werner Forman/Corbis (mask).
32: National Gallery Collection; By Kind
Permission of the Trustees of the National
Gallery, London/Corbis (Turner); Georgia
O'Keefe/Art Resource; Newscom (Hopper);
Archivo Iconografico, S.A./Corbis (Brueghel).
33: National Gallery of Australia (de Kooning);
Eric Lessing/Art Resource (Picasso); Burstin
Collection/Corbis (Rembrandt); Library of
Congress (Lang).
Books: 34: Eric Cahan (Paolini); Newcom
(*Eragon*). **36:** Time Life Pictures/Getty Images
(Carroll). **37:** Jay Colton (book); Bettmann
Archive/Corbis (Golding); Bettmann/Corbis.
Buildings & Landmarks: 40: AP Photo/D Box Inc.
41: Simon Kwong/Reuters (Taipai);
Bettmann/Corbis (tunnel). **42:** Archivo
Iconografico, S.A./Corbis (Versailles); Fergus
O'Brien/Getty Images; AP Photo (Eiffel Tower).
43: Glen Allison/Getty Images (Wat); John
Slater/Corbis (Great Wall); Vladimir
Pcholkin/Getty Images (Stonehenge). **44:** Philip
Gould/Corbis (Lin); Time Life Pictures/Getty
Images. **45:** Bettmann/Corbis; Hulton Archive
By Getty Images.
Calendars & Holidays: 46: Jane Sanders. **47:**
Joseph Sohm; Chromosohm Inc/Corbis; Jane
Sanders (illustration). **48:** Linda Solovic; Jen
Kraemer-Smith. **49:** Rita Maas/Getty Images;
Gary Buss/Getty Images;Ted Spiegel/Corbis.
50: AP Photo/Dario Lopez-Mills; AFP/Newscom.
51: AP Photo/Rajesh Nirgude; Felipe Galindo
(illustration). **53:** Brad Holland (gemstones);
Felipe Galindo (Sun); Time Life Pictures/Getty
Images.
Computers & the Internet: 54, 55: Dean
Macadam. **56:** Felipe Galindo (illustrations);
Newscom. **57:** Jane Sanders (illustrations);
Zuma Press/Newscom; Reuters/Corbis. **59:**
Felipe Galindo (illustration); Bettmann/Corbis.
Dance & Theater: 60: AP Photo/Steven Senne;
Newscom. **61:** Ted Spiegal/Corbis; Claro Cortez
IV/Reuters/Corbis (hip-hop); Bettmann/Corbis
(Native Americans); Felipe Galindo
(illustration); **62:** Jane Sanders. **63:** Jane
Sanders; Newscom.
Dinosaurs: 64: Photo Researchers Inc.; Royalty-
Free/Corbis (*T.rex*); Jonathan Blair/Corbis
(*Triceratops*). **65:** Jim Zuckerman/Corbis;
Royalty-Free Corbis. **66:** Marcos
Brindicci/Reuters (2); Felipe Galindo
(illustration). **67:** National Museum of Natural
History (2); Bettmann/Corbis.
Disasters: 68: Lucy Nicholson/Reuters (2).
69: Newscom; Felipe Galindo (illustration).
70: Time-Life Pictures/Getty Images.
71: Reuters/Daniel Aguilar. **72:** Corbis (Chicago);
The Mariners Museum-AP/Wide World Photos;
Newscom. **73:** Jess Christensen/Reuters (9/11);
Reuters/William Philpott.

Presidents: 192–198: Christie's Images/Corbis (Washington); John Trumbull/NPG/SI (Adams); Mather Brown/NPG/SI beq. of Charles Francis Adams (Jefferson); Chester Harding/NPG/SI (Madison); John Vanderlyn/NPG/SI (Monroe) George Caleb Bingham/NPG/SI (Adams); Ralph Eleaser Whiteside Earl/NPG/SI gift of Andrew W. Mellon (Jackson); Mathew B. Brady/NPG/SI (Van Buren); Albert Gallatin Hoit/NPG/SI (Harrison); LOC (Tyler); Max Westfield/NPG/SI (Polk); James Reid Lambdin/ NPG/SI gift of Barry Bingham Sr. (Taylor); NPG/SI (Fillmore); George Peter Healy/NPG/SI gift of Andrew W. Mellon (Pierce); George Peter Healy/NPG/SI gift of Andrew W. Mellon (Buchanan); William Judkins Thomson; George Peter Healy/NPG/SI (Lincoln); Washington Bogart Cooper/NPG/SI; Thomas Le Clear/NPG/SI gift of Mrs. Grant (Grant); Bettmann/Corbis (Hayes); Ole Peter Hansen Balling/NPG/SI gift of IBM; Ole Peter Hansen Balling/NPG/SI gift of Mrs. H.N. Blue; Anders Zorn/NPG/SI (Cleveland); LOC (Harrison); LOC (Cleveland); Adolfo Muller-Ury/NPG/SI (McKinley); Adrian Lamb/NPG/SI gift of T.R. Assoc. (Roosevelt); William Valentine Schevill/NPG/SI gift of W.E. Schevill (Taft); Edmund Tarbell/ NPG/SI (Wilson); Margaret Lindsay Williams/NPG/SI (Harding). Joseph E. Burgess/NPG/SI gift of Phi Gamma Delta (Coolidge); Douglas Chandor/NPG/SI (Hoover); Oscar White/Corbis (FDR); Greta Kempton/NPG/SI (Truman); Thomas Edgar Stephens/NPG/SI gift of Ailsa Mellon Bruce (Eisenhower); JFK Presidential Library (Kennedy); Peter Hurd/NPG/SI gift of the artist (Johnson); Norman Rockwell/NPG/SI gift of Nixon Foundation (Nixon); Everett R. Kinstler/NPG/SI gift of Ford Foundation (Ford); Jimmy Carter Presidential Library (Carter); Ronald Reagan Presidential Library (Reagan); Ronald N. Sherr/NPG/SI gift of Mr. & Mrs. R.E. Krueger (Bush). **199:** Bettmann/Corbis (Clinton); Eric Draper/White House (G.W. Bush); Greg Smith/Corbis (Bush family); John Trumball/NPG/SI (John Adams); The Corcoran Gallery of Arts/Corbis (John Q. Adams); LOC (B. Harrison); Albert Gallatin Hoit /NPG/SI (W. Harrison); Chester Harding/NPG/SI (Madison); James Reid Lambdin/NPG/SI Gift of Barry Bingham Sr. (Taylor); Bettmann/Corbis (Roosevelts). **200:** Dallas & John Heaton/Corbis (White House); Felipe Galindo (illustration). **201:** Time Life Pictures/Getty Images (Lincoln); Jim Mahan (JFK).
Religion: 202: Phil Schermeister/Corbis (crucifix); Werner H. Miller/Corbis.
203: Steve Raymer/Asia Images (Koran); Royalty-Free Corbis (2). **204:** Reuters/Jeff J. Mitchell (Pope); AFP/Newscom (bishop).
205: Hulton Archive By Getty Images.
Science: 206: David Paul Morris.
207: Thomas Gagliano (DNA); Barrington Brown/Photo Researchers. **208:** Art Wolfe/Getty

Images; PunchStock; Yann Artches-Bertrand.
209: Aaron Horowitz/Corbis. **210** Todd Morrison/Corbis. **214:** Corbis. **215:** TIME Picture Collection/Getty Images (gold); Bettmann/Corbis.
Space: 216: NASA; Antonio Cidadao (Moon).
217–219: NASA (Mercury, Venus, Earth); NASA (Mars); Univ. of Arizona/JPL/NASA (Jupiter); Reta Beebe, D. Gilmore, L. Bergeron and NASA (Saturn); JPL/NASA (Uranus); NASA (Neptune); Dr. Albrecht, ESA/ESO/NASA. **220–221:** Felipe Galindo. **222:** Lin Hui Xinhua/AP; AFP/Getty Images; Jane Sanders (puzzle). **223:** Corbis (*Sputnik*); George Shelten/NASA (Glenn); Roger Ressmeyer/Corbis (shuttle); NASA (space station). **224:** Reuters/David Grey (solar eclipse); Felipe Galindo (Sun); Jane Sanders. **225:** NASA (asteroid); StockTrek/Corbis (galaxy); Chris Hondros/Newscom.
Sports: 226: AFP/Newscom; AP Photo/CP/Andrew Vaughn.
227: AP Photo/Michael Probst. **228:** EPA/C.J. Gunther; AP Photo (Paige); Reuters/Newscom (A-Rod). **229:** AP Photo/John Harrel; AP Photo/Pablo Martinez Monsivais (Jordan). **230:** Newscom (Brady); Jane Sanders (puzzle). **231:** Felipe Galindo. **232:** Reuters/Newscom; Greg Sorber-The Journal/AP. **233:** Gary Bogdon/Corbis. **234:** AFP/Newcom (Gretzky); Reuters/Corbis. **235:** Scott Hallerman/Getty Images (Wie); Lewis Forra/EPA/Landov.
236: Reuters/Laszlo Balogh (Postal); AP Photo/Amy Sancetta (Chechi); Bevilacqua Guiliano/Corbis Sygma (Comaneci). **237:** AP Photo/Chris Polk. **238:** AP (Fleming); Bettmann/Corbis (Seattle Slew); Felipe Galindo. **239:** AP Photo/Jan Pitman; Bettmann/Corbis (Ruth).
U.S.: 240: Nick Ut/AP; Bettmann/Corbis.
241: Joe Lertola (map). **242:** Felipe Galindo.
243: PD; Felipe Galindo. **244:** Smithsonian Institution/Armed Forces; AFP/Corbis (pledge).
246: Felipe Galindo; Bill Ross/Corbis (Times Square). **247:** Jane Sanders. **248–274:** Joe Lertola (maps). **275:** AFP/Corbis **277:** Time Life Pictures/Getty Images.
Volunteering: 278: Courtesy Youth Volunteer Corps; courtesy Youth Service America.
279: Courtesy J.Hordan Logan; courtesy Children for Children. **280:** AP Photo/Mary Altaffer; Jane Kleveland. **281:** Corbis.
Weather: 282: Karl Merton Ferron/Baltimore *Sun*/AP. **283:** Joe Skipper/Reuters; AFP/Newcom.
284: PD; Brad Holland. **285:** Jose Luis Pelaz/Corbis. **286:** William James Warren/Corbis.
287: The Granger Collection.
World: 288: PunchStock (U.N. flag); John Stanmeyer/VII Agency. **289:** Christies (China figure); PunchStock (visa); John Stanmeyer/VII Agency. **290:** Jane Sanders (top); Felipe Galindo (bottom). **291–323:** Information Please (flags). **323:** Corbis (U.N.). **324–338:** Joe Lertola (maps). **339:** Peter Turnley/Corbis; David Rubinger/Corbis.